Farm to Factory

THE PRINCETON ECONOMIC HISTORY
OF THE WESTERN WORLD

Joel Mokyr, Editor

Farm to Factory

A REINTERPRETATION OF THE SOVIET INDUSTRIAL REVOLUTION

Robert C. Allen

PRINCETON UNIVERSITY PRESS
PRINCETON AND OXFORD

Copyright © 2003 by Princeton University Press
Published by Princeton University Press, 41 William Street,
Princeton, New Jersey 08540
In the United Kingdom: Princeton University Press, 3 Market Place,
Woodstock, Oxfordshire OX20 1SY

LIBRARY OF CONGRESS CATALOGING-IN-PUBLICATION DATA

Allen, Robert C., 1947–
    Farm to factory : a reinterpretation of the Soviet industrial revolution /
Robert C. Allen.
        p.   cm. — (The Princeton economic history of the Western world)
    Includes bibliographical references and index.
    ISBN 0-691-00696-2 (cloth : alk. paper)
    1. Soviet Union—Economic policy.   2. Soviet Union—Economic conditions.
    3. Industrialization—Soviet Union.   I. Title.   II. Series.

    HC335.A655 2003
    330.947′0842—dc21   2002042718

British Library Cataloging-in-Publication Data is available

This book has been composed in Sabon

Printed on acid-free paper. ∞

www.pupress.princeton.edu

Mk   10 9 8 7 6 5 4 3 2 1

For Dianne

Contents

Figures

Tables

Acknowledgments

Writing this book had much in common with Soviet industrialization. While I had lectured on Soviet history for some time and had even begun to collect some data, my Soviet project began in earnest on 1 January 1994 with a Five-Year Plan to learn Russian. It was as successful as many Soviet plans: the maximal objectives were not achieved—I was not able to converse in Russian in two years—but great progress was made, and by the end I was able to work with Russian materials. At the same time, I was also trying to model the Soviet economy, so there were conflicting objectives that were difficult to reconcile. Planning was certainly "taut" and day-to-day events "chaotic" but without "overambitious" plans, how much would have been achieved?

There were costs as well. Defining objectives in terms of output targets implied a soft budget constraint for my time: the Soviet project acted as a vacuum cleaner, drawing me away from my family and out of our household economy. Since that was governed by a competing set of objectives emphasizing home improvement projects, there was confusion about what to do and no simple resolution mechanism. My greatest debts are to my wife, Dianne Frank, and my son Matthew for putting up with unfinished construction and a dad often too intent on working.

I could not have accomplished this project without the encouragement and support of several people. I sent Ho Hunter drafts of some early papers, and he answered with an insightful and enthusiastic letter. Then he got me involved in a trip to Moscow that was an eye opener. Later he helped me present my work to the American Association for the Advancement of Slavic Studies. Without Ho's support, I might not have persisted, and I remain grateful to him.

Other people also gave me valuable support. Gideon Rosenbluth edited a volume with me that included a first stab at interpreting Soviet history. Gideon's questions and his sympathy have both made a contribution. Peter Temin has talked Soviet history with me at lunch over the years. I thank him for his penetrating questions and good advice, which—to my loss—I have not always followed. Jeff Williamson has hired me—twice!—which has given me the chance to work at Harvard, where I learned a lot about general equilibrium. Likewise, Gilles Postel-Vinay hired me as a Researcher at the Institut National de la Recherche Agronomique in Ivry-sur-Seine, where I worked out my first simulation model. He also sponsored my work in *Annales*. His questions and his patronage helped focus me on the task. Anne Gorsuch was a constant source of enlightenment by patiently listening to my ideas and explaining Soviet history to me. Joel Mokyr has given me exceptional support as the editor of the *Journal of Economic History* as well as this series. I am grateful to all of these people for their encouragement as well as for their critical thoughts.

I have benefited greatly from the comments and questions I have received at seminars and conferences at the Universities of British Columbia, California, Copenhagen, Illinois, Michigan, Warwick, and at Harvard, Yale, and Moscow State, and Northwestern Universities. I particularly thank the participants at my seminar at Institut National de la Recherche Agronomique. I presented an early and primitive version of my simulation model. The audience pointed out seven deficiencies with it. The comments were a bit daunting. I was doubtful that I could fix the model, but in the end I did, and it is the basis of this book.

Two lectures helped me extend the temporal scope of the argument. Avner Offer invited me to give the Hicks lecture at Oxford University, where I spoke on the late imperial economy. James MacKinnon invited me to give the Innis lecture to the Canadian Economics Association, where I discussed the post–World War II growth slowdown. I am grateful to Avner and James for these opportunities.

I thank several people and institutions for providing me an office and research support: Timothy Colton, Marshall Goldman, and the Russian Research Center at Harvard University, Peter Timmer and the Harvard Institute for International Development, and the Warden and Fellows of All Souls College.

This book contains material that was previously published in copyrighted academic journals. I am grateful to the publishers for the right to reprint this material: portions of Chapters 1 and 10 were published in my "Innis Lecture: The Rise and Decline of the Soviet Economy," *Canadian Journal of Economics*, vol. 34, 2001, pp. 859–81 (Basil Blackwell), portions of Chapter 7 in "The Standard of Living in the Soviet Union, 1928–40," *Journal of Economic History*, vol. 58, 1998, pp. 1063–89 (Cambridge University Press), portions of Chapter 8 in "Capital Accumulation, the Soft Budget Constraint, and Soviet Industrialization," *European Review of Economic History*, vol. 2, 1998, pp. 1–24 (Cambridge University Press), and portions of Chapter 4 in "Agricultural Marketing and the Possibilities for Industrialisation in the Soviet Union in the 1930s," *Explorations in Economic History*, vol. 34, pp. 387–410 (Elsevier Science).

I thank Abram Bergson, Leonid Borodkin, Paul David, Chris Davis, Evsey Domar, David Green, Sheila Fitzpatrick, Paul Gregory, Avner Greif,

Gregory Grossman, Cormac Ó Gráda, Sheila Johannson, Seth Klein, Paul Krause, Carol Leonard, Mary MacKinnon, Larry Neal, Hugh Neary, Patrick O'Brien, Gunnar Persson, Peter Timmer, and Gavin Wright for helpful comments, discussions, and suggestions. Ian Keay and Victoria Annable provided excellent research assistance, and I benefited from grants from the Social Sciences and Humanities Research Council of Canada and the International Research and Exchanges Board.

I am particularly grateful to Mark Baker, Stan Engerman, Anne Gorsuch, David Hoffman, Tracy MacDonald, and Jean-Laurent Rosenthal for reading the manuscript. Their comments were a great help.

Needless to say, the remaining errors are my own.

Farm to Factory

CHAPTER ONE

Soviet Development in World-Historical Perspective

The twentieth century was brief: it began with the Russian revolution of 1917 and ended with the dissolution of the Soviet Union on Christmas Day, 1991. Other events were important, of course—Hitler's rise to power, world war, the dissolution of the European empires, America's world hegemony—but these developments were powerfully influenced by the economic growth and political challenge of the USSR. With the end of communist rule and the dissolution of the Soviet Union, the world has entered a new era.

Death requires a postmortem, and the death of a country is no exception. The Soviet Union was a great social experiment with political, social, demographic, and economic dimensions. This book focuses on the economic issues—socialized ownership, investment strategy, agricultural organization, the growth of income, and consumption. What worked? What failed? And why? What lessons does Soviet history have to teach?

Discussion of Soviet economic performance has often been highly judgmental even when the underlying research has been dispassionately social-scientific. This was inevitable since political and intellectual life in the twentieth century was dominated by the contest between capitalism and socialism. Until Stalin's barbarities were exposed in the 1950s, the Soviet Union was the paradigm of socialism, and, even after that, there were few alternative examples of "actually existing socialism" to contemplate. Perhaps especially for the dreamers of a "better, truer" socialism, it is important to perform the autopsy on the last attempt.

But at the start of the twenty-first century, the failure of the Soviet Union has called into question any search for an alternative to capitalism. Most postmortems on the Soviet Union conclude that its economic model was hopelessly misguided. Rosefielde (1996, p. 980) was vehement and specific: "Stalin's economic programme thus must be judged a colossal failure. Administrative command planning proved inferior to market capitalism, growth was illusory, the nation's material welfare deteriorated during the 1930s and after some improvement lapsed into protracted stagnation." Harrison was more measured: "despite the Soviet great leap forward of 1928–37, . . . the USSR did not win the expected decisive victory in the economic race with the capitalist powers" (Davies, Harrison, and Wheatcroft 1994, p. 56). Malia (1994, p. 10) criticized the attempt to figure out what went wrong on the grounds that "the whole enterprise, quite simple, *was* wrong from the outset."

Overall judgments like these are generalized from conclusions on the major issues in Soviet economic history. The complete case for failure makes the following claims:

1. The Soviet growth rate was not impressively high when seen in a world context (Khanin 1988, 1991). Certainly many capitalist countries have done as well, including the European periphery, Japan and, more recently, the East Asian Tigers. The crimes of Stalin brought no economic advantage.

2. Even before 1917, the Russian economy had taken off on a trajectory of modern economic growth that would have achieved a west European standard of living by the 1980s had the Bolshevik revolution not derailed the process (Gregory 1994; Mironov 2000). Whatever the apparent success of Soviet communism, it did less well than Russian capitalism might have done.

3. The increased output achieved under the Communists was limited to steel, machinery, and military equipment. Consumption was driven down in the 1930s to free resources for investment and armaments, and living standards grew at an abnormally low rate throughout the communist period. This is the expected result of an economy run by dictators whose aim was personal aggrandizement and world power rather than the welfare of the working class — a group whose interests would have been better served by a continuation of capitalism (Tucker 1977; Bergson 1961; Chapman 1963).

4. The collectivization of agriculture in the 1930s is a particularly vicious example of these tendencies. Herding the peasants into collectives, deporting the best farmers, and terrorizing the countryside did allow the regime to squeeze resources for investment out of agriculture, but the result was mass starvation and ruined farms (Nove and Morrison 1982; Conquest 1986; Fitzpatrick 1994; Viola 1996).

5. Soviet socialism was economically irrational because it was driven by ideology, bureaucratic infighting, and despotic caprice. Ignoring prices led to massive misallocation of resources that depressed performance, judging enterprises by output instead of profits meant bloated payrolls and excessive costs, allowing planners instead of consumers to direct the economy unnaturally tilted the balance of production from consumption to investment and the military (Kornai 1992; Hunter and Szyrmer 1992; Malia 1994).

6. The growth slowdown after 1970 showed the ultimate weakness of socialism: while it could function in a mediocre way to build the smokestack industries of the first industrial revolution, it was incapable of the sustained technological advance required for the postindustrial age. Therefore, the system collapsed (Berliner 1976; Goldman 1983; Kornai 1992).

These claims make a formidable indictment, but all of them are contestable. (1) Some commentators have noted that Soviet growth was exceptionally rapid (Nove 1990, p. 387; Gregory and Stuart 1986, p. 422). (2) Leading historians of Russia have been pessimistic about the growth prospects of the empire of the tsars (Gerschenkron 1965; Owen 1995). (3) Most commentators accept that consumption grew rapidly in the Soviet Union after World War II (Gregory and Stuart 1986, pp. 347–50), and published evidence already points to consumption growth between 1928 and 1940 (Hunter and Szyrmer 1992; Wheatcroft 1999; Nove 1990, p. 242), although the case is rarely made. (4) While collectivization has few defenders, not all commentators have dismissed Soviet agriculture as hopelessly inefficient (Johnson and Brooks 1983), and there is a powerful argument that it accelerated industrialization (Nove 1962). (5) Soviet policies had a coherence that is often overlooked (Erhlich 1960). (6) The growth slowdown in the 1970s and 1980s had many possible causes, some of which imply deep-seated failures of Soviet institutions (perhaps the incentives to adopt new technologies is an example), while others (like the diversion of research and development personnel to the military) are incidental. Although the usual judgment on the Soviet economy is negative, these divergent views show that the question is still a live one.

These issues define the agenda for this book. To explore them, the argument is developed along three axes. The first is careful reconstruction of the quantitative dimensions of Soviet growth. Here my work builds on that of the early pioneers of Soviet economic and demographic statistics — Lorrimer (1946), Bergson (1961), Chapman (1963), Hunter and Szyrmer (1992), Karcz (1957, 1967, 1979), Kaplan (1969), Moorsteen and Powell (1966), Nutter (1962), and their associates and students like Gregory (1982) — although my conclusions differ in important respects from theirs, most notably with regard to consumption.

The second axis is international comparisons. These are the only way to see Soviet performance in perspective. The Bolsheviks measured the USSR against the United States, and during the Cold War the Americans did the same. I compare the Soviet Union to the advanced, capitalist countries, too, but I emphasize comparisons with less developed countries as well. In many respects, the Soviet Union in the 1920s had more in common with Asia, the Middle East, and Latin America than it did with Germany or the United States. These similarities underlay the attraction of the Soviet development model to leaders of Third World countries in the 1950s, 1960s, and 1970s: if the USSR could transform itself from an agrarian backwater into a superpower, maybe their country could do the same. Indeed, when compared to poor, Third World countries, Soviet performance was extremely good even taking account of the post-1970 growth slowdown. This record prompts one to look for policies and institutions that worked well rather than the usual cataloguing of reasons why the system was bound to fail. It also raises the question of whether there are positive lessons to learn from the Soviet experience.

The third axis is "what if?" (counterfactual) questions. These have always been central to an assessment of Soviet institutions and policies. The forced collectivization of agriculture is a case in point. It was not preordained: agrarian policy was heatedly debated in the 1920s. We can, therefore, ask how Soviet development would have differed had agriculture not been collectivized. This is Nove's (1962) famous question: "Was Stalin Really Necessary?" An even harder question is how successful Russia would have been had the 1917 revolution never happened. As unhistorical—and difficult—as these questions may be, it is only by engaging them that we can establish the historical import of momentous decisions like collectivization. This book uses economic and computer models to simulate counterfactual development in a way that is as systematic as possible.

The study of counterfactuals is also important for the light it throws on the "Soviet development model." What institutions worked and which failed? Could the model have been modified to make it more attractive and to raise living standards more rapidly? Should the negative assessment of Soviet performance be accepted without qualification, or were there aspects of economic organization that might be salvaged for the future? Questions like these require counterfactual investigation, and that is another reason it is pursued here.

SOVIET PERFORMANCE IN A WORLD-HISTORICAL CONTEXT

What was typical and what was unique in Soviet economic development? How well did the USSR perform compared to other countries in the twentieth century? The simplest indicator is gross domestic product (GDP) per head. Angus Maddison (1995) has pushed the data for the fifty-six largest economies[1] back to 1820.[2] These estimates establish four important points about the evolution of the world economy since 1820 and Russia's place in it.

First, the dominant tendency has been income divergence; that is, the

TABLE 1.1
GDP per Person around the World, 1820–1989 (1990 U.S. dollars)

	1820	1870	1900	1913	1928	1940	1950	1970	1989
USSR	751	1023	1218	1488	1370	2144	2874	5569	7078
W. Europe	1292	2110	3092	3704	4267	4901	5123	11080	16925
offshoots	1205	2440	4022	5237	6379	6813	9255	14372	21226
Mediterranean Periphery	1108	1436	1853	2263	2737	2866	2867	8273	13435
Northern Periphery	1000	1561	2221	2652	3139	3925	5244	10214	15866
Eastern Europe	748	1041	1345	1694	1947	1997	2145	4338	5916
Latin America Southern Core	–	–	2443	3439	3975	3923	4683	6710	6566
Latin America rest	723	725	899	1095	1332	1483	1883	3329	4886
China	523	523	652	688	779	778	614	1092	2649
Japan	704	741	1135	1334	1917	2765	1873	9448	17757
Taiwan & S Korea	–	–	828	909	1174	1548	888	2360	8827
S.E. Asia	–	–	790	977	1197	1183	941	1411	2644
South Asia	531	558	626	661	664	646	589	852	1237
Middle East	–	–	–	759	719	963	1038	1725	2919
Black Africa	–	–	–	440	527	559	537	810	799

Source: Computed from Maddison (1995).

countries that were rich in 1820 grew faster than the countries that were poor (Pritchett 1997). As a result, the gap between rich and poor countries has widened. Broadly speaking, there were two trajectories through the twentieth century: a country could become an advanced industrial economy or it could become an underdeveloped economy. A country's path depended, in large measure, on its starting point. Table 1.1 illustrates this pattern for broad groups of countries. In 1820, the rich countries were in western Europe (with an income of $1292), the "offshoots," that is, the United States, Canada, Australia, and New Zealand ($1205), the northern periphery of Ireland and Scandinavia ($1000), and the Mediterranean periphery of Spain, Greece, and Portugal ($1050). The rest of the world—including Russia—lagged behind with an income between $525 and $750. While there has been growth almost everywhere, the countries that were richest in 1820 grew fastest. Thus, in 1820, western Europe was two and a half times richer than South Asia; by 1989, the lead had grown to 15 times. Per capita GDP rose by a factor of 10 to 20 in the rich countries while the least successful regions—Latin America, South and Southeast Asia, and Black Africa—saw only a doubling or tripling of output per head. Divergence—not convergence—has been the dominant tendency since the industrial revolution.

Second, within the group of rich countries there has been some convergence of income as the peripheral and—it should be emphasized—small countries on the fringe of western Europe caught up with the core. Convergence has lately received much attention from economists who were initially hopeful that it characterized the whole world. The simplest explanation is that convergence represents the diffusion of the industrial revolution. This is also the most optimistic interpretation since modern industry, in principle, can spread anywhere. While technological diffusion undoubtedly played a role, it is also clear that the growth of GDP per capita in countries like Ireland and Sweden owed much to massive emigration (O'Rourke and Williamson 1999), which cut the denominator in income per head. It was the small size of these countries that allowed big fractions of their populations to move to the offshoots. This source of convergence could not operate on a world scale.

Third, the division between the rich countries and the poor countries has been exceptionally stable. Very few countries have switched groups. Japan is remarkable for outstripping the poor countries and joining the rich. Possibly, Taiwan and South Korea, Japan's former colonies, are doing the same thing. In contrast, the southern cone of Latin America—Chile, Argentina, and Uruguay—has gone the other way. In the late nineteenth century, they were as rich as the advanced countries of Europe and were closely integrated into the world economy. Subsequent growth has been slow, and they have fallen into the company of the poor countries. Otherwise, the divisions have been stable.

Fourth, the Soviet Union grew rapidly in comparison to the other countries of the world. This stands out for the 1928–70 period, when the planning system was working well and also obtains—less dramatically—when comparisons are made over the whole 1928–89 period.

Figure 1.1 shows the relevant facts. The vertical axis shows the growth rate (the factor by which GDP per head grew from 1928 to 1970), and the horizontal axis shows 1928 income. The Organisation for Economic Co-operation and Development (OECD) points lie to the right of the graph in view of their higher 1928 incomes.[3] There is also a downward trend in the OECD points characteristic of income convergence (the poorer OECD countries in 1928 had a higher income growth factor). The trend line is the OECD "catch-up regression." The non-OECD points are clustered in the lower left of the graph. These countries had low incomes in 1928 and low growth rates to 1970, so they failed to catch up with the leaders.

The Soviet Union (with a 1928 income of $1370 and a growth factor of 4.1) was the non-OECD country that did the best in Figure 1.1. Its

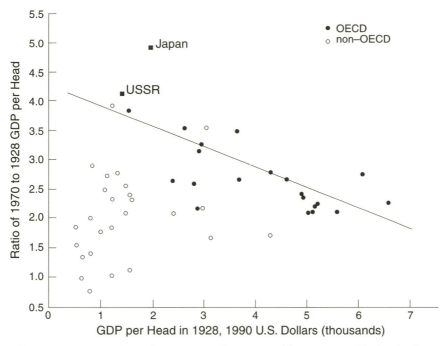

Fig. 1.1. Economic Growth, 1928–70. *Source*: Maddison (1995). Turkey is classified as a non-OECD country.

growth factor was also higher than that of all OECD countries except Japan. Soviet performance exceeded the OECD catch-up regression, which is a more stringent standard since its value is higher for poor countries than for rich. Figure 1.1 shows that the USSR performed exceptionally well over the 1928–70 period if it is classified as a less developed country and also outperforms the average OECD country even allowing for catch-up.

These conclusions hold, with some emendations, if the comparisons are extended to 1989, the year before the "reform" process began to cut GDP per head. The Soviet economy grew slowly in the 1970s and 1980s, so adding those years to the balance is unfavorable to the USSR. Nevertheless, the previous years of fast growth meant that the USSR's overall record from 1928 to 1989 was still better than that of all major non-OECD countries with the exception of Taiwan and South Korea—the leaders of the East Asian miracle.

The long-run record is reviewed regionally in Figures 1.2–1.5. Figure 1.2 compares Soviet income per head to that of the rich countries of the

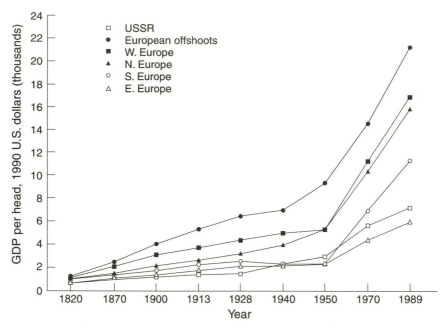

Fig. 1.2. USSR versus Europe and Its Offshoots. *Source*: Table 1.1.

West. Russia started from a lower base and did not catch up, although the Soviet Union grew faster than the West after 1928 and cut the gap that had opened up at the start of the planning period.

Figure 1.3 compares the USSR to East Asia. The Soviet Union does worse by this comparison than by any other, for Japan is the one country that had a mid-nineteenth-century income of less than $750 and that caught up with the advanced countries of the West. Japan was unique. In recent decades, Taiwan and South Korea have grown very rapidly and have overtaken the Soviet Union, although they have not yet caught up with the West. Their recent success recapitulates their performance as Japanese colonies, when output rose from $828 in 1900 to $1548 in 1940. The East Asian miracle has long-standing roots that involve cultural and political factors that are not easily replicated; it is much more than a few simple policies that are geographically transportable.

The rest of the world is poor and has an unimpressive growth record. Figure 1.4 compares Soviet income levels to those in Latin America. The southern cone (Argentina, Chile, and Uruguay) had a European standard of living in the late nineteenth century, but has achieved only limited growth since. By 1989, these countries were surpassed by the USSR. The rest of Latin America started off poor in 1820 and grew at about

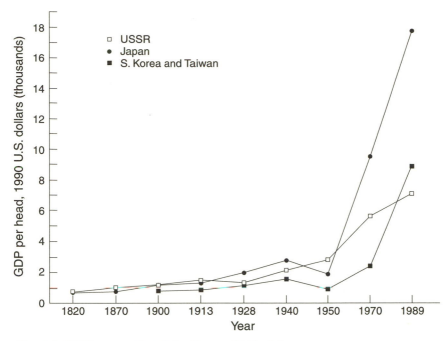

Fig. 1.3. USSR versus East Asia. *Source*: Table 1.1.

the same rate as Russia and the USSR to 1928. Thereafter the Soviet Union grew faster and realized a higher level of income in 1989.

Soviet performance is much more impressive when the rest of the world is the standard (Figure 1.5). In the late nineteenth century, Southeast Asia (Indonesia, Thailand, and the Philippines) grew, like Russia, through integration into the world economy. Growth then slowed until very recent years. The Middle East (here represented by Turkey, Egypt, and Morocco) and China made little progress for much of the century but have also begun to grow in the past generation. GDP growth in South Asia (India, Pakistan, Bangladesh, and Burma) was more lethargic and almost negligible in Black Africa, which remains at a preindustrial income level. As Figure 1.5 makes clear, the Soviet Union grew rapidly since 1928 and had achieved an income level in 1989 several times that of any of these regions.

This point can be buttressed by comparing incomes in Soviet Central Asia (Kazakhstan, Kyrgyzstan, Tajikistan, Turkmenistan, and Uzbekistan) and the north Caucuses republics (Armenia, Azerbaijan, and Georgia) with those in adjoining parts of the middle East and South Asia. These Soviet republics were always the poorest in the USSR and were in

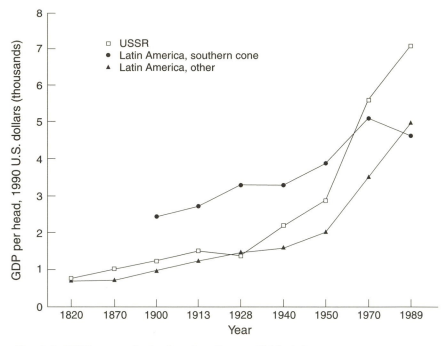

Fig. 1.4. USSR versus Latin America. *Source*: Table 1.1.

a pristinely premodern state in the 1920s that was no more advanced than neighboring regions outside the Soviet Union. In 1989, these republics were still the poorest of the USSR, but they had attained a per capita GDP of $5257 per year.[4] This exceeded incomes in the most developed neighboring states—for example, Turkey with an average income of $3989 or Iran with an income of $3662—to say nothing of the poorer neighbors like Pakistan at $1542 or war-torn Afghanistan, which Maddison guessed had an income of $1000 per head. The Soviet populations in Central Asia and the north Caucuses experienced substantially more income growth than their counterparts in neighboring countries who started the twentieth century in similar circumstances.

As noted, however, the overall impressive record is an amalgam of two very different experiences. Leaving aside the war-torn 1940s, GDP grew at 5 to 6 percent per year from 1928 to 1970. The growth rate dropped to 3.7 percent in 1970–75, then to 2.6 percent in 1975–80, and finally reached 2.0 percent in 1980–85. The latter was effectively nil on a per capita basis. While the energy crisis and the Third World debt crisis hurt many countries in this period, the Soviet growth slowdown was unusually sharp. A major challenge of Soviet economic his-

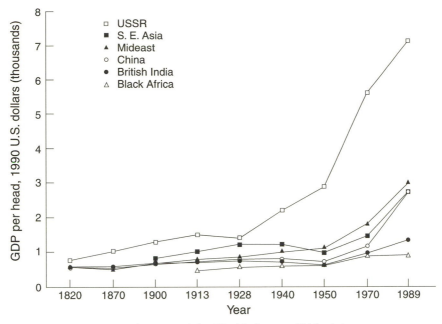

Fig. 1.5. USSR versus the Rest of the World. *Source*: Table 1.1.

tory is to explain how the rapid growth before 1970 turned into the slowdown of the past twenty years. Did the growth slowdown indicate a fundamental contradiction of the Soviet system, or was it due to external factors or policy errors that might have been avoided?

RUSSIA'S PLACE IN THE WORLD

Which is the right group for assessing Soviet performance: the rich capitalist countries of western Europe and its offshoots, or the poor countries of Asia, Latin America, and Africa? Russia's place in the world has been debated since the late Middle Ages. Little thought was given to the question before the late seventeenth century, when it was assumed that Russia straddled Europe and Asia with the line of division following one or another of the great rivers through what is now called European Russia. It was only after Peter the Great's drive to modernize the country that it was reconceptualized as a great empire — on the Western pattern — with its center in Europe and its colonies in Asia, and it was only in the eighteenth century that the continental boundary was pushed east to the Urals. With that relabeling, the Slavic regions were rebaptized as European. This division was hotly contested in the nineteenth century by the Slavophiles, who wanted to distinguish Slavic Russia from Europe and designate Russia as a third great continent like Europe and Asia. Both the communist and postcommunist Westernizers have reaffirmed Peter the Great's cartography, but the important point is its artificiality. Looking at a map is not enough to decide whether Russia is European or Asian (Bassin 1991, 1993).

What is at issue is the inevitability (and desirability) of Russia's catching up with the West. The vision is Eurocentric: implicitly, it is assumed that industrialization is an essentially European phenomenon that all European countries will eventually experience. The process started in Britain in the eighteenth century, spread to northwestern Europe by 1850, and reached southern and eastern Europe by 1900. The Communists thought they were accelerating Russia's growth, while the anti-Communists thought that the 1917 revolution stalled the process, which would resume after 1991. No one expected much growth outside of Europe, so Russia's future depended on its classification. Both parties thought that Russia would become a replica — indeed, the Communists thought an improved version — of the West because both insisted that Russia was European.

The history of world incomes since 1800 provides some evidence in favor of this model. Within Europe, there has been convergence, and Europe has done better than most other regions. Japan's stellar performance is, of course, a challenge, that can be handled by identifying some "European" aspect of Japanese life — Western-style "feudalism" for Marxists or a "capitalist spirit" for Weberians — that sets it apart from the rest of the Third World.

While the classification of Russia can be endlessly debated, there are good reasons for seeing it as non-European rather than European. In the first place, objective indicators point in that direction.

The first is income in the early nineteenth century. As noted in the previous section, the capitalist core and its offshoots already had incomes of $1200 per head and the Mediterranean and Scandinavian peripheries were $1000 per head or more. Russia and the rest of the world had per capita incomes of $750 or less.

The second is economic structure. In 1928, for instance, the rich capitalist countries had far more evolved economies. The share of the population in agriculture was about one-quarter in the western European core and about one-fifth in the offshoots. In the Mediterranean and northern peripheries — the backward parts of Europe soon to catch up with the leaders — the agricultural fraction was about one-half. Likewise, Japan had only half of its population in agriculture. These fractions represent a considerable reduction from the value of three-quarters, which is commonly observed in premodern economies.[5]

Outside of the OECD, few countries had made much progress. In most countries, about three-quarters of the population was agricultural. That was the proportion in the Russian Empire in 1913. Industrial collapse during the civil war (1918–21) pushed it up to 82 percent in 1926 (Davies 1990, p. 251). In keeping with their higher incomes at the time, the agricultural fraction was much lower in Argentina, Chile, Venezuela, and Czechoslovakia.

Third, the rich and poor countries have also had very different demographic regimes. Hajnal (1965) has famously argued for the distinction between European and non-European family structures. The patterns show up in censuses around 1900. In the European pattern, the average woman was in her late 20s when she first married and many women, indeed, never married. In the non-European pattern, virtually all women married, and they married young — mostly before the age of 20. This distinction is of tremendous importance. Beyond its cultural significance, fertility rates and population growth were greater where the non-European pattern predominated.

Where did Russia fit into this scheme? The geographical division was marked by a line from St. Petersburg to Trieste. North and west of that line, the European pattern was the norm, while the non-European pattern predominated to the south and east. Thus, with the exception of the Baltic and the Polish provinces, the Russian Empire was squarely in the non-European zone. It is important to emphasize that the Slavic heartland, as well as Central Asia and Siberia, were non-European by this criterion. So far as demography was concerned, the Slavophiles were right — Russia was not European.

The predominant historiographical tradition attributes Russia's high fertility to peculiarly Russian institutions, notably the peasant commune. These periodically redivided land among their members to equalize holdings. There was, consequently, no penalty for large families, and, indeed, many children served to expand a family's importance by securing more land at the next repartition (Gerschenkron 1965, p. 755; Pavlorsky 1930, p. 83; Violin 1970, p. 92; Heer 1968; Chojnacka 1976, pp. 210–11). Hoch (1994) has questioned this consensus, and the analysis in Chapter 6 shows that Russia's large families were the result of the same traditional, patriarchal values that have led to large families in many poor, non-European countries.

In the twentieth century, countries where the non-European pattern predominated had population explosions that have frustrated development efforts and contributed to the divergence in per capita income. The demographic patterns c. 1900 suggest that Russia's destiny was closer to India's than to Germany's.

RUSSIAN COMPARISONS: LAW AND SOCIETY

A similar conclusion obtains if we shift from economic and demographic indicators to cultural, legal, and political considerations. Free market development requires private property, nonintrusive government, and — more generally — a broad social space that is free of government interference and in which private individuals can pursue their objectives in competitive and cooperative fashions. Successful capitalism is underpinned by a vigorous "civil society" (Seligman 1992; Putnam 1993). These were the characteristic institutions of Western states but not of tsarist Russia.

The civil society view differs from standard Marxist analysis, which attributes the ascendancy of the West to the rise of capitalism, which, in turn, is attributed, by this school, to the concentration of property ownership in the hands of a rich minority as the working majority loses its wealth. The civil society view also differs from neoliberal theories (e.g., North and Thomas 1973) that emphasize the importance of clearly defined property rights, irrespective of who owns them. The civil society view is more Tocquevillian: economic success is facilitated by widespread property ownership. Widespread property ownership promoted economic efficiency, particularly in agriculture, since greater output or lower costs translated directly into higher income for owner-occupying farmers and, thereby, gave them an incentive to innovate. Widespread property ownership also contributed to economic independence and allowed parents to invest in schooling and training for their children. Economic independence also promoted active citizenship, including participation in politics and voluntary associations. The result was more effective government and a vibrant "civil society." A social sphere that allowed economic competition and voluntary cooperation independent of the state depended on widespread property ownership.

The West had it, but Russia did not. The differences between the two parts of Europe evolved over centuries. After the Norman conquest in 1066, England had the most centralized monarchy in Europe. In the twelfth century, Henry II effected a legal revolution that allowed free men to defend their title to freehold property in royal courts rather than in those of their feudal superiors. This was an important step in establishing secure private ownership of land. The high-handed behavior of the Angevin kings led to the confrontation between King John and the barons at Runnymede in 1215 when the king conceded the Magna Carta, which was an important first step in limiting the power of the Crown. Conflict between peasants, lords, and the monarch led to the extension of peasant proprietorship through copyholds and beneficial leases in the sixteenth and seventeenth centuries (Allen 1992). The civil war and the Glorious Revolution secured the primacy of Parliament over the Crown. The widespread ownership of private property and the establishment of representative government (if not democracy) was the basis of civil society independent of the state.

On the Continent, widespread property ownership also evolved but through different channels. In late medieval France, for instance, the weakness of the king led to the consolidation of peasant title as well as the consolidation of noble property and to the creation of municipal, provincial, and ecclesiastical privileges that were immune to the pretensions of the later absolutist monarchs (Bloch 1931; Epstein 2000). In many parts of the Low Countries and in Germany, conflicts between the emperor, kings, nobles, and cities resulted in the securing of property by the upper classes and also by policies that protected peasant title (De Vries 1976; Thoen 1993). As in England, legal regimes and social patterns conducive to market-oriented development emerged.

Russian history did not replicate this pattern. By the eighteenth century, power was concentrated in the hands of the tsar, the nobility was dependent with little scope for self-directed action, and the peasantry was reduced to a serfdom little above slavery.[6] Liberals as well as Marxists regarded this social structure as a cause of underdevelopment.

The origins of serfdom run back to the fifteenth century. At the time, serfdom was disappearing in western Europe, as it was being imposed in eastern Europe. Russian serfdom can be seen as a response to a small population in a vast territory. About 10 million people lived in European Russia in 1400—one-twelfth of the population of the European part of the Russian Empire in 1913 (Bairoch et al. 1988, p. 297; McEvedy and Jones 1978, p. 82). In the Middle Ages, much of Russia was controlled by the Tatars as part of the Mongol Empire, and the duchy of Moscow controlled only a small territory around that city. In the fifteenth and sixteenth centuries, the grand prince, who adopted the title of tsar,[7] vastly expanded his territories at the expense first of the Tatars, and, then, of the Polish state that ruled western Russia and Ukraine. By 1800, the Russian Empire was nearing its maximum geographical extent in Europe, but its population was only 30 million—still less than one-quarter of its 1913 value (McEvedy and Jones 1978, p. 82).

With a very low population throughout the early modern period, Russia was a frontier society like nineteenth-century North America (Bassin 1993). Abundant land meant that new farms could be easily established. As a result, land commanded no rent; the nobility could extract little income from tenants, who would relocate if much was asked. Labor was the scarce factor of production, and the nobility could be supported only by preventing the peasants from fleeing. Once immobilized, they could be forced to pay rent and work the lords' land without compensation. One feature of the settlement process worked in the lords' favor: as new arrivals, the peasants lacked a history of collective resistance to noble demands, and this made them easier to enserf (Brenner 1989). Serfdom (or slavery) was not the inevitable consequence of free land—slavery was the rule in the Southern United States but not the Northern states and peasant resistance had played a role in ending serfdom in western Europe after the Black Death[8]—but the tsar had the political power and will to tie the Russian peasants to the land so that they could be exploited by the nobility and the state (Domar 1970; Crummey 1987) . The Ulozhneie of 1649 was the decree that accomplished that.[9]

The result was a society in which the "rule of law" was a tool by which the tsar and nobles exploited the peasants rather than an impartial umpire defining the rules of the game in which social equals pursued mutually advantageous relationships and exchanges. Yakovlev (1995, p. 5), for instance, claimed that "the basic cultural fact of Russian history is that in people's consciousness, the law never was associated with moral truth." It "was harsh and oppressive, unjust and cruel . . . the law of serfdom." According to Owen (1998, pp. 24–25), "The various codes of laws issued from 1497 onward indicated the vigour with which Tsarist bureaucrats sought to regiment society by means of statutory compulsion and restriction. The law functioned as an administrative device not as a set of rules to be obeyed by state officials." Russia had "rule *by* law" rather than "the rule *of* law" (Hedlund 2001, p. 222). The sphere for cooperation and voluntary exchange was, thereby, restricted, and business was inhibited by the meddling and interference of state officials. Since the seventeenth century an independent "civil society" has been the impossible dream of Russian liberals.

MISSING PREREQUISITES

Tsarist Russia lacked the social, legal, and economic institutions that theorists of economic growth have argued are prerequisites for capitalist development. Indeed, much of the rest of the world lacked—and still lacks—them as well. From the policy perspective, two responses are possible. One is to create the missing prerequisites. This is a favorite of development agencies. The second is to create substitutes for the missing prerequisites. This is an old idea to economic historians—especially historians of Russia—for Gerschenkron (1962) explored it a generation ago. At the time, entrepreneurship was regarded as a prerequisite for growth, and Russia was supposed to have been held back by a lack of the entrepreneurial spirit. Gerschenkron argued that state promotion was substituted for the missing entrepreneurs, so industrial growth proceeded in the late empire despite the lack of this prerequisite. Not much is heard about the entrepreneurial spirit today, but the same logic applies to other missing prerequisites. In reality, societies can invent around them, so development need not be impeded.

Russia's path to industrial society was based on the state's creating policies and institutions to substitute for the prerequisites that characterized Western economies. At the end of the seventeenth century, Russia was already falling behind the advanced countries of western Europe. Rising agricultural productivity and world empires were leading to extensive urbanization and manufacturing growth in the Netherlands and England. Russia did attempt to replicate this success in what has become the characteristic pattern. Instead of a broadly based, market-oriented process of development, Tsar Peter the Great (1682–1725) embarked on a state-directed program of importing Western technology. Hundreds of factories were established to produce mainly military products. While the great city of St. Petersburg was created, the modernization efforts had little impact on the structure of the economy, which remained overwhelmingly agricultural. In 1800, only 5 percent of the population lived in towns of 5000 people or more (Bairoch et al. 1988, p. 259). Indeed, the overall impact of Peter the Great may have been negative, for he extended serfdom and made it more rigorous rather than promoting a civil society capable of independent initiative.

With a weak private sector, economic development depended on state promotion and direction. Following defeat in the Crimean War, Tsar Alexander II abolished serfdom in the 1860s. In the late nineteenth century, the state promoted the construction of a vast railroad system and pursued an industrial policy to build the iron, coal, and engineering industries to supply its needs. Tariffs were used to encourage cotton spinning and weaving and later the cultivation of cotton plants east of the Caspian Sea. There was some growth, to be sure, but, I argue, the economic and demographic transformation was limited. The tsars did not lay the groundwork for rapid, capitalist development. In the absence of the communist revolution and the Five-Year Plans, Russia would have remained as backward as much of Latin America or, indeed, South Asia.

That fate was avoided by Stalin's economic institutions. They were a further installment of the use of state direction to cause growth in an economy that would have stagnated if left to its own devices. Most of this book is concerned with how Stalin's industrial revolution was accomplished, establishing its costs and benefits, and considering some alternative socialist strategies that would have avoided the catastrophes of Stalinism. Finally, the book explores the economic slowdown of the 1970s and 1980s that was one of the causes of the system's collapse.

PART ONE

The Economy before Stalin

CHAPTER TWO

Economic Growth before 1917

The 1917 revolution was preceded by half a century of economic expansion. In 1820, Russian income per head was $749 (1990 dollars), which was on a par with the less developed countries of Asia, Africa, and Latin America, and significantly behind western Europe. Russia did not languish like many poor countries but was one of the first to try to catch up with the West. It made some progress — by 1913 its income had risen to $1488 per head — but the West was a moving target, and, on a percentage basis, Russia was farther behind in 1913 than it had been in 1820. Nonetheless, a start had been made.

But was it a satisfactory start? The imperial expansion raises some big questions: Why did it occur? Would it have continued had Russia remained a capitalist state? Was there a connection between tsarist growth and the revolutions that shook the country? Scholars and analysts have argued the issues since the late nineteenth century. I distinguish four positions: Lenin's, Gerschenkron's, those of a school (including Carstensen and Owen) that I call the business historians, and the optimist tradition, in particular, the views of Gregory.

Lenin's views are important because of his great influence and because of the historical theses he propounded. He argued that economic growth required the emergence of capitalism. The abolition of serfdom in the 1860s was a first step, but the terms of the emancipation inhibited the transition to capitalism and slowed the growth of the economy. The nobles were compensated for the loss of their serfs with government bonds that were serviced by redemption payments levied on each village. Recent research suggests that peasants were significantly overcharged for their land (Gerschenkron 1965; Domar and Machina 1984; Domar 1989). The village taxed its members to finance the redemption payments, and, to collect those taxes, the commune had control over the movements of its members. In most of the empire, the allotment land granted to the peasants at emancipation was given to the commune, which had the right to reallocate it among its members. The emancipation of the serfs slowed economic growth by reinforcing communal ownership, by preventing the emergence of a labor market, and by reducing the demand for manufactures since self-sufficient peasants bought few commodities.

Lenin, however, was optimistic that growth would occur. He believed that capitalist farming was more productive than peasant cultivation. As a result, he thought that the egalitarian commune was splintering into a few large-scale farmers and a mass of landless laborers. This process, which Lenin called "peasant differentiation," spurred industrial development by freeing labor. A domestic market for manufactures was also created since large-scale farmers purchased factory-made implements and since landless laborers bought food and clothing instead of producing their own. Thus, Lenin was confident that capitalism was emerging and that the Russian economy was taking off. He was equally certain, however, that capitalism would collapse in revolution since rapid technical progress would depress urban wages and since polarization in the countryside would lead to rebellion. The revolutions of 1905–7 and 1917 seemed to confirm that prediction. Or do they?

Alexander Gerschenkron was less confident than Lenin that Russia was embarked on self-sustaining growth. Like Lenin, he traced Russia's problems back to the peasant land commune, which he criticized for similar reasons. Gerschenkron, however, parted company with Lenin over the question of peasant differentiation. While Lenin traced the domestic market to that process, Gerschenkron argued, instead, that the state provided the demand for factory products through its program of railroad building. By 1913, Russia had 70,156 kilometers of track—one of the largest networks in the world (Khromov 1950, p. 462). High tariffs channeled the demand for rails and locomotives to Russian producers. Industrial output surged upward with producer goods comprising an unusually large share of the total. To Gerschenkron, Russian growth was a precarious achievement that depended crucially on state promotion and failed to create widespread prosperity. Persisting rural poverty lay behind the revolutions of 1905–7 and 1917.

Another pessimistic tradition has developed from studies of Russian businesses and their interactions with the state. These investigations show how state policy and Russian culture frustrated entrepreneurship and blocked the emergence of a Western, commercial society. In contrast to Gerschenkron's analysis, "Russia was not so much demand-constrained and therefore in need of a substitute market as it was constrained by institutions and policies." These included "uncertainty of property rights and limited access to capital, markets, and skills" (Carstensen and Guroff 1983, p. 355). Corporation law is a blatant example. Instead of incorporation by registration—the usual mode in advanced countries and Japan—Russia's "concessionary system of incorporation obstructed the free establishment of corporations by delaying the granting of charters." Restrictions on ownership and activities were often imposed in the charters granted. More generally, business success depended significantly on state support. Tariffs, subsidies, and interest rates were altered arbitrarily and capriciously by the bureaucracy (Owen 1995, pp. 21–22). Imperial policy was not based on the Smithian notion that the interplay of self-interested producers advanced the public interest. Instead, the state manipulated private firms to such a degree that the possibility of spontaneous growth was frustrated.

Economic historians and analysts have recently emphasized that clearly defined property rights and a stable legal environment promote capitalist growth, while arbitrary regulation, high transaction costs, and corruption inhibit it (North and Thomas 1973; North 1990). The legal situation and business environment of imperial Russia failed to meet these conditions. "However vigorous the economic policies of the Tsarist government, they did not lay a firm foundation of legality" (Owen 1995, p. 28). In this respect, Russia in 1900 was much like Russia in 2000 and, indeed, like many of the unsuccessful capitalist countries of the Third World.

These characteristics of Russian policy were not accidental but reflected widespread and long-standing anticapitalist sentiments and the — ultimately reactionary — interests of the tsar. McDaniel (1988, p. 17) observed that "the strength and legitimacy of capitalism depend upon a triad of institutions that were poorly developed in Russia because of its autocratic political structure: private property, law, and contract. Without these there were no firm bases for entrepreneurial initiative and authority." Carstensen and Guroff (1983, pp. 353–54) distinguished three schools that contended for influence with the tsar. The traditionalists, like Plehve, opposed industrialization and modernization, including Western systems of property and law. The industrializers like Witte sought industrialization without modernization. "But these industrializers were rarely willing to permit, let alone promote, significant institutional transformations, especially those that tended to diminish the power and legitimacy of the center." Finally, the modernizers like Stolypin were the most inclined to transform basic Russian institutions. While Stolypin did launch an agrarian reform, this group was the weakest, and Stolypin was already being undermined by traditionalists before his assassination. In this respect, it is interesting that the heirs to the Russian throne were subjected to lectures in economics, which extolled the virtues of private property and limited government. While Nicholas II wrote a satisfactory examination on the material, he did not put it into practice later in life (Owen 1995, p. 28; Anan'ich 1983, p. 136).

While many commentators have been pessimistic about the imperial economy, there has been an optimistic school claiming the country was launched on rapid economic growth in the Western manner. Mironov (2000) has disputed the pessimism of the business historians and argued, instead, that Russia was developing a legal system and civic society that would have ultimately produced western European-style development. Gregory (1994) has advanced a similarly optimistic interpretation of Russia's economic prospects. His work commands respect because of his empirical contributions to two issues. The first is his estimate of Russian national income from 1885 to 1913, which accurately charts the growth of the economy and shows that it was rapid. The second is his finding that agricultural productivity was rising and that, indeed, the increase in agricultural output made a major contribution to the rise in GDP. Rising productivity challenges Gerschenkron's pessimism based on the supposed immobility of the land commune.

Gregory's empirical findings have changed the terms of the debate, but his interpretations are open to question. He claims that Russia was embarked on "modern economic growth" that was spontaneous (not rooted in state promotion or special features of the period), that raised living standards, and that could be expected to continue through the twentieth century. Since the economy was performing so well, it provides no explanation for the 1917 revolution. "The linkage between economics and politics has always been weak. Misinterpretations and misunderstandings are typically at their worst when economics is used to explain the dynamics of revolution" (Gregory 1994, p. 7). Had capitalist growth continued, Gregory is optimistic that Russia would have achieved a standard of living like that of western Europe by 1990.

This chapter argues that pessimism is the appropriate response to the imperial economy. I offer a more articulated analysis of the sources of growth and the distribution of income than the optimists have presented, and this analysis leads to pessimistic conclusions. While GDP per head certainly went up, the progress was largely due to an agricultural boom that was tied to special features of the world economy in the nineteenth century. Industrial growth made only a small contribution, and much of that was due to state promotion that could not be relied on in the long run. Furthermore, the growth process gave rise to serious conflicts of interest between the main social classes, and those conflicts were fault lines in 1917. It took failure in the First World War, the incompetence and the authoritarianism of the tsar, and the effectiveness of Bolshevik organization to create a revolution, but the imperial economy was fertile ground for radical politics.

Modern Economic Growth?

The most persuasive evidence that Russia was embarked on modern economic growth is the increase in national income, which grew at 3.3 percent per year (1.7 percent per head) from 1885 to 1913 (Gregory

TABLE 2.1
Structure of the Russian Economy, 1885 and 1913
(value added in 1913 prices)

	1885 VA		1913 VA	
Agriculture	5044	58.7%	10294	50.7%
Heavy industry	175	2.0%	1632	8.0%
Light industry	400	4.6%	1391	6.9%
Handicrafts	565	6.5%	1311	6.5%
Transportation/communications	199	2.3%	1173	5.8%
Construction	445	5.1%	1035	5.1%
Trade	869	10.1%	1640	8.1%
Government	186	2.2%	565	2.8%
Housing	386	4.5%	743	3.7%
Medical	47	0.5%	126	0.6%
Domestic service	206	2.4%	264	1.3%
Utilities	71	0.8%	118	0.6%
National income	8594		20292	

Sources: Gregory (1982, p. 73). Gregory's category of factory industry was subdivided into heavy and light industry in proportion to employment (Falkus 1968, p. 58). Heavy industry was taken to be quarrying, mining, metallurgy and machines, wood, chemicals, and motive power. Growth rates for heavy and light industry from Kafengauz (1994, p. 292, col. 15, and p. 297, col. 20). Kafengauz's (1994, pp. 151, 165) sample has a similar employment breakdown for light and heavy industry to the overall figures shown by Falkus.

1982, pp. 56–57, variant 2). Total output growth was high by world standards and per capita growth was on a par with western Europe and North America. Russia also shared other characteristics of a developing country, like a rising investment rate.

The case for the success of the Russian economy becomes much weaker when structural change is analyzed. About three-quarters of the population were peasant farmers in 1913 — scarcely down from the 1861 level. Conversely, the proportion of Russians living in towns of 5000 or more increased from about 6 percent in 1800 to 7 percent in 1850 and reached only 14 percent in 1913 (Bairoch 1988, pp. 221, 290). The population statistics show little evidence of structural transformation.

It is the same story when GDP is broken down by sector of origin (Table 2.1). Agriculture accounted for 59 percent of the economy in 1885, and its share only slid to 51 percent in 1913. At the same time, the industrial share rose from 6.6 percent to 14.9 percent, thus taking up the slack and matching the growth in the urban population. Russia was developing a modern economy, but the pace was glacial.

TABLE 2.2
Growth of the Russian Economy by Sector, 1885–1913

	Output growth factor	Increased value added	Percentage of increased value added
Agriculture	2.04	5250	44.9%
Heavy industry	9.31	1457	12.5
Light industry	3.48	991	8.5%
Handicrafts	2.80	746	6.4%
Transportation/communications	5.88	974	8.3%
Construction	2.33	590	5.0%
Trade	1.89	771	6.6%
Government	3.03	379	3.2%
Housing	1.92	357	3.0%
Medical	2.70	79	0.7%
Domestic service	1.28	58	0.5%
Utilities	1.67	47	0.4%
National income	2.36	11698	100.0%

Sources: See Table 2.1.

The central role of agriculture is even clearer in Table 2.2, which shows the growth rates of the sectors and their absolute contributions to the rise in real output. Agricultural production doubled, and the large size of the sector meant that its expansion accounted for 45 percent of the growth in the whole economy. Since grain was the main cargo of the railroads and since the wholesaling of grain was a major activity of the trade sector, agriculture probably accounted for over half of the growth in the Russian economy. Light industry and handicrafts accounted for another fifth of the growth, with cotton textiles accounting for much of that. Finally, heavy industry and construction, which were at the center of the investment process, accounted for almost another fifth. The greater importance of heavy industry compared to light industry is a point in Gerschenkron's favor.

Gregory, however, used these figures to contradict Gerschenkron's pessimistic assessment of Russian agriculture. Gregory's argument was correct, but its range extends farther than he intended, for it calls into question his own conclusion that Russia had embarked on modern economic growth. This portentous term suggests that Russians had boarded an express elevator that would whisk them to the age of high mass consumption. Russia's expansion, however, was never so grand. It is more aptly described as a one-off resource boom with a veneer of some tariff-induced industrialization.

AGRICULTURAL EXPANSION

The central problem in explaining the growth of the imperial economy has to do with the growth of its agriculture. That growth was due to three features of the late nineteenth century: the integration of the world economy, building Russia's railroads (itself part of world integration), and improvements in agricultural productivity (possibly due to market integration).

The international economy became highly integrated in the late nineteenth century. Ocean shipping rates collapsed as steam replaced sail in the world's merchant marine. There was a narrowing in the difference between wheat prices at exporting points like Buenos Aires, Chicago, and Odessa and European destinations like Liverpool. Prices fell in Europe, and, after 1896, rose on the periphery. At the same time, railroad building cheapened the cost of shipping grain from farms to the coast. The result was a further rise in wheat prices in the Russian interior that linked Russian farmers closely to the international market (Metzer 1974). The implications of world integration are vividly conveyed by the observation of an official of the Russian Ministry of Finance in 1903:

> On the market place in Nikolayev I had an opportunity to observe a fact which a short time ago would have been altogether incredible. The peasants on arrival at the market with their grain were asking: "What is the price in America according to the latest telegram?" And what is still more surprising they know how to convert cents per bushel into kopecks per pood (Quoted by Metzer 1974, p. 549).

Rising agricultural prices resulted in a dramatic improvement in agriculture's terms of trade. Figure 2.1 shows the ratio of wholesale agricultural prices to wholesale industrial prices.[1] It rose about 35 percent from the mid-1890s, when wheat prices were at their nadir, to 1913.

The rise in farm prices led to the dramatic expansion in agriculture shown in Table 2.2. Cultivation was extended into the steppes of south Russia and into western Siberia. Cheap transportation meant that regional production patterns became more specialized as each region focused its efforts on those crops that it could grow relatively well (Metzer 1974). The rise in wheat prices (in conjunction with the prior construction of the Canadian Pacific Railroad) was responsible for Canada's "wheat boom" and the settlement of the Canadian prairies. Railroads and rising wheat prices had the same impact in western Siberia and the Russian steppes.

The effect of rising prices was reinforced by a rise in agricultural productivity; that is, output grew faster than the inputs. From the mid-1880s to the First World War, agricultural output increased at 2.8 per-

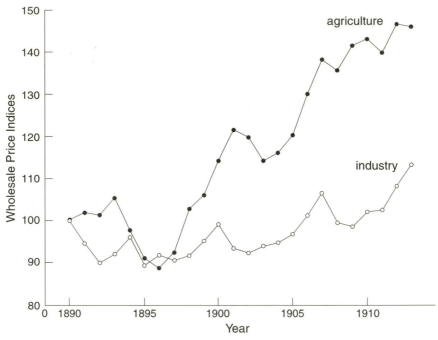

Fig. 2.1. Agricultural and Industrial Prices, 1890–1913. *Source*: See note 1 in Chapter 2.

cent per year. Over roughly the same period, the cultivated area grew by 1.3 percent per year, the agricultural labor force grew at 1.4 percent per year, and farm capital grew at 2.3 percent per year.[2] With equal weights, inputs grew at 2.0 percent per year, so productivity grew at 0.8 percent, that is, the growth of output (2.8%) less the growth of inputs (2.0%).

This high rate of productivity growth calls into question the view held by both liberals and Marxists that the Russian agricultural commune impeded agricultural modernization (Kingston-Mann and Mixter 1991; cf. Kerans 2000). Criticism of the commune included a negative critique of its farming system. As in the West, the arable land surrounding most Russian villages was divided into three great fields, which functioned as units of crop rotation. One field was planted with wheat or rye, one with barley or oats, and the third was left fallow. The land was shifted between these courses from year to year. Each farm consisted of strips scattered evenly across the three fields — useful protection from variations in the weather. In addition, farmers had a meadow to provide hay for winter feed for the livestock and a common on which they were grazed in a village herd. The village community governed the operation of the system. In the histories of western Europe, the open field system has often been attacked as a drag on productivity (Allen 1992). One of the aims of the Stolypin reforms, for instance, was to replace it with enclosed farming, which was regarded as superior.

While this system was the norm in grain-growing areas across Europe, the Russian village community had additional responsibilities since it often owned much of the land. In the Baltic provinces, Ukraine, and Siberia, a high proportion of the farmland was privately owned in "hereditary tenure" by individual peasants. On the other hand, in Russia proper most of the peasant land—the allotment land plus some later purchases from the nobility—was owned by the commune ("communal tenure"). The commune had the authority to reassign land among its members, and, indeed, redistribution was a common practice (Atkinson 1983, pp. 74–75; Shanin 1986, p. 76; Hoch 1989). To liberals, this was a counterproductive limitation on private property that retarded productivity growth by reducing the incentive to improve the soil. While Marx entertained the possibility that the Russian land commune might be a form of socialist ownership (Shanin 1983), most Bolsheviks denounced it as a feudal remnant through which the emerging rural bourgeoisie exploited landless laborers. Neither the liberals nor the Marxists expected productivity to rise in Russian agriculture, so the finding of substantial productivity growth challenges both traditions.

Rising crop yields were one of the major manifestations of productivity growth, but their history has ambiguous implications for the performance of Russian agriculture. Comparisons of Russian yields with those in western Europe have often been used to discredit Russian farming[3]—around 1910, for instance, the yield of wheat in England was about 2 tons per hectare (30 bushels per acre),[4] while it was only 700 kg per hectare (about 10 bushels per acre) in Russia—but those comparisons are beside the point since climatic and soil conditions were so different. A more appropriate comparison group for Russia are the Canadian prairie provinces and the northern plains of the United States. In this region, winters are cold, summers are hot, and the climate is dry, just as in Russia. Productivity in the USSR and North America will be analyzed in Chapter 4, but some of the conclusions are relevant here. At first glance, Russia seems to have done well in the late nineteenth century, for yields rose from 400 kg/hectare in the 1880s to 700 kg by the First World War. The significance of this advance, however, is called into question by comparisons with North America. In North Dakota, for instance, the yield of wheat was considerably higher (perhaps one ton per hectare) in the 1880s, and then fell to 700 kg/hectare by 1913. There are two explanations for the high yields of the 1880s: cultivation was being extended onto virgin prairie, which was exceptionally fertile, and rainfall was unusually high, which was critical given the arid conditions. By the 1920s, yields dropped as soil nutrients were consumed and rainfall slackened.

Why were Russian yields so low in the 1880s? They are consistent with information from earlier periods showing low yield-seed ratios (Kahan 1985, pp. 49–50), so it is hard to argue that the low yields of the 1880s reflected either errors in the data or cyclically low rainfall. It is puzzling why the breakup of the steppes did not cause high yields, but much wheat in the 1880s was still produced in northern districts more suited to rye, and low productivity in those districts may explain the national average. Russian farmers were apparently very inefficient in the 1880s, but they closed the gap with North Dakota by the First World War. In that sense, Russian agriculture performed well, but the progress was generated from a puzzlingly low base and failed to achieve an exceptionally high level. If the advance was due to changes in the regional distribution of production, then it was also due to integration into the world economy.

INDUSTRIAL DEVELOPMENT

While rising agricultural output was the main source of growth in the Russian economy, the increased production of consumer goods — cotton textiles, in particular — and producer goods like locomotives and steel rails also played a role. By itself, the integration of the world economy would have militated against the industrialization of Russia. Cheaper transportation lowered the prices at which English manufacturers could deliver cotton and steel to Russian ports. The combination of higher prices for agricultural goods and lower prices for manufactures would have drawn resources from industry to farming, thus deindustrializing the country. Tariffs were one solution to this problem.

A protectionist trade policy was probably necessary to establish heavy industry in developing countries in the late nineteenth century. India is a case in point. The British built a rail system in India as large as Russia's, but all the rails, locomotives, and rolling stock were imported from the United Kingdom, so that the Indian railroads provided no stimulus to the growth of iron, steel, or engineering industries in India (Headrick 1988, pp. 81–91, 276–98). In Russia, however, tariffs and state procurement policies ensured that Russian industry would smelt the iron ore, roll the rails, and forge the locomotives for the country's railroads. The result was a nine fold increase in the output of heavy industry.

The situation was different in textiles. Tariff protection was a common response to cheap British cotton, and it worked in Russia as it did in other parts of Europe and North America. However, in very-low-wage countries, the British could be beaten at their own game. Thus, India, China, and Japan developed substantial cotton textile industries without tariffs by operating English machinery with cheap local labor. These industries could successfully compete against the British in export markets. Production was initially limited to spinning, and the yarn was woven by hand in the countryside. Tariffs meant that Russia may have proceeded faster to factory weaving than it otherwise would have, but Asian history suggests that the tariff was not necessary for textile production (Morris 1983, pp. 555, 572–83).

Russia promoted cotton more aggressively than steel or engineering. Tariffs on most industrial goods were high from the 1880s to the First World War, and Russian prices exceeded world prices by a premium that remained stable for most goods. The exception was cotton textiles, whose price rose continuously and kept pace with the price of agricultural goods. There were two reasons for this. First, cotton textiles were lightly processed farm products—raw cotton made up three-fourths of the cost of cotton cloth (Odell 1912, p. 30)—and the price of raw cotton rose in step with the prices of other agricultural goods. Second, once the cotton textile industry was established in the Russian Empire, the state sought to promote the cotton-growing industry in Central Asia. Import substitution was repeated at the raw material stage as a tariff was introduced on raw cotton, and the tariff on cloth was raised to offset the higher cost (Odell 1912, p. 22). Higher prices for manufactured consumer goods contributed to stagnating real wages, as we will see.[5]

Russian tariffs introduced a new element into explanations of industrial expansion: domestic demand. With domestic prices above world prices, Russian entrepreneurs never found it profitable to export. The tariff guaranteed them the home market but condemned them to it at the same time. Thus, one reason that there were so few cotton mills in Russia in 1861 is that it was not profitable to erect them since the country was so poor that there was no demand for the cloth. There was a good reason that "The Process of the Formation of a Home Market for Large-Scale Industry" was the subtitle of Lenin's book on *The Development of Capitalism in Russia*. While Lenin may not have been right about how the domestic market emerged, it was essential in explaining the growth of consumer goods output.

The demand for consumer goods had an urban component and a rural component. Only one-tenth of the population lived in cities, but their incomes were all in cash and spent in shops. The rural population spent much less per head, but it was so large that rural spending was about equal to urban spending. Gosplan statisticians worked this out in detail in the 1920s and showed, for instance, that 55 percent of the sales of nonfood consumer goods went to the agricultural population (Wheatcroft and Davies 1985, p. 211). The situation was roughly the same before the First World War. To explain the growth of the consumer goods industries (including trade, housing, etc.), it is necessary to explain the growth of rural and urban demand.

Lenin is famous for propounding the theory that the "differentiation of the peasantry" was responsible for the growth in rural demand. Lenin believed that peasants cultivating moderate-size farms with only the labor of their families were in decline as rural society polarized into a small group of large-scale farmers and a mass of landless laborers. Late-nineteenth-century budget studies showed that the middle sort of peasants were the most self-sufficient and spent a smaller fraction of their income than either landless laborers or capitalist farmers. Consequently, Lenin reasoned that "the differentiation of the peasantry creates a home market for capitalism" (Lenin 1894, p. 181). The creation of the home market was decisive for the growth of the consumer goods industries. "Only this fact that a home market is created by the differentiation of the peasantry can explain, for example, the enormous growth of the home market for cotton goods, the manufacture of which has grown so rapidly in the post-Reform period along with the wholesale ruin of the peasantry" (Lenin 1894, p. 181 n.).

While Lenin provides a plausible link between changes in rural social structure and industrialization, the argument is ultimately unconvincing. It was true that the poorest and the richest peasants spent bigger fractions of their income on consumer goods, but it does not follow that the differentiation of the peasantry had a big impact on demand. A test of the theory is to compare the average spending on consumer goods across all peasant income levels with the spending of the average peasant. It turns out that the difference is minor. The reason is that the poor had little money, and the rich were not numerous, so that the spending that would have resulted from a society of perfectly equalized family farms was scarcely less than that generated by the actual farm size distribution in the early twentieth century. Peasant differentiation, in other words, made little contribution to the growth of the domestic market.

What mattered for the growth in rural demand was the volume and price of farm output. Urban demand depended on the heavy industries called into being by the state's railroad policy and by the cotton industry created by high tariffs. As workers spent their incomes, the consumer goods industries grew even more. The size of the consumer goods industries ultimately depended on the factors causing growth in the Russian economy as a whole—world wheat prices, agricultural productivity, railroad building, and the use of tariffs to promote Russian industry. The growth of light industry, in other words, was a derivative phenomenon with no independent momentum of its own.

The same conclusion applies to foreign investment in Russian manufacturing. This was substantial by 1913, but it was not an independent source of growth. The world capital market was highly integrated, so investment was available to many countries on equal terms. Investment flows, therefore, followed business opportunities. Causation did not run from foreign investment to the growth of the Russian economy. Rather, the growth of demand in Russia sucked in capital.

COULD THE RUSSIAN BOOM HAVE CONTINUED?

Gregory's optimistic assessment of the imperial economy raises the possibility that it would have outperformed the Soviet economy: "It makes sense to consider what would have occurred had the administrative-command system never been installed — if the tsarist economy had continued to develop after the conclusion of World War I on the foundations created during the final decades of the Russian empire." "What if" questions are notoriously hard to answer, especially when the counterfactual extends over a long period and involves major changes in economic and social institutions. But Gregory contends, "From a purely technical statistical analysis, it is hard to imagine that the result would have been inferior" to what actually happened — a 1989 per capita GDP of $7070. Gregory goes further, however, to claim that "it is hard to imagine a scenario in which the area of former imperial Russia would not today be a world economic power offering living standards to its citizens relatively close to those of Western Europe." This is a much stronger claim, for GDP per capita was about $18,000 in western Europe in 1989.[6]

A little arithmetic clarifies the issues. If the imperial growth performance had continued through the twentieth century, then per capita GDP in the Soviet Union would have continued to grow at the rate of 1.7 percent per year when it would have reached $5358 in 1989 — a good deal less than the $7070 actually achieved by the Soviets. An extrapolation of the imperial growth record to 1989, therefore, would not have equaled the performance of the administrative-command system. To have equaled that performance, capitalist Russia would have had to raise its growth rate to 2.1 percent per person per year. That may not be an implausible possibility — German per capita income grew at 1.8 percent per year from 1885 to 1913 and 2.1 percent per year from 1913 to 1989, and the records of other west European countries were similar. If the Russian growth rate would have increased in step with western Europe's, then the implication is that Russians did no better under communism than they would have under capitalism, but, by the same token, they did no worse.

But to assume that the Russian growth rate would have risen like Germany's is to beg the question. Most countries experienced economic growth in the twentieth century, but growth was fastest in the countries like Germany that were rich at the beginning of the century and slow in the poor countries of Asia, Africa, and Latin America. In terms of economic structure and income level, Russia was a poor country in 1913, so the likely inference is that it would have grown less rapidly than the West.

Comparing Russia to the other wheat-exporting economies does not inspire confidence either. In India, Argentina, Australia, and Canada, there was no sustained growth in GDP per head from 1913 until about 1940, when World War II began to push it up. India has experienced little growth since. Argentina is remarkable for its fall from grace: in 1913, it was a leading economy, far more prosperous and urbanized than Russia, but today it is one of the poor countries of the world. Australia, of course, has done much better, but it, too, has experienced a large fall in income relative to the United States. Only Canada has been an unqualified success. What the history of these countries suggests is that success in the twentieth century required more than success as a wheat exporter in 1913.

If it is hard to argue that the Russian growth rate would have increased in step with Germany's, it is even harder to argue that Russia would have closed the gap with western Europe since that would have required even faster growth. The claim that capitalism would have produced a standard of living like that in France or Britain implies that per capita GDP would have grown at 3.3 percent per year from 1913 to 1989—the rate necessary to go from $1488 in 1913 to $18,000 in 1989. Only one country in the world did anything like that: Japan. It had an income per head similar to Russia's in 1913 and realized a western European level of output by 1989. Why should we believe that capitalist Russia would have been like Japan and ended up at the very top of the world league table rather than somewhere in the middle or even at the bottom?

One thing is clear: the nineteenth-century sources of growth had run their course, and the most important had reversed direction. The prime mover behind the agricultural expansion had been the rise in the price of wheat. After World War I, wheat prices collapsed, and the expansion of wheat acreage ceased around the globe. During the Depression of the 1930s, wheat prices hit rock bottom, and land was falling out of cultivation. Stalin is infamous for offering Soviet peasants low prices for grain, but it is none too clear that prices in the Ukraine were any lower than prices in Saskatchewan at the same time. If capitalism had continued in Russia, the wheat boom would have ended there, just as it did in Canada, Australia, and Argentina. Income growth slowed dramatically in these countries and the same fate awaited Russia.

Rising agricultural productivity was not a likely source of farm expansion either. By 1913, Russian peasants had reached the level of yields that was normal on the American plains and Canadian prairies. That level remained flat until after the Second World War, when the extensive use of chemical fertilizers pushed yields higher, an advance in which the Soviets also participated.[7] But the important point is that there were few chances for Russian farmers to raise yields before 1950, so further progress in that direction was out of the question.

Industrial expansion had also contributed to economic growth before 1913, and the prospects for that sector were also dim. The growth of heavy industry depended on railroad building, and that activity had run its course since so much of the network had already been constructed. Between 1870 and 1913, the length of track increased at a rate of 4.5 percent per year, from 10.7 thousand kilometers to 70.2 thousand. The network doubled again by the late 1980s, but the annual rate of expansion dropped to 1.0 percent[8] The poor prospects of agriculture make even that rate of construction unlikely. Why lay more track if it is not profitable to farm the land? By 1913, railroad building had run out of steam as an engine of growth.

Light industry provided the best chance for expansion. Japan forged ahead in the early twentieth century by exporting cotton goods. Russia might have done the same, had Russia's high tariffs not raised prices above world levels and made exports impossible. Russia was locked into the domestic market, which was not promising given the likely collapse of agriculture. Reversing the tariff policy would not have been easy since duties had been imposed on raw cotton to promote its cultivation in Central Asia and tariffs on finished goods had been raised accordingly to maintain effective protection. Success in the world market would have required free trade in raw cotton and jeopardized Russia's growers — neither an inviting nor a likely prospect.

Limping through the twentieth century with high tariffs and slow growth was the most likely scenario for Russia. The parallel with Latin America is compelling. The collapse in primary product prices after World War I cut growth in most of the continent. Attempts to industrialize through tariff-induced import substitution created large cities but only slow growth. With the other sources of growth exhausted, this was capitalist Russia's best chance. Argentina — indeed, India — was a more likely model for Russia's future than France or Germany.

Recent investigations of economic growth have emphasized the importance of education for success in the twentieth century (Barro 1991). One reason that Latin America fell behind Europe and North America was the low level of literacy and education. Ninety percent of the population of Canada, the United States, and western Europe was literate around the First World War (UNESCO 1953, p. 55; 1975, pp. 89, 108, 121). In Argentina, the fraction was 64 percent, in Chile, it was 50 percent, in Brazil 35 percent, and in Mexico 34 percent (UNESCO 1957, pp. 86, 136, 50, 95). While Latin America lagged behind Europe, it was ahead of much of Asia and the Middle East. Only 7 percent of the Indian population was literate, and the Egyptian proportion was at 8 percent (UNESCO 1957, pp. 58, 52). With 38 percent of its population literate, Russia in 1913 was ahead of the most backward parts of Asia, but near the bottom of the Latin American league table and far behind the industrially advanced countries. Progress had been made in Russia — in 1897, only 21 percent of the adults were literate — but the shortfall was still immense (Crisp 1978, pp. 389, 391; Brooks 1982). The low level of educational attainment cast a pall over Russia's economic prospects.

The only way for Russia to have avoided a Latin American outcome was to emulate Japan. That was not likely. As noted, Japan developed an internationally competitive cotton textile industry by avoiding tariffs. This policy had been forced on it by the Western powers and was not a policy followed by Russia (Lockwood 1968, pp. 19, 539).

More generally, the challenge of the West provoked in Japan a far-reaching modernization of social, economic, and political institutions. Russia was instead governed by a repressive autocrat dedicated to preserving traditional prerogatives. From 1870 to 1910, Japan pushed its adult literacy rate from 30 percent to 70 percent through compulsory education (Taira 1978, pp. 196–97). Russia was at least a generation behind. Bureaucrats arbitrarily intervened in business decisions, sowing uncertainty and raising transaction costs. Political repression exacerbated class tensions and inhibited the formation of the informal networks and voluntary associations that Robert Putnam (1993, pp. 152–62) has recently argued were essential to capitalist growth. These associations are the basis of the "civic society" that is notably absent in postcommunist Russia. The empire of the tsars was similar. The business historians have emphasized how the state inhibited the development of modern capitalist activity. "Autocratic government and cultural hostility to the West appear to have combined to hinder the emergence of institutions of capitalism and of attitudes conducive to corporate enterprise." For these reasons, Owen (1995, pp. 11–12) insisted "on resemblances between imperial Russia and the post-Soviet states on the one hand and Third World countries on the other." These legal and cultural contrasts are the counterparts to the different income trajectories followed by these regions since 1913.[9] The tsar was not wise enough to lead Russia down a Japanese course of modernization, nor was the society supple enough to follow. It is impossible to be precise, but—in the absence of the communist revolution and the Five-Year Plans—Russia's fate would have been somewhere between India's and Argentina's.

INCOME DISTRIBUTION

The rate of growth of a poor economy is one criterion for assessing its performance; the distribution of income is another. Many Western countries have a large literature investigating whether the working class shared in the gains from economic growth; the Russian historical literature is remarkable for the slightness of such research despite its manifest relevance to political events.[10] Urban and rural living standards must both be considered.

Urban Living Standards

The urban working class revolted in 1905 and in 1917 with devastating effect. The 1917 revolt had many causes, including tsarist oppression, Bolshevik organizing, and the First World War. The character of tsarist economic development, however, was a facilitating factor. While per capita income in Russia had increased 69 percent between 1883 and 1913 and output per worker in industry rose 2.4 fold[11] from 1887 to 1913, there was no increase in real wages. The imperial economy was a classic case where the gains from growth did *not* trickle down to the working class.

The simplest measure of working-class living standards is the real wage—the ratio of nominal wages to consumer prices. Nominal wage series are available for several groups of Russian workers: factory workers, railroad employees, and building tradesmen, in particular.[12] Little information is available on earnings in the handicraft sector or in various service occupations.[13] In some cases, like factory workers and railway employees, the sources report average annual earnings. In other cases, like building workers, the rate per day is reported. The former are more immediately indicative of the standard of living. I have calculated annual earnings for building workers on the assumption that they worked 150 days per year, that is, during the summer months. Nominal earnings rose about one-third from 1885 to 1913.

But did earnings rise more than consumer prices? These were rising in step with world food prices and with tariff-inflated Russian textile prices. To adjust for inflation, earnings have been deflated either by the

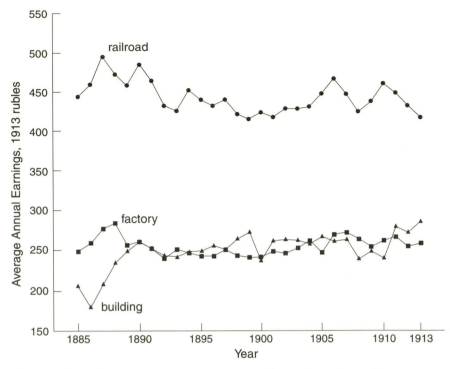

Fig. 2.2. Real Wages, 1885–1913. *Source*: See notes 12 and 14 in Chapter 2.

long-term (1853–1913) St. Petersburg retail price index or the Podtri-agin price index.[14] Figure 2.2 plots the real annual earnings of railway workers, factory workers, and building workers from 1885 to 1913. The absence of real wage growth is impressive. There is, perhaps, some suggestion of a real earnings decline among the railway workers, and a suggestion of a real gain for the St. Petersburg building workers in the mid-1880s. That gain, however, is an illusion. The St. Petersburg build-ing wage series runs back to 1853, and Figure 2.3 shows real wages of those workers from 1853 to 1913. There were ups and downs but no rising trend over this period. The important conclusion is that workers in Russia's factories, railroads, and construction industry did not receive rising incomes in step with the economic growth of the country.

It is not unusual for real wages to remain constant through an eco-nomic boom. The history of real wages in the British industrial revolu-tion has been the subject of extended research. While views have varied considerably, the emerging consensus is that real wages were constant from 1780 to 1820.[15] The movements of the real wage in the industrial revolution were minor perturbations in a series that was roughly con-

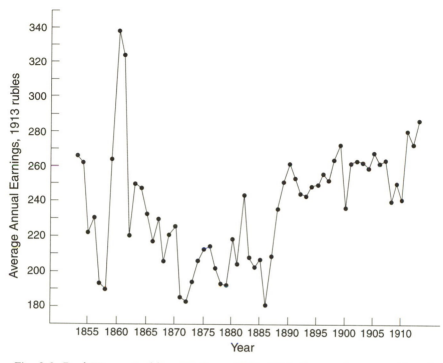

Fig. 2.3. Real Wages, Building Workers, 1853–1913. *Source*: See notes 12 and 14 in Chapter 2.

stant from the end of the Middle Ages until 1870. The same was true of the Low Countries (Allen 2001a). From 1870 to 1913, however, real wages rose in most European countries and in New World countries like Canada, the United States, and Argentina. Within Europe, the industrialized core had the highest real wages, but the rise in living standards was faster in Denmark, Norway, Sweden, Ireland, and Italy as they gained on the core. Not all peripheral economies were so successful, however. Spain and Portugal were like Russia in having constant real wages (Williamson 1995). Real wage growth was common in Europe but not automatic.

Rising real wages were associated with industrialization in the late nineteenth century. The core economies of northwestern Europe, which had the highest real wages, also had the most developed economies. It is striking that economic modernization, as measured by the fraction of the population in agriculture, discriminates between those countries in Europe with rising real wages and those where real wages failed to grow. In the backward countries, the agricultural share was above 60 percent and showed little decline, whereas in the countries with rising real wages, the agricultural share usually fell from 1870 to 1913 and was significantly below 60 percent at the end of the period. Thus, in Russia, the agricultural fraction was 75 percent in 1913 and perhaps higher in 1870. In Spain, 65 percent of the population was agricultural in 1870, and the fraction only declined to 60 percent in 1913. In Portugal the agricultural share was 67 percent in 1900—we have no 1870 value—and 61 percent in 1913. (The shares were lower in Iberia than in Russia because of the urbanization that accompanied the Spanish and Portuguese empires of the early modern period.) In contrast, in Italy, the agricultural share of the population was 61 percent in 1870 and dropped to 54 percent in 1913. The corresponding figures were 57 percent and 47 percent for Denmark, 76 percent and 48 percent for Sweden, and 64 percent and 49 percent for Norway. The Irish share remained constant throughout at 54 percent—a value that may, in any event, not be as significant due to Ireland's proximity to, and union with, Great Britain. Thus, rapid economic development was a prerequisite for rising real wages.

Sir Arthur Lewis's (1954) famous model of economic development with unlimited supplies of labor provides a theoretical context that illuminates these generalizations. Lewis conceptually divided the economy into two sectors: a modern sector, including factory industry, where production proceeds with labor and capital; and a traditional sector, including peasant agriculture, where production uses land and labor. Growth occurs as capital is accumulated, and the modern sector expands by drawing labor from the traditional sector. Lewis thought this labor could be removed from the traditional sector without a loss of output. A minimal wage would suffice to attract this surplus labor to factory jobs. This transfer would continue until all the surplus labor was absorbed. After that, farm output would fall as labor was withdrawn from agriculture, so further transfers would require rising wages to match the rising productivity of rural labor. Lewis thus envisioned a two-phase history of growth and inequality. Inequality increased in the first phase as GDP per head rose and real wages remained constant; in the second phase, inequality narrowed as real wages also advanced.

The application of this theory to Europe is straightforward: while economic growth was significant in western Europe from 1500 to 1870, structural transformation was not extensive enough to move the region out of Lewis's first phase. The Victorian boom finally pushed western Europe past the turning point, but eastern Europe and much of southern Europe remained behind. Rising real wages in western Europe meant that workers benefited from capitalist development, and that prosperity underpinned the reorientation of their politics toward social democracy.

Russian development, while impressive by some standards, was not swift enough to raise the real incomes of Russian workers or to turn them into social democrats. It took more than unequal development to produce the 1917 revolution, but the character of tsarist development invited a radical response. Many other peripheral countries have had unstable political histories with cleavages along class lines.

Rural Living Standards

The revolutions of 1905–7 and 1917 were rural revolts as well as urban ones. In both cases, the demands of the peasants were the same: they wanted ownership of all of the land, and they wanted that ownership vested in the commune rather than divided among the peasants individually. The latter demand came to the fore in 1917 after state policy had shifted from supporting the commune before 1905–7 to undermining it thereafter. The rural revolts, like their urban counterparts, reflected fundamental economic conflicts in Russian society. The details, however, were quite different.

A long-standing approach to the peasant revolutions is to see them as examples of "agricultural involution." Rapid population growth in the context of a fixed land supply and backward technology led to small farms, low output per worker, and low peasant incomes. Revolution was the result of rural poverty, and expropriating the nobles was the logical political program.[16]

The evidence for this view is mixed. It is usually supported by the fact that allotment land grew very little while the peasant population certainly exploded. As a result, each peasant had less allotment land to farm, as the involutionists claim. Arrears in redemption payments are also cited as direct evidence of impoverishment. This view of Russian agriculture is consistent with Gerschenkron's vision of slow agricultural output growth and static productivity caused by communal land tenure, but it is hard to square with Gregory's findings that output was growing rapidly and that productivity was rising. Indeed, the fall in allotment land per peasant is only part of the land story since the expansion of Russian agriculture into the steppes and western Siberia meant that the amount of cultivated land was rising. More allotment land—and especially more noble land—fell under the plow. From 1885 to 1913, the farmed area grew almost as fast as the population (1.3 percent per year versus 1.4 percent). Livestock was rising even faster (1.7 percent per year).

In addition, the increases in wheat prices and farm output raise the possibility that peasant living standards were rising rather than falling, as the involutionists claim. Gregory (1980) has shown that the average

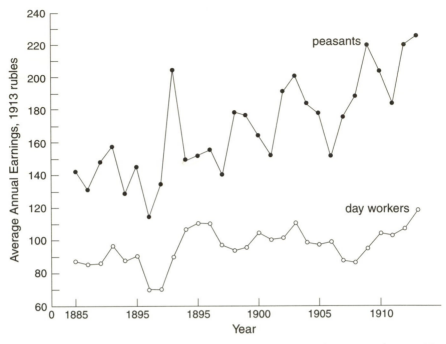

Fig. 2.4. Real Earnings, Agriculture, 1885–1913. *Source*: See text and notes 17 and 18 in Chapter 2. Real agricultural wage rate is the average daily wage for both sexes shown by Strumilin (1957, p. 396, column 7) deflated by the St. Petersburg consumer price index including rent.

peasant's consumption of grain and potatoes increased from 1885 to 1913. Of course, as he notes, peasant consumption included meat and manufactured goods as well. These can be incorporated into the analysis by calculating the value of farm output (net of seed, animal feed, and redemption payments) per peasant.[17] Deflating this series with a consumer price index measures peasant living standards.[18]

Figure 2.4 shows the evolution of real farm income per peasant household from 1885 to 1913. The trend is clearly upward. On the assumption that the average household consisted of five members, the average income of a peasant family in 1913 was still less than the annual earnings of the average factory worker, although the gap was less than it had been in the 1880s. The peasants were still poor, but they were doing better.

If their standard of living was improving, why did the peasants revolt? Peasant income consisted of the return to all of the factors of production that they owned—their land, their labor, and their livestock.

The economic and political divisions in the countryside are revealed by examining factor returns separately. Figure 2.4 shows the real wage of farm laborers. It rose slightly from the mid-1880s to the early 1890s and not at all between 1896 and 1913. Farm labor did not participate in the Russian agricultural boom.[19] In contrast, Anfimov (1959, p. 134) has shown that the average rent of a dessiatyn of land on an annual lease rose from 6.92 rubles in 1887–88 to 13.72 rubles in 1912–14. Deflating these values by the Podtriagin price index shows that real rents rose by 49 percent. Shanin (1986, p. 147) summarizes several authorities to the effect that the rental price of land rose seven fold between 1861 and 1901 — almost a five fold increase in real terms when deflated by the St. Petersburg consumer price index. Owning land was the way to participate in the Russian wheat boom.

The involutionists attribute the rise in Russian land values to population growth, which drove down the land-labor ratio. However, as we have seen, farm land per peasant changed little. Instead, land values were rising because farm output and prices were growing.

The history of real estate prices in Russia was similar to that of other frontier economies that exported wheat — Canada, the United States, Australia, and Argentina. Falling world transportation costs created a tightly integrated world grain market. Prices rose in the exporting countries like Canada and Russia and fell in the free trade importing countries of western Europe like England. As a result, land values dropped 40 percent in England between 1877 and 1912, while they rose three times in the United States and Australia (O'Rourke 1997, p. 787). (French and German tariffs on grain limited the price decline and the resulting drop in land values.) Land values in Russia rose, and the figures cited by Shanin (1986, p. 147) showed an increase even greater than that in the United States and Australia.

Owning land was the key to riches, which is why landownership was the central issue for the peasants. Why should they buy the land from the nobles or pay rent for it if they could have it for free? A stickier question, however, was which peasants should own the land and on what terms. Before the revolution of 1905–7, most peasant-owned farmland in Russia was held by communal tenure. Only in the Baltic provinces and right-bank Ukraine was hereditary (i.e., individual) tenure the norm. The state supported communal tenure as a bulwark of stability since it was supposed to ensure that everyone had land. The revolution of 1905–7 proved, if nothing else, that the commune did not prevent revolution. Thereafter, the Stolypin reforms undermined the commune by encouraging peasants to convert land from communal to hereditary tenure and to exchange their scattered strips in the village fields for consolidated and enclosed farms. The proportion of peasants in communes declined from 71 percent in 1905 to 61 percent in 1915 as about 2.5 million peasants left communes. The share of allotment land held by communes dropped from 83 percent to 71 percent (Atkinson 1983, pp. 81–83). While the commune remained a formidable institution on the eve of the revolution, the Stolypin reforms noticeably weakened it.

Departures from the commune were usually contentious. Most peasants saw them as a threat to equal access to the land.[20] While the issue is a difficult one, there are good reasons for thinking that this fear was well founded. The great debate about peasant differentiation goes to the heart of the matter. In Lenin's view, large farms were more cost-effective than small farms, so that farmers cultivating a large area could afford to pay more to buy or rent land than could small-scale farmers. If true, a competitive land market — the goal of the Stolypin reforms — would have resulted in a polarized rural society in which a relatively small number of people operated large-scale farms employing the labor of the vast mass of the population who would have had little or no land.

There are two reasons why large farms may have been more cost-effective than small farms. The first is that they were more economical in their use of labor, livestock, and implements. Lenin endorsed this view and supported it by citing zemstvo surveys that compared the operations of large and small farms. In *The Development of Capitalism in Russia*, Lenin (1894, pp. 74–75) summarized the results of Postnikov's analysis of farm survey data from south Russia. Postnikov grouped the farms into size categories and for each computed "the number of people working (including hired labourers), and the number of draught animals, implements, etc., per 100 dessiatines of crop area." Comparing the groups showed "that these numbers diminish as the size of the farm increases." In particular, "those cultivating under 5 dessiatines have per 100 dessiatines of allotment land 28 people working, 28 draught animals, 4.7 ploughs and scarifiers, and 10 carts, whereas those cultivating over 50 dessiatines have 7 people working, 14 draught animals, 3.8 ploughs and scarifiers, and 4.3 carts." Overall, Postnikov concluded that "with the increase in the size of the farm and in the area cultivated by the peasant, the expenditures on the maintenance of labour-power, human and animal, progressively decreases, and, among the groups that cultivate large areas, drops to nearly one half per dessiatine under crops of the expenditure among the groups with small cultivated areas." Lenin pointed out that this result applied to grain growing and that it probably did not apply to intensive systems of cultivation or livestock husbandry.

The effect of farm size on efficiency has been a contentious issue in agricultural economics, and some modern investigators have rejected the idea of scale economies based on surveys of contemporary Third

World countries and cross-country comparisons of efficiency (Binswanger and Rosenzweig 1986; Binswanger, Feder, and Deininger 1988; Binswanger and Deininger 1997, p. 1968). On the other hand, data for grain producers in early modern Europe support Lenin's views. Thus, Arthur Young, the English agricultural improver, was the first person ever to carry out a farm survey in the late 1760s. He aimed to ascertain the effect of size on productivity, thus setting the pattern for the zemstvo surveys. Indeed, his data, as recently reanalyzed, show that large farms were more efficient than small farms (Allen 1988; 1992, pp. 159–63, 201–3, 211–27). The source of those efficiency gains was exactly the same as those in south Russia: economies in the use of labor, horses, and implements of about the same magnitude as those established in the Postnikov study. Eighteenth-century French farm accounts, likewise, show similar savings in plow teams and their drivers (Moriceau and Postel-Vinay 1992; Moriceau 1994). It may be that there were significant scale economies in premechanized grain growing, whereas there are not such economies in late-twentieth-century rice growing in South Asia.

An alternative explanation for the greater cost-effectiveness of large-scale farmers is access to cheaper credit. Generally, wealthier people can borrow money at lower interest rates or on easier terms than can poor people. Since large-scale farmers are generally wealthier than small-scale farmers, the large-scale farmers have lower costs due to their access to cheaper capital. This explanation is commonly advanced to explain the advantage of large-scale farmers in South Asia, where technical scale economies seem to be absent. The Peasant Land Bank was established to address the weaknesses of rural credit markets, but a government committee on farm credit still concluded in 1908 that the existing institutions were inadequate to the needs of farmers (Pallott 1999, pp. 222–23). Unequal access to credit is an additional reason to believe that a system of moderately sized farms would be unstable and would collapse into a relatively small number of large farms employing the labor of a landless majority.

Peasants could adopt two very different attitudes to the Stolypin reforms. An enterprising peasant, who thought he would be successful at large-scale farming, could withdraw his land from the commune and expand his farm by renting or purchasing enough land to realize the economies of large-scale production. On the other hand, a less enterprising peasant, who worried he would not succeed, could remain in the commune and resist the reform. Studies of those who left communes show that they came from the extremes of the farm size distribution. A significant number of owners of very small holdings sold their land and left agriculture altogether. A smaller number with large holdings took their land out of the commune (Atkinson 1983, pp. 91–92). They were "the sturdy and the strong"[21] who thought they could succeed in large-scale farming, but they were also a minority. Most peasants who intended to remain as agriculturalists remained in the commune.[22]

The 1917 revolution showed that an overwhelming majority of peasants did not want to gamble on being successful large-scale farmers. In the spring and summer of 1917, the peasants seized all land owned by nobles, the church, and townsmen, four-fifths of the land privately owned by peasants, and most of the land removed from communes pursuant to the Stolypin reforms (Jasny 1949, p. 154; Figes 1990, pp. 239–40, 246–47). These lands were added to those owned by the commune and divided among the members. The result was a radical equalization of land holdings in which large holdings were eliminated and in which those who were landless received some land. Ownership of land and its equal division were the goals of the peasant revolutions. They were understandable responses to the rising value of land in Russia's wheat boom and the chance to become landless in a competitive market for land.

CONCLUSION

A boom in the world market for wheat more than doubled Russian GDP between 1885 and 1913. Railroad building drew peripheral parts of the Russian Empire into the world market and stimulated a rise in agricultural productivity. Agricultural output doubled, and industrial output was pushed up by an aggressive policy of import substitution. Despite these advances, however, the pace of structural transformation was slow, and the bases of rising income were narrow. The exhaustion of these lines of development and changes in the world economy make it unlikely that Russia could have maintained its nineteenth-century rate of growth through the middle of the twentieth century. Furthermore, the rate of industrialization was not high enough compared to the rate of population growth to shift the structure of the economy dramatically away from agriculture. Rising food prices offset the increase in wages caused by the wheat boom. As a result, the benefits of growth did not trickle down to the working class. In the countryside, the rising incomes from rising wheat prices did not yield social peace since land values rose instead of wages. The advantages of large-scale farms meant that even peasants farming allotment land were threatened by the Stolypin reforms that aimed to replace the commune with a free market in land. It is unlikely that capitalism would have continued to bring economic growth to Russia. Moreover, the process of capitalist development was producing such sharp class conflicts that political instability was hardly a surprise.

CHAPTER THREE

The Development Problem in the 1920s

The Bolsheviks seized power on 7 November 1917, but the Soviet industrial revolution did not get under way until the start of the First Five-Year Plan in 1928. "War communism" was Lenin's label for the three years 1918–20, which included the tail end of World War I and the civil war in which the Bolsheviks consolidated their power. By the time the Red Army finally won, the economy was in tatters and Lenin adopted the New Economic Policy (NEP, 1921–28) to promote recovery and conciliate the peasants.

War communism was too chaotic a period to provide useful precedents, but the NEP raises the possibility of alternative models of socialist development. During the NEP, industry was socialized, but agriculture and much trade were in private hands. Markets played a more important role than they did later. While the state was a Communist Party dictatorship, politics were not as authoritarian as they became under Stalin, and political discourse was far more open. This system of social organization proved successful in revitalizing the economy. That experience raises the important question of whether the NEP—a far more attractive society than the one molded by Stalin—would have been a successful basis for rapid industrialization. This is an important question today, and it was vital—and intensely discussed—in the 1920s. Indeed, one of the more remarkable features of the period was the very wide-ranging debate among Preobrazhensky, Trotsky, Bukharin, and other Bolsheviks about the development potential of the NEP and which agrarian and industrial policies should be implemented to achieve rapid economic advance. These ideas defined the policies followed by Stalin, and they remain important and controversial contributions to the theory of economic growth (Sah and Stiglitz 1984, 1986; Blomqvist 1986; Carter 1986).

WAR COMMUNISM AND THE NEW ECONOMIC POLICY

The Bolsheviks seized power under the slogan "peace, land, and bread." These were popular demands, and the state acted quickly to implement them but with mixed results.

Land was dealt with immediately. The peasants had been seizing the property of townsmen, nobles, and the church since the spring of 1917.

One of Lenin's first acts upon taking power was to ratify what the peasants had done with a decree nationalizing all land and transferring its use to the peasants. The communes, which Stolypin had tried to destroy, reasserted themselves. The open fields were reassembled as much land that had been enclosed and converted to hereditary tenure after 1905 was repossessed by communes and divided among their members. The result was a radical equalization of properties as large farms were divided and small holdings enlarged. The peasants, for a time, had realized their long-standing dream of eliminating nobles and unequal farms (Jasny 1949; Male 1971).

Peace proved a more elusive objective. Russian participation in the First World War was ended with the treaty of Brest-Litovsk on 3 March 1918. However, the treaty brought no lasting peace, for war broke out again in the summer between the Bolsheviks and their domestic and international opponents. These included many liberals and radicals (Kenez 1971, 1977; Figes 1989, 1996; Procyk 1995). The Red Army, commanded by Trotsky, only achieved victory in 1920.

Bread—or, more generally, prosperity—was the hardest goal. Economic problems were particularly acute because of the civil war. In 1919, the Bolshevik government controlled only a small territory around Moscow. Taxes could not be collected, so the state financed itself by printing money, and the result was hyperinflation. The imperial government had controlled the grain trade, required peasants to market their surpluses, and rationed bread in the cities. The Bolsheviks continued these practices, and extended them by creating a state monopoly on trade. In the desperate conditions of the time, peasant sales of grain declined, and the state used troops to commandeer surpluses. Grain requisitioning and the disruption of prewar commercial patterns reduced the incentive to sow. When drought struck, the result was the 1921 famine that killed millions.

The urban economy almost disappeared during war communism. Between 1917 and 1920, the output of cigarettes dropped by 78 percent, cotton yarn by 93 percent, pig iron by 96 percent, and horse-driven threshers by 99 percent (Nutter 1962, pp. 420, 438, 454–55). The industrial workforce fell from 2.6 million in 1917 to 1.2 million in 1920 (Nove 1990, p. 57). In 1926, peasants made up 82 percent of the Russian population compared to 72 percent in 1913 (Davies 1990, p. 251).

The Bolshevik government extended its control over the industrial economy even as it collapsed. A decree on 27 November 1917 gave workers' councils control over businesses. The railway unions effectively managed the railways until March 1918, when the state took over. Lenin had all along opposed a "transfer of the railways to the railwaymen" and "the tanneries to the tanners" (Nove 1990, p. 32) since real socialism, in his view, required national planning that was incompatible with labor management. Nationalization, therefore, became the objective of policy. The banks were nationalized in November and December 1917, and combined into a single People's Bank. On 15 December 1917, the Supreme Council of National Economy (VSNKh in Russian) was formed to manage state-owned enterprises. However, by June 1918, only 487 firms had been nationalized, mostly by local action (Nove 1990, p. 45). A nationalization decree was issued, and by September 1919, close to 4000 large-scale firms were in public ownership. In November 1920, small-scale factories and workshops were also nationalized, although there was no capacity for the central direction of these enterprises.

By 1921, the Bolsheviks were in control of most of the country, but the economy was in shambles. Grain output was 56 percent below its 1913 level, livestock production was down 73 percent, and industrial production had dropped 70 percent (Davies 1990, pp. 5–6). Lenin introduced the NEP to reverse this situation as well as to appease the peasants. In many ways, the NEP reflected a retreat from the extreme measures of war communism. The peasants were confirmed in the possession of their farms, the requisitioning of food by the state was replaced by moderate taxation, factory industry was put on a commercial basis and organized as profit-maximizing trusts, private trade was legalized, and economic exchanges between peasants, urban residents, and industry were conducted as market transactions.

The policy was successful in terms of its immediate objectives. Industry and agriculture rebounded; by the late 1920s, output returned to the prewar level.[1] But the policy was deeply controversial in other respects, for it was too moderate to realize Bolshevik ambitions. Three are particularly important for the present discussion.

The first Bolshevik objective was socialism. This was important in itself and was regarded by the revolutionaries as a prerequisite for achieving the other goals. While large-scale industry was nationalized under the NEP, much trade and small-scale industry were in private hands. These activities produced a new class of capitalists and merchants—the Nepmen. Communists did not make a revolution to produce Nepmen.

The situation was no better in the countryside. Agricultural land was effectively owned by communes—precapitalist institutions in the Marxist view—and was inherently unstable for the reason advanced by Lenin before 1917: agriculture exhibited increasing returns to scale, so eventually the village would fracture into a few capitalist farmers—the

Kulaks—and a majority of landless laborers. Like the Nepmen, this emerging group of rural capitalists were considered opponents of the new order.

Industrialization was the second goal of the revolution. While the NEP was a suitable framework for restoring production, the major question—and one still debated—is whether its agrarian settlement or its system of industrial organization was suitable for rapid economic growth. The Bolsheviks were deeply suspicious of peasant agriculture from a technical and economic point of view. They thought that peasants were backward and incapable of modernizing. Furthermore, the medium-size farms that predominated in the mid-1920s were the most self-sufficient and hence the least likely to sell food to the city. Trouble loomed if industry took off and the demand for food ballooned. Peasant farms needed transforming into large-scale, socialized food factories, or so many Bolsheviks thought, but how that was to be achieved and what form they would take were hard to imagine.

So far as industry was concerned, the NEP failed to grasp the advantages that socialism offered a backward country trying to industrialize. NEP industry was state-owned but operated in the capitalist manner. As a result, there were two potential shortcomings. First, in deciding on investments, businesses looked only to their own profits and ignored the advantages their investments created for other firms in the economy. In such a case, socially profitable investments might not be undertaken. Planning could overcome that problem. Second, businesses hired workers only if they generated enough sales to cover their salaries, that is, if the value of their marginal product exceeded their wage. However, in the presence of structural unemployment like that in the Soviet Union, output could be increased by hiring unemployed workers with a positive marginal product even if it was less than the wage. State-owned firms could do this, while private firms would not. Abandoning capitalist employment practices, consequently, could increase growth through employment expansion. The NEP was not well adapted to realize either of these possibilities. Both were realized by Stalin's system of economic organization and proved highly productive.

The third goal was a rapid increase in the standard of living of the population. Socialism would aid it by increasing the rate of economic growth and, thus, the availability of consumer goods. Moreover, socialism would ensure that the gains from growth were distributed to the whole population by increasing the level of employment beyond that achieved by capitalism and by ending exploitation. Marxists were proponents of workfare. They believed that labor created wealth, that everyone had an obligation to work, and that work provided the only legitimate claim on income. The rents and profits received by the nobility and capitalists were transfer payments—an illegitimate form of social welfare payment—not the return for labor. By abolishing un-earned incomes and by requiring everyone to work, income would be more equitably distributed. The imperial pattern of economic growth, in which output per worker rose while real wages remained constant, would be avoided.

Furthermore, socialism would raise the standard of living by making modern health care and education available to the whole population. The provision of education was especially problematic. Traditionalists in many parts of the country objected to the education of girls, for instance, but establishing a nationwide system of schools and requiring attendance would ensure universal education, whatever the wishes of the population.

Was socialism really necessary to realize these goals? Sometimes, they have been achieved by capitalist economies, notably the OECD coun-tries and, more recently, a few in East Asia. The demand problem can be met by the export of manufactures and by their sale to the farm population. The Depression of the 1930s meant that neither of these markets was buoyant for the USSR: the protectionism of the capitalist countries precluded exports of Soviet manufactures, and the collapse of agricultural prices reduced the potential purchasing power of the coun-tryside. The weak rural demand would have been further hampered by the low labor productivity of Russian agriculture, which meant that disposable income was much less than in economically successful wheat-exporting countries like Canada. Slow growth would have pre-cluded a rapid rise in the standard of living since labor markets would not have been tight. Rapid population growth would have compounded the problem. In theory, capitalist development can achieve rapid growth and rising real wages, and sometimes it has in practice, but the poor growth records of many countries discussed in Chapter 1 show that success depends on a favorable conjunction of economic and social con-ditions that has not often been realized. The Soviet growth model side-stepped some of the factors that have prevented successful capitalist development in other times and places.

THE INDUSTRIALIZATION DEBATE

As idle farms and factories resumed production, the pressing question became what to do once full capacity was attained. That was the sub-ject of the industrialization debate. The story of the debate and its rela-tionship to economic events and the leadership struggle within the Communist Party has been skillfully told by several historians.[2] Our interests are different: we are concerned with the ideas underlying Soviet growth (the Soviet development model) as well as the options that were rejected, so we proceed analytically rather than chronologically.

The Soviet Union was a "capital scarce" country in the late 1920s, and the problem could be addressed only by raising investment. Where was that investment to come from? How should it be directed? Since better living standards were also a goal of the Bolsheviks, another key question was: Could investment and consumption be raised together, or would capital accumulation require reducing someone's consumption? If so, whose?

Preferences: Planners' or Consumers'?

To say that the objective of planning was to raise consumption runs counter to a standard distinction in the field of comparative economic systems: that between consumers' preferences and planners' preferences (Bergson 1961, p. 16). The former guide economic activity in the standard models of a capitalist, market economy, while the latter play the corresponding role in a centrally planned economy.

What were the planners' preferences? Raising consumption was a professed goal of the revolution, and that is one possibility. A more widely accepted answer, however, is provided by the totalitarian model of the Soviet Union (Tucker 1977). According to this view, the communist leadership was interested in increasing its power and in controlling all aspects of economic and social life. Those preferences guided the economy and led it to produce investment goods and military equipment rather than consumer goods. In this view, the investment strategy of the Communists was not intended to raise living standards, and so it was no surprise when Bergson (1961) and Chapman (1954, 1963) concluded that consumption per head and real wages declined in the 1930s. The corresponding ideological point is that capitalism is the best system for advancing the interests of the majority.

This critique of communism holds together but is not decisive. In the end the question is factual — did consumption rise or fall in the Soviet Union? — and that issue will be examined in Chapter 7. The logical issues are relevant here as the debate on development strategy is being considered. The totalitarian argument trades on the premise that planners (in this case, Stalin and his associates) had an agenda that was different from that of consumers, and that only the market respected the latter. But there are good reasons to believe that planning can advance consumer objectives in a backward country, and, therefore, the dichotomy between planners' and consumers' preferences may be a false one. There are two issues to consider.

First, market economies can become trapped in low income equilibria due to externalities of investment.[3] Murphy, Schleifer, and Vishny (1989) offer two arguments, the first of which emphasizes consumer demand. There may not be enough cash demand in the preindustrial economy to make it profitable to build a large-scale factory, whereas it would be profitable to build all the factories simultaneously with the wages paid by each providing the cash to buy the products of them all. In such a case, investment would never happen if it were left to individual decision making — since each factory would be unprofitable when analyzed on its own — but planning that took account of all the ramifications could bring about a self-sustaining "big push." (A similar argument holds if coordinated investments lead to a large enough rise in future income to provide the demand that rationalizes the investments.)

Another line of argument emphasizes the interconnection between industries. A railroad, for instance, is a large fixed investment that makes investments in other industries more profitable. Building the railroad may be unprofitable if those other industries are not built (for in that case the railroad would have little traffic) while, at the same time, the other industries may be unprofitable without the extension of the market provided by the railroad. Under these circumstances, no railroad and no industry is an equilibrium for a capitalist economy. Planning that coordinates investment can produce an equilibrium with industrialization.

Second, the future trajectory of consumption depends on the course of development and thus on the rate of investment. In a market economy, investment is determined by the "rate of time preference" of potential savers, according to standard theories (Ramsey 1928; Bergson 1961, p. 26). While these theories usually abstract from the distribution of income, it is important for the discussion at hand that most saving is, in fact, done only by the well-to-do. In that case, the preferences of the overwhelming majority are irrelevant. In this respect, the term *consumers' preferences* is misleading in that it suggests that everyone — as a consumer — plays an equal role in determining investment. While the society-wide balance of preferences may determine the production of ice cream versus chocolate bars, only a minority chooses between candy and machine tools. Indeed, the majority might prefer a higher savings rate than the rich were willing to bear, in which case, planning could represent the majority — consumers, in the parlance at hand — more effectively than the market.

These points, at the moment, are only abstract ones, but they have real force in understanding Soviet history. I will establish the relevance in steps. The first is Fel'dman's theory of economic growth. His model shows that investment in heavy industry has a pay-off in higher consumption. The model challenges, at the theoretical level, the idea im-

plicit in the totalitarian model of the dichotomy between consumers'
and planners' preferences, for Fel'dman's model implies that the buildup
of heavy industry was necessary for raising the standard of living. Second, Chapter 7 examines the actual history of consumption and shows
that the standard of living rose from 1928 to 1940 as, indeed, it has
since the 1950s. The factual basis of the totalitarian model is, thus,
wrong. Third, the simulation model in Chapter 8 tailors the Fel'dman
model to Soviet history and shows that building up heavy industry, in
fact, contributed to the rise in the standard of living. The analysis shows
that other factors were at work as well. Collectivization played a role,
which is analyzed fully in Chapter 9, but, more important, substituting
plan targets and soft budget constraints for profit maximization led to a
more rapid growth in investment and living standards than would have
been obtained with the conventional capitalist employment relation.

The Fel'dman Model

G. A. Fel'dman was an economist in Gosplan. In 1928, he published a
two-part article in the Gosplan journal *Planovoe Khoziaistvo* that developed a mathematical model of capital accumulation.[4] Fel'dman's
model focused on internal sources of investment — exporting wheat to
import machinery received scant consideration. Instead, Fel'dman analyzed the situation in which growth requires a country to produce its
own structures and equipment. The questions were: How could capital
be accumulated? Was there a trade-off between rapid accumulation and
the standard of living? The surprising answer was that you could have
your cake and eat it too: by expanding the investment goods industries,
high investment and rising consumption could be achieved together.
This insight became the basis of socialist economic development.

Fel'dman's model elaborated Marx's division of the economy into
two sectors, consumer goods and producer goods. The former included
food and clothing that sustained workers, while the latter included construction and machinery that could either be invested to expand the
capital stock or be consumed as housing, hospitals, bicycles, or military
equipment. The split of producer goods output between consumption
and investment was the main issue explored by the model.

To examine the implications of that division, Fel'dman specified
highly simplified production functions in which output depended only
on a sector's capital stock:

$$y_t^p = ak_t^p \tag{1}$$

$$y_t^c = bk_t^c \tag{2}$$

where y_t^p is producer goods output at time t, k_t^p is the producer goods capital stock, and the superscripts c in equation 2 indicate the corresponding variables for the consumer goods sector. a and b are the input-output coefficients that relate production to capital.

The key question was how producer goods output should be divided between consumer and producer goods. Let e be the fraction of producer goods output reinvested in that sector. In that case, investment I in the two sectors is the following:

$$I_t^p = ey_t^p \tag{3}$$

$$I_t^c = (1 - e)y_t^p \tag{4}$$

The point of the model is to see how different values of e affect the accumulation of capital and the evolution of consumption. Output in each sector grows in proportion to its capital, and that evolution is governed by the following equations:

$$k_t^p = (1 - d)\, k_{t-1}^p + I_t^p \tag{5}$$

$$k_t^c = (1 - d)\, k_{t-1}^c + I_t^c \tag{6}$$

In these equations, d is the depreciation rate of capital, so $(1 - d)k$ is the amount of capital that survives from one year to the next. Adding investment I_t to that gives the new capital stock.

Substituting equations 1–4 into 5 and 6 gives equations for the growth of the capital stock in terms of earlier values:

$$k_t^p = \frac{(1 - d)}{(1 - ea)} k_{t-1}^p \tag{7}$$

$$k_t^c = (1 - d)\, k_{t-1}^c + \frac{(1 - e)\,(1 - d)\,a}{(1 - ea)} k_{t-1}^p \tag{8}$$

Since output is proportional to the capital stock, the growth of producer goods and consumer goods is also governed by these equations.

What do they tell us about economic growth? Equation 7 shows that the producer goods sector feeds on itself. The capital stock and output of producer goods at any time depend only on the capital stock in the preceding time period and the fraction of output reinvested in itself. Increasing e, that is, reinvesting more of the output of the producer goods industry in itself, increases the growth rate of the producer goods sector. But what happens to consumption? Do high levels of producer goods output exact a high price in terms of consumption?

The surprising answer is no, as shown by equation 8. The first term

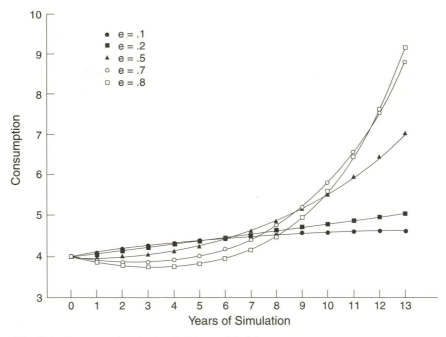

Fig. 3.1. Consumption in the Fel'dman Model

indicates that the capital stock in consumer goods depends on the size of the stock in the preceding period, while the second term indicates that the capital stock in the consumer goods sector also depends on the capital stock in the producer goods sector in the preceding period. The second term creates the possibility of spillover: as the size of the producer goods sector gets larger, it permits a rapid growth in consumption. This is the economists' rationale for building up heavy industry in the Five-Year Plans.

Figure 3.1 shows simulations of these equations that illustrate the trade-off between consumption and investment. Parameter values are plausible ones for the Soviet Union, and the simulations extend over thirteen years, so they are suggestive as to what might have happened in the USSR between 1928 and 1941. There was always a trade-off between consumption and investment in the sense that higher values of e imply lower levels of consumption initially followed by higher values at the end of the thirteen-year period. What is most surprising, however, is that this trade-off does not necessarily imply a fall in consumption. For values of e up to about one-half, consumption never drops below its initial value.

The Fel'dman model opens up several intriguing possibilities — that capital can be accumulated entirely from indigenous sources, that the pace of accumulation is governed by the fraction of producer goods output reinvested in the producer goods sector, and that an accumulation strategy based on an increase in e need not necessarily lower anyone's standard of living. These ideas were key ones underlying Stalin's industrial revolution, although their realization was far from perfect.

Preobrazhensky's Questions

While Fel'dman provides a mathematical model of the development process that provided guidance for the Five-year Plans, his contribution is not nearly as famous as that of Preobrazhensky (1926), who wrote several years earlier. Preobrazhensky was also a proponent of rapid industrialization based on the expansion of heavy industry, but he set the problem in a broader social and political context. Like Fel'dman, he analyzed the economy in terms of two sectors—in this case, agriculture and industry. The former consisted largely of peasant farms, while the latter was state-owned enterprises. Preobrazhensky hoped that the socialized sector would eventually absorb agriculture, and his formulation highlighted that competition.

Preobrazhensky's theory began with the view that there was "huge disguised unemployment in the countryside" and that an aim of development was "the gradual absorption of the surplus population of the country."[5] While there was some possibility of expanding employment in agriculture through intensification, "the key to the solution of all basic problems" was industrialization. This would eventually rebound to the benefit of agriculture as the capacity to produce farm machinery expanded. Preobrazhensky was impressed by the possibilities opened up by socialist planning to coordinate investment across industries in a more effective manner than a free market with its atomistic competitors. Thus, he contrasted socialism's "chain connection in the movement of the whole complex" with the "method of capitalist guerrilla warfare, private initiative, and competition"—vivid language suggestive of Murphy, Schleifer, and Vishny (1989). Of course, coordinated investments across interlinked industries implied a "big push" and a high level of investment.

Preobrazhensky was the first of the superindustrializers who argued for the rapid expansion of heavy industry. As in Fel'dman's theory, however, the ultimate reason for increasing the producer goods industries was to expand the consumer goods industries and thus increase consumption. The reasons were political as well as economic. "If the system does not satisfy a certain minimum of wants, . . . the masses would think of a system that would better satisfy their wants. Herein lies the greatest danger and that is why we are so anxious about the volume of investment."

Preobrazhensky's investment strategy would strain the state budget, which would have to pay for the new plants and equipment. Where were the funds to come from? Preobrazhensky believed they should be extracted from agriculture in a process of "primitive socialist accumulation" that paralleled Marx's (1867) vision of the emergence of capitalism from feudalism. According to Marx, the primitive accumulation of capital was a process in which peasant proprietors lost ownership of their land, livestock, and agricultural implements to their feudal lords. The peasants became wage earners, the lords became capitalists, and the wealth they expropriated from their former peasants became the first capital. Preobrazhesnsky thought that the socialist state should extract a surplus from peasant agriculture to finance the accumulation of socialized capital. Peasant proprietorship would disappear as the peasants were converted to wage laborers, and the state would create capital by investing the income siphoned out of agriculture.

Direct taxation (as in the NEP and in other countries like Japan)[6] would have been one way for the state to extract a surplus from agriculture, but Preobrazhensky rejected it: "The way of direct taxation is the most dangerous way, leading to a break with the peasants." Instead, he proposed a pricing policy to effect "unequal exchange." The Soviet state had great market power since it was the major supplier of factory-produced consumer goods and a major buyer of grain. Preobrazhesnky proposed that it raise the price of consumer goods and lower the price paid for grain in order to extract the agricultural surplus and pay for investment. Financing investment, recruiting a labor force, and expanding socialism at the expense of peasant proprietorship could all be accomplished with one policy.

Bukharin's Response

Rapid industrialization at the expense of the peasantry suffered from two related problems, one political and one economic. The political problem was the potential alienation of the peasants. Preobrazhensky proposed turning the terms of trade against agriculture since it was a less visible method of surplus extraction than direct taxation. But the peasants were no fools and would know if the price structure was manipulated to their disadvantage, so the political problem remained. Moreover, they possessed a potent response to deterioritating terms of trade—a retreat into self-sufficiency by reducing their sales of farm products and their purchases of manufactured goods. Without food for the workers and industrial raw materials, Preobrazhensky's Big Push would grind to a Big Halt. That was the economic problem, and it was a recurring worry throughout the 1920s.

The alternative approach to the Big Push was the concurrent development of agriculture and industry, and Bukharin advocated various forms of that strategy during the industrialization debate. "The greatest sustained speed is achieved when industry develops on the basis provided by the rapidly growing agriculture."[7] He advocated a pricing policy the reverse of Preobrazhensky's, namely, a reduction in the price of manufactures (i.e., an improvement in agriculture's terms of trade) in order to increase peasant marketings as well as to increase their purchases of manufactured consumer goods above pre-1913 levels. Greater demand would stimulate production and industrial profits that could pay for investment. He also advocated measures to raise agricultural productivity. These included removing prohibitions on the use of hired labor in agriculture to encourage investment by the rich peasants. It was in this context that Bukharin repeated the slogan of the reactionary Guizot, "enrichissez-vous." "We have to tell the whole peasantry, all its strata: get rich, accumulate, develop your economy." This offended many Communists, who were more concerned to eliminate Kulaks than to strengthen them. Bukharin, however, felt that a classless society could be achieved in the countryside by peaceful competition. Encouraging cooperatives, for instance, would lower the cost of capital to small farmers and increase the prices they received for their crops. Eventually the Kulaks would be driven out of business. After all, if socialism was really more efficient, the capitalists could be beaten at their own game.

One belief underlying Bukharin's support for balanced growth was his confidence that farm output could be increased at relatively low cost. According to his ally Rykov, "the possibilities of increase in yields even by such relatively elementary devices as replacing the wooden hoe by plough, improvements in seeds, introduction of the simplest agricultural machinery and of fertilizers are tremendous at the present level in our villages." Bukharin was also confident that livestock husbandry could be improved. A big increase in food production would go a long way toward feeding the cities, whatever happened to the peasants' propensity to market. More intensive livestock husbandry and gardening would also provide jobs for underemployed peasants.

The Investment Potential of Surplus Labor

Many economists and politicians participated in the industrialization debate, but this summary of the views of Fel'dman, Bukharin, and Preobrazhensky spans the spectrum and includes the most impressive contributions. In the 1920s, Stalin was an ally of Bukharin. After he came to power, however, Stalin flip-flopped, and he embarked on an extreme version of the Preobrazhensky proposal. The coordination advantages of socialism were realized through central planning and the substitution of output targets for profits as the measure of business success. Investment was pushed up by using the output of the producer goods industries to expand the capital stock of the sector, with the capital in the consumer goods industries growing by a spillover process. The collectivization of agriculture allowed the state to finance investment by turning the terms of trade against farmers. In that sense, the industrialization debate provided the intellectual resources for Stalin's industrial revolution.

The contributions of Fel'dman, Bukharin, and Preobrazhensky, however, did not completely unpack the relationship between surplus labor and capital accumulation. This was only done in 1953 by Ragnar Nurske in his lectures on *Problems of Capital Formation in Underdeveloped Countries*. While writers of the 1920s were aware of the excess population in the countryside, they saw it only as a liability and failed to realize that it was a valuable asset for industrialization. Nurske developed the point by incorporating labor into Fel'dman's otherwise highly abstract model. In Nurske's (1953, pp. 32–47) view, investment and consumption could be increased concurrently if peasants, who were surplus to the needs of agriculture, were put to work on construction projects. This reformulation is critical for explaining the rapid growth of the Soviet Union in the 1930s.

Nurske agreed with Preobrazhensky and Bukharin that a backward country had "large-scale disguised unemployment." In other words, "the same farm output could be got with a smaller labour force . . . without any improvement in technical methods," that is, without "technological advance, more equipment, mechanization, better seeds, improvements in drainage, irrigation, and other such conditions." Nurske expected, however, that the removal of surplus labor would result in organizational changes. In the Soviet Union, as we will see, not only was agriculture radically reorganized, but the use of complementary inputs (notably horses) was actually reduced when labor was shed.

Nurske linked rural unemployment to savings: "The state of disguised unemployment implies at least to some extent a disguised saving potential as well." He distinguished between "the 'unproductive' surplus labourers on the land" and "the 'productive' labourers" who support them. Nurske's key insight was that "the productive labourers are performing 'virtual' saving; they produce more than they consume." However, that "saving runs to waste" since the surplus laborers, who are being fed, produce nothing useful. "If the productive peasants were to send their useless dependants—their cousins, brothers, nephews who now live with them—to work on capital projects and if they continued to feed them there, then their virtual saving would become effective saving." The key to accumulating capital is "taking the surplus people off the land and setting them to work on capital projects—irrigation, drainage, roads, railways, houses, factories, training schemes and so on."

Nurske realized that the reallocation of surplus labor raised the possibility of boosting investment without reducing consumption. "It is possible to increase capital formation without having to cut down the level of consumption." The trick is to create jobs for people who would otherwise be unproductive. This is Fel'dman's conclusion in a more realistic setting.

Farm marketing is a complement to investment in Nurske's view of accumulation. When investment is produced by otherwise unemployed workers, "there is no question of asking the peasants who remain on the land to eat less than before, only of preventing them from eating more." They must "go on feeding their dependants who leave the farms to go to work on capital projects and who, in effect, continue to be dependent for their subsistence on the 'productive' peasants remaining on the farms." Nurske doubted that voluntarism would suffice: "The peasants are not likely to save the surplus voluntarily since they live so close to subsistence." Therefore, "some form of collective saving enforced by the state may prove to be indispensable for the mobilization of the saving potential implicit in disguised unemployment."

While he felt that "peasants are notoriously hard to tax," he indicated three approaches. The first was "through indirect taxation of the things they buy"—a Preobrazhensky proposal, indeed. Second, "Japan kept up a stiff land tax, which was highly effective." The land tax had been rejected by Preobrazhensky as politically unacceptable. The third was Stalin's solution: "This crucial problem of collecting the food seems to be solved in Soviet Russia by the system of collective farms. The word 'collective' has here a double meaning. The collective farm is not only a form of collective organization; it is above all an instrument of collection" of food and fiber.

A Graphical Depiction of Soviet Development

The insights of Fel'dman, Preobrazhensky, Bukharin, and Nurske can be applied to Soviet development with a graphical model that shows how the mobilization of surplus labor can increase investment, consumption, and output concurrently.

Consider the production possibility frontier (ppf) in Figure 3.2. The axes show the production of consumer goods and producer goods, and the ppf curve connects the combinations of consumer and producer

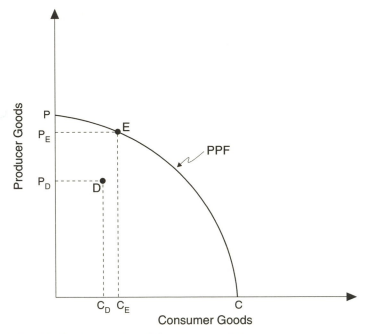

Fig. 3.2. Production Possibility Frontier (PPF)

goods that the economy can produce as resources are shifted from one sector to the other. Thus, consumer goods production will be C if all resources are devoted to that activity, while producer goods production will be P if resources are deployed fully in that direction. Points on the ppf frontier like E represent split allocations where both goods are produced — C_E consumer goods and P_E producer goods. Points on the curve like E represent maximum production potential. Production at interior points like D is also possible, but D represents a situation where resources are underutilized since only C_D consumer goods and P_D producer goods are made.

Economic development in this framework can be conceived as a two-step process (Figure 3.3). In the 1920s, Russia was at a point like D on the interior of the ppf curve since so much labor was inefficiently maintained in agriculture. Shifting labor to industry was the first step in development, for it allowed a simultaneous increase in the production of consumer and investment goods as the economy moved from D to E. The second step (once full employment was achieved) was allocating a high fraction of the additional producer goods to increase the capital in that sector. This investment pattern shifted the ppf curve to ppf′ as the new plant and equipment became operational: the higher the fraction of

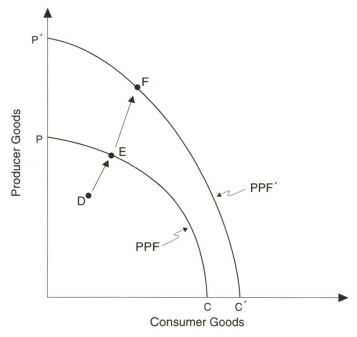

Fig. 3.3. Production Possibility Frontier of Soviet Development

producer goods reinvested in that sector, the higher was the ratio of P' to P and the lower the ratio of C' to C. Once again it was possible to increase both investment and consumption by moving from E to F.

Incorporating labor into the Fel'dman model provides a richer and more realistic framework that retains the essential insight: reinvesting in heavy industry was a strategy that could simultaneously increase investment and consumption. That is the central idea of the Soviet development model.

Did Stalin have this in mind? It is unlikely that he worked his way through Fel'dman's math any more than a Western politician reads the technical papers of his economic advisers. But these ideas were in the air, as the industrialization debate makes clear, and the technical models established the coherence of the arguments.

Fel'dman's model is also important because it precludes a common argument about Stalin's thinking. That argument is that he was not concerned about the well-being of workers since the first Five-Year Plans made heavy industry a priority. However, what Fel'dman's model establishes is that expanding heavy industry is the way to expand consumption since a larger engineering industry can produce the factories to make consumer goods. The important historical question is whether this approach actually delivered the goods in the 1930s. Did consumption rise? Chapter 7 will show that it did. In a schematic sense, therefore, the Soviet industrial revolution reduces to the movement from D to E to F in Figure 3.3.

CHAPTER FOUR

NEP Agriculture and Economic Development

The Soviet Union in the 1920s was a classic underdeveloped economy with too many people on the land and too few working in the city. Industrial investment and mass urbanization were the solutions to the problem. A key question was what role agriculture could play in facilitating or obstructing these processes. It could certainly give up workers, but would it provide the food they would need, once they arrived in the city? The task would be helped if there were an easy way to increase farm output. Was there a technological gap with the West that could be closed by importing a "Green Revolution" technology that would boost food production as much as factory technology could increase manufacturing output? The likelihood of any such progress was one of the disagreements between Bukharin (the optimist) and Preobrazhensky (the pessimist).

Greater farm output would facilitate economic development in other ways. A high rate of industrial investment would require high savings, and agriculture could contribute by increasing its sales. Agriculture's provision of savings to industry equals agricultural sales less its purchases, so anything that increased sales—like greater farm output—would provide resources for industrial investment. If the farm products were sold abroad, they could earn foreign exchange, which would finance the importation of capital equipment as in the late imperial period. A large volume of sales would also contribute to the growth of demand for industrial products since agriculture's sales provided peasants with the cash to buy manufactures. Providing a home market for industry, however, works at cross-purposes to providing savings since a bigger home market means more purchases by agriculture and thus a smaller capital transfer for any level of farm marketing. For that reason, Preobrazhensky was willing to give up on the home market, although Bukharin endorsed it. In any event, a high level of sales was necessary if a large capital transfer and a big home market were both desired. Greater agricultural output would facilitate both.

How feasible was it for Soviet agriculture to make these contributions to industrial development? This chapter concentrates on output expansion, labor release, and increased sales. I compare Russian agriculture in the second decade of the twentieth century with farming on the Great

Plains of North America. The comparison shows that there were tremendous possibilities for reducing farm employment in the USSR, but little chance of increasing output per hectare of farmland. Since the 1960s, farm marketing has not been much of an issue in developing countries because the Green Revolution has allowed large increases in production, so larger sales did not have to come at the expense of the peasants' own consumption. The North American comparisons show that the Soviet Union was not so fortunate, and that the Communists' obsession with marketing had a basis in fact. The final part of the chapter analyzes marketing trends in the USSR from 1913 to 1928 to determine the willingness of Soviet peasants to sell food to the cities. This inquiry indicates that some optimism was warranted, although the situation was problematic. The Communists' concern with farm marketing had some basis in reality, although their fears were overblown.

Comparison of Russian and North American Agriculture: Output

There is a long tradition of regarding Russian agriculture as technologically backward. The case usually rests on comparisons of grain yields in Russia and Ukraine with those in western Europe, which were considerably higher. Such comparisons, however, are off the mark since, in countries such as Britain, soil and climate — and, consequently, the farming system — were so different. To reach a better assessment of Russian performance, the comparison should be made with a region of similar climate and soil. In this chapter, I compare Russian productivity in 1913 with productivity on the Great Plains of North America — a region that includes the Canadian prairie provinces of Manitoba, Saskatchewan, and Alberta, as well as the American states of North Dakota, South Dakota, Montana, and Wyoming. Johnson and Brooks (1983) undertook a very careful assessment of Soviet agriculture in the post–World War II period and compared it with the same region studied here.[1] As in Russia, the climate was cold and dry. While there was some livestock production in both regions, grain was the principal product. Indeed, Russia and the Great Plains both grew rapidly during the world wheat boom from 1896 to 1913. How did Russian farmers compare to their competitors in the most advanced economies of the world? What do the comparisons indicate about the possibilities of modernizing Russian agriculture?

The Russian side of the comparison is based on Prokopovich's (1918, pp. 27–44) estimates of Russian national income in 1913. As part of that exercise, he calculated net agricultural output for the fifty provinces of European Russia. That is a more homogeneous region than the Soviet Union, which includes the very different agricultures of Central Asia and the Caucuses, and one that closely corresponds to the Great Plains of North America. During much of the NEP, agriculture was recovering from the civil war, so the situation is too confused for a good comparison, which is another reason that Prokopovich's work is used instead of Soviet figures for the 1920s. A further advantage of Prokopovich is that he reports all of the details and implicit assumptions underlying his results, and they shed much light on the strengths and weaknesses of Russian farming.

The North American side of the comparison is based on the Canadian and American censuses of 1920 and 1921.[2] The year 1920 was chosen as the year of comparison since it is immediately after the completion of prairie settlement and immediately before the widespread use of gasoline tractors and trucks. Since gasoline vehicles had not yet transformed Russian agriculture, we can compare like with like.

The first object of the exercise is to compare output per hectare in the two regions. There are at least three measures of "hectares" from which to choose. The only figure that is known with certainty in both continents is the number of hectares planted with crops. This, of course, excludes fallow land as well as pasture and meadow. A broader concept that is less well defined is called "improved land" in American and Canadian sources. It includes fallow land, cultivated grasses, meadows, and artificial pastures but excludes "unimproved land." Natural pasture was used for grazing in newly settled parts of the Great Plains and Russian steppes, and that land falls in the "unimproved" category, as does Russian woodland where stock was run even though it did not belong to farms.[3] In practice, then, there are three measures of land: cropped, improved, and improved plus unimproved. The first is clearly too narrow, the third is perhaps too broad. The second is the single best measure of agricultural land, but it is not exhaustive and is not known with certainty. Table 4.1 shows the values of these measures for Russia and the Great Plains. Fortunately, the alternative measures of agricultural land stand in similar proportions to each other in the two countries.

What about output? I begin by consider simple indicators of productivity before considering aggregate measures. Table 4.2 compares crop yields. Russian yields were higher for all crops except oats and maize. Russia's advantage was particularly marked in rye and potatoes, two crops in which it specialized. Russian farmers do well when crop yields are the measure of success.

While grain was the principal product in European Russia and on the Great Plains, animal husbandry was also important. Table 4.3 compares livestock densities. Stocking rates were remarkably similar for cows and

TABLE 4.1
Agricultural Land: Russia versus Plains and Prairies (millions of hectares)

	Russia	Great Plains
Sown	84.4	22.9
Improved	169.7	40.3
Total	349.7	82.3

Sources: Great Plains: U.S. Bureau of the Census (1922, Part 1, pp. 615–36, 643–68; Part 3, pp. 95–116, 149–64) and Canada (1924–28, vol. V, p. 5).
Russia:
sown — Prokopovich (1918, p. 28).
improved and total — Antsiferov (1930, pp. 15, 17–18).
Note: Russia refers to the fifty provinces of European Russia. Great Plains refers to Manitoba, Saskatchewan, Alberta, North Dakota, South Dakota, Montana, and Wyoming.

TABLE 4.2
Crop Yields: Russia versus Plains and Prairies (kilograms per hectare)

	Russia	Plains and Prairies
Wheat	709	696
Rye	794	410
Barley	866	784
Oats	779	945
Corn	1213	1273
Beans	760	519
Potatoes	8656	4096
Sugar beets	22864	20807

Sources: Plains and Prairies — Except for wheat, average reported yields for Manitoba, Saskatchewan, Alberta, North Dakota, South Dakota, Montana, and Wyoming in U.S. Bureau of the Census (1922, Part 1, pp. 615–36, 643–68; Part 3, pp. 95–116, 149–64) and Canada (1924–28, vol. V, pp. 9–17). Wheat yields in the American states were unusually low in the census year, so the average yield of wheat for 1918–22 was used instead of the census value for all states and provinces. North American production was measured in bushels in the censuses. Wheat, rye, and beans were converted to weight at the rate of 60 pounds per bushel; corn, barley, and potatoes were assumed to weigh 50 pounds; while oats was taken to weigh 40 pounds.
Russia — Prokopovich (1918, p. 28). These are average values net of seed. For the grains and beans, 117 kg per hectare of seed was added to Prokopovich's figure based on Wheatcroft (1990a, p. 269). For potatoes, 2000 kg per hectare was added following Johnson and Kahan (1959, p. 236).

TABLE 4.3
Livestock Densities: Russia versus Plains and Prairies
(animals per hectare, as indicated)

	North America		Russia	
	Per cropped hectare	Per improved hectare	Per cropped hectare	Per improved hectare
Horses	.21	.12	.29	.14
Cows	.16	.09	.19	.09
Calves less than 1 year	.10	.06	.12	.06
Calves, 1–2 years	.09	.05	.07	.04
Cattle, 2 + years	.05	.03	.10	.05
Sheep, adult	.19	.11	.56	.28
Swine, adult	.10	.06	.11	.05

Sources: U.S. Bureau of the Census (1922, Part 1, pp. 615–36, 643–68; Part 3, pp. 95–116, 149–64) and Canada (1924–28, vol. V, pp. 26–27, 46–49).

pigs. European farmers usually maintained flocks of sheep, and Russians were no exception, for sheep densities were much higher there than in North America. Russian farms had surprisingly many beef cattle.

The productivity of Russian animals, however, was generally less than North American ones. The weakness of Russian livestock husbandry was particularly striking in the case of beef cattle and undid their lead in numbers. Full-grown beef cattle in North America, for instance, gave 220 kg of meat, while their Russian counterparts gave only 164 kg. Likewise, North America calves gave 45 kg of veal versus 29 kg in Russia. The North American advantage was less for cows (1066 liters of milk per year on the Great Plains versus 923 litres in Russia) and pigs (57 kg versus 49 kg). Russian sheep gave 2.1 kg of wool per fleece, while American sheep gave 3.8 kg. The only comparison in which Russia was ahead was meat per sheep—18 kg on the Great Plains versus 20 kg in Russia—and this surely was due to the Russians slaughtering older stock.[4]

The lower productivity of Russian livestock may have reflected breeding, but also reflected scanty nutrition. Gosplan "norms" for the 1920s indicate that Russian horses were fed 400 kg of grain per year. In contrast, Canadian horses received 1125 kg. The disproportion extended to other animals. Canadian cows, for instance, received 400 kg of grain and 90 kg of roots, while Russian cows got only 75 kg of grain and 80 kg of potatoes.[5] A low standard of living for cattle went hand in hand with a low standard of living for people and stunted the growth of both.

The Russian feed situation was even worse before the First World War. In the imperial period, the working horses ate all of the oats crop (21 percent of the country's grain in 1913)—and even then got only 400 kg per head—while other stock subsisted on grass and hay.[6] In contrast, livestock on the Great Plains ate all of the barley and maize grown in the region, as well as all of the oats.[7] High feeding rates in North America reduced the net output of grain on the plains and prairies but increased the productivity of pigs and cattle.

Table 4.3 raises one further point that requires particular attention, and that relates to horses. Except in the small number of cases where ponies were sold to city dwellers or the army for riding and carting, horses were agricultural implements. Horses, in other words, represented costs rather than benefits, so it was better to have fewer horses, all other things being equal. It is impressive that the number of horses per hectare of cropped land (the relevant measure since horses were kept as draught animals) was 40 percent higher in Russia than in North America. The disproportion is even greater if the comparison is confined to grain-producing states or provinces, where there were .14–.17 horses per hectare in contrast to .29 in Russia.

The main reason for the large number of horses in Russia was the smallness of its farms. Every farmer wanted his own horse, so he could proceed quickly when weather was favorable. Not every peasant succeeded in this wish, but enough did to push up the average number of horses per hectare on small farms. Fewer horses were kept per hectare on large peasant farms, as Lenin noted in his analysis of peasant differentiation, and on noble estates. Indeed, the 1917 Russian census of agriculture showed .16 horses per hectare on large estates, while peasants kept .27 horses per hectare. The rule of thumb was 5–6 dessiatines per horse, or .15–.18 horses per hectare (Antsiferov 1930, pp. 123–25). With so many farms less than 5–6 dessiatines and with each peasant eager for his own horse, the Russian countryside was as overpopulated with horses as it was with people. A high ratio of horses per hectare meant that the horses worked relatively few hours per year. Chayanov (1966, p. 155) pointed out that the only reason Russian horses could survive on their scanty rations was because they were idle much of the time. But even at 400 kg of grain a head, each horse ate as much as two humans, so the cost in terms of food was substantial.

To form an overall comparison of output per hectare in Russian and North American agriculture, it is necessary to compute the total value of farm output and divide it by the land area. Table 4.4 shows production valued at the prewar Russian prices used by Prokopovich and at 1920 prices from the Canadian census. By and large the results are similar. The comparisons using improved land may be the most revealing.

Using ruble valuations, total output per hectare is virtually the same in Russia and North America. When output is valued in dollars, Russia comes out 8 percent higher. Russia has a slight lead in crop output, but North America has an offsetting advantage in livestock products.

Table 4.2 suggests that there was little prospect of increasing the output per hectare of Russian agriculture during the 1920s. The low level of yields on the Great Plains and Canadian prairies did not reflect a failure to conduct agricultural research. On the contrary, Olmstead and Rhode (2002) have emphasized that there was widespread experimentation with new seed varieties to control pests and disease as well as to find varieties of wheat that would grow in the harsh conditions of the Great Plains. It is ironic that some of the leading varieties—for example, Kubanka and Kharkof—were imported from Russia, which was thus setting the limits on North American agriculture rather than the reverse (Olmstead and Rhode 2002, pp. 11, 12n. 37). With other new varieties, the gains were modest. Marquis wheat, which was important for the settlement of Saskatchewan, only increased yields by 14 percent. Its greatest contribution was cutting the growing time by 8 percent, which permitted cultivation to move north (Ward 1990, p. 44). These were small improvements. It also needs emphasizing that they required a system of state-run experiment stations and decades of testing, including trials on many varieties that did not prove successful. North American farmers had no high-yield technology that would quickly increase the Russian food supply.

Under these circumstances, the history of wheat yields on the Great Plains provides a counterfactual experiment showing the possibilities open to Soviet agriculture. They were modest. Figure 4.1 shows the history of wheat yields in North Dakota and Russia/USSR from the late nineteenth century through the twentieth. As noted in Chapter 2, yields were about 1200 kg/hectare in North Dakota before 1900 and only 500 kg in Russia. In both regions, yields converged to about 700 kg/hectare in the 1920s and 1930s although they could drop much lower due to drought or political turmoil. After World War II, yields rose several fold in both North America and the USSR when fertilizers transformed the situation. Figure 4.1 conveys two important lessons about Soviet agriculture. The first is that its productivity history, as measured by yields per acre, has been indistinguishable from that of environmentally similar regions in North America. There is no evidence of Soviet failure in this regard. Second, before the 1950s, there was no prospect of increasing food production by raising yields in the Soviet Union.

Likewise with livestock. More meat and milk could be produced by feeding the sheep and cattle better, but even here the gains were not dramatic and came at high cost. Better breeds might gain weight more

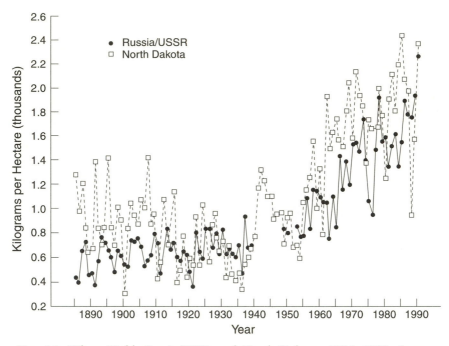

Fig. 4.1. Wheat Yield, Russia/USSR and North Dakota, 1885–1990. *Source*: The North Dakota yields are from U.S. Department of Agriculture (1955), U.S. Department of Agriculture, *Agricultural Statistics*, various years, U.S. Bureau of the Census, *Statistical Abstract of the United States*, various years. Russian and Soviet statistics from Bennett (1933), United Nations FAO, *Production Yearbook*, various years. Soviet wheat yields in the 1930s extrapolated from yields of all grains together.

rapidly, but in the event would also require more feed. And improving the quality of Russian livestock was bound to be a slow process under any system of social organization. There was no Green Revolution technology that could provide a quick fix to Russian agriculture and that would increase farm output at the rapid rates achieved in many developing countries since the 1960s.

LABOR

North America did have a technological lead in agriculture, but it involved machinery and raised output per worker rather than per hectare. Importing that technology would have freed up farm labor, but it would not have helped to feed Soviet cities.

The North American lead is seen by comparing employment per hectare in the two continents. Ideally, one would measure the total hours worked in agriculture, perhaps adjusting hours for differences in the efficiency of different workers, but such precision is impossible. The best we can do is use the total number of farms, which indicates the number of farm families. There were about 16 million peasant families in European Russia in 1913, and 481,399 farms were enumerated in the Canadian and American censuses. The Russian figure may overstate the labor input in agriculture to the degree that members of these families were working part-time outside of agriculture, and the North American figure may understate labor since part-time workers were hired during harvests, and threshing was done by contractors rather than by the farmers themselves, as in Russia. The number of these additional workers was small, however (Ward 1990, pp. 126–28).

Juxtaposing the Russian and North American figures of land and farms highlights the fundamental difference between their agricultures—the difference in farm size. In North America, the average farm was 84 improved hectares, while it was only 11 hectares in Russia.

These results have important implications for labor productivity when they are combined with the earlier findings on production. Output per worker in agriculture equals output per hectare multiplied by hectares per worker. Table 4.4 shows that output per hectare was similar in Russia and the Great Plains, while employment per hectare was about eight times higher in Russia than in North America. The implication is that output per worker was eight times greater on the Great Plains. The weakness of Russian agriculture was not so much in the biological aspects that determined output per hectare and yield per animal as in the organizational and mechanical dimensions that determined farm employment.

How could North American farmers cultivate eight times as much land as Russian farmers? Part of the answer is mechanization. Without horse-drawn reapers and steam threshers, American and Canadian farms would have been much smaller. But that is not the whole answer. Even with their primitive technology, fewer Russians could have cultivated the land. This was true in 1913 and even more so during the NEP. The communal features of Russian agriculture acted like a giant sponge, soaking up labor by creating small farms.

Before we can gauge "overpopulation" or rural unemployment, it is necessary to establish the labor requirements of Russian and North American farm technology. The implements used by most Russian peasants in 1900 were similar to those used by American farmers in the early nineteenth century. The soil was worked with wooden plows. Land was sometimes harrowed by dragging a branch across it. Grain was broadcast by hand, harvested with sickles, and threshed with "the

TABLE 4.4
Output per Hectare: Russia versus Plains and Prairies

A. Output valued in rubles	Canada and United States			Russia		
	Cropped	Improved	All	Cropped	Improved	All
Crops	25.1	14.2	7.0	31.8	15.8	7.7
Livestock	16.6	9.4	4.6	15.8	7.8	3.8
Total	41.7	23.7	11.6	47.6	23.6	11.5

B. Output valued in dollars	Canada and United States			Russia		
	Cropped	Improved	All	Cropped	Improved	All
Crops	26.5	15.0	7.4	37.6	18.7	9.1
Livestock	16.0	9.1	4.4	15.0	7.4	3.6
Total	42.5	24.1	11.8	52.6	26.1	12.7

Sources: Canada and United States same source as Tables 4.1 and 4.2. The trickiest part was estimating meat production. Canada (1924–28, vol. V, pp. 52–53) reported number of animals sold and slaughtered on farms. Corresponding figures were estimated for U.S. states based on herd size. Meat per animal computed from statistics on number of animals slaughtered and dressed meat produced in Leacy (1983). Beef cattle were rated at 485 kg, calves at 100 kg, hogs at 125 kg, and lambs at 40 kg.
Russia: Prokopovich (1918, pp. 27–44).

flail, pitchfork, shovel, and winnowing sheet" (U.S. Commissioner of Labor 1899, p. 86). By 1900, steel gang plows and disc harrows had replaced wooden implements in North America, seeds were drilled, grain was harvested with horse-drawn reapers and binders, and the crop was threshed by steam.

Several studies of the impact of these changes on labor requirements in North American agriculture are available, and they can be compared with surveys of Russian farms. A consistent picture of the impact of machinery on labor requirements emerges (Table 4.5). The U.S. Commissioner of Labor's (1899) comparison of hand and machine methods found that the agricultural methods of the 1830s required about 64 hours of labor per acre, or 20 man-days of work per hectare assuming an 8-hour day. Gosplan arrived at a similar figure for Soviet peasants in the 1920s (Kahan 1959, p. 452 n. 6). Its surveys indicated that they used an average of 20.8 man-days per hectare (where "man," indeed,

TABLE 4.5
Labor Requirement for a Hectare of Grain (man-days per operation)

	Traditional implements	Modern machinery
1st plowing	2.0	.50
1st harrowing	0.625	.125
2nd plowing	2.0	—
2nd harrowing	0.625	—
Seeding	0.5	.14
3rd harrowing	0.625	—
Harvesting	4.0	.14
Carting	1.0	1.0
Threshing	8.0	.375
Total	19.375	2.28

Sources and Notes:

Traditional implements

Plowing times shown here are consistent with Chayanov (1966, pp. 183, 190), who indicates 2 days per desyatina, and U.S. Commissioner of Labor (1899, p. 81), who indicates 5–8 hours per acre for primitive plowing. Eight hours per acre implies 2.0 days per hectare at 10 hours per day.

Harrowing—Chayanov (1966, p. 183) shows only one-third day per desyatina. U.S. Commissioner of Labor (1899, pp. 82, 85) shows 2.5 hours per acre.

seeding—time shown here for seeding and harrowing from U.S. Commissioner of Labor (1899, p. 85). Chayanov gives 2 days per desyatina for seeding and for one plowing.

harvesting—Chayanov (1966, p. 183), gives 6 days per desyatina (5.5 per hectare) but 4.3 days per desyatina on p. 189. The latter implies 4 days per hectare, which is consistent with U.S. Commissioner of Labor (1899, p. 85)—16 hours per acre on a 10-hour day.

carting—Chayanov (1966, p. 183).

threshing—Chayanov (1966, p. 183) gives 9 days for threshing, winnowing, and sorting, and 5.5 days on p. 190. U.S. Commissioner of Labor (1899, pp. 86–87) gives a broad range of estimates of which 32 hours per acre (8 days per hectare at 10 hours per day) is representative.

Modern machinery

plowing—Ward (1990) gives 4.8 acres per day (roughly 2 hours per acre) consistent with gang plow figures in U.S. Commissioner of Labor (1899, p. 81). Two hours per acre implies .5 man-days per hectare at 10 hours/day and one operator per plow. Land was only plowed once on Great Plains.

harrowing—Ward (1990, p. 85) reports 20 acres per day and U.S. Commissioner of Labor (1899, p. 82) about a half hour per acre.

seeding—Ward (1990, p. 83) reports 18 acres/day. U.S. Commissioner of Labor (1899, p. 85) gives only 15–20 minutes per acre.

harvesting—U.S. Commissioner of Labor (1899, p. 85) gives one hour per acre (.25 man-days per hectare). Ward (1990, p. 94) reports 17.5 acres per day, or .14 days per hectare.

threshing—U.S. Commissioner of Labor (1899, pp. 86–87) suggests 1.5 hours per acre, which implies .375 man-days per hectare. This is much more than Ward's (1990, p. 103) times, which are limited to the operating time of the thresher and do not include setup.

refers to an adult male equivalent). Chayanov (1966, pp. 183, 190) summarized surveys by several other Russian investigators that point to similar results.

In contrast, much less labor was required when machines were used. By the early twentieth century, hours per hectare had been cut by almost 90 percent (Table 4.5). Reductions were made in most operations, and the number of plowings and harrowings had been slashed since the larger horse-drawn implements worked the soil to a greater depth and pulverized it more completely. The labor economies shown in Table 4.5 were necessary for North Americans to operate such large farms.

But equipment was not the only reason Russian farms were so small; indeed, they were too small even in terms of the hand technology customarily used. Applying the Gosplan norm of 20.8 man-days per hectare to Russian agriculture as described by Prokopovich implies the need for 17.8 million years of work in the fifty provinces of European Russia.[8] With 16 million peasant families in the region, there were about 39.7 million adult male equivalent years of labor available.[9] By this reckoning, the peasant population was 2.2 times too large for the needs of farming, even without considering organization or mechanization.

Annual balances of this sort need refinement in view of the seasonal fluctuations in employment. Labor demand peaked at the harvest with the trough in the winter. The farm population was much greater than the needs of agriculture outside of high summer, and the surplus labor was redeployed to logging, hunting, and the kustar industry.

What was the employment situation during the peak? Chayanov (1966, p. 189) estimated that "4.3 working days are spent in harvesting one desyatina" of wheat or rye — almost exactly four days per hectare. If "the possible harvesting period is 10 days," then each worker can reap 2.5 hectares and bind and stack the sheaves. At this harvesting rate, which is consistent with North American practice using sickles early in the nineteenth century, 18.6 million reapers were required to harvest the wheat and rye grown in European Russia in 1913.[10] This requirement is less than half of the available labor supply (39.7 million workers). This, of course, is a best-case scenario. Farmers tried to harvest the crop in less than ten days since bad weather always threatened to close this window of opportunity. While the matter is intrinsically uncertain, the labor supply appears to have exceeded demand at its peak in August. The equalization of holdings and the deurbanization following the 1917 revolution led to even more excess labor during the harvest.

It is significant that reaping was the first farm task to be mechanized in the United States and that improvements in North American harvesting technology were continuous in the late nineteenth century. By 1900, when it took a Canadian or an American only .14 man-days to reap a hectare, one farmer could harvest 70 hectares of grain in a ten-day harvest period. That was the single most important reason that farm sizes were so much larger on the Great Plains than in Russia. The reductions in labor time for other operations meant that bottlenecks did not emerge elsewhere in the farming calendar. The cumulative results were striking. If we apply the Gosplan labor norms to North American agriculture, we find that 4.3 million adult male equivalents would have been required to cultivate the Great Plains in 1920–21. Yet farming was conducted by only 481,399 families. How did Americans and Canadians do it? They did it with machines.

Russian farmers were not ignorant of the advantages of economizing labor. Peasant differentiation in the nineteenth century had been driven by the economies of large-scale production, including savings on labor costs when tasks could be organized as group efforts as well as by reducing the number of horses per hectare. The availability of machinery gave further advantages to large-scale farmers. These included, first, the ability to borrow money at lower cost than small-scale (and thus poorer) peasants. This advantage, which had always existed, came to the fore as buying machinery became a more important issue. Second, machines were profitable only on large farms where the savings in labor costs exceeded the interest and depreciation on the machine. Horse-drawn reapers, drills, rakes, and threshers became cost-effective only when farms exceeded 20–30 hectares.[11] The availablity of machines, consequently, provided an incentive for farmers to increase their operations above the breakeven size and reduce employment in consequence. Many cultivators were already moving in that direction: close to half a million horse-drawn reapers were made in the Soviet Union in the 1920s (Nutter 1962, p. 437). The revitalized communes of the NEP had the power to limit the growth in farm size. Without those interventions, there would have been more big farms, more landless laborers, and more rural unemployment as agriculture was mechanized. This has been a common pattern in developing countries during the Green Revolution, and it was the fate that awaited Russian farmers had the 1917 revolution not overturned the Stolypin reforms.

During the NEP, the Russian countryside was overpopulated and destined to become more so. As farmers bought horse-drawn reapers, August labor requirements fell, leading to even more surplus labor on a year-round basis. Looking ahead to the late 1930s, when tractors replaced horses and sickles gave way to combined harvesters, the overpopulation looks immense. By the standards of North American agriculture, surplus labor was even greater.

History has performed a "natural test" of the surplus labor hypothesis. During the 1930s, about 25 million people moved from the country to the city, and perhaps as many as 10 million died in the famine following collectivization. Another 30 million Soviet citizens were killed during the Second World War. By 1950, the urban population was restored, so the war deaths were absorbed by the countryside. Population growth made good some of these losses, but the rural population in 1950 was about 17 million less than it had been in 1928. Not much farm equipment survived the Second World War. Only in 1950 was the tractor stock restored to its 1940 level (Miller 1970, p. 56). Despite the loss in workers and the destruction of capital, farm output was nonetheless 10 percent greater in 1950 than it had been in 1928 (Johnson and Kahan 1959, pp. 204–5). T. W. Schultz (1964, pp. 63–70) has argued that there was no surplus labor in Indian agriculture around 1920 since output and the sown acreage fell as a standard production function would imply in view of the fall in population during the influenza epidemic of 1918–19. The same logic, however, points to significant surplus labor in Soviet agriculture.

Farm Marketing

Russian agriculture could release a considerable number of workers without any loss in output, and the number released could be increased further by mechanization, especially of the harvest. But if the peasants moved to the cities and took up factory jobs, they would have to be fed and supplied with agricultural raw materials. There was some scope to boost farm sales by raising farm production if livestock numbers continued to increase as they had in the 1920s, but the possibilities were otherwise limited since there was little scope for increasing grain or livestock yields or the cultivated land. To increase sales, farmers would have to sell a greater fraction of their crop.

That was a problematic requirement. If people leave the countryside, then food production per rural resident will rise. In order for the city population to eat as it did in the country, the peasants would have to sell *all* of the increase in food per person that arose from rural-urban migration. Only in that way would new workers arrive at their factory jobs with their food parcels on their backs, to use Nurske's memorable phrase. But the peasants were poor and their calorie intake was low, so it is unlikely in the extreme that they would voluntarily sell all of the increment in food.[12] In that case, urban residents would have to bid up the price of food, and agriculture's terms of trade would improve—the reverse of the Preobrazhensky proposal. Would the countryside, thereby, hold the city for ransom? Would the growth of industry be choked off by rising food prices?

As we have seen, these questions were at the heart of the industrialization debate, and farm marketing was a recurring political issue during the NEP.[13] The scissors crisis in 1923 emphasized that peasant marketings — by which I mean the net sales from agriculture to the rest of the economy — had fallen markedly since the prewar period. While there was a recovery in the next few years, extrarural sales were 24 percent lower in 1928 than they had been in 1913, as shown in Table 4.6. Throughout the 1920s grain procurements were a particularly acute problem, and the relationship between peasants and the state became increasingly strained. The culmination was forced collectivization and obligatory deliveries at prices dictated by the state. This solved the marketing problem — extrarural sales of farm produce rose 92 percent between 1928 and 1937 — but at great cost to the peasants, many of whom were deported, or executed, or perished in the famine of 1933.

In order to gauge the seriousness of the farm marketing problem, we must explain the decline in farm marketing in the 1920s. There are four possible explanations. The first emphasizes the elimination of large estates and Kulak farms following the revolution (Jasny 1949, pp. 151–60). In contrast to small peasant farms, these were seen by many Bolsheviks as the main sources of marketed output. Their replacement by large socialized production units was seen as the countermove to restore marketings. While attractive in some respects — for example, the farm size distribution did change as the theory postulates — this view suffers from the grave problem that marketings in the 1920s fell for all farm size categories (Harrison 1990, p. 113). The shift in the farm size distribution was thus not the decisive factor.

A second explanation for the decline in marketings has been proposed by Davies (1980, p. 39) and reiterated by Wheatcroft (1990a). These historians concentrate on grain marketings, which did fall dramatically as shown in Table 4.6, and explain the decline as a response to a fall in the price of grain relative to other crops. "There is no mystery about the reasons for the grain shortage. The attempts of the government to control and hold down grain prices naturally increased the attractiveness of converting grain surpluses to livestock, whose value could be realized on the less restricted private market" (Wheatcroft 1990a, p. 99).

The problem with this explanation is that the decline in marketing embraced many products, including livestock products, as shown in Table 4.6. Milk output did rise 8 percent between 1913 and 1928, but meat marketings rose only 3 percent, egg marketings fell 41 percent, and wool marketings dropped 32 percent. (The 1913 values of extrarural sales of hides are too unreliable to sustain detailed comparisons.) Furthermore, the marketing problem was not limited to these crops.

TABLE 4.6
Agricultural Marketings, 1913, 1928, and 1937

	1913	1928	1937
Plant foods			
Grain	18100	8330	28940
Potatoes	4730	2910	11690
Vegetables	3000	2000	4500
Animal foods			
Milk	5810	6250	6970
Meat	1420	1459	1162
Eggs	6700	3970	3036
Industrial inputs			
Flax fiber	246	120	320
Sunflower seeds	420	1070	1287
Wool	72	49	79
Hides, large	10000	11200	10300
Hides, small	30000	34000	31200
Cotton	738	690	2573
Sugar beets	10850	9780	21450
Total value (mill 1927–28 rubles)	3334	2565	4918

Sources:
prices—*Kontrol'nye Tsifry*, 1929–30, pp. 581–82.
1913 figures:
grain—extrarural sales from Wheatcroft (1990a, p. 269).
other products except vegetables and hides—Jasny (1949, pp. 78, 223).
Vegetables and hides are very rough estimates based on production and later patterns.
1927–28 figures:
grain—Barsov (1969, p. 103). This figure is extravillage sales.
other products—Bergson (1961, p. 327), Karcz (1957, p. 26), Karcz (1979, p. 102), Jasny (1949, p. 223). There are some minor variations in these sources. *Note*: Meat consumption adjusted to include game, poultry, and the like.
1937 figures:
grain—collections (from Davies, Harrison, and Wheatcroft 1994, p. 290) less 3 million tons. This is approximately the adjustment from collections to extravillage sales implied by Barsov's (1969, p. 103) figures for 1928–32.
other products—Karcz (1979, p. 103) except flax fiber, which was from Bergson (1963, p. 329). *Note*: Karcz's sales of meat, milk, and eggs adjusted to remove sales to agriculturalists by dividing by the coefficients on p. 98.
Notes:
(1) Volumes shown are in thousands of tons except eggs, which are in millions, and hides, which are in thousands.
(2) Meat is deadweight and includes poultry, game, and so on, as well as beef, mutton, and pork.

TABLE 4.7
Peasants' Consumption of Agricultural Output, 1913, 1928, and 1937

	1913	1928	1937
Plant foods			
Grain	27400	27700	27051
Potatoes	3562	14246	17060
Vegetables	3880	7262	7820
Animal foods			
Milk	15912	21099	16460
Meat	2633	3441	1795
Eggs	2684	5966	4344
Industrial inputs			
Flax fiber	63	180	18
Sunflower seeds	294	985	402
Wool	101	124	27
Hides, large	4420	6100	500
Hides, small	31116	38123	800
Cotton	0	0	0
Sugar beets	0	0	0
Total value (mill 1927–28 rubles)	4514	6072	4762

Sources: Peasants' consumption calculated as gross production minus marketings (from Table 4.6) minus losses on the farm and utilization of the commodity for seed and feed.

Gross production from Wheatcroft (1983, pp. 42–43) and Davies, Harrison, and Wheatcroft (1994, pp. 287–88). "Low estimate" of grain used. Hide production estimated from a regression of hide production on meat output.

Note: Meat is deadweight and includes poultry, game, and so on, as well as beef, mutton, and pork. "Losses, feed, and seed," from Allen (1997, p. 391).

Potato marketings fell by 38 percent, sugar beet marketings by 10 percent, cotton marketings by 7 percent, and flax fiber marketings by 51 percent. Table 4.7 shows where most of these declines were going — into consumption by the peasants. They were eating (not selling) more milk, meat, eggs, and potatoes. More flax and wool were being processed by the peasant economy than before the war. Thus, the change in behavior that so worried the Bolsheviks in the 1920s was not confined to grain (although problems were particularly acute there) but affected many crops to varying degrees. In this chapter, I generalize from that fact and analyze changes in aggregate output, marketings, and consumption rather than focus on the record of individual commodities or advance hypotheses tailored to particular products.

The third explanation for the decline in marketing is the decline in "surplus extraction" (taxes and rents) that followed the revolution. Indeed, between 1913 and 1928, real taxes and rents fell 51 percent (Allen 1997). Most of this decline was in rents. One hypothesis about peasants is that they sold produce in order to get the cash to pay their taxes and rents, so declines in those items led to less marketing (Ghatak and Ingersent 1984, pp. 44–47).

The fourth explanation for the decline in marketings goes back to the scissors crisis of 1923. That hypothesis attributes the fall in marketing to a deterioration in the agricultural terms of trade, that is, to a fall in the price of farm products relative to manufactured goods (or, to put the matter the other way, a relative rise in the price of manufactures). Underlying this view is the belief that peasants sold produce to get cash to buy manufactured goods as well as to pay their taxes. When the relative price of manufactures rose, the peasants bought less of them and consumed more farm produce instead. During the 1920s the Soviet state tried to manipulate the terms of trade in favor of the peasantry in order to induce more marketings. By the mid-1920s industrial goods prices were being lowered by fiat to accomplish this effect. The main result, however, was shortages of manufactured goods in socialized stores — and peasant complaints about the inability to buy at official prices! — rather than greater marketing (Johnson and Temin 1993; Gregory 1994).

While the terms of trade argument has an important lineage, it seems to suffer from a fatal problem — by several measures the terms of trade had returned to their 1913 parity by 1928. Figure 4.2 plots three measures of the terms of trade. The ratio of wholesale agricultural to industrial prices was 47 percent lower in 1922–23 than in 1913, but by the late 1920s, the ratio was close to the prewar value of 1. The free market retail price index shows an even more extreme pattern: while manufactured goods prices had inflated 80 percent more than food prices between 1913 and 1922–23, the free market retail index indicates they had returned to parity by 1928. A calculation of the retail terms of trade including controlled prices in state and cooperative shops shows a roughly similar pattern.[14]

Neither of these terms of trade indices is the relevant one, however. The peasants sold their produce in wholesale markets, but bought their manufactures in retail markets. The relevant index of the terms of trade is, therefore, the ratio of the wholesale price of agricultural goods to the retail price of nonfood manufactured goods. This ratio, which I call the transaction terms of trade, was 53 percent below its 1913 value in 1922–23 and was still 35 percent below that value in 1928.

Was the decline in the transaction terms of trade large enough to account for changes in farm marketings in the 1920s, or were other

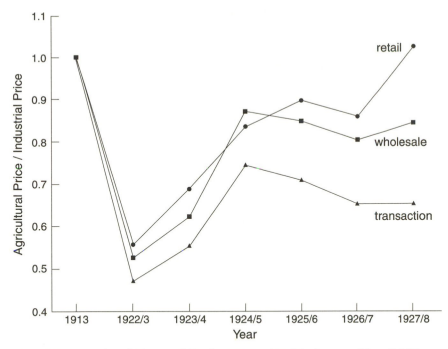

Fig. 4.2. Agricultural Terms of Trade, 1913–1927/28. *Source*: Allen (1997, p. 409) gives the reciprocals of the series plotted here.

factors involved? The price responsiveness of farm marketing has been the subject of much speculation but little estimation. The views range from Millar's (1970a, 1976) conjecture that peasant demand for manufactures — and consequently their supply of produce for sale — was price inelastic to Hunter's (1988) argument that grain production could have been substantially increased at low cost if only the peasants had not killed off so many horses in the early 1930s.[15]

One might look for guidance to the development economics literature, for the determinants of marketing were hotly debated in the 1960s before the huge output increases of the Green Revolution rendered the whole matter irrelevant.[16] Unfortunately, there is little consensus in that literature either. Negative as well as positive marketing elasticities have been obtained. The consistent findings in this literature are, first, that marketing increases with farm size, a view that many Bolsheviks would have endorsed, and, second, that marketing increased with the level of output for farms of any size, an implication of the model developed in this chapter.

In view of this diversity of results, estimating the price responsiveness of farm marketing is the first step in evaluating the early Bolshevik concerns about inadequate farm marketing as an obstacle to industrial development.[17] I estimate responsiveness with a model that is calibrated with data for 1913 and 1928.[18] The model takes agricultural output as given and treats peasants as consumers. They sell farm goods in order to get money to pay taxes and to buy manufactured goods. An indifference curve specifies their readiness to shift consumption between the two types of goods, and the empirical problem is to estimate that willingness from data on prices and consumption patterns.

In the event, the peasants were quite willing to trade off manufactured goods for agricultural ones; they did not, in other words, have the rigid preferences suggested by Millar. As a result, the price elasticity of marketing was high. A 10 percent rise in the price of agricultural goods induced a 7 percent increase in marketing. A high supply elasticity like this calls into question the Bolshevik pessimism that rapid industrialization would founder on the peasants' unwillingness to sell to the city.

But how good is the model? It is fitted to data for 1913 and 1928, so it necessarily explains the decline in marketing over that period. A good test of the model is to see how well it simulates the evolution of marketing during the 1920s. Figure 4.3 compares the evolution of extrarural marketings implied by my model of peasant behavior[19] with Wheatcroft's (1990a, p. 279) index of marketings[20] calculated from the *Kontrol'nye tsifry*. The two series agree to an impressive degree. It is particularly significant that the model simulates the very low level of marketings during the scissors crisis of 1923, for these are distinctly "out of sample" forecasts. This correspondence is consistent with the model of peasant behavior presented here.

The model of peasant behavior can also be used to account for the decline in marketings between 1913 and 1928. Three factors affected the level of extrarural sales: the increase in agricultural production from 1913 to 1928 tended to increase marketings by giving peasants more income, thereby allowing them to purchase more manufactures.[21] This effect was offset by the decline in surplus extraction, which reduced the peasants' need to market, and the deterioration in the terms of trade, which made manufactured goods more expensive. The decline in surplus extraction was responsible for about one-quarter of the decline in marketing, while the deterioration in the terms of trade accounted for the three other quarters.[22]

So why did the terms of trade deteriorate? Soviet wholesale and export prices of grain tracked Chicago and Liverpool prices as closely in the 1920s as they had before World War I, and world market prices in the mid-1920s showed little change from pre-1913 levels. Soviet studies in the 1920s indicated that Russian farmers got about 70 percent of the

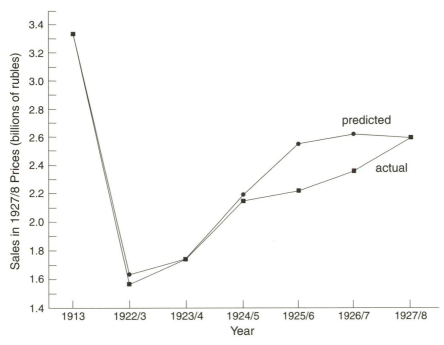

Fig. 4.3. Extrarural Sales: Actual and Predicted. *Source*: The "actual" series equals Wheatcroft's (1990a, p. 279) index number of marketed production (relative to its 1913 value) multiplied by the level of marketings in 1913 shown in Table 4.6. The "predicted" series is that implied by the model in Allen (1997). See that paper and the text for an explanation of the model.

world market price in 1913.[23] The difference, which consists of transportation costs to the points of export like Odessa and wholesale markups, is entirely credible. The price of wheat received by farmers on the Canadian prairies in 1920 was 66 percent of the Kansas City and British price for the same reasons.[24]

The scissors crisis may well have been due to low prices offered by state procurement agencies since, in 1923, the Soviet procurement price for wheat equaled only 41 percent of the world price. In later years, prices were raised and averaged 67 percent of the Liverpool price from 1924 to 1928. There were fluctuations in the average, and it dipped to 60 percent in 1926 and 1927. With the possible exception of 1923, neither a fall in the world market price nor an onerous procurement policy was responsible for low farm marketings.

The reason that agriculture's terms of trade were lower in the mid-1920s than they had been earlier was the high price of manufactured

goods. The high prices were due to a rise in the retail prices of manufactures relative to wholesale prices. By the mid-1920s, the Soviet government could dictate the wholesale prices of factory industry and controlled enough of the grain trade to set the prices received by most
farmers. As a result, wholesale price inflation was effectively eliminated.
However, private traders were still important in retailing, and their
prices were not controlled. The growth in purchasing power as the
economy rebounded from the trough of the civil war was the cause of
the inflation in retail prices. Johnson and Temin (1993) have emphasized the inability of Soviet leaders to think in terms of macroeconomic
balance, and their attempts to deal with the explosion in demand by
controlling prices is a good example. It resulted, first, in shortages of
manufactured goods at official prices (the "goods famine"), the low
level of farm marketings, and ultimately in the abandonment of the
NEP. It is particularly ironic that the rise in manufactured goods prices
enriched Nepmen rather than the state, as Preobrazhensky had hoped.

CONCLUSION

The evidence reviewed in this chapter highlights three issues pertaining
to the future prospects of Russian agriculture and the role it could play
during rapid industrialization.

The model of farm marketing sketched here indicates that Russian
farmers were willing to increase sales substantially in response to moderate price increases. This finding raises the possibility that Russian
peasants would have voluntarily supplied Soviet cities with enough food
and raw materials to permit rapid industrialization. The obligatory deliveries at low prices that Stalin imposed on Russia's farmers may not
have been necessary to feed the cities on reasonable terms. An exact
resolution requires determining the growth in food demand that rapid
industrialization would entail, how much that demand increase would
drive up prices and how much food would then be sold, and, finally,
how much the price increases would have limited other aspects of rapid
development like rural-urban migration. Establishing these magnitudes
requires a multisectoral simulation model like that used in Chapter 8,
where these issues are probed.

Second, there was little possibility of increasing Soviet agricultural
production in basic foodstuffs. Using North America as the standard
shows no scope for increasing crop yields. Livestock husbandry was
more productive on the Great Plains, but improvements in that area
would require breed improvements that could not be accomplished
swiftly. Output could be raised only by extending grain production to
marginal areas like Khruschev's problematic virgin lands campaign or

by reducing the number of horses in Russian agriculture. The latter would have required farm consolidation, and that would have threatened the egalitarian land distribution of the NEP.

Third, there was considerable scope to reduce employment in Russian agriculture — probably under the conditions of the NEP and certainly if tractors and combines were introduced on a large scale. Whether this contribution to industrialization could be realized without social dislocation in the countryside was a difficult problem. The 1917 revolution gave the peasants what they had long desired — elimination of the nobility, effective ownership of the land, and equal land distribution — but the situation was intrinsically unstable. Farms in the 1920s were smaller than the breakeven size for horse-drawn reapers. If the Stolypin reforms had remained in effect, large-scale farmers with reapers would have driven small-scale farmers out of business. Only the ability of the communes to prevent the accumulation of land kept this from happening. The advent of tractors and combine harvesters would have had even more disruptive effects. Russian agriculture in the 1920s was like that of India in the 1970s, when Green Revolution technology threatened a great increase in rural inequality. To mitigate these effects, there was a case for communal organization to manage farm mechanization. Unfortunately, this was not the problem that Stalin sought to address when collective farms were imposed on the peasantry, but it was one that enlightened socialism should have anticipated.

PART TWO

Stalin's Industrial Revolution

CHAPTER FIVE

Planning, Collectivization, and Rapid Growth

The Soviet industrial revolution began on 1 October 1928, when the First Five-Year Plan went into operation. Lenin's death four years earlier launched a struggle for his succession. Through adroit maneuvering, Stalin gradually eliminated all opponents — Trotsky, Bukharin, and their allies. In the mid-1920s, Stalin presented himself as an economic moderate allied with Bukharin and opposed to the superindustrializers like Trotsky. Once he had achieved power, however, Stalin pursued an industrialization strategy more extravagant than any imagined in 1924 or 1925. In short order, the institutions that defined the Soviet economic system — Five-Year Plans, soft budget constraints, collectivized agriculture — were put in place. These institutions launched an unprecedentedly rapid industrial revolution.

The Direction of Economic Activity by Central Plans

Central planning was an innovation of the First Five-Year Plan. During the early 1920s, Soviet firms were organized in trusts and instructed to maximize profits. Gosplan, which eventually came to direct the economy, was created in 1921. At the outset, it undertook precocious statistical studies and compiled national income statistics. By the late 1920s, Gosplan was publishing an annual volume called *Control Figures*, which projected future trends and guidelines, but did not provide detailed plans.

The First Five-Year Plan replaced guidelines with directives. The plan sketched out a scenario for the growth of the economy. By the 1930s, ministries were translating the plan into practice by setting annual output targets for sectors of the economy and parceling them out to individual firms. While productivity, costs, and employment were all targeted, output was given the most weight. "Material balances" were constructed in an effort to ensure consistency across firms — would planned steel production, for instance, equal steel requirements? — but these exercises were of questionable utility since targets were so often missed. Price setting was also centralized, but prices had little relevance to decision making or resource allocation when planning focused on output targets and investment allocation.

Substituting output targets for profits as the principal enterprise objective had momentous implications. For one thing, it marked the end

TABLE 5.1
Targets and Their Fulfillment: Heavy Industry

	1927–28	1932–33	1937	1940
Pig iron				
Target	—	10.0	16.0	18.6
Result	3.3	6.2	14.5	14.9
Crude petroleum				
Target	—	21.7	44.3	39.7
Result	11.7	21.4	28.5	31.1
Cement				
Target	—	6271	7500	8308
Result	1849	3478	5454	5675
Electric power				
Target	—	22000	38000	56014
Result	5050	13540	36173	48309
Coal				
Target	—	75000	152500	188000
Result	35400	64360	127968	165923
Motor vehicles				
Target	—	130.0	200.0	303.0
Result	0.7	23.9	199.9	145.4
Machine tools				
Target	—	—	40000	54000
Result	2098	19720	36120	44000

Source: Zaleski (1971, pp. 306–11; 1980, pp. 524–29).
Note: The target for 1932–33 is the "maximum goal."

of cost controls in industry. Since achieving targets might involve negative profits and since prices no longer reflected scarcity or monopoly power, a corollary of planning was the liberal provision of bank credits to keep firms solvent. So the soft budget constraint, which had first appeared in the mid-1920s as the state tried to lower industrial prices to encourage agricultural marketing (Johnson and Temin 1993), became a general feature of Soviet industrial organization.

The importance of soft budget constraints increased with the ambitiousness of the targets, and in the 1930s Soviet targets were certainly challenging. The original targets of the First Five-Year Plan were replaced by "optimal" targets and then by "maximal" targets that were even more demanding. Higher and higher targets were set in later plans. Tables 5.1 and 5.2 report targets and results for some important indus-

TABLE 5.2
Targets and Their Fulfillment: Light Industry

	1927–28	1932–33	1937	1940
Woolen fabrics				
Target	—	270.0	220.0	145.4
Result	96.6	88.7	108.3	119.7
Cotton yarn				
Target	—	620.0	611.0	675.0
Result	328.0	355.1	532.9	649.9
Leather shoes				
Target	—	145.0	191.0	224.8
Result	103.0	86.9	182.9	189.5
Soap (40 percent fatty acid)				
Target	—	—	1000.0	721.0
Result	360.0	357.2	495.0	700.0
Fish catch				
Target	—	—	1800.0	1969.0
Result	840.0	1333.0	1609.0	1404.0

Source: Zaleski (1971, pp. 306–11; 1980, pp. 524–29).
Note: The target for 1932–33 is the "maximum goal."

tries. An outstanding fact was that targets were rarely met.[1] Setting targets at unattainable levels — "taut" planning — belies the claim that Soviet planning matched the production and utilization of materials across the economy. Instead, targets were a motivational tool. This was an outstanding feature of 1928–32, when the approved targets of the First Five-Year Plan were quickly replaced by ever higher targets in annual plans. Coherence gave way to exhortation.

In the short run, the strategy may have worked. Consider the iron and steel industry, which was a priority. In 1927–28, the Soviet Union made 3.3 million tons of pig iron. The first version of the First Plan called for 8.0 million tons to be smelted in 1932–33, the optimal version raised that to 10.0 million, and this was raised again in 1932 to 15–16 million tons. None of these targets was realized — 6.6 million tons were actually made in 1932 — but a doubling of production in little more than four years was no mean achievement (Nove 1990, pp. 137, 180). Indeed, the original target was hit in 1933, and the optimal target in 1934 (Nutter 1962, p. 420), so performance did not lag far behind plan. The Second Plan reiterated the amended target of 1932 (16 million tons) and applied it to 1937, and actual production came close at

14.5 million tons. There was little more production during the Third Plan, however, despite a further increase in the target.

The rush to meet targets led to great increases in employment and apparent inefficiency in the utilization of labor. High targets were difficult to hit, and managers scrambled for inputs to increase production. More workers helped so long as they had a positive marginal product, and the soft budget constraint allowed firms to expand employment beyond the point where the value of the marginal product equaled the wage. Stringent targets pushed firms to raise output, and soft budgets meant that cost was not an issue.

The comparison of targets and output also reveals a second feature of Soviet targets: they were adjusted in light of the performance of firms in the preceding plan. Thus, when output grew and approached the target, a new, higher target was set. If output failed to reach the target, it was only slightly increased or even lowered. While this may appear to be just "common sense," managers came to realize that fulfilling a target resulted in a higher target in the future. That prospect, in turn, led them to build up reserves of labor, equipment, and materials to meet higher future targets without strain (Kornai 1992, p. 223). Such behavior lowered productivity (output with respect to inputs), and contradicted the motivational effect of targets. The incentive to hoard inputs had serious implications for aggregate performance in the late Soviet period that will be considered in Chapter 10.

CAPITAL ACCUMULATION

Plan targets were chosen in order to accelerate the economic development of the Soviet Union. While the plans envisioned an increase in consumption, the emphasis in the 1930s was on building an industrial society. Accumulating physical capital — structures and machinery — was the prioity, and investment allocation was the key planning issue of the 1930s. Complementary investments in human capital (education and training) were also undertaken.

The necessary machinery for the Soviet industrial revolution could have been obtained in two ways. The first was exporting grain and light manufactures and using the resulting foreign exchange to import capital equipment. The second was developing heavy industry in the USSR itself, from the outset, by using the products of heavy industry to expand the capital stock of that sector. The First Five-Year Plan adopted in 1928 called for the pursuit of both policies, and exports of farm products and consumer goods were initially promoted. Grain exports were increased from 200,000 tons in 1929 to 5 million in 1930 and 1931. However, the collapse in world commodity prices and the protectionism

TABLE 5.3
Investment Allocation, 1929–34 (millions of rubles)

	Average per year	Investment percentage
Agriculture	3243	0
Light industry	1252	0
Iron and steel	1854	70
Nonferrous metals	184	18
Machine building	1807	86
Construction materials	60	60
Chemicals	459	23
Wood	212	34
Paper	105	12
Electric power	498	9
Coal	353	16
Petroleum	558	4
Transportation	2969	11
Communications	171	2
Trade	294	0
Education	256	0
Health	172	0
Municipal services	533	0
Housing	357	0
Total	15617	23

Source: Socialist Construction (1936, p. 346).

of Germany, Britain, and the United States made export-led growth infeasible. Grain exports were curtailed in the mid-1930s (Davies, Harrison, and Wheatcroft 1994, pp. 206–15, 316). By default, if not design, the Soviet Union adopted a development strategy based on enlarging the capital goods sector.

Table 5.3 shows the average distribution of investment across the Soviet economy from 1929 to 1934. About one-fifth of investment went into agriculture. Otherwise, the emphasis was on heavy industry—56 percent of investment went to metals, machinery, construction materials, chemicals, and fuels. Only 6 percent was spent on housing and municipal services (the latter included the construction of electrical distributions systems) despite the vast increase in city size. The underinvestment in cities was a major factor behind the harsh character of life.

It would, nonetheless, be a mistake to conclude that there was negligible investment in consumer goods. An input-output table of the Soviet economy was used to allocate capital and labor between investment and consumption, and the fraction of investment in each industry imputable to economy-wide investment is also shown in Table 5.3. Investment required machinery, iron and steel, and construction materials (both directly and as inputs into requisite products). In the event, 70 percent of the iron and steel and 86 percent of the machinery were attributed to investment in the 1930s. In contrast, the products of agriculture and light industry were used for consumption. These assignments are not surprising. What is less expected is that little electric power or petroleum was used in the accumulation process. Most of that was consumed as well. Likewise, most transportation involved shipping grain. The upshot was that 23 percent of investment, by this reckoning, went into producer goods and 77 percent into consumer goods despite the favored position of heavy industry in the investment plan.

Twenty-three percent of investment in the producer goods sector, nonetheless, represented a major change from the capital stock at the end of the NEP. Applying the same allocation procedure to 1928 capital stock implies that only 7 percent of it was in the producer goods sector. Housing and agriculture comprised substantially bigger fractions of the capital stock in 1928 than did the investment allocation of the early Five-Year Plans.

Channeling investment back into the industries that produce investment goods generated a rapid rate of physical capital accumulation, as predicted by the Fel'dman model. The investment rate[2] rose from 8 percent in 1928 to 14 percent in 1932 and peaked at 17 percent in 1936. Sir Arthur Lewis (1954), the Nobel Prize-winning economist, observed that an industrial revolution required that the investment rate rise from 5 percent to 10 percent or more. The Soviet Union crossed that threshold in the 1930s. The result was a very rapid increase in the capital stock. From 1928 to 1939, it grew at 9 percent per year.[3] On the industrial front, this was achieved by building or extending thousands of factories, mines, hydroelectric plants, and the like.

The investment rate did flag, however, with the approach of World War II. As metals, chemicals, and machinery were allocated to military production instead of further expansion of the capital stock, investment dropped back to 14 percent of GDP. Soviet growth would have been more impressive had it not been for the war.

HUMAN CAPITAL

The Soviet Union accumulated human capital as well as physical capital at a high rate. Educational attainment was quite limited in Russia in 1917, especially in rural districts. While the Russian Empire possessed a few significant universities, the 1897 census showed only 21 percent of the adult population as literate (Crisp 1978, p. 389). Most schooling was confined to the cities. Some extension of primary education occurred immediately before the First World War, but only 38 percent of the adults were literate in 1918 (Crisp 1978, p. 391).

The Soviet government promoted education both for broad cultural reasons and for narrow economic ones. The former are well known, the latter less so. Soviet research on the economics of education built on work done before 1917. Several empirical studies on earnings had been undertaken, and they showed that literate workers had higher earnings than illiterates at every age. In 1924, S. G. Strumilin published a remarkable paper based on a sample of 2602 lathe operators. It was intentionally a prewar sample to eliminate the effect of the post-1917 compression of wages that obscured the relationship between education and productivity. Strumilin estimated an equation in which skill (a transform of earnings) depended on age, job experience, and years of education. The inquiry showed a high return to education, and Strumilin developed a procedure to compare the costs and social benefits of incremental years of schooling. He concluded that "a more profitable 'capital' investment would be difficult to think of even in a country of such immense possibilities as our Soviet Russia" (Kahan 1965, p. 9).

This was not an academic finding without import for policy since Strumilin was a leading Gosplan economist and author of the First Five-Year Plan. His view, expressed in 1929, "that the expenditures of the state budget to raise the cultural level of the country ought to be considered along with the expenditures on technical reconstruction of production as capital expenditures, and as equal in terms of their importance to our economy," was translated into policy (Kahan 1965, p. 10). The First and Second Plans had long sections devoted to the importance of education and training for the industrialization of the country, and set ambitious goals to increase literacy and skill. Primary and secondary education were extended, and adult literacy programs were pushed vigorously. According to the 1926 census, 51 percent of the adult population was literate, and that fraction increased to 81 percent in 1939. The gains were particularly dramatic for women. In 1897, a man was three times as likely as a woman to be literate. By 1939, the differential had almost disappeared (Russian Academy of Sciences, 1992, table 8). The gains were not confined to literacy but included secondary, technical, and university education.

COLLECTIVIZATION OF AGRICULTURE

The agricultural revolution of the 1930s was an outgrowth of the marketing crises of the mid-1920s. From 1926 on, the state collected less grain than it had hoped. In the previous chapter, I argued that the shortfall in purchases resulted from the high price of manufactured goods relative to farm products. Stalin, however, favored the view that the farm size distribution determined the propensity to market. According to this view, extrarural sales were lower in the 1920s than they had been before the war primarily because of the elimination of large gentry and Kulak farms after 1917 and the corresponding expansion of medium-sized, self-sufficient peasant farms. The long-run solution was the reorganization of the small- and middle-scale peasants into socialized production units — collective farms — which would have a higher propensity to market. In the absence of such a reorganization, the only source of grain was the nonmarketed surpluses of the remaining Kulaks.

While a higher price of agricultural products would induce farmers to sell more, Stalin rejected it for the reasons advanced by Preobrazhensky: the state needed to finance its investment drive by raising the price of manufactures and lowering the price paid for grain. Stalin went further and likened this policy to the tribute paid by Moscow to the Mongols, thus earning his approach the sobriquet of "primitive accumulation by the methods of Tamerlane" (Hughes 1996, pp. 14–15).

Most of the potential grain surplus was in the hands of the more prosperous peasants, so they became the target of state policy. Building socialism, according to Stalin, required the "intensification of the class struggle" against the Kulaks. From December 1927 on, he pushed the application of the "Ural-Siberian" method of grain collection. This is usually taken to be simply requisitioning food, but Hughes (1996) has emphasized that the policy was subtler. Each village was taxed grain, but the village could assign the burden among its members. Generally, a majority of peasants had incomes less than the average, and this poor majority forced the wealthy peasants to pay the tax. Tribute and class struggle were successfully combined to extract the agricultural surplus.

In June 1929, about one million people were members of collective farms, and most of those were loosely organized. In November of that year, the central committee announced that a spontaneous movement to join collectives was under way, and that it should be pressed forward. A frantic and ill-planned organizing campaign was launched in which thousands of officials attempted to induce the peasantry to vote to establish collective farms (voluntarism was still the official policy). There was no central directive as to what kind of collectives should be created — were clothes to be shared as well as horses? (Fitzpatrick 1994, p. 50) — and the organizers were put under intense pressure to produce agreement. "Excesses" occurred. By March 1930, almost 60 percent of the peasants had been herded into collectives. On 2 March 1930, Stalin published his famous letter "Dizzy with Success," in which he condemned the zealots for going too far. Thousands of peasant households quit the collectives, and the fraction collectivized dropped below one-quarter by midsummer (Nove 1990, pp. 150–66, 408 n. 24).

The collectivization drive of 1929–30 was accompanied by war on the Kulaks — their "liquidation as a class." Putative Kulaks, including "ideological Kulaks," that is, simply opponents of collectivization, were divided into three groups. The first category were sent to concentration camps and their families exiled to Siberia; the second category were deported with their families to remote regions; the third category were allowed to remain in the localities but were given the worst land. The first two categories lost all of their property, while the last retained items essential to cultivation. Millions were deported under these provisions; others were arrested and, in some cases, killed.

While the peasants felt free to leave the collective farms in the summer of 1930, the respite was short lived. In the next three years, the cultivators were dragooned back. By 1933, two-thirds of the peasants were members, and they cultivated 85 percent of the land. By then, the "artel" was adopted as the organizational standard. With this model, most of the land, all of the horses, and many of the other livestock were transferred to the collective. Peasants retained ownership of their houses, a cow and some swine, and small plots on which they could raise their stock and cultivate produce for their own use or for sale to city residents in farmers' markets — called "collective farm markets" after their legalization in 1932. A significant proportion of the Soviet Union's livestock products and vegetables were sold on the collective farm market since those were the items in which the peasants specialized. The collective farms received quotas for grain, meat, and the like to be sold to state procurement agencies at prices dictated by the state. Excess production — if there was any — could be sold on the collective farm market. The net income of the collective farms was divided among members in proportion to days worked (although not all days were rated equally). About half of farm cash income came from sales to state procurement agencies; farmers' markets accounted for the other half.

Collectivization was widely unpopular among the peasants. Perhaps the village taxation of the Ural-Siberian method was tolerable for a poor majority since it could push the burden onto the richer minority, but collectivization threatened every peasant with land, and so alienated the majority. Peasant resistance took many forms, and women were particularly active in leading it. Passive resistance was widespread, including the slaughter of livestock and a reduction in sowing (Fitzpatrick 1994; Viola 1996). Between 1929 and 1933, the number of horses dropped by 15.3 million (47%), cattle by 24.7 million (42%), sheep and goats by 69.8 million (65%), and pigs by 9.5 million (49%) (Davies, Harrison, and Wheatcroft 1994, p. 289). Stalin saw this as an act of war: "The fact that the sabotage was silent and apparently gentle (no blood was spilt) does not change the fact that the honourable cultivators in reality were making a 'silent' war against Soviet power. War by starvation . . ." (quoted by Nove 1990, p. 166). Stalin answered in kind. Grain production fell in 1931–33, but the state maintained its delivery quotas. The result was famine in places like Ukraine where grain was the focus of agriculture.

A longer-run response of the state to the rebellion of the peasants was to nationalize much of grain production. Collective farms were still nominally responsible for growing grain, but plowing and (by the late 1930s) harvesting were mechanized. The tractors and combines were owned by Machine Tractor Stations, which were state firms, and the collective farms contracted with them to cultivate the land. The key tasks in growing grain were, thus, transferred from the peasant economy to state employees. These were often young men from the villages who learned some mechanical skills and then moved on to city jobs.

Mechanizing agriculture revolutionized family relations. Labor requirements in grain growing dropped from 20.8 man-days per hectare in the 1920s to 10.6 days in 1937 (Johnson and Kahan 1959, pp. 214–15). This was still four times the labor required on North American farms (Table 4.5), but the tractors and combines were, nonetheless, decisive in driving the "excess population" to the cities. Men had traditionally done the plowing and the harvesting, so it was men who were rendered unemployed by the mechanization of Soviet farming. The division of labor of the peasant family was thus unbalanced. Furthermore, the harvest peak in labor demand was eliminated, so permanent migration to the cities was possible, and many men took advantage of the opportunity. Despite the decline in labor requirements, however, days worked in Soviet agriculture did not fall (Kahan 1959). Collective farms became employers of last resort, providing a meager subsistence to women and children, the old and the infirm.

While collectivization forced many men off the land, it did not result in increased output. Net output (production less the seed and fodder use of crops) fell 21 percent between 1928 and 1932 (Table 5.4). After recovery in the late 1930s, output was only 10 percent higher than it had been in 1928. Much of this increase was due to irrigation in Central Asia and the resulting increase in cotton production. In the absence of collectivization, there is no reason to believe that grain production would have been any greater in the late 1930s since Soviet grain yields were on a par with those in climatically similar parts of North America (Figure 4.1). Livestock production would surely have been greater, however. Total farm output might have been 29 percent to 46 percent higher,

depending on what one assumes about horse numbers and mechanization.[4]

In contrast to production, farm sales grew steadily. They had dropped
by 9 percent from 1928 to 1932. By 1937, they bounced back to 62
percent above the 1928 level and by 1939 the advance reached 89 percent. Most of these increases were compulsory sales to state procurement agencies or payments to Machine Tractor Stations for plowing
and harvesting.

Stagnant production with rising sales looks like Preobrazhensky in
action. The situation was more complex, however, for his plan to turn
the terms of trade against agriculture was incompletely implemented.
The real prices paid to peasants on their compulsory sales fell during
the First Five-Year Plan since nominal prices were not raised and inflation was high (Malafeev 1964, p. 129). However, the impact of this
policy was mitigated by peasant sales directly to city dwellers on collective farm markets. Prices on these markets were unregulated, and inflated rapidly. According to the Soviet historian A. A. Barsov (1969, pp.
108, 123), who is one of the leading revisionists on this question, prices
on farmers' markets increased thirty fold between 1928 and 1932. Averaging them with the state procurement prices implies a 3.13 fold increase in the average price received by peasants on their sales. Over the
same period, Barsov calculated that the prices paid by peasants for
manufactures increased by a factor of only 2.4. Hence, the remarkable
revisionist conclusion that agriculture's terms of trade improved during
the First Five-Year Plan.

It was a closer contest over a longer time frame, but the revisionist
view still prevails. Collective farm market prices slumped in the mid-
1930s, and prices in shops were raised in 1936 and 1937, so that the
same prices prevailed in all retail channels, and markets cleared at
posted prices. Agricultural procurement prices were also increased. The
upshot was that the average price received by farmers increased by a
factor of 6.2 between 1928 and 1937, while the price of manufactured
consumer goods rose by a factor of 4.22. Agriculture did slightly better
than manufacturing during the first two Five-Year Plans.[5]

That would seem to be the end of Preobrazhensky, but he cannot be
banished so easily. While the average price received by farmers kept
pace with the inflation in nonfood manufactures, it did not keep pace
with food prices, which rose eight fold between 1928 and 1937. This
inflation was due to the extraordinary urban growth of the period. Instead of letting the peasants reap those rising food prices as higher income, the state imposed a high sales tax (the turnover tax) on consumer
goods. This tax drove a wedge between the prices that urban residents

paid for food and the prices that farmers received for their crops. These tax collections financed the investment boom. If agriculture's terms of trade were measured with retail prices rather than the prices received by peasants, agriculture would appear to have done even better than Barsov's calculations indicate. It was precisely for that reason that Stalin could pump a surplus out of the sector. Stalinism really was Preobrazhensky in action.

In addition, the revisionist interpretation of farm prices is too aggregative to reveal all of the inequities of Stalin's procurement policy. Grain producers fared worse than livestock or cotton producers. While grain prices increased, they did not keep up with inflation: from 1928 to 1937, for instance, the real price of grain (averaged across all marketings) dropped 32 percent. In contrast, the real price of meat rose 81 percent over the same period.[6] One reason that meat producers did better was that meat was sold mainly on the free market. The more sales passed through state hands, the more the state could put Preobrazhensky into practice.

INDUSTRIAL REVOLUTION

Central planning, raising the investment rate, and collectivizing agriculture accelerated economic growth to 5.3 percent per year from 1928 to 1940—an impressive rate even by the standards of the East Asian miracle. The urban economy boomed, while the countryside suffered.[7] Agriculture showed very little growth. The superindustrialization strategy of Preobrazhensky and Fel'dman called for reinvesting the output of the producer goods industries back into themselves, so they (and the capital stock) would grow rapidly. Machinery was the archetypal producer good, and, indeed, machinery output increased over eleven fold between 1928 and 1937. Partly because it started from such a low level, however, the production of military equipment leapt up by a factor of 70 from 1928 to 1940. After 1937, machinery production fell, as the arms buildup came at the expense of the civilian economy. Fear of the Nazis put Preobrazhensky into reverse.

While the Soviets were famous for denigrating the importance of services, their output increased about three fold during 1928–40. Construction activity—central to the investment drive—was intense from 1928 to 1937, but then ceased growing as war preparations received priority. Transportation grew rapidly throughout the period. Education and health services grew at 12 percent per year. The last three years of the 1930s witnessed a large increase in the military. The growth in housing was minimal throughout, as was the growth in retailing and restaurants.

TABLE 5.4
GDP Growth by Sector, 1928–40

	1937 value added	1928	1932	1937	1940
Agriculture	107.2	1.00	.79	1.08	1.10
Industry					
Factory consumer goods	15.4	1.00	1.12	1.79	1.80
Kustar consumer goods	.2	1.00	.29	.11	.11
Materials	39.0	1.00	1.84	3.49	4.00
Machines	6.0	1.00	2.99	11.40	8.26
Military	5.0	1.00	1.50	25.00	70.00
Services					
Construction	10.5	1.00	1.73	2.72	2.75
Transport and communication	16.8	1.00	2.08	3.58	4.12
Trade and restaurants	86.4	1.00	1.16	1.73	1.69
Government and services	48.4	1.00	1.35	1.88	2.47
Industrial output		1.00	1.46	2.94	3.53
GDP index	334.9	1.00	1.07	1.63	1.78

Sources: Income originating in the sectors from Bergson (1953, p. 123) with amendments, including: For agriculture, Bergson's "incomes other than wages" was replaced with "farm income in kind" in Table 7.3. A deduction of 7 billion rubles was made for purchases from other sectors. For industry and construction, value added in military products and construction from Moorsteen and Powell (1966, pp. 621–22). Consumer goods from Table 9.1 and kustar at half the value of goods produced shown in Table 7.3. Materials calculated as a residual for the sector. Trade and restaurants includes turnover taxes. Government and services is a residual. The figure is close to Bergson's.

Sectoral growth rates:

agriculture—my calculations. See Appendix C.

consumer goods—Table A.1, "shops" and "rural mft'rs."

materials—Nutter (1962, p. 525).

machinery—total excluding miscellaneous from Nutter (1962, p. 526).

construction, transportation and communications, government and services—Moorsteen and Powell (1966, pp. 621–22).

trade and restaurants—Moorsteen and Powell (1966, p. 635). nominal series deflated with my implicit consumer price index explained in Chapter 7.

The materials sector—steel, coal, oil, chemicals, cement, and so on—made up a bigger share of Soviet industry than either machinery or munitions, and the output of materials grew rapidly, if less dramatically, than machinery and munitions.

Ferrous metals were a high priority. Pig iron production grew from 3.3 million tons in 1927–28 to 14.9 million in 1940, and steel ingots increased from 4.3 million tons to 18.3 million tons. In the case of pig iron, for instance, the increase in production was realized by building or rebuilding 42 blast furnaces. The Soviets aimed to emulate the best American practice, and hired the Freyn Engineering firm of Chicago and the McKee firm of Cleveland, Ohio, for technical guidance. With their assistance, Russian engineers designed a furnace of about 930 cubic meters and built 22 of them early in the 1930s. They next designed a 1200 cubic meter furnace and then a 1300 cubic meter furnace in 1937, of which 5 were built. These were of comparable size to the leading American furnaces of the day.[8]

The four fold increase in iron and steel output was achieved by rebuilding old mills and, especially, by constructing entirely new works on "green field" sites. About one-third of the new iron smelting capacity, for instance, came from the addition or rebuilding of blast furnaces at Ukrainian works dating back to the nineteenth century. These included the Alchevsk, Denpropetrovsk, Enakievo, Iuzovka, Kerch, and Makeevka iron and steel mills. Two-thirds of the capacity expansion was realized by brand-new plants. Krivoi Rog, Azovstal, and Zaparozhstal were built in south Russia to smelt Kerch and Krivoi Rog ore with Donets coal. Novo-Lipetsk, Novo-Tula, and the reconstructed Kosaya Gora plants were built near Moscow to smelt foundry pig iron, and Novo-Tagil was built in the Urals.

The most famous new plants were Kuznetsk and Magnitogorsk in Siberia. They were among the largest construction projects of the 1930s and embodied foreign technology on a grand scale: Magnitogorsk, for instance, was based on the Gary, Indiana, works of the U.S. Steel Corporation (Davies, Harrison, and Wheatcroft 1994, p. 188). These two mills alone accounted for one-third of the growth in Soviet iron and steel production in this period. New cities sprang up around these plants. The population of Kuznetsk rose from 3894 in 1926 to 169,538 in 1939. Magnitogorsk was an empty steppe in 1926 but contained 145,870 people in 1939.

Light industry, as well as heavy industry, was targeted for growth in the 1930s, but the scheduled rate of expansion for consumer goods was less than for steel or machinery. In the event, performance was often worse than planned, particularly during the First Five-Year Plan, as the comparison of 1932 targets and output indicates (Tables 5.1 and 5.2). Many commentators have argued that food and textiles were never accorded the same priority as concrete and steel, so the weak performance of the consumer goods sector was to be expected. Zaleski (1980, p. 504) suggests that the planned increases in consumer goods were essentially fraudulent exercises in public relations to whip up enthusiasm for plans that were really focused on heavy industry.

The Fel'dman model suggests another reason for devoting resources to investment: it would ultimately—indeed, quickly—result in more consumer goods than an investment strategy that targeted them. The simulations of Chapter 3 established the theoretical possibility. Chapter 7 explores what really happened to living standards in the 1930s, and Table 5.4 summarizes one of the important findings: the production of factory-made consumer goods was 79 percent higher in 1937 than it had been in 1928. The gain from 1928 to 1932 was only 14 percent, however. The question, then, is why consumer goods output was so limited in the First Five-Year Plan. One reason was that it took time, first, to build the engineering works, second, to make the power looms, and the like, for the consumer goods industries, and, third, to erect the textile and other mills to house the new machinery. Five years, in other words, was too short a period for the Fel'dman strategy to bear fruit. Such considerations would have limited the growth in consumer goods output between 1928 and 1932, whatever else happened.

In addition, however, the collapse of agriculture crippled consumer goods production by cutting the raw material input. The most important consumer goods were processed foods (sausage and bread, for instance) and textiles (mostly cotton and wool), and their production depended on the supply of grain, meat, and fiber. The disastrous drive to collectivize agriculture reduced farm production, cut marketings, and, thereby, limited consumer goods output.

The handicraft sector was the greatest casualty. In 1913, kustar production amounted to 6.5 percent of the Russian economy and remained important in the 1920s. Roughly half of the wool, flax, and sheep hides were turned into textiles and leather goods by handicraft producers (Wheatcroft and Davies 1985, pp. 392–93, 400–1, 404–5). The fall in livestock numbers in the early 1930s eliminated handicraft production as the falling raw material supply met the rising demands of state procurement agencies, leaving nothing for the craftsmen to process.

Consequently, wool was a problematic industry throughout the 1930s. In 1928, half of production was processed by the peasants themselves and did not enter the industrial sector. The 65 percent drop in the number of sheep between 1929 and 1933 cut the wool clip proportionately. The situation was so dire that even state procurements fell. A reduction in raw wool imports and an increase in exports further reduced the supply of wool to the factories. Factory cloth output dropped, and it is difficult to see how even the reduced volume of production could have been woven without a significant admixture of cotton in the wool cloth. Targets were cut back to more "realistic" levels but were never achieved. The increase in sheep numbers after 1933 generated enough wool for the fabric produced in the late 1930s (without adding cotton or other fiber) but allowed no scope for much increase. Wool production was held back not because capital and labor were allocated to heavy industry but because the collectivization catastrophe meant that there was not enough raw material to expand production.

The story was similar with leather shoes. Again, about half of the hides produced in the Soviet Union before 1928 had been tanned and fashioned by peasants outside of the industrial sector. When livestock numbers fell in the early 1930s, the peasant producers were squeezed out of business, and the industrial supply was also limited. As a result, shoe production fell slightly during the First Five-Year Plan. The restoration of livestock numbers after 1933 relaxed the raw material constraint, leather production expanded, and, with that, the production of leather shoes increased.

Cotton manufactures were also dependent on an agricultural raw material — but it was a plant, not an animal — and escaped the output collapse in European Russia. There was some check to growth in the raw cotton supply because imports were cut during the First Five-Year Plan, but the irrigation of Uzbekistan yielded a rising supply, and yarn, fabrics, and knitwear rose accordingly.

URBANIZATION

The tripling of industrial output in the 1930s implied rapid urbanization, and, indeed, the city population doubled from 1928 to 1940. Remote development projects like Magnitogorsk and Kuznetsk created cities where only herdsmen had lived before. Most of the new urbanites, however, lived in the established cities of the USSR. The population of Moscow, for instance, increased from 2.0 to 4.1 million between 1926 and 1940, and that of Leningrad rose from 1.7 to 3.2 million in the same period. The populations of many other cities doubled or tripled (Lorimer 1946, pp. 250–51).

Table 5.5 shows the history of the rural and urban populations. The rural population dropped abruptly in 1933 because of the collectivization famine, and was about 7 million less in 1939 than it had been in 1928. At the same time the urban population almost doubled from 28.1 to 54.7 million. Most of this increase was due to rural-urban migration, which totaled 23 million in the period (Lorimer 1946, p. 150).

Several factors were responsible for the high rate of migration to the cities. Urban wages were relatively high. Even though agriculture's terms of trade were improving, the Stalinist procurement system kept rural incomes below levels they otherwise would have achieved. Soft budget constraints meant that industrial enterprises could greatly expand employment without lowering wages. The very rapid growth in

TABLE 5.5
The Urban Transition, 1928–39 (millions of people)

	Urban	Rural
1928	28.1	121.9
1929	29.5	123.2
1930	31.2	123.6
1931	34.2	122.5
1932	38.6	119.4
1933	41.6	116.4
1934	42.7	116.3
1935	45.4	114.4
1936	48.2	112.8
1937	50.2	112.8
1938	52.4	113.8
1939	54.7	114.8

Source: See Appendix C.

urban jobs was a magnet for rural migrants. On the supply side, the mechanization of plowing and harvesting eliminated both the harvest peak in labor demand and the traditional male jobs in the countryside, so the economic tie with the village evaporated for many men. Collectivization further increased the propensity to move. It became clear to rural residents that the future lay in the city, not the country.

State policy had contradictory effects on migration from the countryside to the cities and remote industrial projects. On the one hand, passports were introduced during the collectivization famine in an effort to reduce migration to the cities. These regulations had little impact initially, although they may have introduced some measure of control by the late 1930s (Fitzpatrick 1993, p. 32). On the other hand, migration was increased through state coercion. Dekulakization forced significant numbers out of the countryside. Arrests during the Terror of the late 1930s further swelled the numbers in the Gulag. The inmates of forced labor camps were mainly working age men. Rosefielde (1981, p. 76) averred that "their effect on Soviet industrialization could not have been trivial." Without forced labor, growth would have been much less. This issue has been debated for years.[9]

The question hinges on the number of prisoners and their productivity compared to the civilian workforce. Estimates have varied widely. Dallin and Nikolaevsky (1947) argued for as many as 12 million inmates, and others have posited more. Rosefielde (1981, p. 65) estimated 9 million. On the other hand, Jasny (1951) put the number of inmates at 3.5 million in 1940 based on a careful study of the Fourth Five-Year

Plan. Bergson (1961, pp. 443, 447) concurred and estimated the Gulag workforce at 3 million in 1937 and 3.5 million in 1940. Recently, the results of the 1937 and 1939 censuses, as well as secret police (known as NKVD in Russian) statistics, have become available. These sources indicate a convict population of about 3 million (Getty, Rittersporn, and Zemskov 1993, p. 1020; Davies, Harrison, and Wheatcroft 1994, p. 70). Rosefielde (1981) argued that 9 million inmates amounted to 23 percent of the nonagricultural workforce and concluded, in consequence, that forced labor was fundamental to Stalin's industrial revolution. This calculation treats convicts as equal in productivity to the non-incarcerated population. Jasny (1951, p. 418), however, concluded that "somewhat more than two concentration-camp inmates were needed to do the work of one free laborer" when account is taken of waste of skills, lack of equipment, poor nutrition, low motivation of the Gulag population, as well as the need for camp guards and administration. If, in 1937, there were 3.0 million convicts, who were equivalent in productivity to 1.5 million free workers, then the labor derived from the convicts was 5 percent of civilian, nonfarm labor and only 2 percent of the labor in the whole economy. These fractions were not large enough to be decisive.

This conclusion is consistent with the industrial and regional distribution of convict employment. They were employed mainly in construction, timber harvesting, and mining, particularly in remote areas (Jasny 1951). Convicts did manual, unskilled work even if they had skills. Convict labor was used to dig the Moscow–Volga canal but was otherwise peripheral to Moscow life (Hoffman 1994, p. 51). Even in Magnitogorsk, a remote project by any standard, the convict population was only about 30,000, 12 percent of a total population of a quarter million in 1932 (Kotkin 1995, pp. 72–73, 133). By the late 1930s, the convict population had fallen, although many convicts continued to live in the camps (Kotkin 1995, p. 461 n. 139). In Chapter 9, I argue that state terrorism did play a role in accelerating rural-urban migration. But forced labor per se did not account for much Soviet growth.

Soviet cities grew far faster than the amenities needed to make urban life satisfactory. The situation in a new town like Magnitorgorsk was extreme. People lived in tents at first and later in overcrowded barracks or huts made from bits of cast-off wood and metal and dug into the frozen earth. Public services were virtually nonexistent. The situation was scarcely better in Moscow. The capital, with its subway and impressive public buildings, was the showcase of Russian cities. Here the lucky workers lived in overcrowded apartments. Most of the new arrivals, however, lived like their counterparts in Magnitorgorsk—in barracks or squalid shanty towns miles from public transport, running water, sewer lines, central heating, or electricity. Pigs walked the streets, and the lucky ones had gardens. The country had come to the city, and the city became the country. The parallels with cities in the Third World are obvious, and the conditions are reminiscent of Engels' (1845, pp. 45–74) description of Manchester in 1844.

The immediate cause of bad housing and poor sanitation was the concentration of investment on industrial capacity at the expense of urban infrastructure (Williamson 1990, pp. 267–309). Most countries, as noted, experience this shortfall as they industrialize. The real question is how rapidly housing quality and sanitation catch up with industrial employment. After the Second World War, the sanitary problems of Soviet cities were rectified, and housing improved greatly, although apartments were never large. Slums remain widespread in most of the Third World.

CONCLUSION

The agrarian transformation and the industrial development of the Soviet Union were linked. The countryside supplied the city with labor and food, and the new urban workers were used to produce more consumer goods and, especially, more capital goods. These were used to build and equip more factories, creating more jobs for refugees from the countryside and yet more steel, cloth, and weaponry. Industrial output would not have increased rapidly without rapid urbanization or without the sharp increases in producer goods that equipped the new urbanites for work.

The industrialization debate of the 1920s prefigured some of what happened in the 1930s. The concentration of resources on heavy industry to the detriment of agriculture was reminiscent of Preobrazhensky's thinking. Agriculture was also squeezed, although not quite in the way he had envisioned. Stalin kept procurement prices low during the First Five-Year Plan, but urban farmers' markets were a safety valve. Their prices were unregulated, and inflation was so extreme that agriculture's terms of trade improved from 1928 to 1932. Increases in procurement prices in the mid-1930s meant continued improvement in agriculture's position insofar as prices were concerned. The inflation in agricultural wholesale prices, however, did not keep pace with the inflation in retail food prices. The state used the turnover tax to divert much of that increase from peasants to the state. This way of financing investment was certainly in the spirit of Preobrazhensky.

The policies that were mainly responsible for rapid growth were the allocation of investment goods to make ever more factories, and the shift in enterprise management from profit maximization to output targeting. Both pushed up the rate of investment—the former by tilting production toward the machinery, steel, and concrete needed to expand industrial capacity, and the latter by providing factory jobs for anyone looking for work. Increasing industrial employment was critical for increasing industrial output.

Collectivization played a contradictory role in this process. Its impact on farm production was negative in the early 1930s, and that falloff reduced GDP and checked the production of consumer goods. That was an important reason why living standards were low during the First Five-Year Plan. The system of compulsory sales to state agencies did guarantee a high level of marketing, however much was produced, but it remains an open question whether the total volume of food sold in the late 1930s was greater than it would have been if the free market of the NEP had continued: a lower marketing fraction might have been offset by a greater volume of production. In a perverse way, however, collectivization did accelerate industrialization, and that was by driving people off the land. Without collectivization, rural-urban migration would have been less, the cities would have been smaller, and factory output would have been reduced. Soviet industrialization was anchored on a rapid transfer of labor from farm to factory, and collectivization sped up that process.

CHAPTER SIX

The Population History of the USSR

Economic growth means more GDP per head. This ratio can be raised either by increasing GDP or by reducing the number of heads. Much of this book explains how the Soviets pushed up the GDP growth rate. This chapter analyzes the growth in population. Mortality was extraordinary in the famine during collectivization and the Second World War. Did the USSR achieve a high income per head because Stalin — with help from Hitler — cut the denominator as well as pushing up the numerator?

In many respects, the Soviet Union in the early twentieth century was like the underdeveloped countries of Asia, Africa, and Latin America. Per capita income was low, and an overwhelming share of the population was in agriculture. The demographic similarities were equally striking. Fertility was very high. The average woman in the late empire gave birth to seven children. High fertility was rooted in universal marriage at a young age. In a famous essay, Hajnal (1965) contrasted the "European marriage pattern" of northwestern Europe with the "non-European pattern." The former was characterized by a high average age of women at first marriage and far from universal marriage; universal marriage at a young age characterized the rest of the world. Fertility and population growth were lower with the European pattern than the non-European. What is of great importance for the present discussion is that the line dividing the two regions ran from St. Petersburg to Trieste. With the exception of the Baltic republics and the Catholic fringe on the Polish border, the Soviet Union was firmly in the non-European camp.

In the twentieth century, most Third World countries experienced a population explosion. Between 1928 and 1989, population increased three fold in India, Indonesia, and Bangladesh, about four fold in Turkey and Morocco, and close to five fold or even more in Brazil, Mexico, Pakistan, the Philippines, Thailand, and Venezuela. With its high fertility regime, the Soviet Union was headed for the same fate. If Soviet population growth had been like the Third World's, the USSR would have contained close to a billion people in 1989 rather than the 288 million actually present. Income per head would surely have been less.

And yet, between 1928 and 1989, the Soviet population rose by only 70 percent.[1] A central question in twentieth-century Russian history is why the USSR did *not* have a population explosion. This question is different from the one usually pursued by historians of the USSR, who have been mainly concerned with measuring the number of "excess deaths" (deaths beyond those that would have occurred given normal mortality rates) due to collectivization, forced labor, Stalinist repression, and the Second World War. If such deaths were great enough, they could account for the absence of a Soviet population explosion. The famine following collectivization and the Second World War were, indeed, enormous catastrophes that reduced the long-run growth of the population. They were not large enough, however, to explain why the Soviet Union did not have a population explosion. The main reason was the rapid decline in the birth rate during the Stalinist period. This drop occurred *despite* Soviet population policy, which was emphatically pro-natal (Goldman 1993). It should be stressed, moreover, that fertility did not fall due to declining living standards or political oppression; indeed, poverty and oppression typically breed children. Instead, fertility fell in the USSR for the same reasons it drops anywhere in the Third World: the creation of a modern urban society and the education of women. Of course, these changes were the results of communist policies and ideology but not the repression of the Stalinist regime.[2]

POPULATION STATISTICS

Demographic history requires accurate censuses, and it is fortunate that the First Five-Year Plans were bracketed by them.[3] A fine census was taken in 1926, and volumes of detailed tabulations were published. The next census was in 1937, but the total population count was millions less than Gosplan projections made prior to the collectivization famine. Stalin was shocked and ordered the 1937 census suppressed as "unscientific." Another census was taken in 1939, but only a few basic results were made public. Significantly, the population count of 1939 confirmed the low figure of 1937 but was published anyway.[4]

The 1926 and 1939 censuses were the basis of earlier work on Soviet population such as Lorimer's (1946) reconstruction and the figures used by Bergson (1961) in his magisterial estimates of the size of the Soviet economy. They remain accurate in broad outline. With glasnost, the 1937 census has been published as well as more results from the 1939 census. These figures have resolved many controversial questions such as the size of the convict population and have permitted more detailed demographic reconstructions. While the opening of the archives has enriched our understanding of Soviet population history, it has not overturned the insights of scholars like Lorimer and Bergson.

Demographic analysis requires more than just censuses. Ideally, they should be linked together with records of the number of births (broken down by the age of the mother) and of deaths broken down by the age of the deceased. The age structures of the population in successive censuses guide this linking since the number of 18-year-old men in 1937 equals the number of 7-year old boys in 1926 minus deaths and net emigration. Since few males normally died between 7 and 18 and since emigration from the USSR was usually negligible, reconstructing the population in this detail identifies the "excess deaths" due to Stalinist repression and war. Fortunately, the Soviet statisticians Andreev, Darskii, and Khar'kova (1990, 1992) have reconstructed Soviet population history between 1920 and 1959 in this way. Their research is the basis of the analysis undertaken here.

THE HISTORY OF VITAL RATES: THE DEMOGRAPHIC TRANSITION

In the absence of migration, a population grows when births exceed deaths, and that was the case in Russia for centuries. If we can believe the estimates, the population of "European Russia" grew at .5 percent per year from 1500 to 1850 (McEvedy and Jones, 1978, p. 79). In the last half of the nineteenth century, for which the data are more reliable, the growth rate accelerated to 1.6 percent per year. This high rate of growth was due to a remarkably high birth rate of about fifty births per thousand people per year. This rate was as high as that of any Third World country at the peak of its population explosion. The rate was also much above that of western European countries at any time for which we have evidence. This difference underscores the pertinence of the comparisons with less developed countries. A death rate of thirty-four per thousand gives population growth of 1.6 percent.

And yet the Soviet population explosion fizzled out. The explanation lies in the history of birth and death rates shown in Figure 6.1. The nineteenth-century figures, which are five-year averages and thus obscure many crises like the famine of 1891–92, show the great excess of births over deaths. Coale, Anderson, and Harm (1979, pp. 16–17) noted the fall in the birth rate between 1900 and 1913 and suggested that the fertility transition was under way before the First World War. The upsurge in fertility in the 1920s calls this view into question, however.[5] With the First Five-Year Plan in 1928, the situation changed dramatically. Birth rates and death rates began a race downward, with the course interrupted by dramatic reversals and accelerations. Most of the catastrophes of the twentieth century show up in this figure, including the following:

The First World War (1914–17). Close to 4 million Russians perished due to World War I. The population rose from 140 to 143 million during 1914—an expansion consistent with the birth and death rates of 1910–13—and remained at that level through 1917. Despite a fall in

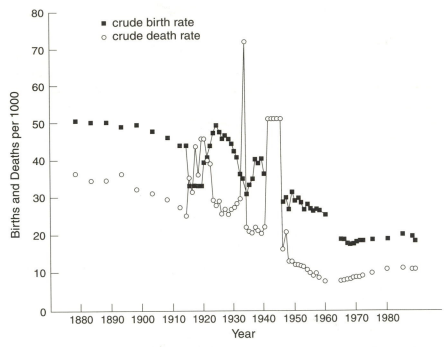

Fig. 6.1. Birth and Death Rates, 1880–1989. *Source*: Pre-1913 figures from Rashin (1956, pp. 154, 172). Figures for 1914–19 estimated as described in text. Davies, Harrison, and Wheatcroft (1994, pp. 77–78) for World War II. Other figures for 1920–58, from Andreev, Darski, and Khar'kova (1992, pp. 129, 131). Later figures from *Narodnoe Khozyaistvo* (1972, p. 18), Karasik (1992, p. 112).

the birth rate, population stability implies 3.8 million deaths in excess of the number expected from prewar mortality rates.[6] These included 2 million soldiers killed at the front, and many wounded who later died in the rear. It is not clear how many civilians died because of the war since death rates did not rise in cities where this has been studied (Davies, Harrison, and Wheatcroft 1994, pp. 57–64).

Civil War (1918–22). The years following the 1917 revolution claimed millions of lives. Between the beginning of 1918 and the end of 1922, the population fell by about 4 million, which implies that excess deaths amounted to 9.7 million or more.[7] About one million soldiers died in the civil war following the revolution. Social breakdown resulted in millions of civilian deaths first from typhus, typhoid, and dysentery, and then millions more from famine, influenza, and other diseases in 1920–22 (Davies, Harrison, and Wheatcroft 1994, pp. 62–64).

Collectivization famine (1933). The fall in agricultural output follow-ing collectivization in the early 1930s in conjunction with the enforce-ment of high compulsory deliveries resulted in famine in 1933, espe-cially in the Ukraine and north Caucuses. Credible estimates of "excess mortality" are in the range of 4–9 million. An exact determination is difficult since high estimates are generated by positing undocumented events like a rise in unregistered births accompanied by a rise in un-registered infant deaths. Figure 6.1 is based on Andreev, Darskii, and Khar'kova's estimate of 7.3 million excess deaths (Davies, Harrison, and Wheatcroft, 1994, p. 76), which results in the most dramatic rise in the crude death rate in Russia in the twentieth century. It might also be noted that the birth rate dips in the mid-1930s but rebounds by the end of the decade, suggesting that the famine had ramifications for fertility as well as mortality. The drop in fertility might, however, have had less sinister causes such as the very-large-scale migration of men to con-struction sites during the period.

Great Terror (1937–39). Estimates of the number of arrests and exe-cutions during Stalin's purges have varied widely, but a consensus is emerging based on archival research and demographic reconstruction. Both NKVD statistics and the census returns indicate that the number of people in prison or Gulag labor camps reached a maximum of about 3 million in the late 1930s (Getty, Rittersporn and Zemskov 1993, p. 1020; Davies, Harrison, and Wheatcroft 1994, p. 70). This figure is not much different from those worked out by Jasny (1951) (and extended by Bergson 1961, pp. 443, 447) from a close reading of the 1940 Five-Year Plan. Executions and deaths in prison amounted to 826,000 in 1937–38 and accounted for the excess of mortality in those years above that of 1936.[8] While the times were desperate, the excess deaths associ-ated with the Great Terror equaled only 13 percent of total deaths, so that the rise in the crude death rate in 1937–38 is almost imperceptible in Figure 6.1.

World War II (1941–45). Deaths due to the German invasion were enormous — between 25 and 30 million (Harrison 1996, pp. 160–61). Davies, Harrison, and Wheatcroft (1994, p. 78) estimate that total deaths (normal and excess) amounted to 41.8 million in the four and a half years of struggle, and that figure has been used to calculate the average crude death rate for the war years shown in Figure 6.1. While this rate is less than the peak following collectivization, the true war peak may be obscured since an annual breakdown is not available. In any event, the crude death rate for the war shown in Figure 6.1 was sustained over four and a half years and so had more significant long-term effects than the deaths due to collectivization in 1933.

Indeed, as we will see, one of the most substantial long-run effects of

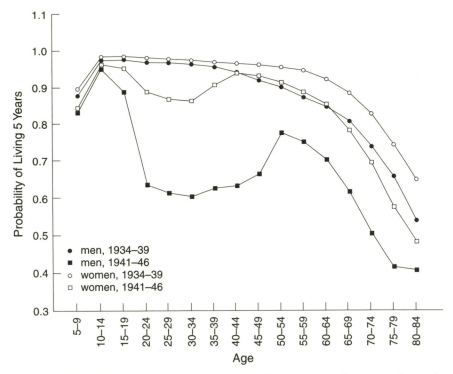

Fig. 6.2. The Chance of Surviving World War II. *Source*: Andreev, Darskii, and Khar'kova (1992). These probabilities are calculated from the age structures of 1934, 1939, 1941 and 1946. See text for calculation details.

the war was a reduction in fertility—both during the war and after. Figure 6.2 contrasts the age-specific mortality rates of the 1930s with the rates during the war. Under peacetime conditions, mortality for people aged 20 to 49 was slight. During the war, about 15 percent of women aged 20 to 49 died, while the mortality of men in the same age group reached the incredible rate of 40 percent.[9] The disproportion in death rates meant that many women could not marry after the war, depressing fertility.

BIRTHS, DEATHS, AND POPULATION GROWTH

Figure 6.1 highlights two reasons why the Soviet population has not grown more rapidly. First, the mortality peaks have cut the growth in population below what it would otherwise have been. The mortality peaks offset the drop in "normal" mortality that has also occurred and which, on its own, would have accelerated population growth. Second, the fertility rate has fallen. Why that has occurred is a question that will be pursued later, but it may also have been the result of events like collectivization and the Second World War.

The first step in sorting out why the Soviet population has not grown more rapidly is to determine the relative importance of excess mortality and declining fertility as explanatory factors. The method we will use is simulation. Since population change equals births minus deaths, we can rerun history by starting with the 1926 population—a census year and the initial year in our simulations—and by then adding the births and subtracting the deaths that would occur in each succeeding year under alternative scenarios. If we used the historical course of birth and death rates, we should simulate the actual history of the Soviet population. Such a simulation is a test of the model.

The impact of catastrophes like the collectivization famine can be gauged by repeating the simulations with alternative trajectories of births and deaths. The impact of the collectivization famine, for instance, can be ascertained by rerunning the simulation and using normal death rates for 1933 instead of the extraordinary mortality rates that were actually experienced in that year. In these simulations we do not use the crude vital rates shown in Figure 6.1. Instead, the exercise is fine-tuned by using age-specific birth and death rates. In that way, for instance, we can track the effects on fertility of the heavy mortality of 20- to 49-year-olds during World War II.

Figure 6.3 contrasts the actual history of the Soviet population with the trajectory that is simulated using the actual age-specific birth and death rates.[10] In interpreting this and the other graphs, it should be remembered that the sharp jump in population in 1940 reflects the annexations of territory in 1939 and 1940. The close correspondence between the two series confirms the consistency of the demographic data and the soundness of the modeling.

What does the model imply about the evolution of the Soviet population under alternative conditions? We begin by removing the worst demographic catastrophes associated with Stalin: collectivization and the Second World War.[11] Both of these catastrophes affected the population by reducing fertility as well as by raising mortality.

Figure 6.4 shows the actual growth of the Soviet population, and the growth that would have occurred without the excess mortality associated with collectivization and, in addition, without the fertility decline of the mid-1930s. Removing the excess mortality raises the 1989 population from 288 million to 304 million and removing the reduction in fertility during 1932–36—which may not have been entirely due to collectivization—further raises the 1989 population to 315 million.

The fertility effect deserves emphasis since it is unusual. Often the

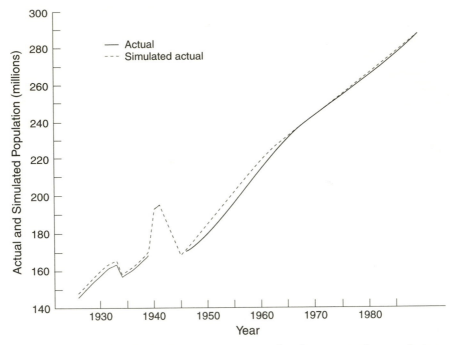

Fig. 6.3. Simulating Soviet Population. *Note*: This figure tests the population simulation modeling by comparing the actual history of the population with the simulated history using historical trajectories of all relevant parameters. The close similarity of the lines in the figure indicates the success of the model. The large jump in population in 1940 reflects the annexation of the Baltic republics and parts of Poland.

heightened mortality of a famine has no impact on the long-run history of a population since it is the very old and very young who die. As a result, the share of the population aged 15–45 increases. Since those are the people who bear children, the famine raises the fertility rate, and the increased number of births offsets the deaths caused by the famine (Charbonneau and Larose 1979). Death rates did rise disproportionately for children and the elderly in the Soviet Union, but the decline in the birth rate short-circuited the standard correction mechanism. Consequently, collectivization exerted a persisting effect on the size of the Soviet population. In 1989, the population was 288 million — 27 million (9%) less than it would have been without collectivization.

The Second World War had a greater effect on the size of the population. Figure 6.5 simulates the population without the excess mortality of the war and, in addition, without the reduction in fertility during and

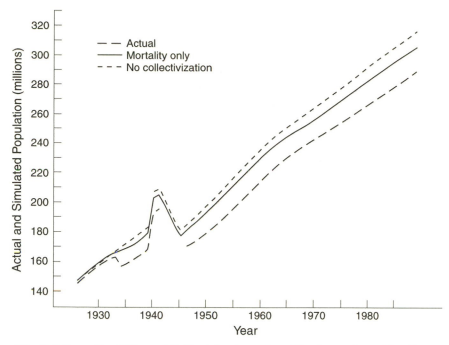

Fig. 6.4. Long-Run Effect of Collectivization. *Note:* The figure shows the effects of collectivization on the Soviet population, first, from heightened mortality, and, second, from reduced fertility as well. The simulation labeled "no mortality" shows how the population would have evolved if age-specific death rates had not leaped up in 1933. Between 1932 and 1936, age-specific fertility rates dropped and then recovered. In the simulation labeled "no collectivization," the actual age-specific fertility rates for 1932–36 are replaced with values linearly interpolated between 1931 and 1937. The heightened mortality of 1933 is also removed in this simulation.

after the war. Eliminating the wartime mortality raises the 1989 population to 329 million, and eliminating the shortfall in fertility raises it by a further 34 million to 363 million. The fertility effect (34 million) was almost as large as the mortality effect (41 million). World War II cut the Soviet population by 21 percent.

Figure 6.7 shows the results of a combined simulation in which the adverse fertility and mortality effects of war and collectivization are removed from Soviet demographic history. This simulation shows how the population would have grown if it were subject only to the "normal" fertility and mortality rates. The 1989 population under this simulation would have been 394 million instead of the 288 million actually

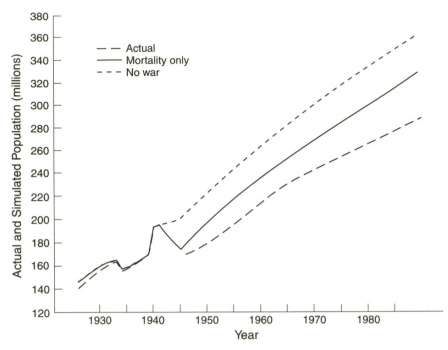

Fig. 6.5. Long-Run Effect of World War II. *Note*: The figure shows the effects of World War II on the Soviet population, first, from heightened mortality, and, second, from reduced fertility as well. The fertility impact reflects the higher death rate of men than women during the war.

alive. The impact of collectivization and the Second World War was to reduce the 1989 population of the Soviet Union by 27 percent.

This reduction goes partway toward explaining why the Soviet Union did not have a population explosion like that of the Third World. The Soviet population grew by a factor of 1.7 from 1928 to 1989.[12] Without collectivization or war, that factor would have increased to 2.3. This is still much less than the three to five fold increase commonly observed in developing countries. The evolution of the "normal" fertility and mortality rates explains why the Soviet population did not grow faster. Both rates fell sharply as Figure 6.1 indicates. The fall in mortality tended to increase the rate of population growth and so cannot explain the absence of a population explosion. (Indeed, the fall in "normal" mortality is an indicator of rising living standards.) The key development shown in Figure 6.1 that checked the population growth was the dramatic reduction in fertility. In the 1920s, the average woman gave birth to almost seven children. That number dropped to two and a half in the

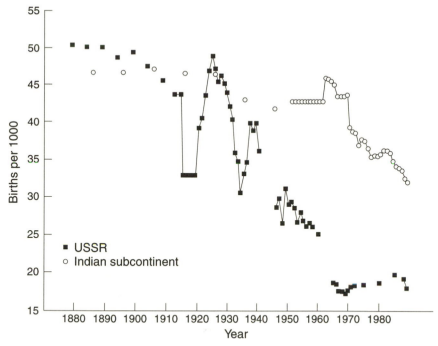

Fig. 6.6. Birth Rate, USSR and Indian Subcontinent. *Sources*: Pre-1950 rates for India from Kumar and Desai (1983, pp. 501, 508). Post-1950 rates from United Nations, *Demographic Yearbook*, various years. For Soviet rates, see sources to Figure 6.1.

1980s — a fertility rate marginally higher than the value implying zero population growth. Explaining the fertility transition is the key to explaining why there was no population explosion.

Sorting out the relative importance of the fertility transition, on the one hand, and of war and collectivization, on the other, depends on what one thinks the fertility rate might have been in a counterfactual scenario. This is a difficult judgment. To fix the bounds on the possible, consider the history of fertility in the Indian subcontinent, a region with a relatively modest population explosion. Figure 6.6 compares the crude birth rate in Russia and the Soviet Union with that in India, Pakistan, and Bangladesh since the mid-nineteenth century. Both regions had rates of about fifty per thousand early in the twentieth century. The rate in the Indian subcontinent continued at close to that level until the 1970s, when it began to drop. The rate of descent is similar to that in the Soviet Union after 1928. The fertility decline was most pronounced in India, where the crude birth rate dipped to thirty-one per thousand in

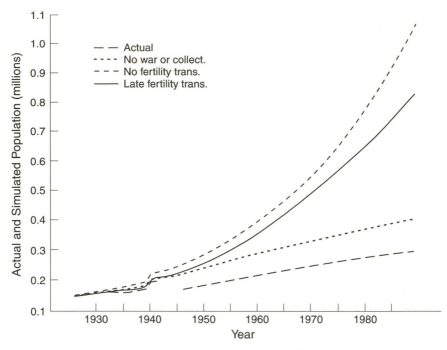

Fig. 6.7. Effect of Collectivization, War, and Fertility Transition on Soviet Population. *Note*: The figure shows how the Soviet population would have grown without collectivization, World War II, and the rapid fertility transition of the Stalinist period. Reduced fertility was much more important than the heightened mortality of collectivization or World War II in explaining the absence of a population explosion.

1989. Fertility in Pakistan and Bangladesh remained above forty per thousand through the 1980s.

Fertility in South Asia suggests two counterfactuals for Russia. The most extreme is a continuation of the high fertility rates of the 1920s through the 1980s. A more modest extrapolation assumes a history of fertility like India's, that is, a continuation of the fertility rates of the 1920s until 1970, at which point fertility drops as it did in the Soviet Union after 1928. (For closer correspondence with the Indian case, all of the age-specific mortality rates in this simulation were increased 25 percent to close the gap between the Indian and the lower Soviet crude death rates.) The results of these counterfactuals are shown in Figure 6.7, where they are contrasted with the population evolution that would have occurred without the excess mortality and deficient fertility associated with Stalinism and the Second World War. Assuming no fertility transition implies a 1989 population of 1.1 billion in the Soviet Union. A delayed fertility transition (in conjunction with higher mortality) as in India implies a 1989 population of 825 million. Both simulated values are significantly higher than the projected "normal" population of 394 million and the actual population of 288 million. It is difficult to choose among the high fertility scenarios, but the simulations make it clear that fertility decline has been of greater importance than Stalinism or World War II in preventing a Third World-style population explosion in the Soviet Union.

THE FERTILITY TRANSITION

The Soviet fertility transition was important and unusually fast. It took only a generation (from the mid-1920s to the mid-1950s) for the number of births per woman to fall from almost seven to three. Only East Asia has had a comparably rapid transition. In China, for instance, the total fertility rate fell from 5.9 in 1960–65 to 2.4 in 1985–89 and similar declines occurred in North and South Korea (Rele and Alam, 1993, p. 20).

The first substantial investigation of Soviet fertility was *Human Fertility in Russia* (1979) by Ansley Coale, Barbara Anderson, and Erna Harm. This was the Soviet portion of the European Fertility Project, which aimed to measure the fertility decline across Europe in a consistent fashion and to test whether falling fertility was the result of economic development. The surprising conclusion was that fertility fell independently of modernization. While educated urbanites were usually the first group in a country to begin to reduce the size of their families, family limitation sometimes began at an early date in very poor countries. Consequently, there was little relation between the onset of fertility decline and economic development. Furthermore, the trend to small families quickly spread from the cities to the countryside, where it bore no relation to education or economic development.

Coale, Anderson, and Harm's study of Soviet fertility was based on the censuses of 1897, 1926, 1939, 1959, and 1970. Valuable work was done measuring the decline in fertility and decomposing it into changes in the proportion of women marrying, the average age at marriage, and the number of children per marriage. Considerable attention was given to contrasting developments in rural and urban areas. Some correlations between marital fertility rates and social variables like literacy were estimated from census cross sections, but the surface was only scratched in this regard. Coale, Anderson, and Harm found only slight evidence that education and economic development lowered fertility, and emphasized instead the independent spread of Western ideas favoring lower fertility and the maintenance of non-Western cultural values supporting large families. In this regard, Coale, Anderson, and Harm were particularly impressed by the persistence of high fertility among non-European nationalities in the Soviet Union despite the spread of education and economic development to these groups.

In the 1980s, Soviet fertility was studied by analyzing post–World War II Soviet censuses. Kuniansky (1983) and Berliner (1983, 1989) modeled fertility and labor force participation in a human capital framework, that is, the decision to have a child was analyzed like the decision to work or to buy consumer goods and was influenced by the same variables. Kuniansky (1983) estimated such a model with oblast level data from the 1970 census and found that increases in male education raised fertility while increases in female education slightly lowered it. Berliner (1983, 1989) also estimated models of fertility and labor force participation using the 1970 census. His results were more equivocal, but he (1989) found some evidence that higher education for women lowered fertility. Both Kuniansky and Berliner were surprised that the impact of women's education was so small.

Jones and Grupp (1987) also studied Soviet fertility by statistically analyzing post–World War II censuses. In contrast to Coale, Anderson, and Harm, they strongly endorsed the view that modernization led to lower fertility and gave the theory a feminist twist. They argued that fertility was high in nineteenth-century Russia and in late-twentieth-century Central Asia because of the dominance of patriarchal families. In these families, the decisions were taken by the leading men, and they wanted children for their contribution to family production and for the prestige they brought. When Soviet demographers in the 1970s asked women who were from traditional backgrounds and who were born in the nineteenth century how many children they had wanted, the usual responses were "the more the better" and "however many God gives" (Jones and Grupp 1987, pp. 36–37). Education changed that attitude. By increasing women's ability to earn income outside the home, education also increased their bargaining power within the family. Consequently, fertility fell.

The Soviet fertility transition was rapid, but was it faster than transitions in developing countries once the speed of modernization is taken into account? This question can be answered by using the findings of a recent international study undertaken by Paul Schultz (1997).[13] The results are striking. The fertility transition in the Soviet Union is explained by the same factors that account for fertility decline in the Third World, and the speed of the Soviet fertility transition is explained by the speed of development of the Soviet economy and society.

   Schultz's study is based on a sample of eighty countries in 1972, 1982, and 1988 (although some countries did not appear in every year). For these countries, Schultz measured the total fertility rate (the variable to be explained) and a variety of explanatory variables including the number of years of women's education, the years of men's education, GDP per adult, the percentage of the population living in cities, the percentage of the labor force in agriculture, the religious composition of the population, per capita calorie consumption, and child mortality. A variety of family planning and other variables were also analyzed but proved to have no statistical significance. Many models were estimated, but I concentrate on the reduced form models in which fertility was expressed as a function of education, economic, and religious variables.[14] Table 6.1, equation 1, shows a typical result, which I refer to as the Third World Equation.

   The coefficients of the Third World Equation highlight the factors explaining fertility transitions. Education is the key. The coefficient of women's education is negative, implying that more education for women lowers fertility. In contrast, men's education has a positive coefficient, so more education for men increases fertility. Why the contrary result? Several interpretations are possible. Like Kuniansky and Berliner, Schultz analyzes fertility as though children were products that parents were buying. More men's education means that the wages of men are higher so they choose more children as they would choose to buy more of most goods. The effect of women's education is more complicated, however, since women were usually the primary caretakers of children. Higher women's education raises the income of women which (a) tends to increase the demand for children as with men's education, but (b) which also raises the opportunity cost of women's time and thus the cost of raising children. In other words, if women take care of children instead of working, the cost of the child care is higher when women have greater earning power due to more education since they give up more wage income when they care for childen. This effect dominates the income effect and means that more education for women leads to fewer children.

   Other interpretations of the education coefficients are possible, in particular, the feminist theory of Jones and Grupp. If men are educated while women are not, the dependence of women is increased, and patriarchy is reinforced. Raising the education of women relative to that of men reduces the dependence of women. Indeed, in their statistical investigations, Jones and Grupp use the ratio of women's education to men's education as an explanatory variable, which they call an index of emancipation, and it is highly significant in explaining fertility in the Soviet Union. One attraction of the Jones–Grupp interpretation is that its logic

TABLE 6.1
Schultz-type Equations

	1	2	3
Constant	5.79	5.861 (28.886)	5.480 (19.875)
Female education	−.551	−0.444 (−2.661)	−3.481 (−8.174)
Male education	.179	0.160 (.718)	2.409 (4.871)
Log of GDP per adult	.517	—	—
% population urban	−.0084	−0.0228 (−5.369)	−.02410 (−6.096)
% labor force in agriculture	.019	—	—
Catholic % of population	.0115	—	—
Protestant % of population	.0239	—	—
Muslim % of population	.0119	0.0146 (4.801)	.0135 (4.337)
Calories per day	−.0035	—	—
Calories per day squared	.00053	—	—
Female education squared	—	—	.2884 (6.232)
Male education squared	—	—	−.1572 (−2.199)
R^2		.603	.680

Sources: equation 1–Schultz (1997, p. 398) equation 4. See the original source for detailed definitions and statistical apparatus. I have omitted the dummy variables for 1982 and 1988 and the family planning variable. The coefficients of these variables are very small and statistically insignificant.

equations 2 and 3–estimated from Russian and Soviet censuses.

Note: The dependent variable is the total fertility rate. T-ratios in parentheses.

is more consistent with Soviet history since their approach does not presume that women gave up work when they had children.

The other coefficients in the Third World Equation deserve comment. Fertility increases with GDP per adult since, in Schultz's interpretation, the rise in GDP represents income growth that raises the demand for children. Urbanization and the decline in agriculture reduce the demand

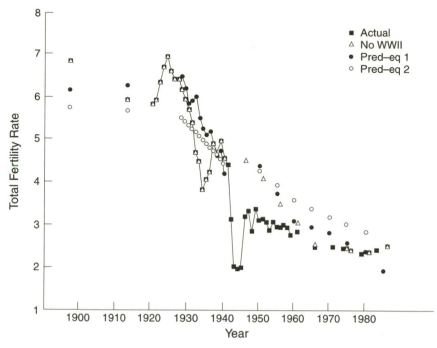

Fig. 6.8. Explaining the Soviet Fertility Transition. *Note*: The points labeled "actual" show the historical evolution of the total fertility rate. The points "no World War II" adjust the points for high male deaths by conditioning fertility on the male population rather than the female, as is the usual procedure. This is the line that the models should explain. The line "predicted by equation 1" shows the predicted total fertility rate from Schultz's study as given in Table 6.1, equation 1. The line "predicted by equation 2" shows the corresponding predictions from the abbreviated Schultz-type equation estimated from Russian and Soviet data. Equation 1 tracks the adjusted fertility rate best.

for children—hardly unusual results. The religious variables indicate that Catholics, Protestants, and Muslims have more children than adherents of other religions, even taking into account the economic variables. Increased calorie consumption per head tends to cut fertility by lowering child mortality and thus reducing the number of births required to achieve a desired family size. These variables nuance the effect of the education variables, which are the decisive ones.

To test whether the Soviet fertility transition was like that in other developing countries, the Third World Equation was used to predict fertility in the USSR during the twentieth century. The result is shown in Figure 6.8, where four lines are plotted. One is the measured total fertility rate. The second is the measured rate corrected for the high number of male deaths in World War II. This curve is computed by dividing the number of births by the number of men in each age group since men—not women—were the limiting factor on fertility after the war. This curve is somewhat higher than the first in the 1950s and 1960s and is the measure of fertility that the Third World Equation should replicate if Soviet fertility conforms to the international pattern. The third line is the prediction of the Third World Equation. Clearly, this line is close to the actual Soviet experience, which shows that it was not unusual once the pace of economic and social development is taken into account.

Actual Soviet experience, of course, was more volatile than the predictions of the Third World Equation, which includes only the impact of underlying, structural factors. Some of the deviations from predictions are significant. Thus, Soviet fertility at the end of the 1920s and the end of the 1930s was consistent with the experience of many countries, while the low fertility of the mid-1930s is a deviation from the expected level. That discrepancy was the reason for treating the low level of fertility in the mid-1930s as "deficient fertility" attributable to collectivization and simulated in Figures 6.4 and 6.7. It might, however, have been due to a high rate of male migration to the cities, in which case, the previous simulations overstated the impact of collectivization on population change.

The Third World Equation was estimated with data from developing countries in the late twentieth century. Do Soviet data reveal the same patterns? This possibility has been explored by estimating abbreviated versions of the Third World Equation with data sets based on the European Fertility Project. Cross sections of subnational data—provinces, oblasts, krai, republics, and so on—from the 1897, 1939, and 1959 censuses were used. For these districts, which I will refer to as "provinces," it was possible to measure the total fertility rate (the dependent variable) and the most important explanatory variables—women's education, men's education, urbanization, and the religious composition of the population. GDP per adult, agricultural employment, and per capita calorie consumption could not be measured at the subnational level, but these explanatory variables were less important than the others. While the European Fertility Project was primarily concerned with "European Russia," I have expanded the data set to include the Caucuses, Central Asia, and Siberia, which Coale, Anderson, and Harm treated less comprehensively.

Equation 2 in Table 6.1 is patterned after Schultz's Third World Equation. Notice that the coefficients of the education and religion variables are very similar to the corresponding coefficients in the Third World Equation. The absolute value of the urbanization coefficient is

TABLE 6.2
Jones–Grupp-type Equations

	1	2
Constant	7.519	9.019
	(47.939)	(26.928)
% population urban	−0.0113	−.01031
	(−2.996)	(−2.846)
Muslim % of population	0.0080	.0050
	(3.123)	(1.981)
Emancipation	−3.591	−8.374
	(−16.886)	(−8.587)
Emancipation squared	−	2.993
		(5.015)
R^2	.710	.734

Source: See text.
Notes: The dependent variable is the total fertility rate. Equations are estimated from Russian and Soviet censuses. T-ratios in parentheses.

almost three times greater, however, probably because it is picking up the effect of the decline in agriculture, which appears as a separate variable in the Third World Equation. Similar coefficients imply similar results when Soviet population is simulated with equation 2 in Table 6.1, although the absence of calorie terms in equation 1 leads to a slight underestimate of total fertility in the early twentieth century.

Equation 3 includes men's and women's education raised to the second power. These terms are statistically significant and indicate that the effect of education on fertility dimishes as education increases. Thus, giving all women a primary education was highly effective in reducing the birth rate; further, education had less impact so long as women's education increased in step with men's. Kuniansky (1983) and Berliner (1983, 1989) may have found women's education to have been less important in lowering fertility since their data came from the census of 1970 when educational attainment was high so its variation had only a small impact on fertility. The inclusion of higher-order terms does not lead to significantly improved tracking of the actual fertility rate.

The equations in Table 6.2 are inspired by Jones and Grupp's analysis in which fertility is explained by the ratio of women's education to men's.[15] In both equations a rise in that ratio—which Jones and Grupp interpret as a measure of female emancipation—leads to lower fertility. Simulations of the Soviet fertility rate with either equation in Table 6.2

TABLE 6.3
The Reasons for the Fertility Decline, 1928–60

Causal factor	Implied change in total fertility
Education	−1.62
Calorie consumption	−1.00
Economic transformation	−0.67
Religious composition	−0.12
Total	−3.41

Sources: Values of the independent variables for 1928 and 1960 were substituted into the Third World Equation to predict the total fertility rate. Subtracting the equations evaluated at those dates decomposes changes in the total fertility rate into effects due to changes in each variable. Changes for the full list of variables were as follows:

Women's education	−2.28
Men's education	.66
GDP/adult	.50
Urbanization	−.25
Reduction in agriculture	−.91
Catholics	−.09
Protestants	−.03
Muslims	.00
Calories	−1.00
Change in fertility rate	−3.41

In the main table, education is the sum of the figures shown here for women's education and men's education; economic transformation is the sum of GDP/adult, urbanization, and reduction in agriculture; religious composition is the sum of Catholics, Protestants, and Muslims.

are somewhat less successful than with the equations in Table 6.1: while the Jones–Grupp predictions track actual fertility from 1897 through the 1950s, they overpredict fertility in recent decades, and so are less satisfactory than the other fertility equations.

Since equation 2 in Table 6.1 provides considerable substantiation for Schultz's Third World Equation in the Soviet case, and since the greater list of variables in Third World Equation does a better job of replicating the full course of Soviet fertility history, it will be used to analyze the causes of the fertility decline (Table 6.3). Between 1928 and 1960, the total fertility rate fell by 3.41 (from 6.47 to 3.07 children per women). The increased education of the Soviet population was the most important factor behind this decline, being responsible for a fall of 1.62 children per woman. Improvements in agricultural performance and diet that raised calorie consumption per person and reduced infant mortality were responsible for a reduction in fertility of one child per woman. The economic tranformation of the Soviet Union reduced fertility by a further .67 children per woman. Changes in religious composition—principally the decline of Catholicism due to religious persecution, including the forced amalgamation of the Uniates with the Russian Orthodox Church—made a minor contribution to the fertility transformation. Clearly, education, economic development, and rising living standards were the main factors responsible for smaller families and slower population growth.

One factor notably lacking from this list is birth control. Schultz found that neither family planning programs nor the price of birth control devices had much to do with the fertility transition, and the same was true of the Soviet Union. Birth control practices were primitive, and policies respecting abortion fluctuated wildly, although it has been widely used since 1954 (Jones and Grupp 1987, pp. 266–331; Blum 1994, pp. 133, 165–80). The unimportance of contraceptive technology is less surprising in light of Western experience, where the fertility transition preceded the invention of modern birth control devices. Indeed, marital fertility in the West has been limited for centuries.

CONCLUSION

The Soviet Union escaped the population explosion that occurred in the less developed world during the twentieth century. These population explosions were the result of falling mortality rates combined with persistently high fertility. Normal mortality fell in the Soviet Union just as it did elsewhere. Two factors kept the population in check, however. The first was the decline in fertility; the second was the excess mortality due to collectivization and war. Without the losses of World War II and collectivization, the Soviet population would have been larger, in part because these events also lowered fertility, thereby circumventing the fertility response that usually keeps such catastrophes from permanently lowering populations. The main factor, however, that prevented a population explosion in the Soviet Union was the early and rapid fertility transition. It was due to the education of women, rapid economic development, and increased food availability after agriculture recovered from collectivization. Indeed, rapid development and slow population growth have been mutually reinforcing. If the USSR had not followed this path—if, for instance, industrialization and urbanization had proceeded less rapidly and if schooling had been expanded slowly and provided to men in preference to women—then population growth would have been explosive. At the end of the twentieth century, the population would have approached one billion as in India, where urbanization has been limited and where most women remain illiterate.

CHAPTER SEVEN

The Standard of Living

For most countries, there is little debate about the purpose of industrialization: it is to raise living standards. In Chapter 3 we analyzed the ideas of Preobrazhensky and Fel'dman and showed that they constituted a coherent model in which investing in heavy industry led to higher consumer goods output by increasing the capacity to build consumer goods factories. Simulations of the theoretical model indicated that consumption would rise significantly in the span of a dozen years. Just because the Soviets concentrated resources on heavy industry, in other words, does not mean that they were only interested in tanks and steel. Bukharin claimed that "our economy exists for the consumer, not the consumer for the economy" (quoted by Cohen, 1980, p. 173). If Preobrazhensky and Fel'dman were put into practice, this sentiment could become a reality.

Bukharin, of course, was shot. Did the goal of high consumption die with him? The totalitarian school denies that Stalin ever entertained it. In this view, the aim of Stalinism was power and aggrandizement rather than the betterment of the working class (Tucker 1977). As a result, investment and military spending were increased at the expense of consumption. Tucker (1977, p. 98) characterized Stalinism by quoting the great historian Kliuchevsky, who described earlier phases of state-led industrialization with the phrase "the state swelled up; the people grew lean." Magnitorgorsk, in other words, meant steel for tanks, not for textile machinery. Even historians who are otherwise critical of the totalitarian school have accepted this conclusion: "socialism and scarcity turned out to be inextricably linked" (Fitzpatrick 1999, p. 4).

We cannot dissect Stalin's mind, but we can ascertain the results of Soviet policies. What did happen to consumption during Soviet industrialization? Did it rise or fall? The usual answer depends on the time frame. Between 1950 and 1980, there is little dispute that real per capita consumption grew at almost 3 percent per year despite a huge rise in investment and military spending (U.S. Congress 1982, pp. 72–74). During this period, food consumption increased significantly, as we will see, and the volume of urban housing grew much more rapidly than the city population. The consumer durables revolution even hit the USSR: the number of washing machines per 100 households rose from 21 in

1965 to 75 in 1990, the number of refrigerators grew from 11 to 92 per 100 households over the same period, the number of radios went from 59 to 96, and the number of television sets from 24 to 107 (Fernandez 1997, pp. 312, 314). There were 16 telephones for every 100 people in Russia in the early 1990s. This was less than in western Europe or Japan, where the ratio ranged from 50 to 70, but it greatly exceeded the proportion in Third World countries like Argentina (8), Brazil (1), Iraq (3), or Turkey (6) (Dogan 1995, pp. 367–69). The rapid increase in Soviet consumption is consistent with the prognosis of Fel'dman and Preobrazhensky.

The real question is what happened in the 1930s. Most accounts maintain that the standard of living of the working population declined, or was static at best, during the first Five-Year Plans. The bedrock support for this interpretation is the national income accounting of Bergson and the related calculations of real wages by Chapman. Bergson (1961, p. 251) described the record of per capita consumption as "unimpressive." "Valued at adjusted market prices of 1937" — his preferred measure — "per capita consumption in 1937 is 3 percent below the 1928 level." Furthermore, "students of growth wish to know whether industrialization at Soviet tempos can be consistent with progressively rising consumption standards. If the Soviet experience is any indication, the answer must be in the negative" (Bergson 1961, p. 257). Chapman (1963, p. 165) characterized the history of real wages as a "very poor showing." She felt that the best reading of the evidence indicated "a decline of 6 percent in urban per capita household purchases and a significant decline also in rural per capita household purchases of goods between 1928 and 1937" (Chapman 1963, p. 170). These conclusions have been accepted by many other economists and historians.[1]

In this chapter I argue that the standard pessimism is misplaced. It is true that there was little gain in consumer goods output during the First Five-Year Plan, and the famine of 1932–33 casts a pall over those years as well. But by the late 1930s, per capita consumption was significantly higher than it had been in the 1920s. The experience of 1950–80 was thus anticipated in the 1930s. The rural population did not share in this advance — its standard of living only returned to the 1928 level from the trough of 1932–33 — but the urban population and those millions who moved from the country to the city realized a significant increase in consumption. Since the urban share of the population rose from less than one-fifth in 1928 to almost one-third in 1939, the gain was far from universal but important nonetheless. The improvement was not free — urbanites had to work more hours (another feature of the Preobrazhensky strategy) — but the gain in material welfare was real, nonetheless.

THE SUPPLY OF FOOD

There are many approaches to measuring the standard of living. One of the most basic needs is food. Was enough being produced in the Soviet Union in the 1930s? The question is very much to the point in view of the famine in 1932–33 and, more generally, of the usual grim portrayal of Soviet life.

To judge the world's food supply, the United Nations Food and Agricultural Organization (FAO) produces food balance sheets for all the countries of the world. Publication began in the 1960s, but I have applied the method to Russian data back to 1895.[2] The FAO tracks a variety of nutrients, but I limit myself to calories, which is the most basic. The Russian food balances show how calorie availability has changed over time and allow Soviet performance to be assessed with international comparisons.

The food balances are constructed from the agricultural statistics of food production and from industrial returns of a few products like vegetable oil and raw sugar consumption.[3] In the case of the USSR, I tracked twelve food groups that accounted for most calories consumed: grain (including peas and beans), potatoes, sugar, vegetables, beer, vodka, meat, milk, eggs, vegetable oil, butter,[4] and fish. Domestic availability of each food was calculated as gross production less the quantity used for seed and animal feed, exports, and losses in storage and shipping. Food availability is translated into calorie availability with coefficients reflecting the processing of farm goods into food products and the calorie content of those foods.

The calculations are, of course, imprecise, but they give a general indication of food availability. In the case of the USSR, there are significant questions regarding the manipulation of production figures for political ends. I have used the recent findings of Wheatcroft (1990a) and Davies, Harrison, and Wheatcroft (1994, pp. 114–16). The grain figures, in particular, are based on previously secret records and paint a much bleaker picture than the published statistics. Other elements of the calculation — notably losses — are based on the judgment of authorities like Jasny (1949).

Figure 7.1 plots per capita calorie availability from 1895 to 1989. The long-run trend was upward. Several important periods can be identified.

The first was 1895–1910. Per capita calorie consumption in Russia was about 2100, which is consistent with the experience of many poor countries. At this level, there is always some danger of famine. It is impressive that food availability declined in 1906 and 1907, and that may have contributed to political instability at the time.

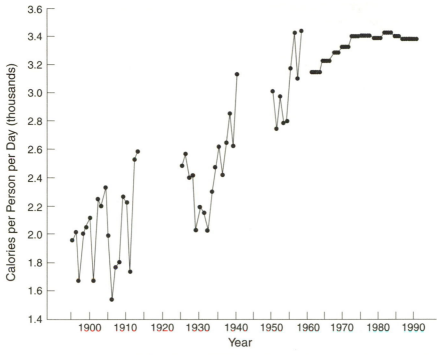

Fig. 7.1. Calorie Availability, Russia/USSR, 1885–1989. *Source*: See text and Appendix C.

The second period was the years immediately before the First World War and the height of the NEP. In this period, calorie availability jumped to 2500 per person per day. There is little information about food production during the period of the civil war, so the causes of the 1921 famine cannot be explored. While the number of years involved is small — so generalization is hazardous — Russian agriculture seems to have been performing better during the peacetime years between 1912 and 1927 than it had in the early twentieth century.

The third period was the First Five-Year Plan. From 1929 to 1932, the calorie availability reverted to the level prevailing from 1895 to 1910. There were several reasons for the deterioration. In 1929–31, the state increased its collection of grain and exported the increment to import machinery (Davies, Harrison, and Wheatcroft 1994, pp. 290, 316). These exports cut into the domestic food supply. From 1930 on, agricultural production slid as collectivization proceeded. The food question, however, was complicated by the slaughter of horses. Since each horse ate as much grain as two people, the loss of 15 million horses between 1929 and 1933 made enough grain available to feed 30 million people. In 1932, however, the fall in food production was so general that calorie availability from almost all food sources dropped. This coincided with the famine, but was not its main cause. Per capita calorie availability in 1932 (2022 calories per person per day) was not much lower than it had been in 1929 (2030 calories) or in many prewar years when there had been no famine. Famines, as Sen (1981) has insisted, are rarely the result of a food availability decline, but are, instead, the results of price movements or policy interventions. In market economies, the cause is usually a rise in food prices relative to earnings. In the Soviet Union, the cause was the conflict between peasants and the state. When the peasants slaughtered livestock and stopped planting and harvesting, the state continued to take grain and the peasants starved.

The fourth period began in 1933 and extended into the 1950s. The decline in food availability was reversed in the Second Five-Year Plan, and the food situation improved dramatically by the late 1930s, when calorie availability reached about 2900 per person per day. This improvement was better than that of South Asian countries during the Green Revolution. In India, for example, food availability increased from 1991 calories per person per day in 1961–63 to 2229 calories in 1988–90. In Pakistan the gain was from 1802 to 2280. Indonesia had one of the best records, with an advance from 1816 to 2605 calories per person per day (Food and Agricultural Organization 1991, vol. 45, p. 238). The Soviet food situation was, of course, desperate during the Second World War, but calorie availability in the early 1950s represented a continuation of the improved situation of the late 1930s.

The final period in the history of the Soviet food supply ran from the late 1950s to the 1980s. Per capita availability rose to about 3400 calories per person per day by c. 1970 and stabilized there. Since 1960, the history of calorie availability in the USSR has paralleled that of Europe as a whole, where it has increased from 3088 in 1961–63 to 3452 in 1988–90 (Food and Agricultural Organization 1991, vol. 45, p. 238).

Economic development has meant an increase in food consumption. Fogel (1991, p. 45) estimated that the average French person consumed 2290 calories per day in 1785 and that the average English person consumed 2700 in 1790. Eighteenth-century French calorie intake was similar to that in contemporary South Asia and to Russia in the early twentieth century. (The higher figure for eighteenth-century England reflects the agricultural revolution of the early modern period that helped launch the first industrial revolution.) By the late twentieth century, calorie consumption in western Europe had risen to 3400 calories per day, and the Russians had matched that increase. The mid- and late 1930s were an important step in that advance. When calorie availability is the metric, the standard of living rose in the late 1930s.

BERGSON'S ESTIMATES REVISITED

Food is important, but people also need shelter, clothing, and many other goods and services. General conclusions regarding living standards require that consumption as a whole be measured. It is important to reexamine the question since much new information has become available since Bergson's work in the 1950s. The upshot of my reassessment is shown in Figure 7.2, which plots my index of per capita consumption from 1928 to 1940. There was a drop during the First Five-Year Plan, but rapid increase thereafter, with the result that consumption per head was 22 percent higher in the late 1930s than in 1928. Figure 7.2 also shows the implications of Hunter and Szyrmer's (1992) reassessment of Soviet national income. Consumption was not their focus, and they adopted a very different aggregation procedure from that used here, but they relied on many of the same agricultural and industrial output series — information not available to Bergson — with the result that they reached conclusions like those advanced here. Indeed, it is difficult to sustain Bergson's pessimistic interpretation of consumption under Stalin on the basis of the information available today.

New information is not the whole story, however. While Bergson's calculations were pathbreaking, they incorporated two debatable procedures that strongly influenced the results. Altering those procedures calls Bergson's pessimistic conclusions into question even without new data.

Table 7.1 summarizes one of Bergson's basic calculations of the standard of living in 1928 and 1937. (He did not estimate consumption annually but only for benchmark years.) The table values goods and services at the prices prevailing in 1937. With that metric, per capita consumption increased by only 3 percent between 1928 and 1937. This result is not Bergson's absolutely lowest estimates (which was minus 3 percent), but it is sufficient to sustain the usual pessimism in historical writing.

In the absence of information on the production of consumer goods, Bergson measured consumption by adjusting expenditures for changes in prices. Two problematic procedures tilted Bergson's calculations toward a low measured growth in per capita consumption. The first was the choice of index number for measuring inflation. Bergson relied on price indices prepared for later publication by Chapman (1963), and

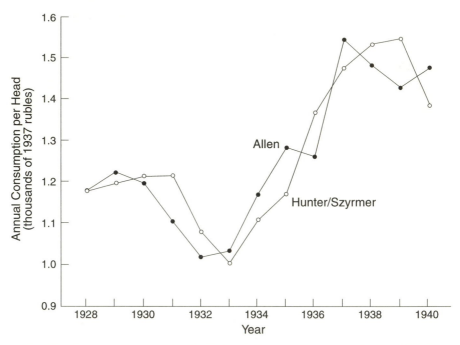

Fig. 7.2. Consumption per Head, 1928–40. *Sources*: See text and Allen (1998c) for my figures. Hunter and Szyrmer (1992, p. 41) present their estimates of rural and urban consumption. The series graphed here is obtained by summing them and dividing by the population.

she calculated a Laspeyres index and a Paasche index using 1937 as the base year.[5] The former uses the 1937 consumption pattern to weight prices, while the latter uses the 1928 consumption pattern. Chapman's Laspeyres price index implies that prices rose by a factor of 5.92 between 1928 and 1937, while her Paasche index increased by 8.69.[6] We can convert 1928 retail sales (12.1 billion rubles) to 1937 prices by multiplying by the price increase. If the Paasche index is used, then 1928 retail sales equal 105.0 (= 8.69 × 12.1) billion rubles in 1937 prices. If the Laspeyres index were used instead, real household purchases in 1928 would be reckoned at only 72.0 (= 5.92 × 12.1) billion rubles in 1937 prices. The implications of these calculations are also shown in Table 7.1: the former implies that consumption per head rose by 3 percent from 1928 to 1937 while the latter implies an increase of 32 percent. Bergson opted for the first result, which supports the pessimistic interpretation of Soviet history. The second would imply a decidedly optimistic view.

Bergson (1961, p. 88) was aware of the implications of the choice of

TABLE 7.1
Bergson's Calculations of Real per Capita Consumption
(1937 and 1928 prices)

	Bergson's preferred Paasche price index (1937 base)		Alternative Laspeyres price index (1937 base)	
	1928	1937	1928	1937
Household purchases in retail markets	105.0	126.0	72.0	126.0
Farm income in kind	35.6	25.0	35.6	25.0
Services	11.1	19.9	11.1	19.9
Total	151.7	170.9	118.7	170.9
Population index	1.00	1.09	1.00	1.09
Indices of real per capita consumption	1.00	1.03	1.00	1.32

Sources: All expenditure figures are from Bergson (1961, p. 48) except for the 72.0 billion rubles shown for household purchases in retail markets in 1928. For that, see the text. The population index is calculated from Bergson (1961, p. 442).

Notes: Services include Bergson's categories of housing, services, and military subsistence. Real per capita consumption is computed as the relative rise in total consumption from 1928 to 1937 divided by the relative rise in population (1.09).

index number, for he reported the calculations with the Laspeyres price index. Nevertheless, he believed that the Paasche index was "logically appropriate" (Bergson 1961, p. 47). He was trying to measure inflation for six benchmark years between 1928 and 1955 with an index number with a 1937 base. Using the Laspeyres index would have imposed the 1937 spending pattern on all of the calculations, while the Paasche index allowed the weights to alter from year to year. For that reason, he felt the Paasche was superior.

The modern theory of index numbers suggests a better procedure. Instead of using Paasche or Laspeyres indices, we should take some sort of average that uses the weights of both years (Diewert 1976; Allen and Diewert 1981). The Fisher Ideal Index (the geometric average of the Paasche and the Laspeyres) is a commmon choice. In the case of multi-year comparisons, chain-linking the Fisher Ideal would solve Bergson's logical problem by allowing the weights to follow the change in consumption patterns over time. This procedure would also use more information in calculating inflation between successive dates and would not arbitrarily privilege the spending pattern in one year as does Bergson's choice of the Paasche index or, indeed, as would a preference for the

TABLE 7.2
Revisions to Bergson's Calculations of Real per Capita Consumption

	Fisher Ideal Price Index		Fisher Ideal Price Index and no rural adjustment	
	1928	1937	1928	1937
Household purchases in retail markets	87.1	126.0	79.1	126.0
Farm income in kind	35.6	25.0	35.6	25.0
Services	11.1	19.9	11.1	19.9
Total	133.8	170.9	125.8	170.9
Population index	1.00	1.09	1.00	1.09
Indices of real per capita consumption	1.00	1.17	1.00	1.25

Sources: Table 7.1 except for household purchases in retail markets, which is described in the text.

Laspeyres. Common sense, as well as modern economic theory, supports the use of indices like the Fisher Ideal. After all, if the Paasche and the Laspeyres indices differ widely, doesn't it make more sense to use an average of the two rather than to rely on one to the exclusion of the other?

Table 7.2, first two columns, puts this theory into practice. Inflation is measured with a Fisher Ideal Index. As a result, per capita consumption grew by 17 percent from 1928 to 1937.

The second problematic procedure underlying Bergson's calculations was an adjustment made by Chapman to the price data used to measure inflation. She collected prices for goods sold in Moscow in 1928, 1937, and later years. While she believed the 1937 prices were representative of all transactions in the Soviet Union, she thought the 1928 prices applied only to state and cooperative shops in urban areas. Consequently, she first raised the 1928 prices to encompass transactions in private shops—a correction that I do not question here[7]—and then adjusted them again to reflect differences between town and country. She believed that prices in rural areas were lower and reduced the price indices accordingly to get values for deflating consumption in the USSR as a whole. The only evidence for lower prices is a loose statement in the First Five-Year Plan that "the 'purchasing power of the ruble in the village' [was] as much as 35 percent higher than in towns" (Hoeffding

1954, p. 65). Chapman assumed that this differential applied to the prices of consumer goods sold in shops, so the rural price of these goods was 75 percent (= 1/1.35) of the urban price.[8] Since she estimated that rural sales amounted to 40 percent of the total, she reduced the 1928 price indices by a factor of .90 (= .6 × 1 + .4 × .75) to get the values of .115 and .168 for Paasche and Laspeyres price indices that she believed characterized all retail sales in the Soviet Union.[9] Shifting these to a 1928 base implies the inflation rates used earlier: 5.95 = 1/.168 and 8.69 = 1/.115.

Chapman's adjustment is hard to accept. As Hoeffding (1954, p. 65) observed, it "is none too clear" what Gosplan meant when it compared rural and urban purchasing power. Hoeffding interpreted the comparison to cover all consumption—in particular, farm income in kind and not just purchases in shops. Indeed, in most places, the prices of agricultural goods (as well as house rents) are less in the country than in the city (Williamson 1988; Hatton and Williamson 1991, pp. 400–1), so Hoeffding's interpretation is plausible. There is, moreover, no reason to believe Chapman's contention that manufactured consumer goods sold for less in rural districts. Indeed, the contrary is more likely. There was excess demand for manufactured consumer goods in state stores in both town and country, and the imbalance was greatest in the country. For that reason, small-scale traders found it profitable to buy goods at controlled prices in urban shops and cart them to the country for resale. Given the added burden of these transport costs, the average price of manufactured consumer goods in the country was probably higher than in the city—not lower as assumed by Chapman (Johnson and Temin 1993; Gregory 1994, pp. 97–98). The simplest procedure is to ignore the downward adjustment Chapman made in urban prices and to treat the Paasche and Laspeyres indices for sales in all urban markets—.168 and .115, respectively—as estimates for the Soviet Union as a whole. It must be recognized, however, that these are lower bound estimates since they understate the price of manufactures sold in rural areas in 1928. Consequently, using .168 and .115 as deflators for 1928 leads to overestimates of 1928 consumption, and, consequently, underestimates of the growth in real retail sales from 1928 to 1937.

Table 7.2, last two columns, shows the result of abandoning the rural-urban adjustment to prices. The Fisher Ideal Index of 1928 prices relative to 1937 prices becomes .153, so prices rose by a factor of 6.54 from 1928 to 1937. As a result, measured consumption per head grows by 25 percent between 1928 and 1937. In contrast to the usual stagnationist view of living standards during the first two Five-Year Plans, this is marked improvement.

TABLE 7.3
Consumption Estimates Aggregating Consumer Goods

| | Services and farm income in kind valued at | | | |
| | Prevailing prices | | Adjusted market prices | |
	1928	1937	1928	1937
Shops and restaurants	61.5	110.0	61.5	110.0
Farmers' markets	3.4	16.0	3.4	16.0
Household purchases in retail markets	64.9	126.0	64.9	126.0
Farm income in kind	35.6	25.0		
— food		78.2	81.3	
— manufactures		7.3	.4	
Services	11.1	19.9	26.3	42.9
Total	111.6	170.9	176.7	250.6
Population index	1.00	1.09	1.00	1.09
Indices of real per capita consumption	1.00	1.40	1.00	1.30

Sources: See text.

Note: Services includes Bergson's categories of services, housing, and military subsistence.

A NEW INDEX OF CONSUMPTION

A slightly larger increase in consumption per head is implied by aggregating the output of consumer goods and by reworking the other elements of the calculation to take advantage of new information. Table 7.3 shows my estimates for 1928 and 1937. I have made no change to Bergson's estimates for services (including housing). The other components of consumption have been computed as follows.

Household Purchases in Shops

Processed foods (bread, sausage, vodka, vegetable oil, etc.) and nonfood consumer goods (cloth, shoes, bicycles, etc.) were sold in shops, and they were the most important retail channel, doing 110 billion rubles of business in 1937. I measured the quantity of goods sold in this way by aggregating the output of manufactured consumer goods.[10] I rely on Nutter's (1962) massive study of Soviet industrial statistics for the output series, and I use his 1928 and 1955 value added prices for valuing output—a procedure equivalent to aggregating by value added. Nutter

(1962, p. 524) presented estimates of the value of output[11] in 1928 and 1937 using both 1928 and 1955 prices. I have extended the calculations to include all years from 1928 to 1940.

When output is measured in 1928 prices, it grew by 93 percent from 1928 to 1937, but growth was only 66 percent when 1955 prices are used. This discrepancy is an example of the Gerschenkron (1947) effect — the industries that were unimportant at the beginning of industrialization were likely both to grow exceptionally rapidly and to have particularly steep reductions in price and cost as technology was modernized. As a result, aggregate growth rates differ depending on whether early or late prices are used for indexing. In the case at hand, consumer durables (bicycles, clocks, phonographs) grew the most rapidly and had the most steeply falling relative prices between 1928 and 1955. The prices of textiles also fell relative to foods, and the production of some textile products, notably hosiery and knitwear, grew very rapidly. Food products in general had the slowest growth and also prices that rose relative to other commodities.

Aggregating quantities presents an "index number problem" just as aggregating prices did. Rather than plump for 1928 or 1955 prices as weights, I have used a geometric average of the two indices. It shows that the output of manufactured consumer goods grew 79 percent between 1928 and 1937. As a result, household purchases in shops in 1928 is reckoned at 61.5 (= 110/1.79) billion rubles in 1937 prices.

Collective Farm Market

The second major retail channel consisted of farmers' markets, where peasants sold produce directly to urban residents. These markets were the principal distribution channel for fresh meat, vegetables, and dairy products. There are official returns for the prices and quantities of goods bought and sold on these markets between 1932 and 1940,[12] and I rely on Malafeev's (1964, p. 402) and Vyltsan's (1966, p. 61) summaries of this material. Barsov's (1969) work was used to extend the index of collective farm market sales back to 1928.[13]

Between 1928 and 1937, sales at farmers' markets increased by a factor of 4.7, so the volume of sales in 1928 was 3.4 (= 16/4.7) billion rubles in 1937 prices. Such a high growth rate is plausible in view of the abolition of private trade in 1930. Prior to that date, peasants could sell to private wholesalers at uncontrolled prices that exceeded state procurement prices, so it was not necessary to sell directly to consumers in farmers' markets to realize high prices. After 1930, however, selling directly to urban consumers in farmers' markets was the only way peasants could realize high prices for their produce, so sales on those markets exploded.

Combining sales in shops and farmers' markets implies that household purchases in retail markets rose from 64.9 billion rubles in 1928 to 126 billion rubles in 1937, all expressed in 1937 prices.[14] As a result, per capita consumption grows by 40 percent, as shown in Table 7.3, columns 1 and 2. However, other issues must be considered before a final conclusion is reached, and they imply a more moderate growth in consumption.

Farm Income in Kind — Food

Some grain was sold to the state or to city residents on the collective farm market, some was used for seed, some was fed to livestock, and some was eaten by rats. The grain left to the peasants for their own consumption was "farm income in kind." Following Bergson, I calculated farm income in kind for the major agricultural products as gross production minus marketings, losses, and utilization as seed and feed. I have altered Bergson's calculations in three ways, reflecting new knowledge. First, Bergson used prices from Karcz (1957), but Karcz has since revised them twice (see Moorsteen and Powell 1966, p. 621; Karcz 1979, p. 105), mainly due to Vyltsan's (1966) publication of prices on the collective farm market. I use Karcz's most recent revisions. Second, Bergson used official Soviet production figures, which Wheatcroft (1990a) and Davies, Harrison, and Wheatcroft (1994, pp. 114–16) have urged should be revised downward. Eliminating Gosplan's upward "corrections" for the late 1920s raises the growth rate of grain consumed on the farm. Third, more satisfactory information on marketing is available due to the work of Barsov and Karcz. These writers have highlighted conceptual issues in measuring marketing and make clear that Bergson's figures for grain marketings are not strictly comparable. His figure for 1928 is net extrarural sales (i.e., sales net of repurchases by the rural population)[15] while the 1937 figure is a gross figure that does not net out those repurchases (Karcz 1957, p. 198). I have used estimates of net sales throughout. These revisions imply a smaller fall in farm income in kind than computed by Bergson.

A tricky question is which prices to use for valuing farm income in kind. The possibilities include procurement prices, the much higher collective farm prices, or an average of the two reflecting the quantities sold at each price. I have used collective farm market prices since they represent the opportunity cost to the peasants. Consider, for instance, a woman who had three eggs. Suppose that the first was sold to the state at the procurement price of 24 kopecks, that the second was sold on the collective farm market for 40 kopecks, and that the third was eaten. What price should be used to value the egg she ate? Clearly, the collective farm market price—not the procurement price or the average price—for she could have sold the egg on the collective farm market for 40 kopecks and bought 40 kopecks' worth of cloth instead.[16]

Farm Income in Kind—Nonfoods

In addition to food, farm income in kind included flax, wool, and hides.[17] In the 1920s, there were substantial rural industries producing a range of textile and leather products for peasant consumption. These industries used half of the raw material. As discussed in Chapter 5, they were squeezed out of business as animals were slaughtered during the collectivization catastrophe.

What were these rural manufactures worth to the peasants? I value wool, flax, and hides at the prices of the manufactures made from them. In the case of wool, for instance, 716,000 centners of wool (in washed condition) were processed by the "agricultural population" in 1928, while 618,000 were processed by industry (Wheatcroft and Davies 1985, pp. 404–5, 459–60). Industry produced 117 million meters of cloth in the same year, and this output required all of its raw wool supply—only a negligible amount was sold as yarn or processed by the factory knitwear and hosiery industry.[18] Hence the raw wool retained by the agricultural population was enough to produce 136 million meters of cloth (= 117 million × 716/618). Analogous calculations indicate a rural production of 190 million meters of linen cloth and 47 million pairs of shoes.

These quantities were valued with 1937 prices from Chapman (1963, pp. 190–95). She reports eight prices for different grades of woolen and worsted cloth. I use the price of "coarse wool baize, solid color" (29.51 rubles per meter) since it was described as coarse and since it was not particularly expensive and so may have been appropriate for rural, handwoven material.[19] The wool cloth was worth 4 billion rubles in 1928. Parallel calculations imply that the value of the linen was 2.5 billion rubles while the shoes were worth 2.4 billion.[20] All told the value of rural production amounted to 8.9 billion rubles in 1928 and .9 billion in 1937—all in 1937 prices.[21] These values are considerably greater than Bergson's estimates.[22]

Total Consumption

Adding up the components gives total consumption in 1928 and 1937 (Table 7.3). It increased by 42 percent, or 30 percent per capita. Advance was not smooth, as Figure 7.2 makes clear.[23] Consumption dropped sharply in 1932 and 1933, recovered during the Second Plan

(1933–37)—indeed, living standards surged forward at the time—and then fell with the approach of the Second World War. The year 1937 has always been regarded as an exceptionally prosperous year since the grain harvest was so large, and Figure 7.2 confirms that view. Between 1928 and 1938, consumption per capita rose 22 percent in the Soviet Union—2.0 percent per year—and that is probably a fairer indicator of the pace of advance than the higher growth rate from 1928 to 1937.

ANNUAL AND SECTORAL ESTIMATES OF CONSUMPTION PER HEAD

The well-being of peasants and workers is such a central question in the 1930s that it is important to measure consumption separately for the farm and nonfarm populations. This requires a consistent decomposition of both consumption and the population, and both divisions are problematic.

So far as the population is concerned, the problem is that many country people were active in both the agricultural and nonagricultural economies. There were four main groups: full-time cultivators; part-time cultivators who also earned money by logging, carting, building, or working in the cities; artisans like millers or handicraft producers who provided cultivators with goods and services often in exchange for food or other produce; and other handicraft producers who specialized in selling goods to the urban sector. Some of these individuals were compensated out of agricultural income and should be included in the denominator when average farm income is calculated. Other individuals were compensated by income earned directly from the urban/industrial sector and should be included in that sector. In practice, I proceed by defining the agricultural population to be full- and part-time cultivators and their families.[24] This treatment of part-time cultivators as full-timers implicitly allows some nonfarming rural residents to be included in the calculation of average income on a full-time equivalent basis. There is bound to be some error in this procedure, but the data do not allow for refinement.

I break down consumption by, first, calculating farm consumption and, then, by computing nonfarm consumption as a residual. Farm consumption equals farm income in kind (as measured in 1937 prices) plus purchases of manufactured consumer goods in shop. I assume that cultivators spent all of their cash incomes, so the value of shop purchases equals farm cash income less agricultural taxes.[25] I express the value of shop purchases in 1937 prices using Malafeev's (1964, p. 407) consumer price index for state and cooperative shops.[26] This index is consistent with the rate of inflation implicit in Table 7.3 for 1928 to 1937.

Table 7.4 shows the per capita income estimates for 1928–39. The

TABLE 7.4
Farm and Nonfarm Consumption per Head, 1928–39 (1937 rubles per person per year)

	Overall	Farm	Nonfarm
1928	1208	940	1727
1929	1225	—	—
1930	1225	—	—
1931	1122	—	—
1932	1052	737	1601
1933	1118	806	1615
1934	1233	840	1855
1935	1334	964	1875
1936	1287	745	2020
1937	1546	1154	2058
1938	1475	992	2079
1939	1450	967	2030

nonagricultural population always had the higher income, so the shift of employment from farm to factory raised average consumption. Some of the gain in average living standards was also due to improvements in nonfarm consumption per head, which grew at 1.9 percent per year from 1928 to 1938. Very little of the gain in average consumption came from improvements in rural living standards. On the farm, consumption per head went up only 5.5 percent between 1928 and 1938. During the collectivization period, average farm consumption had dropped 22 percent below the 1928 level. Remote farming districts specializing in grain probably suffered greater losses, while districts close to cities and specializing in livestock products probably did better since the farmers could sell some produce at the high prices in the collective farm markets.

CONSUMPTION GROWTH AND REAL WAGES

How can the evidence of rising consumption be reconciled with the common view that living standards fell in Soviet cities?

If they are based on statistical evidence, these pessimistic judgments are founded on real wage calculations. The usual case is laid out in Table 7.5, which compares nominal and real earnings for all employees in 1927–28 and 1937. Average earnings in all jobs rose from 690 to 3047 rubles. Prices rose by a factor of 5.1 by my calculations.[27] Dividing the rise in money wages (4.42 = 3047/690) by the increase in the price level (5.1) implies that real earnings dropped 13 percent to equal 87 percent of their 1927–28 value (.87 = 4.42/5.1). The fall in industrial

TABLE 7.5
Real Wage Changes, 1927/28–1937

	Annual earnings			Real rise	1937 real earnings relative rise	
	1927–28	1937	(2)/(1)		to 473	in (5)
Column	(1)	(2)	(3)	(4)	(5)	(6)
All jobs	690	3047	4.41	.87	6.44	1.26
Urban jobs						
Industry	836	3005	3.59	.70	6.53	1.25
Iron ore	739	3143	4.25	.83	6.64	1.30
Coal	759	3626	4.78	.94	7.67	1.50
Ferrous metals	967	3327	3.44	.67	7.03	1.38
Chemicals	808	3165	3.92	.77	6.69	1.31
Textiles	670	2338	2.49	.68	4.94	.97
Food processing	952	2259	2.37	.47	4.77	.94
Construction	1026	3087	3.01	.59	6.53	1.28
Railroads	838	3271	3.90	.77	6.92	1.36
Maritime	888	3397	3.83	.75	7.18	1.41
Communications	751	2356	3.14	.62	4.98	.98
Trade	805	2528	3.14	.62	5.34	1.05
Public eating	623	2045	3.28	.64	4.32	.85
Credit	981	3425	3.49	.68	7.24	1.42
Administration	790	3937	4.98	.98	8.32	1.63
Education	633	3442	5.44	1.07	7.28	1.43
Public health	608	2455	4.04	.79	5.19	1.02
Rural jobs						
State agriculture	286	2121	7.42	1.45	6.05	1.19
Logging	395	1920	4.86	.95	5.48	1.07

Notes:
column (1)—average annual earnings (rubles) in 1927–28 from Zaleski (1971, pp. 318–19).
column (2)—average annual earnings (rubles) in 1937 from Zaleski (1980, pp. 562–65).
column (3)—column (2) divided by column (1).
column (4)–column (3) divided by 5.1, the rate of inflation.
column (5)—column (2) divided by 473 rubles per year except for last two rows, where 1937 earnings are divided by 350 (= 473/1.35) to eliminate the adjustment for urban prices relative to rural.
column (6)—column (5) divided by 5.1, the rate of inflation.

earnings was greater — 30 percent. There was clearly a range of experience across industries. In the urban sector, the two industries whose workers did the best were education, where real incomes rose 7 percent, and public administration, where earnings dropped only 2 percent. The superior performance of these jobs is consistent with Fitzpatrick's view that the new intelligentsia and administration of educated proletarians did well under Stalin.[28] Otherwise, the real wage changes in Table 7.5 would seem to support a pessimistic verdict.

There are, however, three reasons why pessimism is unwarranted. The first is that the real wage comparisons in column 4 are not relevant for most individuals. The real wage change for the category "all employees" indicates the change in consumption possibilities for someone who was the "average wage and salary employee" in both 1927–28 and 1937. The problem is that the "average wage and salary employee" in 1937 was not a wage and salary employee at all in the late 1920s. He or she was a peasant in 1927–28. Between 1927–28 and 1937, total wage and salary employment expanded from 11.3 million to 27 million. The additional workers were peasants. Industrial employment rose from 3.5 million to 10.1 million. All of these new workers had migrated from the countryside to the city. Indeed, the "ruralization" of Soviet cities is a major theme in the social histories of the period (Lewin 1985, pp. 218–21). It must be taken into account in judging real income changes.

To measure the change in the real income of the new arrivals to the cities, we must compare their urban earnings in 1937 to their rural earnings in 1927–28. Fortunately, Hoeffding (1954, pp. 63–72) carefully measured rural earnings at the start of the First Five-Year Plan. He arrived at a figure of 473 rubles (p. 68). This average encompasses full-time farmers, the employed, artisans, and agriculturalists working part-time in the cities. The average has also been inflated by differences in rural and urban prices to make it directly comparable to urban salaries. These adjustments are generous and "may well lead to overstatement" (p. 68). Nonetheless, average rural earnings only equaled 57 percent of the average industrial wage of 836 rubles. The average rural resident who moved to a city and took an average industrial job boosted his or her consumption by 77 percent (836/473). Much of the rise in consumption per head accrued to people making moves like this.

When allowance is made for these moves, the rise in real earnings of many city dwellers is apparent. Columns 5 and 6 in Table 7.5 compare the 1937 earnings to 473 rubles in 1927–28. The average employee (across either all activities or just industry) realized about a 25 percent increase in consumption by moving from the country to the city. There is variation in the result depending on which industry the migrants worked in. Textiles and food processing showed slight falls, while administration, education, credit, and coal mining showed the biggest gains. Fitzpatrick's educated proletarians continue to lead the field by this standard.

A second development also plays a role in reconciling the growth in consumption with the history of real earnings. That factor was an increase in the fraction of urban residents working. Hoffmann (1994, p. 143), for instance, reports that the number of wage earners per family in Moscow rose from 1.37 in 1929 to 1.63 in 1937. This was a 19 percent increase and counteracted much of the fall in real earnings in each industry. Long-term urban residents could maintain their consumption in the 1930s by working more.

A third way by which long-term urban residents could realize higher incomes was by upgrading their skills, moving into higher-income administrative jobs, or through the Stakhanovite movement (Siegelbaum 1988). The latter was the effort by many workers to produce more than the stipulated norms. Breaking quotas resulted in large income gains since earnings depended on production. The experience of established workers may have allowed them to lead the others. In that case, the extra income preserved consumption even as the average wage fell.

The history of wages helps identify the groups who gained from Soviet economic growth in the 1930s and the channels by which the gains were distributed. The urban working class tripled during the first three Five-Year Plans, and the new urban residents realized large gains in real income. Established residents could also raise consumption by working more, upgrading their skills, increasing their productivity, or joining the administrative bureaucracy and educational system. Staying on the farm brought no economic progress.

MORTALITY AND LONGEVITY

If food consumption and the standard of living generally were rising by the mid-1930s, the improvement should be reflected in better health. Longer life — like more education — is a good in itself. As well, greater life expectancy may indicate improvements in nutrition and other aspects of material consumption. The extension of medical services may also have increased longevity, but increases in real income were probably decisive.[29] In the event, the demographic evidence strongly supports the conclusion that the standard of living was rising.[30]

The most careful reconstruction of Soviet population history is that of Andreev, Darskii, and Khar'kova (1990, 1992), and it was the basis of the previous chapter. Figure 6.1 plots their estimate of the crude death rate (the number of deaths per thousand people). The dreadful famine following collectivization stands out starkly: in 1933, the crude

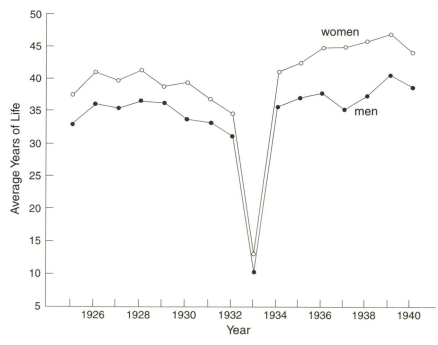

Fig. 7.3. Expectation of Life at Birth, 1925–40. *Source*: Andreev, Darskii, and Khar'kova (1992, p. 148).

death rate jumped to seventy per thousand. Otherwise, the graph shows a long-run improvement in mortality. In the late 1920s, the crude death rate was about twenty-seven per thousand. It rose slightly during the First Five-Year Plan. After the 1933 famine, however, there was a noticeable drop in mortality, and the crude death rate hovered around twenty-one per thousand in the late 1930s. This was a significant improvement on the NEP record.

Crude death rates vary with changes in the age structure of the population. A better indicator of overall mortality is the expectation of life at birth—the longer expected life, the lower mortality across all ages. Figure 7.3 plots life expectancy for men and women from 1925 to 1940 (Andreev, Darskii, Khar'kova 1992, p. 148). The impact of the famine in 1933 is again apparent. In addition, Figure 7.3 confirms the improvement in mortality shown in Figure 6.1, for the long-run trend in expected years of life was sharply upward. The average Soviet woman lived about five years longer in the late 1930s than she had in the mid-1920s; the average man had about three more years of life.[31] Many people died prematurely in the Soviet Union in the 1930s in either the

Great Terror or the collectivization famine; other people lived longer than those who were born a decade or two earlier.

CONCLUSION

The Soviet development model implies that allocating capital to the producer goods sector should lead to higher consumption growth than would otherwise have been possible. Bergson and Chapman called the pertinence of this model into question by propounding the view that consumption per head declined in the 1930s. The history of wages, prices, food production, and mortality do not support that pessimism. Consumption did, indeed, languish during the First Five-Year Plan. The explanation has nothing to do with the logic of accumulation—collectivization was the culprit. Once farm production rebounded from that catastrophe, consumption rose rapidly. By the late 1930s, the production of manufactured consumer goods had increased almost 80 percent.

While this increase is important in understanding the growth of the economy in the 1930s, it also has important implications for the study of politics. The totalitarian model views the state as exclusively oppressive and the population as disaffected and controlled through terror. Historians are questioning this monolithic model. Fitzpatrick (1979) has suggested that the upwardly mobile workers and peasants who formed the new intelligentsia and administrative hierarchy supported Stalinism since they were its beneficiaries. Siegelbaum (1988) has suggested that Stakhanovites also gained from the system and, therefore, had a reason to support it. Thurston (1996) has gone furthest in suggesting that Stalinism enjoyed wide support among urban workers. The formation of political attitudes is complex and not immediately reducible to economics, but the standard of living does matter. What we have shown in this chapter is that many people did benefit materially from the economic development of the 1930s. The gainers included the new administrative elite and the Stakhanovites. The millions who migrated to the industrial cities were a much bigger group of beneficiaries. By the late 1930s, urban residents and industrial workers, teachers and bureaucrats had economic reasons for supporting the Soviet state.

CHAPTER EIGHT

The Causes of Rapid Industrialization

Economic development was very rapid in the Soviet Union during the first three Five-Year Plans (1928–40). GDP grew at 5.3 percent per year from 1928 to 1940, and industrial output increased at 11 percent per annum (Tables A.2 and 5.4). Investment surged and consumption rose sharply. This growth record would be impressive even for recent decades, when expanding world trade has allowed a few countries to industrialize very quickly. For the interwar period, when the capitalist world was mired in Depression and export-led growth was out of the question, the Soviet performance is remarkable. How did they do it?

The review of the economic record in Chapter 5 suggests some answers. Assigning a big fraction of producer goods output to expand the producer goods sector pushed up both consumption and investment in accord with Fel'dman's model; directing enterprises to meet ambitious production targets and relaxing the requirement that revenues cover costs encouraged rapid job expansion; the violent collectivization of agriculture drove people from the country to the city, further expanding industrial employment and output. While these are plausible hypotheses, the question remains whether they were sufficient to explain Stalin's industrial revolution or whether other factors were at play. Moreover, their relative importance is hard to know. An assessment of socialist development varies depending on whether state terrorism or subsidized job creation was the decisive factor behind rapid industrial growth.

The aim of this chapter is to provide a quantitative analysis of these issues. The measuring rod is a multisector simulation model of the Soviet economy. Comparing simulations of alternative policies and institutions identifies the factors that were responsible for rapid development after 1928 and establishes their relative importance. Growth can be simulated with collectivization and without it, for instance, in order to establish its importance. The simulations also help explore some related issues, including the development possibilities of the NEP and the features of socialism that accelerated industrialization under the conditions of the 1930s.

The chapter is organized as follows. First, the simulation model is described. Second, it is used to assess the implications of investing in heavy industry. This policy not only raised the growth rate of output and the capital stock, but it also rapidly raised living standards—an expected result in view of Fel'dman's work. Third, the effect of collectivization on growth is gauged by simulating the impact of investing in heavy industry within the framework of the NEP. The growth prospects were good—but not quite as good—as they were in the collectivized economy. The implication is that collectivization played a positive but secondary role in accelerating Soviet growth. Finally, a version of the NEP model is simulated in which the soft budget constraints that characterized the actual Soviet system are replaced with hard budget constraints. Soviet industry, in other words, is forced to hire workers in accord with a capitalist employment rule rather than the full employment policy followed. As a result, industrial employment and output fall, as does the level of per capita consumption. In toto, these simulations indicate that the main sources of growth were the strategy of heavy industrialization, which rapidly expanded the capital stock, and the ambitious output targets (in conjunction with the soft budget constraints), which led to industrial jobs for people who would otherwise have languished in the countryside or been squandered in a Latin American-style "informal sector." The collectivization of agriculture made only a minor contribution to industrial growth.

The Simulation Model

Since the major weakness of the Soviet economy in 1928 was the small size of its capital stock, the simulation model focuses on the production and allocation of producer goods. In this respect, the model elaborates G. A. Fel'dman's framework by making it more descriptive of the institutions and policies of the USSR in the interwar period. Agriculture is separated from other consumer goods, so the issues debated by Bukharin and Preobrazhensky can be explored. The major markets that existed in the Soviet Union appear in the model: the labor market, the collective farm market, and retail markets for consumer goods. Other decisions, such as the allocation of investment, which were handled administratively, are modeled as such.[1]

The equations of the model are described in Appendix B, so I simply review its salient features here. There are, indeed, three versions of the model—one for the collectivized economy, a second for the NEP economy with the Five-Year Plans grafted on, and a third that introduces a capitalist labor market. I begin with the first since it is supposed to simulate what actually happened and, therefore, is the most closely based on the historical record. The model begins with a solution for 1928 and in each subsequent year a series of equations is solved to determine the values of about fifty variables. Births, deaths, migration, and investment cause the economy to grow from one year to the next and give the model its dynamic character.

The flow chart in Figure 8.1 (see p. 156) shows how the economy is described and highlights the variables that are determined for each year of the simulations. The figure can be approached as follows.

Inputs and Production Sectors

The two columns on the left identify the sectors of the economy — agriculture, consumer goods, and producer goods. The agricultural sector has "excess population," so output is not constrained by the labor supply. There is little point in trying to model agricultural output as a simple economic process since the main determinants of farm production were political factors like resistance to collectivization. Instead, farm production follows its historical trajectory.

Producer goods include machinery (industrial, agricultural, and hospital equipment) and consumer durables like bicycles, military ordnance, and construction. The production of producer goods depends on capital and labor in that sector. Consumer goods output (which includes food and nonfood manufactures, housing, services, and government activity) depends on deliveries of farm products for processing as well as labor and capital.[2] In the computer model, equations (production functions) calculate outputs from the inputs in the sectors.

The quantities of inputs available in any year are largely determined by decisions taken in previous years. Agricultural goods available for processing equal compulsory sales to state procurement agencies in the previous year, the capital stocks are the results of earlier investments, and the industrial labor force depends on earlier births, deaths, and migration. Only the division of the industrial labor force between the producer and consumer goods sectors is determined on an annual basis, and that is done by equating the real marginal product of labor in the two sectors year by year.

The Purchasers

Goods and services are produced for someone's use. There were three types of users in this model: urban households, peasants, and the state. With the exception of the food and fiber retained by the peasants for their own use, all goods and services must be paid for. Key questions are where the groups get their money and what they spend it on.

Urban households earn their income from selling their labor, so household income equals employment in the consumer goods and pro-

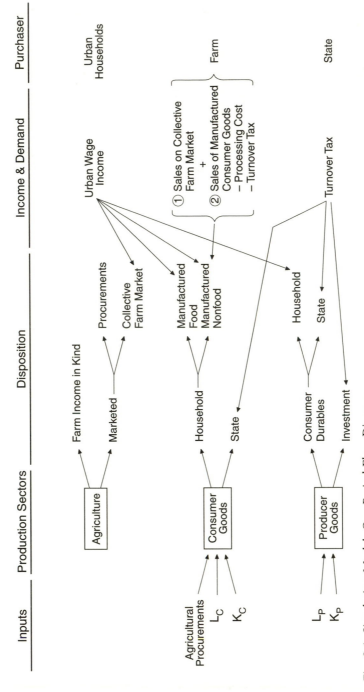

Fig. 8.1. Simulation Model: One Period Flow Diagram

ducer goods industries multiplied by the average wage rate.[3] The house-holds spend their money on fresh food bought directly from farmers on the collective farm market, on food and nonfood goods manufactured by the consumer goods industry, and on consumer durables made by the producer goods industry. Fixed fractions of income are spent on each type of good.[4]

Peasants earned their cash incomes from selling farm products to urban residents on the collective farm market and to state procurement agencies. The revenue they received from procurement agencies equaled the sales of manufactured consumer goods to consumers minus the production cost of those goods minus turnover tax collections.

The state was the third source of demand. It purchased educational, health, administrative, military, police, and other services (treated in the model as output of the consumer goods sector), hospital and military equipment (producer goods output used for consumption), and investment (also producer goods output). Stalin believed in balanced budgets. The turnover tax was the major source of revenue in the 1930s, and the rate was set to balance the budget.

The turnover tax was an important way in which economic policy impinged on the rest of the economy. An increase in investment, for instance, required an increase in taxes. Raising the turnover tax enlarged the gap between the prices that peasants received for their products and the prices they paid for the manufactured goods they bought. In other words, the turnover tax was the administrative device that implemented Preobrazhensky's proposal of turning the terms of trade against agriculture.

Disposition of Output

The central column of the flow chart shows how producers and purchasers exchanged goods and services for income. The output of each sector is broken up into several types of goods and services sold to different buyers on different markets.

Agricultural output is first divided into marketed goods and "farm income in kind," that is, the agricultural produce retained by farmers for their own use. The model of farm marketing developed in Chapter 4 is used for this purpose. Since that market was calibrated with data from 1913 and 1928 and replicates marketing behavior in the 1920s, the simulations that use that model answer the question of what would have happened to Soviet development if peasants had continued to market as they had during the NEP. The procurements of farm products by state agencies are subtracted from total marketings to compute sales on the collective farm market. Setting that supply equal to demand from urban consumers determines the price on the collective farm market.[5]

State purchases of services (education and so forth) are set at their historical values, so the sale of consumer goods to households is calculated by subtracting the state's consumption of services from total consumer goods production. Sales of consumer goods to households are divided into sales of food and nonfood goods using the proportions of value added in the two industries in 1928. These supplies of consumer goods are set equal to the demand from the urban and peasant populations to determine the price of food and nonfood manufactures.

Investment is a residual. It equals the production of producer's goods less the amount consumed as hospital equipment, consumers' durables, and armaments. The consumption of producer goods is not explained by the model: it is set at historical values. By far the most important of these expenditures was armaments, so the procedure incorporates the trade-off between military spending and investment: one more ruble spent on tanks meant one less ruble of investment.

The key question of Fel'dman's growth model—how investment should be divided between the producer goods and consumer goods sectors—is a central issue in the disposition of producer goods. The fraction (e) can be set arbitrarily to simulate the effects of alternative investment strategies.

The state paid for investment and arms purchases. As noted, the turnover tax is set to generate the income needed for these acquisitions.

From One Year to the Next: The Growth of the Factors of Production

In each year of the simulations, the computer solves equations describing the relationships shown in Figure 8.1 (plus a few additional nuances). A simulated trajectory of the economy across the 1930s is built up by solving the equations year after year. One year's solution leads into the next since the inputs with which a year begins depend on the results of the previous year.

With capital, the stock at the beginning of the year equals the stock at the beginning of the previous year plus investment in the year minus depreciation of the previous stock. Different investment strategies (different splits between producer and consumer goods or different levels of arms spending) translate into different levels of investment, which cumulate into different capital stocks and, hence, different levels of output.

Underlying labor supply is a demographic model. It is a simplified version of the one described in Chapter 6. For the rural and urban sectors, consistent trajectories of crude birth rates, "normal" crude death rates, "excess" deaths, and rural-urban migration rates were developed to replicate the history of the rural and urban populations between the 1926 and 1937 and 1939 censuses. The industrial workforce depends on the urban population, which was determined mainly by the history of rural-urban migration. The fraction of the rural population moving to the city depends on the level of urban consumption relative to rural. Different investment strategies affect the rate of growth by changing the turnover tax rate, which, in turn, alters worker and peasant incomes and, thus, rural-urban migration.

Model Validation: Can We Believe It?

The model is complicated. There are three reasons for believing it describes the Soviet economy accurately. First, the main institutions of the economy are represented, and most are described by structural models rather than reduced form regression equations. Second, the sectors perform well in partial equilibrium simulations. For instance, treating agricultural production and the prices of farm products and manufactured consumer goods as exogenous, the model of farm supply replicates the marketing behavior of the 1920s, including the scissors crisis, as shown in Chapter 4. Third, the model accurately simulates the evolution of the main endogenous variables from 1928 to 1939, as will be shown shortly. In view of these results, one can have some confidence in the counterfactual simulations undertaken.

Models of the NEP and Capitalist Employment Relations

The model, as described, is a model of the collectivized economy. It can be used to explore the effect of changing the investment strategy (i.e., the allocation of producer goods) within the institutional structure that actually existed. Analyzing the development possibilities of the NEP requires changes that are more substantial than varying a parameter or two. The model of the NEP replaces obligatory deliveries with a market relationship between town and country, eliminates the antipeasant bias of the Soviet tax system, but preserves many of the agricultural development initiatives (like mechanization and water control) that were actually pursued in the 1930s.

In particular, the NEP model differs from the collectivized model in four main ways. First, I assume that neither the production and livestock losses that accompanied collectivization occurred nor that there was famine and "excess mortality." Second, the turnover tax, which was aimed at the peasants, is replaced with a tax on all cash incomes (farm and nonfarm). Third, farm supply is made a function of the average price (net of tax) received on all marketings. A regression equation is used to divide marketings into sales on farmers' markets and sales to industry for processing. Fourth, a lower migration function is used since dekulakization and other forms of state interference that drove people from the countryside are presumed not to have occurred.

Finally, to analyze the effects of the soft budget constraint and high firm output targets on growth, yet a third model is necessary. This model, which I call the capitalist employment model, is a modification of the NEP model. In both the NEP and the collectivized models, there is a soft budget constraint in that nonagricultural employment equals the urban population multiplied by the fraction of the urban population that was actually employed each year from 1928 to 1939. As a result, there is no unemployment, and the marginal product of labor is less than the wage. In the capitalist employment model, firms pay a high fixed wage and adjust their employment until the marginal product of labor equals that wage. The introduction of a hard budget constraint creates unemployment. Rural-urban migration responds to the expected wage, taking account of unemployment. This view of employment and the labor market is an implementation of the theories of Todaro (1968, 1969) and Harris and Todaro (1970) about labor markets in developing capitalist countries.

Figures 8.2 and 8.3 compare the actual time series of nonagricultural value added and per capita consumption with simulated series from the three models. These simulations are a test of the collectivized model since it represents the actual institutions of the USSR and uses historical parameter values.[6] The model passes the test in view of the correspondence between the actual series and the simulations. For comparison, simulations with the NEP and the capitalist employment models are also shown. While the differences between the various simulations will be analyzed in the remainder of the chapter, it is worth noting now that the NEP and the capitalist employment models imply faster growth than the collectivized model in the early 1930s since the farm output losses following collectivization are avoided in these simulations. By the late 1930s, however, the collectivized model does a bit better than the NEP model, while both of those do very much better than the capitalist employment model.

INVESTING IN HEAVY INDUSTRY

I use the three models, just described, to analyze the implications of alternative institutions and policies for the growth of output and per capita consumption in the Soviet Union in the 1930s. I begin with the model of the collectivized economy—the model that replicates what ac-

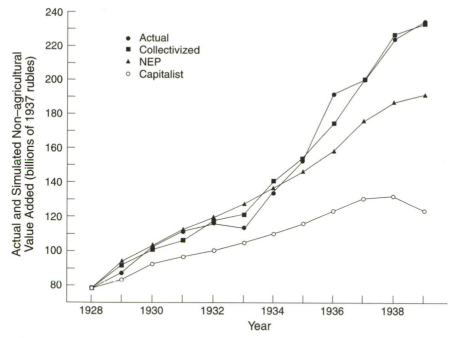

Fig. 8.2. Nonagricultural Value Added. *Note*: The graph contrasts the growth of the nonagricultural economy under alternative economic systems. All simulations assume the same fraction of producer goods expended on expanding that sector.

tually happened — and explore the ramifications of alternative investment strategies to study the sources of capital accumulation, output growth, and rising living standards.

Concentrating investment on heavy industry was a principal strategy for raising the rate of economic growth. Investment could be increased by allocating more of the output of the producer goods industries to investment (rather than consuming it as military equipment, hospital equipment, or consumer durables) and by increasing the proportion of investment that was channeled back into the producer goods industries themselves.

In 1928, investment amounted to 94 percent of the output of the producer goods industries, so there was little scope for increasing capital accumulation by raising that fraction. The investment rate was increased, instead, by raising the proportion of investment that was allocated to the producer goods sector itself. In 1928, about 7 percent of the nonagricultural capital stock was in that sector. From 1929 to 1934, 23 percent of gross investment outside of agriculture was allocated to

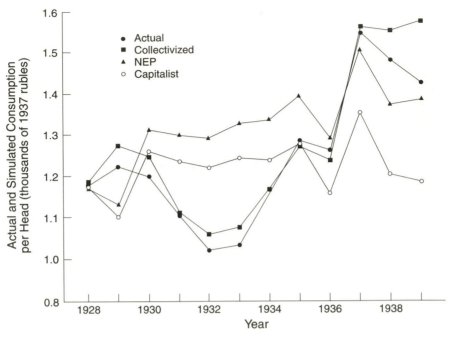

Fig. 8.3. Consumption per Head. *Note*: The graph contrasts the growth of consumption per head under alternative economic systems. All simulations assume the same fraction of producer goods expended on expanding that sector.

those industries.[7] While 23 percent may not have been a huge number, it marked a major departure from previous patterns and signified the drive to develop heavy industry.

The effect of this increase can be seen by simulating Soviet development with alternative values of e, the fraction of investment allocated to the producer goods industries. Tables 8.1–8.4 show the resulting impact on the 1939 values of certain key variables. Evidently, alternative values of e had a significant effect on output and income. The 1939 nonagricultural value added increases from 143.4 billion rubles to 231.9 billion as e rises from .07 to .23. The 1939 capital stock also increases from 201.0 to 343.9 over the same range of e. Channeling more resources into heavy industry resulted in a greater nonagricultural capital stock and level of output.

What is more surprising is the behavior of per capita consumption. The 1939 consumption per head also increased consistently as e was increased. Higher values of e did result in a more rapid growth of the producer goods industry, but that growth spilled back onto the con-

TABLE 8.1
Actual and Simulated Nonagricultural Value Added (billions of 1937 rubles)

	Collectivized soft budget	NEP soft budget	Capitalist employment hard budget
1928, actual	78.4	78.4	78.4
1939, simulated e			
.07	142.4	137.9	84.7
.12	165.2	157.7	99.2
.17	192.0	177.8	115.5
.23	231.9	189.7	122.7
1939, actual	233.2	233.2	233.2

sumer goods industries in the form of higher capital stocks. The possibility for "spill back" was large since 77 percent of investment went to consumer goods. There was, of course, a trade-off. Low values of e implied a slightly larger capital stock in the consumer goods industry from 1929 to 1932, but the difference was minor. The resulting shortfall in consumption with a high value of e was never more than 1 percent of the value implied by a low value of e during the First Five-Year Plan. In other words, increasing the fraction of investment going to the producer goods sector had little cost in terms of lower consumption.

TABLE 8.2
Actual and Simulated Nonagricultural Capital Stock (billions of 1937 rubles)

	Collectivized soft budget	NEP soft budget	Capitalist employment hard budget
1928, actual	136.3	136.3	136.3
1939, simulated e			
.07	201.0	192.7	162.9
.12	237.3	225.1	186.3
.17	281.1	263.6	215.2
.23	343.9	318.0	258.7
1939, actual	344.7	344.7	344.7

TABLE 8.3
Actual and Simulated GDP (billions of 1937 rubles)

	Collectivized soft budget	NEP soft budget	Capitalist employment hard budget
1928, actual	200.9	200.9	200.9
1939, simulated			
e			
.07	270.1	284.8	240.6
.12	293.5	303.6	252.8
.17	321.6	324.0	268.6
.23	364.6	348.3	290.3
1939, actual	344.9	344.9	344.9

A corollary of this conclusion should be stressed: the decline in consumption between 1928 and 1932 was due to the decline in agricultural output and marketing—not the investment strategy. Workers as well as peasants suffered in the early 1930s as the disastrous effects of collectivization rippled through the economy.

By 1939 the advantages of investing in heavy industry were clear. Per capita consumption was 17 percent larger with $e = .23$ than it would have been with $e = .07$. With $e = .23$, the capital stocks of both the producer goods and consumer goods sectors would have been larger.

TABLE 8.4
Actual and Simulated Consumption per Capita (rubles per person per year)

	Collectivized soft budget	NEP soft budget	Capitalist employment hard budget
1928, actual	1177	1177	1177
1939, simulated			
e			
.07	1252	1296	1085
.12	1322	1346	1123
.17	1387	1381	1160
.23	1468	1384	1184
1939, actual	1426	1426	1426

Thus, with $e = .23$, the capital stock of the producer goods sector would have been 60.8 billion versus 14.2 billion rubles with $e = .07$. For consumer goods, the corresponding values are 283.1 billion with $e = .23$ versus 186.7 with $e = .07$. Almost any calculation trading off present and future consumption would have favored an investment strategy to develop heavy industry. The frequent criticism of Soviet investment — that it sacrificed living standards for ever more steel and military ordnance — is off the mark.

While an increase in e accelerated growth in the USSR, this effect was being offset in the 1930s by an increase in the fraction of producer goods output allocated to consumption. The culprit was the military buildup preceding the Second World War. From 1933 to 1939, the fraction of producer goods that were invested declined from 93 percent to 58 percent, while the production of military equipment increased from 4 percent to 41 percent of producer goods output.

This increase in military spending explains one of the well-known features of growth in the late 1930s — the falloff in investment and the slowdown that occurred after 1937. The actual investment rate rose from 1928 to the mid-1930s and then declined for the rest of the decade. This pattern is substantially replicated when investment is simulated using the historical values for exogenous variables. In contrast, I have also simulated the investment rate with a value of e of .23 and with real defense expenditures continuing at the level of 1930. This rate grows continuously throughout the 1930s since there is no diversion of machinery output into tanks, artillery, and military aircraft. Had investment occurred at this rate, nonagricultural value added, the nonagricultural capital stock, GDP, and per capita consumption would all have been about one-fifth greater than their simulated 1939 values. The threat of German invasion significantly retarded Soviet growth.

Thus, the simulations of alternative investment strategies with the model of the collectivized economy show that investment policy was a potent tool for accelerating the growth in output, capital, and living standards. Growth rose more as producer goods output was reinvested in that sector. This result holds true for the other models as well. While enlarging heavy industry was an important source of growth, it was not the only one, as will be shown.

THE GROWTH POSSIBILITIES OF THE NEP

Nothing has been said so far about the impact of collectivization on growth during the 1930s. Did collectivization accelerate, retard, or have no effect on the rate of industrialization? Equivalently, the question can be posed in terms of the NEP. Would the strategy of heavy industrialization have been as effective — or, for that matter, feasible — if it had been undertaken within the institutional arrangements of the NEP?

Answers to these questions have spanned the gamut. On the one hand, it has been argued that collectivization accelerated growth by increasing rural-urban migration, by increasing agricultural marketings, and by mobilizing the agricultural surplus to finance industrial investment. On the other hand, it has been claimed that none of these effects occurred or (if they did) were of any consequence and that collectivization was detrimental to growth since it resulted in huge losses of farm output as livestock was destroyed and grain production collapsed. Rather than begin with these issues, I simulate the effects of alternative investment strategies (values of e) with the NEP version of the model and compare them to those obtained with the collectivized version of the model. The results are shown in Tables 8.1–8.4.

The tables show quite clearly that a high investment strategy ($e = .23$) would have been successful within the framework of the NEP in that the growth rates of output and per capita consumption would have risen dramatically compared to low values of e. Nonetheless, the results would not have been as impressive as they were with collectivization. In 1939, nonagricultural value added was 22 percent higher with collectivization than it would have been if the same investment strategy ($e = .23$) had been undertaken with a continuation of the NEP, and the nonagricultural capital stock would have been 8 percent higher. GDP, however, would have been only 5 percent higher due to the superior performance of agriculture without collectivization.

This result is at considerable variance with the findings of Hunter and Szyrmer (1992, pp. 196–97, 241, 246–51), who have also analyzed Soviet industrialization with a large-scale simulation model. Their analyses of military spending and alternative consumption strategies are not radically different from those presented here, but they came to a much more negative assessment of collectivization. Instead of finding that it gave a modest boost to growth in the 1930s, they concluded that it cut 1940 GDP by about 30 percent and the 1941 capital stock by perhaps 40 percent. The Hunter–Szyrmer model is so complex that the reason for their different findings is not immediately clear. An important factor is probably the treatment of rural-urban migration, which they set at arbitrary rates. In the model of this chapter, the migration rate depends on relative urban-rural consumption and on collectivization, with the result that collectivization pushed up rural-urban migration. That is the reason it promoted industrialization in the model of this chapter, and that effect is not encompassed by the Hunter–Szyrmer simulations. In addition, their model sets rural and urban per capita consumption at predetermined values with the result that a shortfall in agricultural output causes the consumer goods industries to suck capital and labor from the rest of the economy in order to maintain consumption levels. In contrast, the model used here allows the shortfall in farm production during collectivization to cut consumption while investment is maintained. These differences in modeling appear to explain why Hunter and Szyrmer reached their much more negative assessment of collectivization.

The following chapter explores how the findings of this chapter relate to the standard hypotheses that attempted to explain why collectivization retarded — or accelerated — Soviet industrialization. The essential point, however, is the modesty of its overall impact. It did retard growth during the First Five-Year Plan and accelerate it later, but the cumulative effect during the 1930s was only a small boost to economic expansion. The human misery that accompanied collectivization was very large, while the economic gains were meager.

AMBITIOUS OUTPUT TARGETS AND THE SOFT BUDGET CONSTRAINT

Tables 8.1–8.4 indicate that allocating a larger fraction of investment goods to the producer goods industry accelerates the rate of growth of nonagricultural output and of per capita consumption. The effect is of roughly the same magnitude with both the collectivized and the NEP economies. Another feature of these tables is puzzling, however. All show high levels of output in 1939 even with only 7 percent of investment allocated to the producer goods industry. The figures for the collectivized economy implied that real nonagricultural output would have grown 5.6 percent per year from 1928 to 1939, while growth would have been 5.3 percent with a continuation of the NEP. The puzzle is why growth would have been so high with investment so low.

Growth would have been rapid even with low investment because of the employment practices of Soviet enterprises. Profit-maximizing capitalist firms hire workers so long as the value of the marginal product of their labor equals or exceeds the wage paid. During the early 1920s Soviet firms probably operated in this way, but by the late 1920s output targets had replaced profits as the objective. The provision of liberal bank credits — the soft budget constraint — allowed firms to pursue higher output by expanding their workforces beyond the point where the value of the marginal product of labor equaled the wage.

In recent years, the soft budget constraint has been severely criticized for causing "overmanning" and inefficiency in Soviet industry (Kornai 1992, pp. 140–48). These criticisms may have been pertinent in the 1980s with the Soviet economy at full employment. If the growth of new, high-productivity enterprises was limited by an inability to attract labor, then forcing labor out of older, less efficient enterprises by requiring them to cover their costs might have accelerated economic growth. In the 1930s, however, the Soviet Union was not a full employment economy. Structural unemployment in the rural sector was very large and increasing as plowing and harvesting were mechanized (Hoeffding, 1954, p. 66; Kahan 1959, p. 458). With the marginal product of labor equaling zero in the countryside, total output could be increased by finding industrial jobs for otherwise idle farm workers. Under these circumstances, it would have been socially irrational to force firms to restrict their employment to levels where the marginal product of labour equaled the wage. Output could have been expanded by breaking the link that capitalism imposes between the wage and the marginal product of labor. Giving firms high output targets and a soft budget constraint broke that link and was a source of growth in the Soviet Union in the 1930s.

The combination of ambitious output targets and soft budgets meant a great expansion of employment and a growing gap between the marginal product of labor and the wage rate. In 1928, the real wage was about 3200 rubles per year in 1937 prices,[8] while the marginal product of labor was 2750.[9] The marginal product fell quickly to about 1300 rubles per year and then rose slowly to 1650 rubles in 1939, while the real wage declined to 3000 rubles per year in 1937. As a result the marginal product fell from 85 percent of the wage in 1928 to about 50 percent in the 1930s.

To quantify the effect of high output targets and soft budget constraints on overall development, it is necessary to simulate the evolution of the economy with an alternative representation of firm behavior. The simplest alternative is the commonly used Harris–Todaro model of the labor market in less developed capitalist countries, which I will call the capitalist employment model. In this model, it is assumed that urban employers pay a high, exogenous wage. They adjust employment so that the marginal product of labor equals that wage. Rural-urban migration depends on the expected wage, that is, on the fixed wage multiplied by the probability of being employed. Migration continues until urban unemployment rises enough to reduce the expected urban wage to the rural wage.

The Harris–Todaro framework is incorporated into my simulations by fixing the wage rate at 3000 rubles per year in 1937 prices. (Higher values of the wage could be easily defended,[10] and they would produce even more extreme results.) Total wage income is then computed as 3000 rubles multiplied by the number of workers actually employed. Dividing total wage income by the urban population gives the expected wage, which is compared to rural per capita consumption and which drives migration.

One effect of a capitalist employment relation is high unemployment. In 1928, urban unemployment was about 10 percent of the labor force, and it fell to a negligible level during the First Five-Year Plan. In the capitalist employment simulations, however, unemployment rises to over a quarter of the nonagricultural labor force in the 1930s. Implicit in these simulations is a high level of job turnover, so everyone in the urban labor force works for three-fourths of the year and obtains enough income to eke out an existence better than that on the farm. In reality, if there were a capitalist labor market in the Soviet Union, turnover would probably have been less, and some sort of informal sector would have emerged to support the urbanites not employed in modern industry.

The soft budget constraint, therefore, accounts for many of the peculiar features of Soviet urbanization. Unlike capitalist Third World countries, there was little urban unemployment or underemployment and no informal sector. Instead of supporting himself or herself in petty retailing, the typical Soviet urbanite had a job in modern industry. Retailing was "underdeveloped" and industry was "overstaffed." An investment boom with a hard budget constraint produces Latin American-style urbanization.

Did the soft budget constraint promote or retard economic growth? Tables 8.1–8.4 show the simulated 1939 values of nonagricultural value added, the nonagricultural capital stock, GDP, and consumption per capita for the capitalist employment model. As with the collectivized and NEP economies, more investment in heavy industry results in more growth by all measures. What is most important about the simulations of the capitalist employment model, however, is the lower level of performance compared to the other two. At each value of e, performance is much worse. Indeed, with $e = .07$ (when the investment strategy simply replicates the structure of the capital stock on the eve of the First Five-Year Plan), growth is zero or negative on a per capita basis. Nonagricultural output and the capital stock grow 1.6 percent per year— the same as the population—and nonagricultural value added at only 0.7 percent. Consumption per head drops. Even with a high level of investment ($e = .23$), the capitalist employment model generates less growth in nonagricultural output, capital stock, or GDP than either the collectivized or NEP economy. Per capita consumption barely rises in this most favorable scenario. The NEP economy always performs much better than the capitalist economy. Thus, high output targets and the soft budget constraint were important in accelerating growth in the Soviet Union in the 1930s.

CONCLUSION

Tables 8.1–8.4 highlight those factors responsible for rapid Soviet development between 1928 and 1939. Two factors were of cardinal importance: the investment strategy emphasizing heavy industry, and the imposition of high output targets in conjunction with the soft budget constraint.

Consider the following thought experiment. We begin with the economy least like that of the Soviet Union in the 1930s, that is, with the capitalist employment relation and an investment strategy that simply replicates the consumer goods oriented capital stock of the 1920s (i.e., $e = .07$). That economy would generate a 1939 GDP of 240.6 — not much above the 1928 starting value of 200.9 and no increase on a per capita basis. Now let e rise to .23. In that case, 1939 GDP equals 290.3 — a jump of 21 percent. The strategy of investing in heavy industry pays off. Next replace the hard budget constraint with the soft budget constraint. Simulated GDP rises to 348.3 in 1939 — a further gain of 20 percent. The soft budget constraint also pays off. Finally, imagine that the free market relationship between agriculture and industry that characterized the NEP were replaced by the obligatory deliveries and state-imposed prices that characterized collectivization. Simulated GDP would again rise, but only to 364.6 — an additional gain of 5 percent. There is little payoff to collectivization. Since the simulated level of GDP is within 5 percent of the actual 1939 value of 344.9, the thought experiment shows that the investment strategy and the soft budget constraint comprise a complete explanation of Soviet growth — it is not necessary to invoke other factors to account for what happened.

Fairly similar conclusions obtain if the other tables are analyzed in the same way, although collectivization appears to be mildly more important when nonagricultural value added is the standard of assessment and downright counterproductive when consumption per head is the criterion for judging economic performance. As with GDP, collectivization gives only a tiny boost to capital accumulation.

These findings point toward three important conclusions about institutions and Soviet economic development. First, the NEP, which involved the preservation of peasant farming and a market relationship between town and country, was a conducive framework for rapid industrialization. Collectivization made little additional contribution to this system of organization. Second, the autarchic development of the producer goods sector was a viable source of new capital equipment. Exporting wheat and importing machinery — that is, following comparative advantage — was not necessary for rapid growth. Third, the central planning of firm output in conjunction with the soft budget constraint was effective in mobilizing otherwise unemployed labor. This additional employment made a significant contribution to output as well as distributing consumption widely.

On a more general level, the NEP already contained many socialist elements such as the public ownership of industry. The development of central planning and the soft budget constraint during the 1930s further shifted the economy toward socialism. These changes also accelerated the development of the productive forces because they led to greater employment in a labor surplus economy. Of course, this development strategy was the antithesis of the trade- and market-oriented policies advocated so often today.

While the development of socialism was conducive to economic growth in the Soviet Union during the 1930s, the barbaric policies of Stalinism added very little to industrial output. In particular, the collectivization of agriculture—perhaps the archetypical Stalinist policy and the one that resulted in the most avoidable death—made only a modest contribution to growth. Modifying the NEP to include central planning, high employment, and the expansion of heavy industry was a program for growth in capital, output, and per capita living standards. Adding collectivization to that recipe contributed little to growth and corrupted socialism.

CHAPTER NINE

Preobrazhensky in Action

In 1962, Alec Nove (1962, pp. 17–39) published a provocative essay, "Was Stalin Really Necessary?" Nove's answer was "yes" in the sense that rapid industrialization in a socialist state required collectivization. He agreed with Stalin that "an egalitarian land redistribution" like that after the 1917 revolution "strengthens the traditional subsistence sector," thereby "reducing the volume of marketable production, and sometimes of total production" (Nove 1990, p. 114). A system of compulsory sales at prices dictated by the state was the only way to guarantee the flow of cheap food to the cities. Discriminatory pricing, moreover, was necessary to finance industrialization. Finally, "rapid industrialization, especially with priority for heavy industry, meant a reduction in living standards, despite contrary promises in the first five-year plans" (Nove 1962, p. 24). Conflicts between the state and the peasants would necessarily be intense since the purpose of collectivization was to force the farm population to do the saving. Under these circumstances, dictatorship and coercion were inevitable.

Nove's essay sparked a vigorous debate in which revisionist historians—particularly, Barsov (1969), Millar (1970b, 1974), and Ellman (1975)—have called into question the economic premises of Nove's argument. There are two key elements to their critique. First, some farm produce was also sold in the collective farm market, where prices were not controlled and inflation was very high. As a result, the terms of trade actually shifted in agriculture's favor during the First Five-Year Plan, as we saw in Chapter 5. Second, in order for agricultural savings to contribute to nonagricultural investment, it was necessary for agriculture's sales to exceed its purchases. Indeed, the balance of trade equals agricultural savings supplied to the rest of the economy. While there is some debate between Barsov, Millar, and Ellman as to the correct measurement of the trade balance, they agree that it was inconsequentially small, if not zero. By this reading of the evidence, collectivization failed to generate the surplus that Preobrazhensky hoped for and that Nove presumed.

A search for new savers is a further theme of the revisionists. They agree that someone's consumption had to fall for investment to rise. Peasants were the obvious candidates when it was thought that they financed industrialization. However, real wages fell in the First Five-Year Plan, as we have seen, and the revisionists have pointed to that as proof that the workers were the real savers. Stalin may have imagined that he was squeezing the peasants to benefit the workers, but actually he was doing in the people he claimed to be supporting. The totalitarian school maintains that he knew the truth all along.

The results of the previous chapter suggest that these issues merit another look. The simulations showed that the collectivized economy really did grow faster than the alternatives analyzed. Did collectivization promote growth for the reasons advanced by Preobrazhensky and Nove, or were other factors at work? The simulations also showed that industrialization within the framework of the NEP would have been more successful than they had imagined, particularly compared to a high investment policy conducted with an industrial sector organized along capitalist lines. Perhaps Stalin was not really necessary after all?

While Barsov, Millar, and Ellman have greatly advanced our knowledge of Soviet development, they have gone too far in rejecting what Millar called the "standard story." I argue that in key respects, Soviet policy was, indeed, Preobrazhensky in action. However, I do think that, in a larger sense, the revisionists were right. The Preobazhensky policies, important as they were, were only one factor in play, and others were more important in explaining rapid economic development. The simulations of the previous chapter emphasized the importance of the investment strategy and soft budget constraint in accelerating growth. Collectivization, in that framework, played a small role. In this chapter, we extend the analysis and unpack collectivization. It included not only the pricing and budgetary policies proposed by Preobrazhensky but also state terrorism. Terror, rather than tinkering with the price system, explains the rapid growth of the collectivized economy in the simulations of the previous chapter. Stalin — in a most sinister sense — did accelerate growth in the 1930s, but he was not necessary for the slightly slower growth that would have been achievable if the Five-Year Plans had been carried out within the framework of the NEP.

CLEARING THE DECKS: COLLECTIVIZATION AND FARM OUTPUT

We will be considering ways in which collectivization *increased* the rate of economic growth. Before tackling those issues, it is important to assess the argument that collectivization *reduced* economic growth by lowering agricultural output. There are short-run and long-run versions of the argument.

The immediate effect of collectivization was to shrink the economy. Farm output dropped 29 percent between 1929 and 1932 as peasants stopped planting grain and slaughtered livestock rather than turn the animals over to the collectives. Factory-produced consumer goods fell due to shortages of agricultural inputs. These effects were highlighted in Chapter 5, and they account for the superior performance of the NEP economy during the mid-1930s. By the later 1930s, however, the production of the collective farms had rebounded and eliminated the advantage of the NEP.

In the longer term, it is claimed that the slaughtering of horses by peasants in the early 1930s required rapid mechanization to make up for the lost draft animals, and this diverted machinery from the creation of industrial capital. While tractor output soared, the significance of this fact is not entirely clear. Tractorization was planned anyway. Equipment investment in agriculture was only a small fraction of capital formation during the 1930s (Moorsteen and Powell 1966, pp. 358, 429). Furthermore, it is not obvious that the fall in horse numbers between 1930 and 1935 hurt grain production since the small farms of the NEP used many more horses per hectare than did large-scale grain farms, as shown in Chapter 4. Moreover, since a horse ate as much grain as two people, the fall in horse numbers freed enough grain to feed 30 million people, and that is one reason that per capita calorie consumption fell only slightly during the First Five-Year Plan (Figure 7.1). In the absence of much scope for raising grain yields—they were as high in the 1930s as those on the Great Plains of North America and there was no output raising technology in sight—reducing the grain fed to horses was the main way of increasing net output per hectare. It is worth noting that "farm draft animals consumed the output of roughly 22 percent of all cropland harvested [in the United States] over the 1880 to 1920 period" (Olmstead and Rhode 2001, pp. 664–65) and a similar loss was incurred in the Soviet Union.

In the long run, it is claimed that collectivization created a set of institutions inimical to productivity growth. This argument, whatever its merit, requires a longer time frame than the 1930s to be effective. Moreover, the claim is intrinsically dubious. The record of Soviet agriculture so far as the adoption of new techniques goes is not unimpressive; the level of yields and their rate of growth are on a par with those in environmentally comparable regions in North America, as is output per hectare generally (Johnson and Brooks 1983). Figure 4.1 compares the growth in wheat yields in the Soviet Union and North Dakota. Over the long term, the histories were identical. Yields were flat in both places until after World War II, when they advanced together as farmers in both countries increased their use of fertilizers at the same rate. There is no negative yield performance in the Soviet Union to attribute to collectivization.

Moreover, productivity growth in agriculture involves institutions besides farmers. Water control, for instance, involves public agencies that dam rivers and build irrigation systems; mechanization involves the industrial sector; and the invention of biological technology is generally performed by specialized research institutions that are usually socialized since the new knowledge is a public good. American examples include the Army Corps of Engineers that builds dams, John Deere that makes tractors, and the University of California that solved the viticultural problems of California wine industry. During the 1930s, agricultural development meant mechanization and irrigation, and the Soviets actively pursued those possibilities. Hence, it is not self-evident that the preservation of peasant farming in the Soviet Union would have led to more output or higher productivity.

The upshot of these considerations is that collectivization had an immediate negative impact on agricultural output in the early 1930s. This reduction in output lowered industrial production and GDP. Food production did not fall drastically since the drop in livestock numbers freed food for human consumption. (The famine was caused by the way the state distributed food rather than the total available.) By the late 1930s, farm production was restored. It is not clear that the performance of Soviet agriculture would have been any better in the rest of the twentieth century had it not been collectivized.

PREOBRAZHENSKY IN ACTION: THE STATE BUDGET

Against this background, we can explore why collectivization accelerated economic growth by the late 1930s. The place to begin is with Preobrazhensky's proposals. He advocated that the state cut the price it paid for grain and other farm products while raising the price it charged for consumer goods. This policy would generate the cash to pay for industrial investment at the expense of the peasantry.

The first place to look for evidence of this policy is in the state's finances. Indeed, Soviet taxation was reorganized in 1930 to make Preobrazhensky's proposals feasible (Holzman 1955; Fitzpatrick 1994). The main source of revenue became the "turnover tax," which was a manufacturers' sales tax imposed mainly on consumer goods. The cotton, grain, and meat sold by farmers to state procurement agencies were turned into cloth, bread, and sausages by the consumer goods industries. The turnover tax was added to their costs and prices. Higher investment required a higher turnover tax, which raised the price of consumer goods relative to the procurement price of farm products. The turnover tax became the administrative device that put Preobrazhensky's pricing policy into practice.

The turnover tax raised a lot of money. In 1937, retail purchases in shops of cloth, bread, sausage, and so forth amounted to 110 billion rubles (Table 9.1). It cost 17 billion rubles to convert the raw agricultural products into the processed food and fibre. The difference is 93 billion rubles (110 billion − 17 billion). Without the turnover tax (or some equally confiscatory device), this would have accrued to farmers as income. In the event, the turnover tax absorbed 76 of the 96 billion rubles, leaving only 17 billion rubles for farmers. This was what they received from procurement agencies for their compulsory sales and Machine Tractor Station (MTS) payments. In other words, the state took 82 percent of the 93 billion rubles of net income generated by consumer buying.

This was a lot of money relative to state expenditures. In 1937, all public agencies spent 118 billion rubles, which included 56 billion rubles of investment in fixed and circulating capital. The turnover tax thus financed all of the investment in the Soviet economy and 20 billion rubles of other spending as well. During the First Five-Year Plan, agricultural taxation amounted to only half of investment, but agricultural taxes and turnover tax receipts exceeded investment from 1933 on.[1] Agricultural taxation was involuntary savings, and it financed Stalin's industrial revolution during the Second and Third Five-Year Plans, if not the First. State finances were Preobrazhensky in action.

Preobrazhensky in Action: The Trade Surplus and the Agricultural Surplus

Did the turnover tax lead to a capital transfer from the country to the city and a decline in agriculture's terms of trade in accord with Preobrazhensky's model? The revisionist literature says no, but there are serious index number issues that must be addressed and their resolution has a strong bearing on the answer.

Table 9.1 sets out the relevant figures for 1928 and 1937. These include retail purchases, tax receipts, farm agricultural incomes, purchases, and allocations of capital equipment. Retail purchases in 1937 and their division into processing costs, turnover tax receipts, and payments to farmers have just been reviewed. In addition to the 17 billion rubles the farmers received on sales to state agencies, they earned 16 billion rubles on collective farm market sales, so their total cash income was 33 billion rubles.

To calculate agriculture's trade balance, we need to compare the sector's imports to its exports. On the assumption that farmers spent their entire cash incomes, their imports of consumer goods equaled 33 billion

TABLE 9.1

Sales and Purchases by Soviet Farmers, 1928 and 1937 (billions of rubles in current prices)

	1928	1937
Retail sales in shops	11.3	110
Less value added in processing	6.3	17
Net sales of agricultural goods	5.0	93
Less taxes	2.5	76
Farmers' sales to traders or state	2.5	17
Plus farmers' sales on free market	.8	16
Farm cash including purchases of manufactures	3.3	33
Plus farm equipment purchases	.6	2
Total farm imports	3.9	35

Sources:
1928:

retail sales: Bergson (1961, p. 46). Deduction of .8 from 12.1 billion in 1928 for farmers' sales on free market.

farmers' cash income: sale of agricultural goods (Hoeffding 1954, p. 14).

Farmers' sales on free market estimated as total marketings less procurements (Zaleski 1971, pp. 313–38; Jasny 1949, pp. 78–79, 228) multiplied by corresponding prices (Karcz 1979, p. 105; Barsov 1969). Farmers' sales to traders or state calculated as 3.3 less .8.

Taxes: excise taxes plus agricultural tax (Holzman 1955).

Net sales of agricultural goods: taxes plus farmers' sales to traders or state.

Value added in processing is a residual.

1937:

retail sales—Bergson (1961, p. 46).

agricultural machinery investment—Moorsteen and Powell (1966, p. 429).

turnover tax receipts, spending by public agencies, and investment—Bergson (1953, p. 20).

value added in processing—calculated as a residual.

rubles. In addition, 2 billion rubles of equipment were shipped to the farm sector by the state, so total imports were 35 billion rubles.

There are two ways to value exports, and they imply very different conclusions about agriculture's trade balance. The first is to value exports inclusive of the turnover tax. In that case, exports equaled 109 billion rubles (93 billion of net sales plus 16 billion on collective farm market sales), so agriculture had an export surplus of 74 billion rubles (= 109 − 35). This surplus exceeds total investment (56 billion rubles). By this reckoning, agriculture provided all the savings for economic development. Preobrazhensky would have been delighted.

This is not the revisionist conclusion, however, because they would read Table 9.1 in a different way. It is all a question of the value placed on farm sales, and in their work, Barsov, Millar, and Ellman value them at the prices farmers received, that is, exclusive of the turnover tax. This procedure implies that farm exports were worth 33 billion rubles (17 billion of receipts from state procurement agencies and 16 billion from collective farm market sales). With imports at 35 billion, agriculture had a small import surplus of two billion rubles. Thus, the revisionist conclusion that agriculture was not a source of capital for the rest of the economy, but a small drain.

One can always debate which prices to use in computing an index number. However, if you use the prices received by farmers, then you leave out of consideration the forced savings accomplished by taxation. Given that procedure, it is no wonder that Barsov, Millar, and Ellman concluded that agriculture was providing no savings to the rest of the economy. What their calculation measures is the voluntary savings of the peasants minus the cost of agricultural mechanization. Since the peasants were very poor, they did not save much, and that is what the calculations of Barsov, Millar, and Ellman establish. But this procedure misses the total contribution that agriculture made to savings.

The Incidence of the Turnover Tax

But was it really farmers who paid the tax? Putting a tax on bread might reduce the income of the farmer, but it might equally raise the price paid by the consumer. In the second case, it is the consumer who pays the tax. Did the turnover tax lower the income of peasants, or cut the real earnings of workers by increasing the prices of bread and clothing?

When a sales tax (like the turnover tax) is imposed, its burden does not depend on whether the buyer or the seller is the designated bearer. What matters is how the prices received by the buyer and the seller compare to the price in the alternative situation of no tax. The tax can be analyzed by imagining that either party paid the tax, and the implied changes in price will be the same.

Figure 9.1 diagrams the tax incidence problem.[2] Panel 1 shows the supply curve of farm marketings (S) and the urban demand for those products in 1928 (D_{28}). The intersection of those curves determines the level of marketings (M_{28}) and their price in 1928 (P_{28}). These are baseline values.

Panel 2 shows the situation in 1937. For simplicity, I show supply as unchanged. The investment boom, however, meant a large increase in urban demand to D_{37}. Were there no turnover tax, the price of agri-

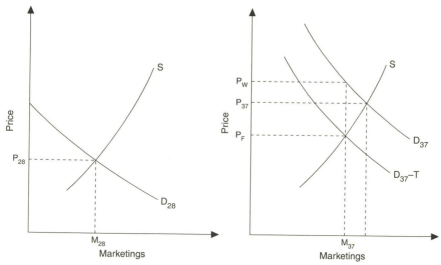

Fig. 9.1. The Effect of the Turnover Tax

cultural products would have risen to P_{37}. However, the turnover tax (T) was imposed, and it reduced the price received by farmers P_f to the price paid by urban consumers minus the tax ($P_w - T$). If we treat the turnover tax as being paid by consumers, its impact on farmers is represented in the diagram by a reduction in demand to $D_{37} - T$. Intersection of that curve with the supply curve determines the price received by farmers P_f, the level of marketings M_{37}, and the price paid by consumers P_w, which is the price on the urban demand curve corresponding to M_{37} and which equals P_f plus T.[3]

The prices P_f and P_w in Figure 9.2 correspond to the two ways of valuing farm sales, just discussed. Valuing sales at the net prices paid by consumers corresponds to using P_w in Figure 9.2, while valuing sales at the price received by farmers corresponds to using price P_f. The difference corresponds to the turnover tax.

In partial equilibrium analyses of tax incidence, the burden of the tax is determined by the price elasticities of supply and demand. In the model used here, the price elasticity of supply in 1930 was about .7, while the demand elasticity was 1. Those figures imply that the tax was shifted onto farmers as Stalin intended.

This conclusion is borne out by simulations, which take account of ramifications between sectors. The simulations with the collectivization model show that a rise in investment increased urban consumption and reduced peasant consumption. In contrast, the corresponding simulations with the NEP and capitalist models show constant ratios of farm and nonfarm consumption. These simulations confirm that it was, indeed, the peasants who bore the tax.

PREOBRAZHENSKY IN ACTION: THE TERMS OF TRADE AND AGRICULTURAL MARKETING

One important implication of the diagram relates to the calculation of agriculture's terms of trade during Stalin's industrial revolution. A major item in the revisionist case is the finding that the terms of trade improved. That is true, but Figure 9.2 calls its significance into question. The revisionist conclusion follows from comparing P_f to P_{28}. However, P_{37} was the price that would have obtained had the Stalinist procurement system not been imposed, and P_{37} was greatly in excess of P_f. P_w, the actual retail price, was even higher. The urban boom meant a huge growth in the demand for food, and it led to great inflation in urban markets. The Stalinist procurement system siphoned off much of that increase to finance investment, leaving the peasants with less income growth than they would have had otherwise. In that important sense, the revisionists have gone too far. Soviet price policy in the 1930s really was Preobrazhensky in action.

Table 9.1 contrasts the relationship of consumers and farmers in 1937 with their predecessors in 1928. While the numbers are fragile, they indicate the differential price movements. Between 1928 and 1937, retail sales rose from 11.3 billion to 110 billion rubles. The production of those goods required the purchase of farm goods worth 5 and 93 billion rubles, respectively. Over this period, the volume of goods sold to wholesalers, processors, and state procurement agencies rose by a factor of 2.09 in 1937 average prices. The net price paid by consumers on these sales rose by a factor of 8.9 ($= (93/5)/2.09$). It will be noted that the state appropriated much of this gain since excise and agricultural taxes rose from 2.5 billion to 76 billion rubles. Farm revenue on these sales, after tax, rose from 2.5 billion to 17 billion. Prices received by farmers rose by a factor of 3.3 ($= (17/2.5)/2.09$). Total farm incomes included direct sales to consumers in farmers' markets. Adding these to the other sales indicates that total cash income rose from 3.3 billion in 1928 to 32 billion in 1937. Dividing this gain by the factor by which total marketings grew implies that the average price received by farmers across all sales rose by a factor of 6.2 ($= (33/3.3)/1.62$) between 1928 and 1937.

Comparing these different measures of agricultural price inflation to the inflation in the price of manufactured consumer goods indicates the terms of trade arguments of the various schools. The price of manufactured goods increased by a factor of 4.22. This exceeded the 3.3 fold increase in the price paid by procurement agencies. If we only look at obligatory deliveries and MTS charges, agriculture's terms of trade declined. That is the "standard story" of collectivization.

The insight of Barsov and the other revisionists is that sales in farmers' markets must also be included. The average price increase across all marketing categories was 6.2 fold. This exceeded the inflation in manufactured goods (4.22) and establishes the revisionists' case that the terms of trade of agriculture were improving.

There is a third comparison, however, and that is with the price that farmers would have gotten if the state had not intervened between them and the consumer. Without turnover and agricultural taxes, farm prices would have risen by a factor of 8.9. The state took most of the gain that the farmers might otherwise have gotten, and that was Preobrazhensky's idea.

Farm Marketing

Collective farms led to a much higher level of farm marketing than would have obtained under the NEP in the early 1930s, but by the end of the decade, the difference between the two systems would not have been great. The agricultural collapse of the early 1930s meant that agricultural production under collectivization remained less than it would have been had the NEP continued throughout the decade. However, collective farms marketed a higher fraction of their crop. Extrarural sales were higher with a system of collective farms for most of the 1930s, but by the end of the decade, the NEP would have caught up. These sales were part of the capital transfer from agriculture to industry.

The marketing advantage of the collective farm system was not necessary for economic growth, however. Industrialization, NEP-style, would have been somewhat less intense and cities would have grown less rapidly, so the urban demand for food would have been less. While peasants would have retained a larger fraction of their output, sales to the cities would have been adequate for the considerable growth that would have taken place. Had the NEP continued, livestock products would have constituted a larger fraction of farm output, and that implies differences in marketing channels. My simulations of the NEP, indeed, show a higher level of sales on farmers' markets (where livestock products were mainly sold in the 1930s) and a correspondingly reduced sale of agricultural goods to industry, a point noted in the previous section. Thus, the continuation of the NEP would have implied smaller manufactured consumer goods industries in the 1930s, but a larger provision of fresh food. In the event, urban consumption per capita from both sources combined would have been higher under a continuation of the NEP.[4]

Were There Savers?

One thing on which Nove and his critics agree is that someone had to save to make Stalin's industrial revolution possible. Nove thought it was the peasants, while the revisionists speculate it was urban workers. While consumption by both peasants and city dwellers fell at the end of the First Five-Year Plan, it recovered by the late 1930s, and average consumption was a fifth higher than in 1928. With a rising trend like this, it is hard to say that consumption was being cut back to increase investment.

Moreover, there is no evidence that consumer goods output was being reduced in order to free up resources to expand the metal working, machinery, and construction industries. On the contrary, employment grew in the consumer goods industries. Kahan's (1959) estimates of Soviet agricultural labor show that the number of days worked in 1933 was 2 percent above the 1926–29 average. From 1934 to 1938, employment increased to 8–14 percent above the 1926–29 level. The labor that left the countryside was surplus to the needs of agriculture.

Employment also increased in the consumer goods industries, the most important of which were processing farm products. In textiles, for instance, employment rose from 1.9 million in 1927–28 to 2 million in 1933 to 2.6 million in 1937. In food and allied products, the corresponding figures were .8 million in 1927/8, 1.1 million 1933, and 1.5 million in 1937 (Nutter 1962, pp. 501–2). There is no evidence of resource reallocation from agriculture — or consumer goods generally — to the production of investment goods.

The main reasons for believing that resources were being redeployed from consumer goods to producer goods were the famine of 1932–33 and the drop in urban real wages at the same time. However, these developments were due to the collapse of agricultural output in the immediate aftermath of collectivization. As a result, free market food prices shot up (lowering urban real wages) and there was a famine in grain-growing areas. Death by starvation, however, is not resource reallocation. The fall in consumption in the early 1930s reflects a disastrous agricultural policy rather than a transfer of productive farm workers to city jobs.

There are two reasons why it was not necessary to lower consumption below the 1928 level in order to raise investment during the early Five-Year Plans. The first is the Keynesian observation that investment and consumption can be increased concurrently by giving jobs to unemployed workers. Mobilizing peasant labor was a key to Stalin's industrial revolution. The second reason is made clear by the Fel'dman model. The choice between consuming or investing producer goods output (bicycles versus machine tools) had an immediate impact on the level of consumption, of course, and, thus, posed a trade-off. However, the choice between allocating the investment goods between the consumer goods and producer goods industries had no immediate impact on consumption (although it affected the possibilities in future years). By increasing the fraction of investment goods going into the producer goods sector, investment could be increased without reducing consumption. This argument was illustrated by Figure 3.3.

Mobilizing the Labor Surplus

Soviet policy in the 1930s followed the Preobrazhensky blueprint in many respects: the investment boom was financed by taxing farm products, there was a capital transfer from agriculture to industry, the procurement system siphoned off consumer purchasing power rather than passing it on to farmers. But none of these changes, in themselves, resulted in steel mills or textile factories. An alchemy was required to change the grain amassed by the state into industrial plant and equipment. That alchemy was rural-urban migration. It created the industrial workforce that built the industrial capacity.

The most important effect of collectivization was to increase the rate of rural-urban migration. It, indeed, was exceptionally high during the 1930s. Between 1928 and 1939, the urban population increased from about 28 million to 55 million. 84 percent of this increase was due to rural-urban migration—an exceptionally large proportion (Lorimer 1946, pp. 147–50). During the 1930s, rural-urban migration rates averaged close to 2 percent per year (Lorimer 1946, p. 150; Eason 1963, p. 72), again a very high rate in comparison to developing countries in recent decades. Moreover, the new arrivals were employed in construction and large-scale industry, where they produced the machinery and structures needed to build a modern economy. To the degree that collectivization accelerated rural-urban migration, it contributed to industrialization by swelling the urban labor force.

Table 9.2 contrasts the simulated histories of the rural and urban populations under collectivization and NEP-style institutions. The differences are remarkable. Under collectivization, the rural population fell absolutely, especially during the famine. The urban population increased from 28 million in 1928 to 58.5 million in 1939, a growth close to the actual (cf. Table 5.5). Had rapid industrialization been undertaken within the framework of the NEP, the rural population would have expanded by about 11 million between 1928 and 1939, while the urban population would have grown from 28 million to 44 million. The growth in the industrial labor force—compared to the experience under

TABLE 9.2
The Urban Transition, Actual and Simulations (millions of people)

	Actual		Simulated collectivized		Simulated NEP-style	
	Urban	Rural	Urban	Rural	Urban	Rural
1928	28.1	121.9	28.1	121.9	28.1	121.9
1929	29.5	123.2	29.5	123.3	29.5	123.2
1930	31.2	123.6	30.3	124.6	30.8	124.5
1931	34.2	122.5	32.0	124.7	32.2	125.6
1932	38.6	119.4	33.8	124.3	33.3	126.7
1933	41.6	116.4	36.8	121.3	34.6	127.4
1934	42.7	116.3	42.3	116.8	36.0	127.8
1935	45.4	114.4	47.0	112.9	37.5	127.8
1936	48.2	112.8	50.8	110.3	39.0	127.9
1937	50.2	112.8	53.3	109.7	40.6	128.7
1938	52.4	113.8	56.2	110.1	42.6	130.2
1939	54.7	114.8	59.4	110.1	44.5	131.7

collectivization—would have been reduced accordingly. In 1939, the simulated nonagricultural labor force (including soldiers and inmates of forced labor camps) was 40 million with collectivization and would have been 30 million under a continuation of the NEP. The rapid urbanization that would have occurred had the investment rate been pushed up within the context of the NEP was significant and accounts for its development potential; the advantage that collectivization had over the NEP reflects the additional urbanization it would have entailed.

Collectivization increased rural-urban migration for two reasons: the income gain from migrating was greater than it would have been had the NEP continued (especially during the early 1930s), and the probability of migrating at any income differential was higher due to Stalinist terror, which included forced relocations, the expropriation of peasant property, and the attacks on traditional religion, culture, and rural values (Fitzpatrick 1994; Viola 1996). Farm mechanization also played a role. The future lay in the cities; the peasants knew it, and so they moved.

It is remarkable that terrorism explains most of the advantage that collectivization had over the NEP. We can see this by simulating growth under "peaceful collectivization." Suppose that the peasants really had wanted collective farms, so they did not resist collectivization. In that case, there would have been no slaughter of livestock, no reduction in sowing, no war with the state, and no famine. We can remove these elements from our model of collectivization, so that the collectivized economy is identical to the NEP economy except for the differences in marketing and taxation. Simulations with the model of peaceful collectivization show the trajectory of the Soviet economy if collectivization had proceeded without conflict.

One might have expected that peaceful collectivization would have resulted in more economic growth since the agricultural collapse would have been avoided, but that is true only briefly. By 1939, nonagricultural value added would have reached only 212 billion rubles with peaceful collectivization, and the capital stock would have accumulated to only 325 billion. These values are midway between those for the NEP simulations and the collectivized simulations shown in Tables 8.1 and 8.2. Thus, peaceful collectivization added very little to the growth possibilities of the NEP, and was, indeed, inferior to forced collectivization. In other words, collectivization pushed up the rate of industrialization because it produced a social catastrophe in the countryside, not in spite of it.

How could disaster be good for growth? The answer is simple: forced collectivization drove people from the countryside and put them to work in industry. With peaceful collectivization, the urban population would have only reached 48 million in 1939 instead of 58.5 million with forced collectivization, and the industrial workforce would have only been 33 million instead of 40 million. Collectivization raised economic growth above the NEP rate by accelerating rural-urban migration.

But both of these systems of organization would have grown faster than an economy of capitalist firms in the industrial sector. Why? The answer is not rural-urban migration, for the simulated trajectories of rural and urban population are very close for the NEP and capitalist economies. The difference between the two lies in the level of urban employment (Table 9.3). Soft budget constraints meant that everyone in the labor force got a job in the NEP simulations while about one-quarter of them remain unemployed in the simulations with the capitalist employment relationship. The marginal product of these extra workers was low, as we noted in the previous chapter, but it was positive, and they made a significant contribution to increasing output and investment.

There were thus two sides to mobilizing the surplus agricultural population. The first was increasing the rate of rural-urban migration, so the rural unemployed would be available for industrial work. The second was providing them with jobs. Soft budget constraints meant that the NEP and the collectivized economy performed the second function better than the capitalist economy, and, therefore, had an edge in output, consumption, and investment. The terrorism of collectivization meant that the collectivized economy performed the first task better than a continuation of the NEP and accounts for the marginally superior results of the collectivized economy.

TABLE 9.3
Simulated Urban/Industrial Employment (millions of people)

	Collectivized	Peaceful collectivized	NEP-style	Capitalist
1928	12.3	12.3	12.3	12.3
1929	16.1	16.1	16.0	12.1
1930	18.1	18.1	18.1	14.1
1931	20.9	20.3	20.4	14.5
1932	22.2	21.0	21.2	14.9
1933	24.0	21.9	22.1	15.3
1934	25.4	22.2	22.5	15.8
1935	27.0	22.9	23.2	16.4
1936	29.0	24.0	24.2	17.1
1937	34.7	28.2	27.8	18.3
1938	37.7	30.7	30.0	18.7
1939	39.8	33.3	30.8	18.6

CONCLUSION

The concept of labor mobilization unites the various aspects of the collectivization debate. Insufficient capital was a fundamental cause of the backwardness of the Soviet economy in the 1920s, and converting peasants to masons and machinists was a solution to that problem. Nurske's (1953) model of accumulation through the redeployment of surplus farm labor provides a good interpretation of the process. The advantage that collectivization, particularly forced collectivization, had over other policies was that it maximized the rate of rural-urban migration. Requiring farmers to sell their crops to state agencies guaranteed that the new urban workers would be fed. Those sales of food can be regarded as a capital transfer if the accounts are done in the right way. That was Preobrazhensky's logic, and it worked.

But this chapter also illuminates why the NEP was also a feasible system for economic development. Farm marketings would have been almost as great under the NEP as they were with collectivization. Rural-urban migration would also have been substantial. The simulations of the NEP economy assume soft budget constraints and they give the NEP a strong advantage over the capitalist economy in terms of urban/industrial job creation. A high rate of job creation would have contributed to economic success had industrialization been undertaken within the framework of the NEP.

PART THREE

After Stalin

CHAPTER TEN

The Soviet Climacteric

The human and material losses of the Second World War were enormous for the USSR. Both GDP and population fell by almost one-fifth.[1] GDP did not recover to the preinvasion level until 1948. Close to a decade of economic growth had been lost.

The mid-1950s saw a resumption of the prewar growth trajectory, as the Fel'dman strategy of increasing the size of the producer goods sector was pursued with renewed vigor. The investment share was pushed from 22 percent of GDP in 1950 to about 39 percent in 1980.[2] Although the share of household consumption in GDP slipped from 60 percent to 54 percent, the economy expanded so much that total consumption increased by a factor of 3.5 and consumption per head grew by 2.9 percent per year.[3] While an American lifestyle remained a distant dream, the improvement was substantial, and most people reached a standard of living considerably above that of workers and peasants in many less developed countries. The Fel'dman strategy continued to pay off.

Growth began to slow in the 1960s, and success turned to failure after 1970, when the growth rate dropped dramatically. GNP grew in excess of 5 percent per year from 1928 to 1970, but the annual rate dropped to 3.7 percent in 1970–75, then to 2.6 percent in 1975–80, finally hitting 2.0 percent in 1980–85 (Table 10.1). The rapid growth before 1970 was due to exceptional growth of the capital stock, a big increase in employment (especially in the 1930s), and some expansion of the cultivated acreage. Productivity grew at a rate like that of the East Asian economies during their boom. Indeed, the sources of high-speed growth in the USSR look much like those of South Korea or Taiwan (Young 1995).

The growth slowdown was the result of deterioration in all sources of growth. Employment growth plummeted, and there was a reduction in land under cultivation. The growth of the capital stock declined, although it still grew faster than the other inputs. The slowdown in accumulation was not due to a drop in the investment rate, which continued to rise, but to the decline in GDP growth. Most dramatically, total factor productivity (TFP) growth went negative.

Why did the economy, which grew so rapidly from the 1920s into the

TABLE 10.1
Inputs, Output, and Productivity, 1928–85

	1928–40	1950–60	1960–70	1970–75	1975–80	1980–85
GNP	5.8	5.7	5.2	3.7	2.6	2.0
Labor	3.3	1.2	1.7	1.7	1.2	.7
Capital	9.0	9.5	8.0	7.9	6.8	6.3
Land	1.6	3.3	.2	1.0	−.1	−.1
Total inputs	4.0	4.0	3.7	3.7	3.0	2.5
Productivity	1.7	1.6	1.5	0.0	−.4	−.5

Source: Ofer (1987, pp. 1778–79).
Note: To emphasize the long-run trends, the figures for the 1940s have been omitted. Growth rates in that decade were very low due to World War II.

1960s, perform so badly in the 1970s and the 1980s? The question is approached by most observers, both East and West, in terms of a standard paradigm — that of extensive and intensive growth. From the 1920s to the 1960s, the essential tasks were mobilizing unemployed farm workers and providing them with capital. Stalin's institutions were well suited to that purpose. However, once the deficiency of capital was rectified and full employment was achieved, the economic problem changed to one of increasing output from the available resources. Stalin's institutions proved inimical to technological progress, and the economy stagnated.

This paradigm has been used by many Western scholars, including Amann and Cooper (1986, p. 1) in their authoritative assessment of Soviet technology: "A successful transition has not yet been made from the stage of 'extensive development' to one of 'intensive development.'" Why not? "At the heart of the problem is the failure of the central planning mechanism, which took shape in the 1930s under Stalin's political direction, to promote rapid technical progress." President Gorbachev (1987, pp. 20, 28, 39, 46) used the same paradigm in explaining the "declining rates of growth and economic stagnation." Central planning was created "to build up industry, especially heavy industry and the power and machine-building industries, from scratch." The system was successful. However, "the management system which took shape in the thirties and forties began gradually to contradict the demands and conditions of economic progress. . . . It became more and more of a hindrance, and gave rise to the braking mechanism which did us so much harm later." Central planning needed to be replaced by a management system whose "emphasis has been shifted from new construction to the technical retooling of enterprises, to saving the resources, and sharply raising the quality of output." In Gorbachev's thinking, technological progress had replaced resource mobilization as the basic problem.

Gorbachev's analysis leaves many issues to explore. The first is the changing context of policy formation. Gorbachev, essentially, argued that central planning was appropriate for the surplus labor economy of the 1930s but became inappropriate once full employment was achieved. Was the end of surplus labor really sufficient to explain the growth slowdown? Several prominent economists have investigated this possibility and concluded the answer was "yes," and I begin with their analysis. In the limit, this research implies that the Soviet climacteric was inevitable but reflected no errors in policy or failures of economic institutions. This conclusion goes too far, however, and I investigate alternative explanations for why the Soviets failed to increase output more rapidly in the 1970s. The possibilities include errors in investment, the depletion of natural resources, inadequate incentives for firms to minimize costs, and failures in research and development. I argue that it was no coincidence that the growth slowdown followed the end of surplus labor and the full exploitation of the natural resources of European Russia. The new era posed new challenges, and the Soviet leadership failed to meet them. Errors in investment policy led to the waste of capital on a grand scale. The result was rapid input growth, little output growth, and falling productivity. International developments also contributed to the productivity decline. The arms race with the United States diverted R&D resources from the civilian economy to the military and cut the rate of technical progress.

THE END OF LABOR SURPLUS

Rapid growth in the 1930s was based on expanding the industrial sector by mobilizing labor that would otherwise have been unemployed. The theoretical counterpart was Fel'dman's assumption that capital was the only limiting factor in production. This assumption was substantially true through the 1950s but became increasingly unrealistic thereafter. The end of freely available labor meant that capital accumulation ran into diminishing returns: while output had grown as rapidly as capital in the surplus labor phase, it grew less rapidly—and increasingly so—once labor became a scarce resource. As a result, capital accumulation lost potency as a source of growth. This process was explored theoretically in the famous Solow (1956)–Swan (1956) one-sector growth model, and its implications for Soviet history will be considered shortly.

A key empirical question is how abruptly diminishing returns cut the impact of capital accumulation on output growth. This issue was first explored by Weitzman (1970) in a revolutionary analysis of the declining Soviet growth rate. While growth was still very rapid when Weitzman wrote, the slowdown had begun, and most analysts attributed the slackening to a declining rate of productivity growth as in Table 10.1. This, in turn, was attributed to deficiencies in the planning system, incentive problems, and so forth.

The TFP measures in Table 10.1 assume constant shares for the inputs, and, thus, implicitly assume that the production function was Cobb-Douglas. In this case, if the wage of labor rises one percent with respect to the price of capital, firms respond by cutting their use of labor relative to capital by one percent. The reduction in the quantity of labor exactly offsets the rise in its price—conversely for capital—thus preserving constant shares. With the Cobb-Douglas function, the "elasticity of substitution"—the relative change in the capital-labor ratio induced by a one percent change in their relative price—equals one. In contrast, the elasticity of substitution would be zero if production technology were wholly inflexible, so that a change in relative factor prices induced no change in the capital-labor ratio. Values between zero and one are possible, as are values greater than one.

Weitzman (1970) called the reality of the productivity decline into question by estimating a production function for the USSR. He concluded that the Cobb-Douglas specification was incorrect, and that the Soviet experience was better represented by a constant elasticity of substitution (CES) function with an elasticity of substitution between capital and labor of .4. This revision in the production model leads to a radically different explanation of the growth slowdown. The problem is no longer a cessation of technical progress but rather the end of surplus labor. The growth slowdown, in other words, does not indicate poor institutional performance. Easterly and Fischer (1995) have redone the econometrics with more recent data and confirmed the elasticity of substitution. They have been reluctant to exonerate Soviet institutions, however.

One attractive feature of the Weitzman–Easterly–Fischer approach is that it can be extended to provide an integrated account of both the success and failure of the Soviet economy. Figure 10.1 is a diagram that tells the story of Soviet history in a simplified form. The depiction is starker than Weitzman's because the isoquants assume fixed proportions—an elasticity of substitution of zero rather than .4—but the logic is more clearly revealed. In this framework, a rise in the investment rate caused rapid growth in the 1930s and 1940s as surplus labor was put to work. By the 1950s, structural unemployment was eliminated and growth slowed as capital accumulation ran into diminishing returns.

The diagram presupposes that fixed quantities of capital and labor are required to produce a unit of GDP as indicated by point Y_1. These

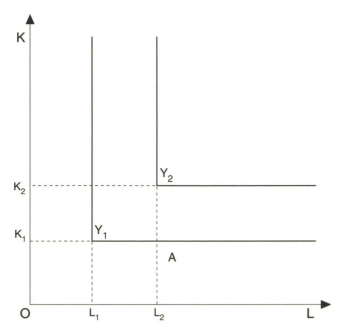

Fig. 10.1. Weitzman Growth Model

proportions are preserved along the diagonal OY_2. More labor (L_2) or capital (K_2) yields no extra output so long as the quantity of the other is fixed. Constant returns to scale is assumed so that doubling the capital (from K_1 to K_2) and labor (from L_1 to L_2) doubles output (from Y_1 to Y_2).

In 1928 the Soviet Union was at a point like A. Output was limited to one unit (Y_1) by the available capital (K_1) and L_2–L_1 units of labor were in surplus. In this case, accumulating capital increased output by moving the economy upward along a vertical line from A to Y_2; indeed, in this period output and capital grew at the same rate.[4] Surplus labor was correspondingly reduced. This shift corresponds to the 1928–70 period, when the USSR grew rapidly by accumulating capital.

The era of high-speed growth ended, however, when the economy reached Y_2, and surplus labor was exhausted. Thereafter, capital accumulation failed to generate growth. As the economy accumulated capital it moved upward along the vertical part of the isoquant, where capital was in surplus and labor constrained production. In that case, output failed to grow. Indeed, there was a quick transition from fast growth to stagnation. In real time, the transition occurred in the late 1960s and early 1970s. One indicator of the change is unfilled vacancies on the first shift, which rose from one percent in 1960, to 4.9 percent in

1970, to 7.3 percent in 1975, then to 9.9 percent in 1980, and finally hit 12.2 percent in 1985 (Rumer 1989, pp. 199–200). In the 1970s, a Gosplan research director reported that 10–12 percent of the increment in real fixed capital was unutilized due to a shortage of labor (Rumer 1989, p. 202), and that proportion could only have increased in the 1980s. The capital stock rose without a corresponding rise in GDP because there was no labor to operate the new capacity.

Weitzman's statistical results support this story in a nuanced fashion. With an elasticity of substitution of .4, the isoquant has a curved corner rather than a right angle. As a result, the growth slowdown takes a decade or two rather than occurring instantaneously. History is more accurately replicated, but the underlying logic is the same as shown in Figure 10.1.

To see how Weitzman's statistical results imply rapid growth followed by an abrupt slowdown, we can embed his production function in a Solow (1956)–Swan (1956) growth model: GDP is a function of the capital stock and labor force, an exogenously given fraction of output is invested, and capital grows as the stock in one year is increased by investment and reduced by depreciation. Production is computed from a CES production function:

$$Y_t = A(hK_t^{-p} + (1 - h)L_t^{-p})^{-1/p} \qquad (1)$$

where Y_t is GDP in year t, K_t is the capital stock, and L_t is the labor, which is assumed equal to the population and to grow at its historical rate. The parameter values are those estimated by Weitzman: $h = .639$, and $p = 1.481389$ implied by an elasticity of substitution of .403. The constant A is chosen to make Y equal its historical value in 1928.

Investment is computed by multiplying GDP (Y_t as given by equation 1) by the historical series of investment rates (s_t):

$$I_t = s_t Y_t \qquad (2)$$

The capital stock is cumulated from investment according to the equation:

$$K_t = (1 - d)K_{t-1} + I_t \qquad (3)$$

where d is the depreciation rate applied to the capital stock in the previous year.

The data for this exercise are derived from Maddison (1995).[5] The Second World War is dealt with in a highly stylized way, namely, by leaving it out: GDP was similar in 1940 and 1948, so the intervening years were omitted, and the capital stock in 1940 was carried over to 1948. The population in the 1930s was interpolated between 1928 and 1948.

The Soviet GDP, labor, and capital stock series imply a plausible productivity history when they are analyzed in the standard Cobb-Douglas

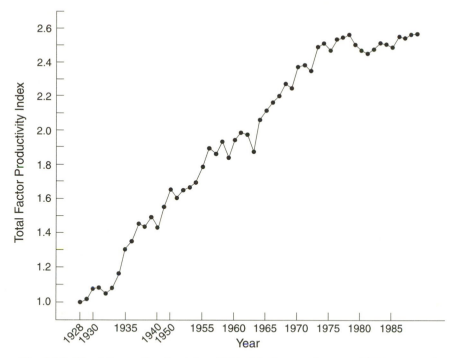

Fig. 10.2. Total Factor Productivity, 1928–89. *Source*: See text. TFP computed with a Cobb-Douglas production function with an employment share of 75 percent and a capital share of 25 percent.

framework. Figure 10.2 shows that TFP growth was negligible during the First Five-Year Plan but rose rapidly in the rest of the 1930s as projects started in the late 1920s were brought to completion. Productivity continued growing until about the 1970s, when progress ceased. The rates of growth in the postwar period are close to those in Table 10.1, but the rate of productivity growth in the 1930s is higher than Table 10.1 because labor was measured by the population, which grew less rapidly than employment as jobs were created for the structurally unemployed. The reconstructed series are consistent with a conventional account of the growth slowdown that emphasizes the falloff in productivity growth.

Figure 10.3 contrasts the actual history of real GDP per head in the Soviet Union between 1928 and 1989 with the series implied by equations 1–3. The correspondence is remarkably close: The series are within 10 percent of each other in 1989 despite the simplicity of the model and the cavalier treatment of the Second World War. The simulation mimics the remarkably fast growth of the Stalinist period and the growth slowdown of the final decades of Soviet power. The import of

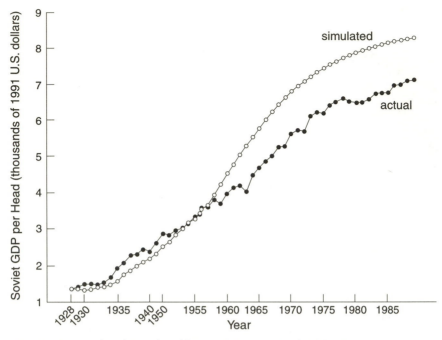

Fig. 10.3. Actual and Simulated Soviet GDP per Head, 1928–89

the simulation is that these facts can be entirely explained by the logic of capital accumulation under the assumption of a low elasticity of substitution between capital and labor.

Figure 10.4 shows why the model captures the main lines of Soviet history. The diagram shows the unit isoquant implied by the Weitzman-style production function. The sharp corner is apparent. In 1928 the Soviet Union was at the right end of the isoquant, with little capital and lots of labor. One percent more capital increased output by .93 percent, while one percent more labor increased it by only .07 percent. These fractions come close to the assumptions of the Fel'dman model—namely, that more labor would generate no growth, while a one percent increase in capital would raise output by the same amount—and that is why its policy prescriptions worked. The Soviet Union moved to the left as accumulation proceeded. The dates at which the economy reached various points are shown in the figure, and it passed the corner in the 1960s as growth began to decelerate. With surplus labor gone, more workers could increase output as could more capital, and, indeed, labor was the greater constraint on output since one percent more labor raised output by .8 percent, while one percent more capital increased it by only

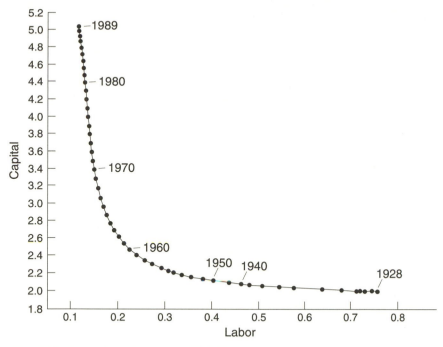

Fig. 10.4. Soviet Unit Isoquant, 1928–89

.2%. The economy no longer corresponded to the assumptions of the Fel'dman model, so the accumulation strategy it implied no longer brought rising prosperity.

DIMINISHING RETURNS TO CAPITAL: CAN WE BELIEVE IT?

Weitzman's explanation is very elegant. It complements the account of rapid development given earlier in this book by advancing one mechanism by which the elimination of surplus labor would cut the rate of growth. But is a low elasticity of substitution really the explanation for the Soviet climacteric?

Weitzman's theory is hard to credit when seen in international perspective. Japan is an important contrast. It may have been even more devastated than the Soviet Union in 1945, and its recovery in the late 1940s was slower. In 1950, GDP per head was $2834 in the USSR and $1873 in Japan. By that time the Soviets had already raised their investment rate to 22 percent — higher than levels in the 1930s — and the Japanese rate was 17 percent. Both countries grew by pushing their investment rates even higher, reaching 35 percent and 38 percent, respectively, in 1989.

With similar investment histories, one would expect similar growth performance if the Weitzman model were the full story. But the growth histories were very different. While output per head flagged in the USSR, it surged upward in Japan and reached a western European level in 1989 ($17,757 in Japan versus $7078 in the USSR). While the capital stock per head was also lower in Japan in 1950, that too quickly surpassed the Soviet level, reaching a value almost twice that of the USSR in 1989.[6] If the Weitzman story had applied in Japan, then growth should have been chocked off as the capital-labor ratio rose. Why was Japan so different?

One difference was in the elasticity of substitution. Weitzman's econometrics imply a value of .403 for Soviet industry, and this value was confirmed by Easterly and Fischer (1995, p. 357) for the whole economy. But .4 is an unusually low value. Evidence for Japan and other advanced capitalist economies suggests a value of 1.0 or even greater (Easterly and Fischer 1995, pp. 359–61; Duffy and Papageorgiou 2000). While simulations using an elasticity of substitution of .403 imply a growth slowdown, simulations with a value of 1.0 do not: with more substitutability between capital and labor, diminishing returns to capital are not substantial enough to cause stagnation, and this is why a high investment rate paid off in Japan but not in the USSR. But why was the elasticity of substitution so low in the Soviet Union? Why was it only the USSR that failed to translate high investment in the 1970s and 1980s into greater output?[7]

Investment Policy and Productivity Slowdown

Weitzman and Easterly and Fischer speculate on reasons why the elasticity of substitution might have been lower in the USSR than elsewhere without coming to firm conclusions. This is good, for, I argue, the value of .4 is an illusion. The low measured value of the elasticity reflects massive errors in Soviet investment strategy rather than a real difference in technology. It was not purely happenstance that these errors occurred in the 1970s and 1980s, for the end of the surplus labor economy posed new management problems, and the party leadership bungled them.

The 1960s saw two changes in investment policy that were highly deleterious. First, investment shifted from the construction of new manufacturing facilities to the modernization of old ones. Second, the depletion of old oil fields and mining districts led to a redirection of investment from Europe to Siberia. Both changes involved huge expenditures, and these accumulated into a rapid growth in the capital stock shown in

Table 10.1. However, the massive accumulation did not lead to more output since the investment was largely wasted.

Under this circumstance, standard econometric techniques give misleading results when applied to Soviet data. Fitting production functions to the inputs and outputs of capitalist firms is justified by the assumption that they minimize costs, so that the observed data are efficient input choices and lie on the firms' isoquants. The assumption of cost minimization did not obtain for the Soviet Union, however. When output per unit of capital and labor in the USSR are plotted as in Figure 10.4, the result is a sharp vertical movement in what appears to be an isoquant. In terms of the post-1970 aggregate data shown in Table 10.1, there is the rapid growth of the capital stock in conjunction with small growth in employment and GDP. Fitting a production function to the data indicates a low elasticity of substitution. This result should be regarded as spurious, however. Whatever the "true" isoquant, the data do not reveal it; instead, they are accounted for by a massive misallocation of investment.

We can get at the role of investment policy by examining input and output growth at the industry level, where there was considerable variation in behavior. Table 10.2 shows total factor productivity growth for major industries. The average TFP growth of these industries shows roughly the same decline as the aggregate Soviet data in Table 10.1, but the average encompasses some satisfactory performances and some disasters. Generally, the industries with good productivity records had capital-output ratios that were fairly stable. In electricity generation, for instance, output increased by a factor of 2.3 from 1965 to 1975, while the capital stock grew 2.2 times. From 1975 to 1985, output increased 1.5 times, while the capital stock grew by 1.7 times. In contrast, industries with poor productivity records showed large increases in the capital stock without reductions in employment or increases in output. In ferrous metals, for instance, the capital stock went up by 67 percent between 1975 and 1985, while employment rose 9 percent, and output grew by only 10 percent. As a result, total factor productivity dropped 11 percent. How could so much capital be poured into the iron and steel industry with such a scant increase in output and no saving of labor?

Two factors explain the difference between steel and electricity. One was the degree of reconstruction investment undertaken: the industries with high levels of reconstruction investment exhibited big increases in capital with little increase in output and, consequently, falling productivity. In 1970, for instance, 20 percent of the investment in electricity generation went to "technical reequipping, reconstruction, and expansion of existing production," while the proportion in ferrous metals was

TABLE 10.2
Productivity Growth (TFP) by Industry, 1965–85 (percentages)

	1965–75	1975–85
Moderately successful		
Gas	30	49
Electricity	30	8
Chemicals	26	10
Poor		
Machine building	20	−1
Construction materials	15	−3
Light industry	12	3
Food	12	−7
Other	−3	2
Disasters		
Coal	7	−24
Oil	35	−21
Ferrous metals	14	−11
Overall	18	−1

Sources:
TFP computed as output divided by a weighted geometric average of the real capital stock (30%) and employment (70%).

Output: CIA's output indices for all industries except coal, oil, and gas where physical output indicators were used. U.S. Congress, Joint Economic Committee (1982, pp. 63–64, 231) and U.S. Central Intelligence Agency (1986, pp. 134, 138, 139; 1987, p. 71).

Employment: *Trud v SSSR: Statisticheskii Sbornik*, 1988, pp. 49–50.

Capital: cumulated from investment. *Narodnoe Khoziaristvo*, 1985, p. 48, reports the capital stock for industry as a whole in 1973 rubles for 1965 and odd years in the 1970s and 1980s. Annual investment for all industry and for the various branches in 1973 rubles were found in *Narodnoe Khoziaristvo*, 1975, p. 508; 1980, p. 338; 1985, p. 368. The last was in 1982 rubles, and those series were used to extend the earlier ones through 1985. The first step was to replicate the capital stock for all industry from the investment data and the 1965 stock value by adding investment and deducting depreciation each year. A search for the implicit depreciation rate showed that a value of 2.1 percent allowed a close reconstruction of the later published capital stock figures. The second step was to determine the capital stock in 1965 in each branch. For most branches, these were taken from U.S. Central Intelligence Agency (1981, p. 59). Fuels, consumer goods, and wood and paper were broken down into the industries shown here by dividing the reported capital stocks among components in proportion to 1965 investment. The third step was to cumulate the capital stock in each branch by adding investment and subtracting depreciation (at 2.1%) each year from 1965 to 1985. The results agree closely with published CIA capital stock figures for the industries.

60 percent. The fractions jumped to 34 percent and 80 percent in the next decade.[8] The second factor was the seriousness of mineral depletion and the investments in Siberian resources that were taken to offset it. The former cut productivity in existing operations and the latter led to vast investments that maintained output with more expensive inputs. These were not issues in electrical generation but plagued the steel industry.

Reconstruction investment was the implication of a guiding principle of Soviet industrial policy, namely, the continued operation of all factories. There were three reasons for this. The first was employment protection: an aim of socialism was to eliminate the unemployment of capitalism. Instead of closing down the old factories, they would be brought up to the efficiency of new ones. The second was the provision of housing and social services: they were normally allocated through the employer, so closing plants would have entailed a reorganization of housing and other services. The third was economic: the Soviets believed they could save on the cost of structures by adding new equipment to established factories. By this means their investment budget could be stretched farther.

While reconstruction expenditure sounds like an efficient way to invest in industry, it proved highly wasteful. The aim of investment is either to increase output or to reduce costs, and replacement investment did neither well. Retrofitting new equipment was a much more expensive way to increase capacity than "green field" investment. The problems are familiar to anyone who has renovated a bathroom: new equipment is intended for new installation and does not conform to the connections, power requirements, or placement of the old models. Space is often an important constraint. New equipment may operate at a higher volume of production, thus requiring a greater flow of raw materials and finished product. These flows cannot be economically handled in the cramped confines of old facilities. For the same reason, the economies attainable from the integration of successive stages of production cannot be achieved when equipment is retrofitted. The renovations are often done by production employees rather than by specialized builders. These problems are all alleviated when new equipment is installed in new facilities. The economies are often enough to cover the costs of the additional new structures: Gosplan, for instance, found that it cost 55 percent more to increase capacity in old works than in green field projects (Rumer 1984, p. 15; 1989, p. 211).

The steel industry provides a graphic example of the distortions introduced by reconstruction investment. Japan showed the world how to boost productivity in steel making. Between 1960 and 1985, Japanese steel production grew from 26.9 to 105.3 million tons,[9] and Japan was renowned as the most efficient producer in the world. Japan's success was achieved by building nine new integrated steel mills on large coastal sites with an average capacity of 9 million tons (Hasegawa 1996, p. 81). The minimum efficient size of a steel mill was 6 million tons per year in this period (Hasegawa 1996, p. 162), and the new Japanese steel mills exceeded that size.

Soviet productivity went up so long as they acted like the Japanese; otherwise, it declined. From 1960 to 1985, Soviet steel production increased by 90 million tons (from 65.3 million to 155 million). About 55.8 million tons of the steel smelted in the USSR in 1980 were made in eight green field plants built in the 1960s and 1970s. Those plants accounted for five-eighths of the increase in output from 1960 to 1980. They were large enough to realize scale economies, but, despite frequent complaints about excessive "giantism" in Soviet industry, they were somewhat smaller than new Japanese steel plants — 7 million tons in the USSR versus 9 million in Japan (Rumer 1989, pp. 51–75). These plants pushed up TFP and accounted for the rise in efficiency in 1965–75 shown in Table 10.2.

Older plants made 58 percent of general purpose Soviet steel[10] and accounted for the remaining three-eighths of the increase in production after 1960. This group included the famous mills like Magnitorgorsk and Kuznetsk constructed in the 1930s as well as mills in the Ukraine dating back to the nineteenth century. Although Magnitogorsk had a capacity of 16 million tons, its plant site was highly congested, its equipment was obsolete, and its high-grade ore deposits were exhausted. The rest of the older plants had capacities between one and five million tons. Not only were these too small to realize scale economies, but their sites were overcrowded. The post-1960 mills had about 140 hectares per million tons of capacity while interwar mills had only 90 (Rumer 1989, p. 56). Furthermore, these investments failed to shake out labor since there was no agreement on employment norms in reengineered plants. Plants in the Russian Republic that received reconstruction investment in the early 1970s actually increased their workforces by 18 percent (Rumer 1989, p. 202).

In the 1960s and 1970s, the Soviets spent their investment budgets wisely in the steel industry. Green field sites were developed, and they greatly increased output. The shift in emphasis to reconstruction of old sites was disastrous. It resulted in little increase in output or reduction in the use of labor or raw materials. The planners were not able to monitor changes in capacity nor did they have objective norms to assess employment levels. As a result, the shift to reconstruction investment allowed firm managers to accumulate labor and capital to meet future output targets. A great deal of money was spent for little gain.

RESOURCE DEPLETION

Reconstruction investment was a great waste of funds, but it was not the only fruitless investment. Three industries had TFP falls of more than 10 percent between 1975 and 1985: coal, oil, and ferrous metals. These were natural resource industries plagued by depletion and burdened by the heavy expense of expanding production in Siberia. Indeed, the development of Siberian natural resources was a vast sink for investment rubles. The Soviet Union is often seen as "blessed" with abundant natural resources. Before the 1970s, this was true in that many of the resources that were being exploited were in European Russia or just east of the Urals, and their exploitation was comparatively cheap. By the 1970s, however, the locus of resource exploitation had shifted to Siberia, where costs were very much higher. By then, the Soviet Union's "abundant" natural resources had become a curse. Resource development swallowed up a large fraction of the investment budget for little increase in GDP.

The problems were acute in iron mining, which accounted for 30 percent of ferrous metal investment (Rumer 1989, p. 205). Between 1960 and 1980, the production of iron ore increased from 142.1 million tons to 502.0 million, making the USSR the world's largest producer. Fifteen open pit mines accounted for 80 percent of the growth in production. These were, of course, giant cones that became narrower as they were pushed deeper into the earth. Each year they were driven down another 5–12 meters. Between 1976 and 1980, the share of ore from mines of less than 200 meters declined from 74 percent to 58 percent (Rumer 1989, p. 151). The iron content dropped from 44.5 percent to 34.7 percent, and the overburden to be removed increased. Between 1977 and 1982 alone, the total rock removed to extract one ton of commercial ore increased from 5 to 8 tons (Rumer 1989, p. 152). As the mines became deeper, the routes to the surface became longer and required more equipment. Likewise, the bottom became correspondingly narrower, causing congestion and reduced productivity on the floor of the mine. Costs rose in step with total production. New mines could be opened but they offered little relief, as the deposits were even more remote.

The problems were even more costly in the energy sector. Coal had traditionally been the most important fuel. The Donbass in the Ukraine was the center of coal mining until the 1960s. Its production peaked in 1976, and exploitation shifted to the lignite deposits of the Kansk-Achinsk Basin in Krasnoiarsk Province. This proved hugely expensive and slashed productivity (Gustafson 1989, pp. 27, 33). Between 1975 and 1985, investment raised the capital stock by 64 percent, but employment increased by a quarter, and output grew by only 4 percent. As a result, TFP dropped by 24 percent!

Oil was an even bigger sponge for capital. Before 1975, the situation appeared trouble free, but the industry failed to meets its exploration targets and then its production targets as exploitation was pushed farther and farther into Siberia. Brezhnev responded with a series of crash programs that brought larger and larger commitments of investment to the oil industry. Between 1975 and 1985, energy as a whole increased its share of the industrial investment budget from 28 percent to 39 percent. This rise understates the capital absorbed by energy, for it excludes pipeline investment, which was tallied as transportation. Before 1975, the aggregate statistics of the oil industry were not troublesome, but thereafter they became a nightmare. In 1975–85, the capital stock was increased by a factor of 2.45, employment rose by a quarter, while output fell by 21 percent. Productivity plummeted. The oil industry sucked in capital at a great rate without yielding up more energy.

There was one success story in the energy sector, and that was natural gas (Gustafson 1989, pp. 137–81). As the oil industry's performance declined in the late 1970s, the decision was taken to develop Siberian gas as an alternative. This was hugely expensive and required capital goods not produced in the USSR, namely, compressors and 1420 mm pipe for the pipelines. Nonetheless, six pipelines (over 20,000 km) were built to connect Siberia to European Russia. The USSR overtook the United States in gas production. The fuel basis of the Soviet electrical generators was overturned. Unlike oil, TFP in the gas industry rose substantially as output increased.

But Siberian gas (including transmission costs) was expensive and does not contradict the main point that the Soviet Union was caught in a Ricardian trap. The depletion of existing raw material sources implied steeply rising costs—including capital costs in particular—if output was increased from either new regions or already exploited ones. There were two solutions to this dilemma: replace expensive domestic raw materials with cheap imports or reduce demand for energy and metals.

Soviet trade policy was very different from that of the advanced capitalist countries when it came to raw materials. Japan was at the opposite pole. It had few minerals, no oil, and only a little coal, so it necessarily relied on imports for these key raw materials. However great an obstacle this may have been to Japan's early development (Yasuba 1996), it was a great boon as transport costs fell after World War II since it meant that Japan could shop around the world for the cheapest minerals and fuel. Economic development efforts in the Third World guaranteed abundant supplies at low prices. Even First World governments around the Pacific Rim rushed to supply Japan with subsidized coal. Not having billions of hectares of tundra to develop made the Japanese economy competitive.

Instead, the Soviets tried to be self-sufficient in everything. To a remarkable extent they succeeded. The output of almost every mineral grew, and the USSR was usually one of the biggest producers in the world. Many of these mines would not have been profitable if they had been evaluated at world prices. But that was not the point in the USSR. There the objectives were self-sufficiency and the full development of the country's natural resources — not creating a surplus of revenue over cost. Early in the development process, when deposits were accessible, this strategy did not involve great waste. But as the sources of supply became more remote, the costs skyrocketed, and vast quantities of investment were committed to projects that brought little gain. These show up as falling productivity in coal, oil, ferrous metals, and "other products," which include nonferrous metals.

The other approach to rising resource costs would have been to cut consumption. In 1980, the USSR consumed .95 tons of oil equivalent per US$1000 of GDP in contrast to the OECD average of .50 tons. Canada, which has a similar climate, consumed .74 tons. In the next eight years, conservation measures in the West reduced energy consumption (to .41 in the OECD as a whole and to .64 in Canada), while consumption in the USSR rose to .99 tons per US$1000.[11]

The rise of Soviet energy consumption did not reflect a lack of concern in planning circles. Since the 1970s, conservation had been part of the official rhetoric. Indeed, some improvement had been made — electrification of the railways, more co-generation, more efficient power plants, and a shift from coal to oil and then to gas (Gustafson 1989, pp. 230–31).

Most Soviet energy was consumed by large industrial customers, which should have made conservation simple, but several obstacles stood in the way. First, there was no agreement as to appropriate norms for energy use. Second, attempts to control energy use by raising its price were hampered by the soft budget constraints of many customers. Third, and most important, the majority of farms, residences, and factories lacked meters to monitor energy consumption. The problem worsened as gas displaced oil since gas meters, in particular, were lacking. An energy conservation program of any sort required the creation of an industry to make meters or their importation on a massive scale (Gustafson 1989, pp. 236–42). The politicians running the economy, however, looked for immediate solutions to the problems they faced, and establishing an industry to make meters, like erecting steel mills to make 1420 mm pipe, would have taken too long to command interest.

Incentives and Firm Behavior

The Soviet energy crisis has important implications for one of the widely held explanations of Soviet decline: poor incentives for decision making (Kornai 1992; Roemer 1994; Bardhan and Roemer 1993). In considering this view, it is important to distinguish between incentives that operated at the level of the business enterprise and those that influenced research and development.

Poor incentives at the industry level can be traced back to the essential features of the planning system: firms were given output targets and managers were rewarded to the degree that they met those targets. These incentives had a mixed impact on output and a clear negative effect on costs.

So far as production is concerned, output quotas did give managers an incentive to expand production subject to two caveats. First, product quality was difficult to monitor so quality was sacrificed for quantity, and, second, managers had an incentive to hold back production in one year, so they would not reveal a great ability to produce that might lead to a higher output quota in the following year. The second adverse effect was reduced by shifting managers among enterprises. While output quotas could be self-defeating, they did tend to increase production.

The impact of output quotas on input use, however, was counterproductive. Under capitalism, where profit maximization was the goal, saving a ruble of inputs increased profit by as much as producing an extra ruble of output, so firms had an incentive to do both. When firms were directed with output targets, however, there was only an incentive to expand output and none to economize on costs. As a result, managers tried to horde inputs (disguising their productive capacity), so they could easily meet future output targets and earn high bonuses. Increasing inputs and restricting production (if that occurred) lowered total factor productivity. Furthermore, there was no reason to economize on inputs that became more expensive.

The importance of these responses for economic performance changed during the course of economic development. In the 1930s when structural unemployment was widespread, the social opportunity cost of labor was less than the wage (low as that was), and it was sensible for firms to increase employment levels beyond the point that conventional cost account would have suggested as appropriate. Then soft budgets promoted growth. But once full employment was realized and new productive capacity could not be brought into use without shaking labor out of outmoded facilities, soft budgets became counterproductive. Similarly with energy and raw materials generally. In the early stages of industrialization, when resources were abundant and cheap, cost accounting did not matter greatly, but by the 1980s, when energy was expensive, economizing on its use was critical.

The difficulty was not that no one was concerned about energy use or employment levels but rather that the feedback loops were longer, ran higher, and were less effective than under capitalism. In capitalist states, these decisions are made by firms in response to price signals. In the Soviet Union, the scarcity had to be recognized by the planners, who then had to act on it.

It is important to see what the planners did and did not do. In the case of energy, the planners recognized that there was an energy problem and decided to increase production in response. They were eminently and impressively successful in this. The Siberian gas industry was created in a few years, six pipelines were built to European Russia, and the energy base of the economy was put on a new footing. This very ambitious investment program was not frustrated by plant managers with their own agendas or by the other ills often attributed to Soviet industry. The gas program was an example of the impressive strength of central planning and illustrates the mechanisms that had been responsible for rapid economic growth since 1928.

The gas program, however, highlights the weakness of the system as well: The decision to expand gas production was fundamentally wrong. Reducing the demand for energy would have been a wiser course. The planners, in this case, meant the highest levels of the Soviet leadership, and their priority was the quick fix rather than a concerted effort to monitor and reduce consumption. The problem with Soviet decision making was not that managers frustrated the plans; rather, the plans were implemented but they were wrong headed.

Why Did the Growth Rate Drop? Technological Failure

Another way in which poor incentives may have retarded Soviet performance was in the invention and application of new technology. The standard critique of Soviet technology was developed by Joe Berliner (1976a, 1976b). "The general problem with the old economic structure" — central planning — "is that it gave maximal encouragement to decision makers to favor established products and processes, and to discriminate against innovations 'as the devil shies away from incense,' in Mr. Brezhnev's words." Berliner (1976b, pp. 437, 444) offered many reasons for this conservatism, including the following. First, research and development was carried out by institutes rather than by the businesses that would use the new products or processes. These institutes either chose their own projects or were assigned projects by higher-level authorities. In either case, projects were not suggested by the production or sales departments of businesses and so research was not directed to meeting the needs of business, and the new techniques produced by the labs were often of little practical use or were too imperfectly developed to be of immediate value. Second, the pricing of new models tended to pass the gains of improved performance on to consumers rather than benefiting the innovating enterprises. Third, managers were rewarded for meeting output targets, so they had little incentive to innovate. "The reason is that the changeover to a new product or a new manufacturing process always results in a slowdown in the current rate of output" and that slowdown threatens the manager's bonus for meeting his output target. Consequently, the lack of information flow between producers and designers could not be solved by creating manufacturing departments in firms since the firm managers found it financially rewarding to transfer the R&D personnel and equipment to current production if that was necessary to meet output targets. For instance, Glavneftemash, which made two-thirds of the USSR's oil field equipment, assigned its research facilities to current production in order to meet the heavy demand for drilling rigs during Brezhnev's oil and gas offensives (Gustafson 1989, p. 190).

Despite its popularity, there are many difficulties with Berliner's incentive arguments about R&D.[12] First, there is a timing problem. The Soviet research and development institutions and the incentives to which they gave rise were long-standing. They did not change around 1970. Easterly and Fischer (1995) note that if they did not change, it is hard to see how they can explain the abrupt drop in productivity.

Second, the disincentives to innovate may not have been as strong as usually believed. Berliner's arguments suggest that no invention would take place, but the situation was never that bleak. The cement industry, admittedly not the most glamorous, is a case in point (Abouchar 1976).

Cement grew fast in the first two Five-Year-Plans, but its geographical pattern was highly inefficient: much cement was produced in central Russia and shipped great distances—at excessive cost—to sites in Siberia. By 1940, these imbalances were being corrected, and the shipping distances were further reduced in the postwar period. Socialist planners are supposed to balance the cost savings from large-scale plants against the added transportation costs from longer shipping routes, and they eventually did so in cement production. Plant design was improved after 1950 as kilns were expanded (realizing scale economies), gas was used more extensively as a fuel (reducing kiln wear, increasing product quality, and saving money), and more powerful grinding equipment (improving quality) was introduced. New plants were larger and incorporated advances in other areas of design.[13] Abouchar (1976, p. 565) concluded that cement was a "rational industry in the post-war period. Progress in technology has been seen in kiln size, fuel mix, use of electric power, and plant scale." Output per worker more than doubled from 1928 to 1950, and then more than doubled again by 1968.

Perhaps most important, the character of invention and innovation was very different from that predicted by Berliner. "The journals in this period contain abundant evidence of experimentation—on the plant sites and not just in central laboratories." The result was further "improvements: more efficient heat transfer apparatus and chimney design modifications to reduce stack loss, two-end kiln feeding, and so on." Despite Berliner's (1976, p. 444) conclusion that "there was very little incentive for self-initiated innovative activity at the enterprise level," much experimentation went on.

Third, there was an external development that coincided with the drop in Soviet productivity and that may explain it. That development was the arms race with the Americans during the Brezhnev period. The magnitude of Soviet military spending and its impact on the economy were heatedly debated in American defense circles during the 1980s (Adams 1992; Firth and Noren 1998; Jacobsen 1987; Noren 1995; Rosefielde 1982; Rowen and Wolf 1990, 1992). After much revision, the CIA concluded that the USSR spent 12 percent of its GDP on defense in 1966–70 against 16 percent in 1981–85 (Davis 1992, p. 193). This increase was probably not large enough to significantly affect the growth rate since even one-for-one ruble substitution of investment for defense spending would only have raised the investment rate by one-ninth (from 36 percent to 40 percent of GDP).

The increase in defense spending may have lowered productivity growth, however, by diverting R&D resources from civilian to military innovation. It is difficult to measure the rate of invention, but the available indicators suggest that it was declining in the USSR, at least for the civilian economy. The Soviets did publish considerable statistics on the number of new prototypes brought into use. While such numbers are always hard to interpret, Kontorovich (1986, 1990) has argued that they indicate the volume of newly available technologies, and Amann (1986) has pressed them into service. They show a decline in the absolute number of new inventions brought into use each year from the 1960s to 1985. Kontorovich (1990, p. 267) has divided these into civilian and military innovations and argued that the fall was largely confined to the civilian sector.

These shifts in the output of the R&D sector reflected a reallocation of inputs to the military. According to Campbell (1990, pp. 141–42), the defense "ministries were absorbing the lion's share of the resource increment in R&D"—in particular, technical employees—"in the decade preceding 1985, starving the civilian R&D function." Moreover, the defense "ministries were winning out over the civilian ministries in the struggle for investment resources," so producing an investment crisis in nondefense machinery production. Kontorovich (1990, p. 267) attributed much of the decline to the arms race — "resources were shifted from civilian to military R&D in 1965–85." Campbell (1990, p. 127) agreed: "resource allocation to the military sector became increasingly burdensome" from 1976 to 1985. "It was an important contributor to the slowdown in economic growth, primarily through its deleterious impact on the civilian machinery industry and on investment."

The same conclusion is supported by industry studies that demonstrate the lack of investment in civilian machinery and trace it back to resource conflicts between the military and civilian economies. The oil and gas industry is a prime example, for it was the priority civilian activity in the 1970s and 1980s. Soviet efforts to increase production were hampered by inadequate industrial support. Throughout the period, oil field equipment continued to be made in the antiquated plants of Glavneftemash. Investment was not available for reconstruction, let alone expansion. The Soviet gas campaign required six new pipelines, and they, in turn, required 21,000 kilometers of 1420 mm diameter pipe. Virtually all of this was imported since it would have taken too long to build the mills for the Soviet steel industry to make it. "In metals as in machinery, the underlying reasons for failure have been abysmal civilian innovation and competition for the best people and the best output from the military-industrial sector (the former obviously aggravated by the latter)." The pipelines also required hundreds of compressors to push the gas from Siberia to Europe. Nevskii Zavod produced a satisfactory 10-megawatt compressor by the mid-1970s, but never managed to produce a reliable 25-megawatt model. The most successful large Soviet compressor was based on a converted jet engine supplied by the Ministry of the Aviation Industry and produced at the Frunze plant. "The chronic problems at Nevskii Zavod (and the lesser but substantial difficulties at the Frunze plant in Sumy) had little to do with high technology; rather, the case illustrates the debilitating effects of competition from military priorities on civilian programs, even high-priority ones." Productivity growth in investment as well as consumer goods industries was stifled by the allocation of resources to the military: "A major reason for the technological stagnation of the civilian machinery sector was the preferential channelling of resources to the ministries making military machinery" (Gustafson 1989, pp. 190, 193, 204–8, 212).

If the Cold War was responsible for the drop in Soviet productivity growth, then it accounts for over half of the Soviet growth slowdown. TFP growth dropped from 1.5 percent per year to −.5 percent between the 1960s and 1980–85. Reversing the productivity slowdown by adding 2 percent to the 1980–85 GNP growth rate increases the latter from

2 percent to 4 percent per year. This is still less than the 5.7 percent growth of the 1960s, but certainly a much better performance.

CONCLUSION

The Soviet Union grew rapidly from 1928 to about 1970 by accumulating capital and creating industrial jobs for people otherwise inefficiently employed in agriculture. The strategy of building up heavy industry and the use of output targets and soft budgets were effective in doing this. The growth rate dropped abruptly after 1970 for external and internal reasons. The external reason was the Cold War, which diverted substantial R&D resources from civilian innovation to the military and cut the rate of productivity growth. The internal reason was the end of the surplus labor economy: unemployment in agriculture had been eliminated and the accessible natural resources of the country had been fully exploited. A new strategy was needed. The Soviet leaders responded to these changes by squandering vast sums on retooling old factories and by throwing additional fortunes into Siberian development. It was as if the United States had decided to maintain the steel and auto industries of the Midwest by retooling the old plants and supplying them with ore and fuel from northern Canada instead of shutting down the Rust Belt and importing cars and steel from brand-new, state-of-the-art plants in Japan supplied with cheap raw materials from the Third World. What the country needed was a policy to close down old factories and shift their employees to new, high-productivity jobs, reductions in the use of energy and industrial materials, and increased involvement in world trade.

The interpretation of the Soviet decline offered here is the reverse of the analyses that emphasize incentive problems and the resulting failure of managers to act in accord with the plans. On the contrary, the plans were implemented; the problem was that they did not make sense. The strength of Soviet socialism was that great changes could be wrought by directives from the top. The expansion of heavy industry and the use of output targets and soft budgets to direct firms were appropriate to the conditions of the 1930s; they were adopted quickly, and led to rapid growth of investment and consumption. By the 1970s, the ratio of good decisions to bad was falling. President Gorbachev was as bold and imaginative as any Soviet leader was likely to be, but his economic reforms did not aim in the right direction. Perhaps the greatest virtue of the market system is that no single individual is in charge of the economy, so no one has to contrive solutions to the challenges that continually arise. The early strength of the Soviet system became its great weakness as the economy stopped growing because of the failure of imagination at the top.

Soviet National Income

The evolution of Soviet national income has received great attention from scholars. Data reliability is a question, and I consider it first. The leading attempts to chart the growth of the Soviet economy are then discussed. Finally, Maddison's (1995) summary of Russian and Soviet national income since 1820 — and the changes I have made to his series — are considered.

I. DATA RELIABILITY

The analysis of this work required developing detailed demographic and economic accounts for the Soviet Union from 1928 to 1939. Ultimately, these series are based on Soviet figures, which have been doubted by some (most recently Khanin 1991). In addressing this concern, it is important to distinguish aggregates like industrial output or net material product from the underlying series of the output of particular commodities. Soviet aggregates have generally been rejected by Western scholars. They are not used in this book; new aggregates in accord with Western definitions have been computed instead. My aggregates are close to those of other recent investigators like Hunter and Szyrmer (1992).

The deeper problem is whether the detailed figures used in constructing the aggregates are reliable or have been falsified for political purposes. Did the Soviets really produce as many tons of steel or pairs of shoes as they claimed? Many Western scholars have investigated this question, however, and the consensus is that the published Soviet figures for the output of individual commodities were basically reliable, although there are some difficulties of interpretation due to changes in definition that are not fully documented (Nutter 1962, pp. 11–51; Hunter and Szyrmer 1992, pp. 64–89, 273; Davis, Harrison, and Wheatcroft 1994, pp. 24–37). It has long been known, for instance, that there was no secret set of books with different figures — the Soviet government did its planning and made its decisions with the same figures that it published.

The opening of the archives has allowed this question to be explored more fully. Grain production figures are particularly problematic. Published figures after 1933 exceeded levels shown by archival sources (Davis, Harrison, and Wheatcroft 1994, pp. 30, 115–17, 286–28, Tauger 1991). Ironically, however, Gosplan "correction factors" raised output estimates for the late 1920s by an even greater percentage, so the published series, while manipulated, actually underestimate the growth rate of grain output. My aggregates are based on the archival sources rather than the figures published at the time.

No similar problems have been discovered with industrial statistics. The most important inquiry has been Harrison's (1996) investigation of military production and expenditure statistics during the Second World War — obviously a sensitive subject. He has compared the published figures with the internal, unpublished records of the production and procurement of weapons. While the archives provide more detail, the published figures are confirmed.

The published statistics can also be tested for internal consistency. For instance, is the production and importation of raw cotton (as shown in the agricultural and trade statistics) consistent with the production of cotton yarn shown in the industrial statistics? And is the production of yarn consistent with the production of cotton cloth, knitwear, and hosiery? Calculations using input-output coefficients from contemporary American censuses of manufactures show that the figures are consistent with each other and, therefore, probably reliable.

Perhaps the figures most likely to have been altered for political reasons were population figures. Stalin expected that socialism would lead to rapid population growth, and official projections in the mid-1930s anticipated this. The results of the 1937 census were a contradiction since they indicated a significantly smaller population than expected. Rather than publish falsified figures, the census was suppressed as "unscientific." The 1939 census confirmed the results of the 1937 census as a comparison of the published totals for 1939 with the unpublished 1937 and 1939 figures reveals. An excessive allowance for undercounting raised the published 1939 population figure less than one percent above a reasonable estimate based on the actual returns (Davis, Harrison, and Wheatcroft 1994, p. 72). Since political manipulation — if that is what it was — was so limited in 1939, past estimates of the Soviet population have been remarkably accurate (Lorimer 1946; Bergson 1961, p. 442; Davis, Harrison, and Wheatcroft 1994, pp. 274–25). As was the case with military production, archival research adds detail, which is critical for some questions like the size of the convict population, but does not change the overall picture indicated by previous Western estimates.

II. Leading Attempts to Chart the Growth of the Soviet Economy

Post–World War II Estimates

The U.S. Central Intelligence Agency has prepared the authoritative estimates of Soviet GDP for this period. Their procedures extend those of

Bergson, which will be considered subsequently. They have been attacked as overstating Soviet growth by liberal Russian economists like Khanin (1988, 1991). A close examination of his work shows little difference between his estimates and those of the CIA for this period. The main burden of Khanin's critique is really directed against Western estimates for 1928–40. The CIA figures are, thus, the only game in town, and I use them as recalibrated by Maddison (1995). His procedures will be discussed later in this appendix.

Interwar Estimates

The 1928–40 period is the main battleground for competing Soviet national income estimates. The data are poorer and the index number problems more severe than for the postwar period. I will comment on the estimates of Bergson (1961), Moorsteen and Powell (1966), Hunter and Szyrmer (1992), Khanin, and myself. Many different national income concepts have been used, and I try to standardize them by comparing gross domestic product. This sometimes requires recalculation or reweighting of the series. The effort is worthwhile, however, because it highlights the differences that can otherwise be overlooked. What becomes clear is that there is little difference between the estimates of Moorsteen and Powell, Hunter and Szyrmer, and myself. All of these series grow considerably faster than those of Bergson and Khanin. I believe that faster growth is a more accurate reading of the situation.

Bergson's figures are the most venerable and have provided a base for later scholars. Bergson and his associates produced baseline figures for 1928, 1937, 1940, 1944, 1950, and 1955. (Major publications included Bergson 1953, 1961; Bergson and Heymann 1954; Hoeffding 1954). Bergson estimated national output by summing the components of aggregate demand — consumption, investment, and government spending. His consumption figures discussed in Chapter 7 were part of that enterprise. In view of my criticisms of those series, it is important to work out the implications of both Bergson's and my own consumption series for the growth in gross domestic product. That is one aim of this appendix.

A second estimate of Soviet national income on an annual basis was made by Moorsteen and Powell (1966, pp. 622–24). They estimated indices of real output by sector — industry, trade, and so forth — and aggregated them with 1937 value added shares derived from Bergson's work. This estimate is widely cited. It grows at the same rate as some of Bergson's national income series, as we will see.

Hunter and Szyrmer's (1992, pp. 34–35) GDP estimates are also based on aggregating output by sector. Their weights derive from their 1928 input-output table of the Soviet economy.

Finally, Khanin (1988) has produced alternative estimates that show Russian growth to have been much lower than Moorsteen and Powell's and Hunter and Szyrmer's. Khanin's estimates will be discussed later.

Before comparing and evaluating these series, I explain my own procedures. They are aimed at reconciling Bergson's approach, which is based on summing the components of aggregate demand, with Moorsteen and Powell's. This involves converting Bergson's benchmark years to an annual series, and, more fundamentally, relating categories like purchases of consumer goods to the output of consumer goods.

Allen's National Income Accounts, 1928–40

The procedure follows that of Bergson's (1961) pioneering work in which gross national product is computed as the sum of the components of final demand. These are household purchases in shops, household purchases in farmers' markets, farm income in kind, housing and privately consumed services, communal services (education and health care), government administration, the NKVD, military subsistence, purchases of military equipment, and gross investment. Tables A.1 and A.2 summarize the results. (Table 5.4 shows a corresponding series of sectoral output and GDP.) All figures are in millions of 1937 rubles. The series were derived in the following manner:

1. *Household purchases in retail markets*
   Bergson's (1961, p. 46) 1937 figure was extrapolated to other years with an index of the volume of manufactured consumer goods produced. The construction of this index is described in detail in Allen (1998c).
2. *Household purchases in farmers' markets*
   Bergson's (1961, p. 46) 1937 figure was extrapolated to other years with an index of the volume of sales on the collective farm market (for 1932–39) and on farmers' markets for earlier years. This index is explained in the discussion of the agricultural database.
3. *Farm income in kind*
   The construction of this index is explained in the discussion of the agricultural database.
4. *Housing and privately consumed services*
   Interpolated from Bergson's (1961, p. 48) estimates for 1928, 1937, and 1940.
5. *Communal services (education and health care)*
   For education, labor costs were estimated by multiplying Moorsteen and Powell's (1966, p. 622) index of the number of educa-

TABLE A.1
Soviet Household Consumption Expenditures, 1928–40
(billions of 1937 rubles)

	Shops	Farmers' m'k't	Serv/house	Mil sub	FIIK food	Rural mft'rs	Total
1928	61.5	3.4	25.5	.8	78.2	8.9	178.4
1929	63.9	3.8	27.2	.8	85.0	8.2	188.9
1930	65.5	12.8	28.8	.8	73.7	6.6	188.2
1931	69.4	9.9	30.5	.8	61.4	4.5	176.4
1932	68.6	4.2	32.1	.8	56.8	2.6	165.1
1933	68.2	4.3	33.8	1.0	58.8	2.3	168.4
1934	79.7	8.6	35.4	1.3	56.9	1.0	182.9
1935	87.2	12.6	37.1	1.6	63.2	1.2	202.8
1936	101.0	15.9	38.7	2.1	43.2	1.0	201.8
1937	110.0	16.0	40.4	2.6	81.2	1.0	251.3
1938	113.7	25.3	40.4	3.4	61.7	.8	245.2
1939	114.3	21.6	40.4	4.4	58.1	1.5	240.3
1940	111.0	12.5	45.0	5.3	78.4	1.0	253.2

Column headings:
shops = household purchases in retail shops
farmers' m'k't = household purchases on collective farm (or farmers') market
serv/house = household purchases of services and housing
mil sub = military subsistence
FIIK-food = farm income in kind
rural mft'rs = rural handicrafts and manufacturers
Notes:
(1) The 1940 figures are supposed to represent economic activity on interwar Soviet territory. Where possible, series have been adjusted to achieve that, but there is a greater likelihood of error in this figure than in others.
(2) Total may not equal sum of columns due to rounding.

tion employees by Bergson's (1961, p. 347) estimate of total wage and salary costs in education in 1937. Bergson (1961, p. 347) reported nonlabor expenses for 1928, 1937, and 1940. These were interpolated for intervening years. Health care was dealt with in the same manner as the data reported in Moorsteen and Powell (1966, p. 622) and Bergson (1961, p. 355).

6. *Government administration*
   Bergson's (1961, p. 359) estimate of total outlays in 1937 was extrapolated to other years using Moorsteen and Powell's (1966, p. 359) index of employment in government administration.

7. *NKVD*
   Bergson (1961, p. 361) presents estimates of total outlays in 1928, 1937, and 1940. These were interpolated—roughly—to

TABLE A.2
Soviet Gross National Expenditures 1928–40 (billions of 1937 rubles)

	Private consu	Govt	Milit	Invest	GDP
1928	178.4	9.4	1.0	11.3	200.1
1929	188.9	11.2	1.1	14.0	215.3
1930	188.2	14.8	1.4	19.4	223.9
1931	176.4	18.4	1.4	21.6	217.8
1932	165.1	21.7	1.4	22.4	210.7
1933	168.4	23.0	1.4	20.5	213.2
1934	182.9	24.5	4.7	23.5	235.6
1935	202.8	26.7	7.5	29.4	266.4
1936	201.8	29.4	13.2	39.9	284.2
1937	251.3	32.3	14.8	36.6	334.9
1938	245.2	34.9	19.9	38.1	338.1
1939	240.3	37.6	29.1	37.9	344.9
1940	253.2	40.3	40.5	37.8	371.9

Column headings:
private consu = household consumption (from Table A.1)
govt = nonmilitary government expenditures (public administration, health care, education, NKVD)
milit = military pay and procurements of munitions
invest = investment in fixed capital
GDP = sum of spending in table
Notes:
(1) Investment and GDP are defined exclusive of livestock and inventory investment. See Moorsteen and Powell (1966, p. 386) for estimates of those components.
(2) The 1940 figures are supposed to represent economic activity on interwar Soviet territory. Where possible, series have been adjusted to achieve that, but there is a greater likelihood of error in this figure than in others.
(3) Total may not equal sum of columns due to rounding.

intervening years on the presumption that the series never went down and that increases were concentrated during the collectivization period and the Party purges.

8. *Military subsistence*
The number of military personnel from Moorsteen and Powell (1966, p. 628) multiplied by 1500 rubles per year from Bergson (1961, p. 60).

9. *Purchases of military equipment*
Bergson's (1961, p. 364) estimate of munitions and other procurements in 1937 was extrapolated to other years using Moorsteen and Powell's (1966, p. 629) index of munitions procurements.

10. *Gross investment*

I use Moorsteen and Powell's (1966, p. 386) series of gross investment in fixed capital including capital repairs. It should be noted that I do not include livestock or inventory changes in my investment or GDP series.

11. *Comparison with other series*

There is considerable overlap between my GDP series and Bergson's. The main difference is in the measurement of consumption. This difference has important implications for the growth of industrial output and GDP, which can be seen by relating aggregate demand to production. This exercise helps adjudicate between the series. While my GDP series grows faster then Bergson's, it grows at a rate similar to those of Moorsteen and Powell (1966, pp. 622–23) and Hunter and Szyrmer (1992, pp. 34–35).

As pointed out in Chapter 7, my consumption series grows more rapidly than Bergson's. Consequently, my series implies faster growth for industrial output and GDP than do Bergson's results. This is not immediately apparent since Bergson did not report estimates of industrial output and because he produced so many estimates of national income using so many different definitions that it is not immediately apparent which one should be used for comparison.

So far as manufactured consumer goods are concerned, there is no question that Bergson's figures imply a growth rate much less than that computed by any other investigator. If we use Bergson's preferred (Paasche) measure of the growth in retail sales given in Table 7.1, first column, and subtract my estimates of sales of fresh food on farmers' markets, we obtain implicit estimates of the volume of manufactured consumer goods in 1928 and 1937—namely, 101.6 and 110 billion rubles. These give a growth rate of only 0.9 percent per year. Kaplan and Moorsteen (1960) calculate a corresponding figure of 5.7 percent using 1950 weights. Nutter's figures (1962) imply a growth rate of 7.6 percent per year using 1928 weights and 5.8 percent using 1955 weights, thus leading to the rate of 6.7 percent per year. Hunter and Szyrmer (1992, p. 34) give a figure of 5.5 percent per year. My estimates indicate a growth rate of 6.7 percent (Table 7.3).

Similar discrepancies between Bergson and other statisticians also arise in the measurement of industrial output and GDP. If we calculate overall industrial growth (including mining and quarrying) by adding estimates of military production, capital equipment, and construction materials to the estimates of manufactured consumer goods, Bergson's figures imply that industrial output grew at the rate of 5.7 percent per year from 1928 to 1937. Various investigators have calculated different figures for this rate (Davies, Harrison, and Wheatcroft 1994, p. 292), but Gregory and Stuart (1986, p. 94) quote a figure of 11.3 percent per year, which is as near a consensus value as possible. Nutter (1962, p. 326) gives a figure of 12.1 percent, and even the Russian economist Khanin (1991, p. 146), many of whose estimates seem implausibly low, reports an industrial growth rate of 10.9 percent for 1928–42. My figures imply a growth rate of 12.7 percent per year.

We can perform the same tests with GDP estimates — with the same result — but the issue is complicated because national income can be measured in various ways. My final estimates of consumption (Table 7.3) followed Bergson's lead in valuing farm income in kind at collective farm market prices and sales from shops at prices paid by consumers — that is, inclusive of the turnover tax. This measurement of consumption corresponds to measuring GDP at purchasers' prices (rather than at factor cost, where the turnover tax would be netted out). Bergson did not actually compute an estimate of GDP at purchasers' prices, but one can do so by adding to his estimate of consumption at "adjusted market prices" (where farm income in kind is valued at collective farm market prices) his estimates of the other components of gross national expenditure at prevailing prices (Bergson 1961, pp. 48, 165). The result is that GDP rises from 248.4 billion 1937 rubles in 1928 to 341.7 billion in 1937 — that is, by only 3.6 percent per year. In contrast, my estimate of GDP at purchasers' prices — which differs from Bergson's mainly in the treatment of consumption — grows at the rate of 5.6 percent per year over the same period (Table 5.4). Moorsteen and Powell (1966, p. 622) have computed GDP growth at factor cost. I have recomputed their index on a purchasers' price basis, and it grows at 6.1 percent per year from 1928 to 1937.[1] Hunter and Szyrmer (1992, p. 34) have computed GDP at 1928 purchasers' prices, and it grew at an average annual rate of 8.3 percent between 1928 and 1937. Among these estimates, Bergson's is clearly the lowest.

A sequence of decisions biased Bergson's national income figures downward. The first was the measurement of consumption by deflating expenditure: "I rely chiefly although not exclusively on the method of deflation as distinct from that involving the aggregation at base year prices of data on the physical volume of different commodities" (Bergson 1961, p. 47). The second was the use of 1937 weights in constructing the consumer price index instead of a Fisher Ideal Index using 1928 and 1937 weights. The third was Chapman's rural-urban "adjustment" to the prices of manufactured consumer goods in 1928. The implications of these decisions were discussed in Chapter 7. All of the subsequent calculators of Soviet national income have been written since much information on industrial and agricultural output has become available, and, and they can, therefore, directly aggregate the output of consumer goods. They do not need to deflate expenditures, as Bergson did, and they can, thereby, avoid the index number problems that bedeviled Bergson's efforts.

The final set of national income estimates to consider is Khanin's (1988). He is the only economist to have produced an estimate on the order of Bergson's. Khanin estimated that net material product grew at the rate of 3.2 percent per year from 1928 to 1941. Unfortunately, Khanin has never explained how he arrived at this figure. Since, as noted, he estimated that industry grew much more rapidly than Bergson's figures imply and since, for some other important sectors, he has used output series that, in other hands, lead to a much more rapid rate of GDP growth, it is not clear how he reached his conclusion. By default, it appears to be a question of weighting, but the weight put on agriculture must have been even larger than that implied by using collective farm market prices for farm income in kind (Harrison 1993; Davies, Harrison, and Wheatcroft 1994, pp. 36–37). How larger weights could be justified is not obvious. Without an explanation of the procedure, Khanin's national income accounting cannot be relied on.

The upshot of this discussion is that Soviet GDP measured at purchasers' prices grew at a rate of about 5.3 percent per year from 1928 to 1940 (Table A.2). This growth rate is higher than Bergson's or Khanin's but a bit less than the 6.0 percent of Moorsteen and Powell (1966, pp. 622–23) and the 6.6 percent computed by Hunter and Szyrmer (1992, p. 35). I have shown why Bergson's figures imply slower growth. Bergson's figures cannot be reconciled with the disaggregated data on the growth of individual goods and services. It is not clear how Khanin arrived at similarly slow growth.

III. Maddison's Very-Long-Term Estimates

In Chapters 1 and 10, I rely on Maddison's estimates of Soviet GDP per head expressed in 1990 U.S. dollars. How reliable are these figures?

It is important to consider this question both in the context of comparing GDP across countries and in the context of the various attempts previously reviewed to measure the real growth of the Soviet economy.

So far as international comparisons are concerned, there have been concerted attempts to convert the national income accounts of many countries to a common standard. Exchange rates were the first recourse but are not satisfactory as they do not reflect purchasing power. The solution has been to survey the prices of the same goods and services across countries and use these to calculate purchasing power parity (PPP) exchange rates. These are used to convert GDP per head to a common standard in a base year. Then the growth rates of GDP per head for each country are used to calculate the base year values forward and backward.

The most encompassing example of this methodology are the widely used Penn World Tables prepared by Irving Kravis, Alan Heston, and Robert Summers at the University of Pennsylvania's Center for International Comparisons. These tables cover more countries (152) back to 1950.

Angus Maddison (1995) has produced a similar set of calculations for fifty-six large countries. These estimates have been extrapolated back to 1820 in many cases. The long-term perspective is useful for this book. It should be noted, however, that Maddison's figures have been criticized — particularly the ones farther back in time. The difficulty is that the various national series are put on a common standard with prices for 1990. In 1820, the price structure was different, and a different price structure might lead to different exchange rates between countries than the ones obtained by extrapolating 1990 rates backward for 170 years (Prados de la Escosura 2000). No one has suggested a superior, practical procedure, however, but these difficulties must be borne in mind.

Given the basic procedure, there are two issues that arise in judging the acceptability of Maddison's estimates of Soviet GDP per head in U.S. dollars. One is the exchange rate and resulting level of GDP in 1990. The one thing that is clear is that Maddison's procedure indicates a relatively low value for Soviet GDP. For instance, he puts Soviet GDP per head at 33 percent of the U.S. level in 1985, while the Penn World Tables put Soviet performance at 43 percent. Using Maddison understates — rather than overstates — Soviet income.

The second issue in judging Maddison's reconstruction is the growth rate of real GDP that he uses to extrapolate the 1990 value backward. For the postwar period, he relies on CIA estimates and for the interwar period on Moorsteen and Powell. These appear to be accurate, as discussed previously. Alternative figures like Khanin's would be a worse choice.

The biggest difficulty with Maddison's reconstruction is in the imperial period before 1913. Maddison relies on Goldsmith's index of Russian agricultural and manufacturing productivity, but it has been superseded by Gregory's (1982) work. Consequently, I have extrapolated Maddison's 1913 estimate of Russian GDP in 1990 dollars back to 1870 using Gregory's (1972, pp. 433, 1982, pp. 56–57, variant 2) estimates of Russian NNP rather than Maddison's. Gregory's figures show faster growth from 1870 to 1913 than Maddison's and imply an 1870 GDP of $749, which is lower. I apply this to 1820 as well since there was no urbanization or other evidence of expansion. This seems more satisfactory than Maddison's assumption that income grew as rapidly from 1820 to 1870 in Russia as in Czechoslovakia, which was urbanizing rapidly in the period. In the end, Maddison and I end up with similar 1820 income levels for Russia.

The Simulation Model of the Soviet Economy

I. INTRODUCTION

The purpose of this appendix is to document the model of the Soviet economy that I have used in Chapters 8 and 9. The data sources used to implement the model are discussed in Appendices A, C, and D.

The aim of the model is to simulate the results of Soviet policies and institutions in order to determine their role in the economic development of the USSR. My point of departure is Domar's (1957) version of Fel'dman's growth model. Fel'dman was a Soviet economist who developed a theoretical model of economic development during the 1920s. The Fel'dman model divides the economy into producer goods and consumer goods sectors. Output in each sector depends only on capital in that sector. Producer goods output can be invested in either the producer goods sector or the consumer goods sector. The more capital invested in the former, the faster the economy grows.

This model is an appropriate place to begin since capital accumulation was the main source of growth in the Soviet Union and since most investment was effected with domestically produced plants and equipment. (While the possibility of exporting farm products and light manufactures and importing capital equipment was considered and, indeed, tried briefly, the 1930s were not a propitious time for export-led growth, so Soviet development quickly became autarkic.)

To assess Soviet policies, the model must be elaborated to more accurately describe Soviet conditions. So I have modified Fel'dman's model in several ways. I divide the economy into four sectors: agriculture, manufactured consumer goods, producer goods, and services (including government). Administrative rules and markets define the relationships between these sectors. The important markets were the labor market (encompassing rural-urban migration and the allocation of labor between industries); consumer goods markets, where the available supply was sold to consumers, and the collective farm market, where peasants sold food to city dwellers. Other important decisions like the allocation of investment or the delivery of farm products to industry were handled by administrative fiat rather than by markets and are so treated in the model.

Indeed, to address issues like collectivization, it is necessary to develop several closely related models. The NEP and the Stalinist (collectivized) system differed in many ways, so comparing them is not a matter of changing the value of one or two parameters. I explain the models in turn.

The issues to be addressed by the models involve feedbacks from one part of the economy to another. Economists have increasingly turned to computable general equilibrium (CGE) models to address issues of this sort. These models are the empirical counterparts to the theoretical general equilibrium models first analyzed by Walras (1874) and later by many other economists dealing with international trade, welfare economics, and other issues. Input-output analysis, developed by Leontief (1941) and others, can be considered a form of applied general equilibrium model, but it was not until the 1960s that computable general equilibrium models of the modern sort were developed. In these models, people, who are conceived to be both consumers and owners of factors of production, are modeled with utility functions that give rise to product demand and factor supply curves. The technology of each industry is represented by a production function, and profit maximization subject to that constraint yields factor demand and product supply curves. Taxes and government spending are also usually part of the model. Solution of the full set of product and factor demand and supply curves yields the "general equilibrium" of the economy—the product and factor price and volume levels that clear all markets simultaneously. The point of the model is usually to determine the effect of some variable—a tax is a common example—by solving the model with and without the tax and comparing the results. My assessment of the turnover tax is in this tradition. Computable general equilibrium models are commonly used by economists studying international trade, economic development, taxation, and so on.[1]

CGE models have also been used by economic historians to study a variety of issues.[2] In the 1960s, the profession inched toward CGE. On the one hand, some important issues were analyzed explicitly with general equilibrium models, but the models were not applied or computable (e.g., Temin 1966, 1971b; Fogel 1967). On the other hand, some calculations—notably Fogel's (1964) social savings calculations—had a general equilibrium flavor, but were not the products of a CGE model. Beginning in the 1970s, genuine CGE models have been formulated. Chambers and Gordon's (1966) analysis of the Canadian wheat boom was a precursor of this work. Williamson with several coauthors has applied the CGE approach to capital accumulation, long-run growth, and the distribution of income in Japan, the United States, and Great Britain (Williamson 1974, 1985; Kelley and Williamson 1974; Williamson and Lindert 1980). Other issues studied include the impact of

American tariffs (James 1978, 1981; Harley 1992) and Canadian tariffs (Percy, Norrie, and Johnston 1982), the Canadian wheat boom (Lewis 1975), the recruitment of the American industrial labor force (Lewis 1979), the role of slave trade in the Atlantic economy (Darity 1982; Findlay 1993), rural depopulation in Ireland (O'Rourke 1991), and the British industrial revolution (Hueckel 1973; Harley 1993). CGE modeling is becoming more and more widely used by economic historians.

A question that always arises with CGE models is whether the complexity of a real economy can be captured by the relatively small number of equations comprising the model, particularly since each sector is often modeled in a highly simplified way. The real issue here is where the crux of the historical problem lies. If the interaction between the sectors of the economy is at the heart of the matter, it is probably better to adopt—certainly to explore—a CGE model incorporating those intersectoral relations. On the other hand, if sectoral interaction is largely irrelevant to the problem analyzed, then CGE is probably pointless, and the economic historian is well advised to develop as rich an analysis as possible of the part of the economy being studied.

Since the analysis of Soviet taxation and procurement policy is fundamentally concerned with the interactions between agriculture and the rest of the economy, I have developed a modified CGE model. Like CGE models, it distinguishes several sectors and specifies the links between them. Retail goods markets, labor markets, and farmers' markets for fresh food were present in the Soviet Union, and I model them as such. However, some decisions like investment policy and some sectoral links like the procurement of farm products by the state were administrative, and I model them in that way. Such a hybrid model captures the essential feedbacks of the Soviet economy, so that the full ramification of policies can be traced out. The decision to direct more investment into heavy industry, for instance, raised the investment rate, which required higher taxes with further implications for farm and nonfarm consumption and rural-urban migration. Capturing these feedbacks is the strength of this model.[3]

There are three steps in constructing a CGE model or a simulation model of the sort used here: the equations of the model must be specified, then the parameters must be estimated, and, finally, the model must be verified by seeing how accurately it replicates history. Only after these steps are finished can the model be altered and resimulated to gauge the impact of institutions or policies on economic development. My model has gone through this process of formulation and verification, and some examples of verification are given in Chapter 8. Here I only give an overview of the structure of the model to clarify the simulations.

II. The Model of the Collectivized Economy

I begin with the model of the collectivized economy. Each year, a series of subprograms are executed in the same order. The following equations specify the collectivization model for 1930–39. For 1928 and 1929 (before forced collectivization), the model incorporates elements of the NEP model (like its migration function), and many variables are set to their historical values since their simulation would be extremely difficult.

1. Demography and Employment

The rural (rurpop) and urban (urbpop) populations are updated by adding births, subtracting normal and "excess" deaths (exdeath), and accounting for migration (mig). The appendage (-1) indicates a lagged value, and the variables beginning with cdr and cdr are crude birth and death rates, respectively. (Cdrrurok is the "normal" crude death rate in rural areas.)

(1) rurpop = rurpop(-1) + $(((\text{cbrrural}(-1) - \text{cdrrurok}(-1))$ *rurpop$(-1))/1000)$ − mig(-1) − exdeath(-1)

(2) urbpop = urbpop(-1) + $(((\text{cbrurban}(-1) - \text{cdrurban}(-1))$ *urbpop$(-1))/1000)$ + mig(-1)

An estimate of the farm population in 1928 is updated by the change in the rural population, and the nonfarm population equals the total population minus the farm population:

(3) farmpop = farmpop(-1) + rurpop − rurpop(-1)

(4) nonfarmpop = rurpop + urbpop − farmpop

The nonagricultural labor force (l) is computed as the urban population multiplied by the observed employment rate (emprate) plus the size of the armed forces (lmil):

(5) l = emprate * urbpop + lmil

2. Investment

One-third of the investment expenditures undertaken in any year (i) are presumed to come into productive use in each of the following three years, so the additions to productive capacity (efinvest) equal one-third of the investment expenditures in the three preceding years:

(6) efinvest = $(\text{i}(-1) + \text{i}(-2) + \text{i}(-3))/3$

Besides agriculture, the model includes two industries, broadly conceived. Producer goods include machinery, structures, military equipment, hospital equipment, and consumer durables. Consumer goods include manufactured consumer goods, housing, private services, and government activities other than the acquisition of military equipment. As in the Fel'dman model, a fraction (e) of new investment is assigned to the producer goods sector (p) increasing its capital stock by dkp, and the remainder is assigned to the consumer goods industry (c):

$$(7) \quad dkp = e * efinvest$$

$$(8) \quad dkc = (1 - e) * efinvest$$

The fraction e was determined from the investment breakdowns for 1929–34 reported in the Soviet statistical abstract *Socialist Construction in the U.S.S.R.* (1936, pp. 346–51). This source subdivided investment for the "total socialist economy" — essentially the entire economy outside of agriculture — by commissariats and branches. The data were first reorganized by industry. Then investment in each industry was multiplied by the fractions shown in Table C.1 that decompose each industry into a producer goods component and a consumer goods component. Summing the investment in the producer goods component and dividing by the total gave an estimate of e for each year. The average value was .23, and there was little variation from year to year. This may not seem like a high number in view of the rhetoric about heavy industrialization, but it is considerably larger than 7 percent, which was the share of the nonagricultural capital stock in the producer goods industry in 1928.

The capital stocks of the two sectors (kp and kc) are updated by adding new investment and subtracting depreciation:

$$(9) \quad kp = dkp + (1 - .015) * kp(-1)$$

$$(10) \quad kc = dkc + (1 - .015) * kc(-1)$$

Investment in these calculations is defined to be gross and inclusive of repair expenditures. With these conventions a depreciation rate of 1.5 percent rationalizes Moorsteen and Powell's (1966, pp. 315, 386) investment and capital stock series.

3. Labor Allocation

The nonagricultural labor force is allocated between the producer goods and consumer goods industries by equating the value of the marginal product of labor (in 1937 prices) in the two sectors. Equation 11 is the marginal product of labor in the consumer goods industry, equation 12 is the marginal product in the producer goods industry, and equation 13 is the nonagricultural labor force. The production functions are explained shortly.

(11) mpp = (83.2513/9.977) * (1 − f − h) *
((lc/9.977) ** (−p−1)) * (f * (kc/126.540) ** (−p)
+ h * (agmfsim(−1)/16006.26) ** (−p) + (1 − f−h) * (lc/9.977)
** (−p)) ** ((−1/p)−1)

(12) mpp = (12.0267/2.368) * (1 − d)
* (((lp)/2.368) ** (−p −1)) * (d * (kp/9.729) ** (−p)
+ (1 − d) * ((lp)/2.368) ** (−p)) ** ((−1/p)−1)

(13) l = lc + lp

4. Supply of Goods

With the labor force and capital stock in each sector determined, output can be calculated from the production functions. The functions are CES functions. The output of producer goods depends on capital and labor in that sector, while the output of consumer goods depends on capital, labor, and the quantity of agricultural products processed (agmfsim). The latter is lagged one year—what was processed in 1930 was harvested in 1929. The intercepts are 1928 output levels (cf. Table C.2). Input indices are normalized by dividing by 1928 values from Table C.2.

(14) yp = 12.0267 * (d * (kp/9.729) ** (−p)
+ (1 − d) * ((lp)/2.368) ** (−p)) ** (−1/p)

(15) yc = 83.2513 * (f * (kc/126.540) ** (−p)
+ h * (agmfsim(−1)/16006.26) ** (−p) + (1 − f−h) * (lc/9.977)
** (−p)) ** (−1/p)

In the simulations d is assumed to be .6 and the elasticity of substitution is taken as .4. This implies that p = 1.5. These values were suggested by Weitzman's (1970) estimates of industry production functions for the Soviet Union in the 1950s and 1960s. The same value for the elasticity of substitution is used in the consumer goods industry as in the producer goods industry. The coefficients of capital, labor, and processed agricultural goods are assumed to be .35, .35, and .30, respectively.

Since consumer goods include services and since consumer durables are producer goods, consumer goods sold in shops (congoods), that is, real retail sales, are defined as:

$$(16)\ \text{congoods} = \text{yc} - \text{yhs} - \text{ygov} - \text{milps} + \text{condur}$$

where yhs is housing and private services, ygov is goverment services (education, health, administration, the secret police), milps is military pay and subsistence, and condur is consumer durables, which are part of producer goods. Yhs, ygov, milps, and condur are all set equal to their actual historical values. Consumer goods sold in shops are subdivided into nonfoods (shpmfsup) and foods (shpfdsup) according to value added weights in their production:

$$(17)\ \text{shpmfsup} = .55 * \text{congoods}$$

$$(18)\ \text{shpfdsup} = .45 * \text{congoods}$$

The output of the producer goods industry includes agricultural equipment (iag), consumer durables (condur), hospital equipment (healtheq), and military equipment (milequip).

All of these deductions are set to equal their historical values.

$$(19)\ \text{it} = \text{yp} - \text{iag} - \text{condur} - \text{healtheq} - \text{milequip}$$

5. Demand for Consumer Goods

Wage income (wagebill) is the main component of income driving the consumer goods market and equals nonagricultural employment multiplied by the average nonagricultural wage (wact):

$$(20)\ \text{wagebill} = 1 * \text{wact}$$

Consumer preferences in the nonfarm sector are assumed to be Cobb-Douglas, so spending on each commodity equals a constant fraction multiplied by income. Purchases on the collective farm market (kolkexp) and food goods purchased in shops (shpfdexp) also depend on wage income and transfer payments. The latter are set to their historical values:

$$(21)\ \text{kolkexp} = .13 * (\text{wagebill} + \text{trans})$$

$$(22)\ \text{shpfdexp} = .42 * (\text{wagebill} + \text{trans})$$

Expenditures on nonfood consumer goods (shpmnexp) are assumed to depend on lagged agricultural income as well—this year's purchases depend on the sales of last year's crop.

$$(23)\ \text{shpmnexp} = .27 * (\text{wagebill} + \text{trans}) + \text{aginc}(-1)$$

6. Consumer Good Market Clearing

In this model the prices of nonfood consumer goods (priceman) and processed food sold in shops (pricefd) are determined by equating supply and demand (equation 18 with 22 and 17 with 23):

$$(24)\ pricefd\ =\ 1.77\ *\ (shpfdexp/shpfdsup)/.1932775$$

$$(25)\ priceman\ =\ 2.42\ *\ (shpmnexp/shpmfsup)/.200383176$$

1.77 and 2.42 are the 1928 values of price indices with bases equal to 1.00 in 1913, and the divisors on the right normalize the indices with respect to those 1928 values.

7. Government Budget Balance

Real government spending (govreal) includes investment (i), hospital (healtheq) and military equipment (milequip), military pay and subsistence (milps), and education, health, adminsitration, and the secret police (ygov):

$$(26)\ govreal\ =\ i\ +\ healtheq\ +\ milequip\ +\ milps\ +\ ygov$$

Real government expenditures are converted to current ruble expenditures by multiplying the real value by the historical ratio of nominal to real values (govnomrl):

$$(27)\ govnom\ =\ govreal\ *\ govnomrl$$

The government budget was balanced by adjusting the turnover tax. A regression equation indicates the required turnover tax receipts (in current rubles) as a function of government spending in current rubles:

$$(28)\ turntax\ =\ exp(-1.51876\ +\ 1.240056\ *\ log(govnom))$$

8. Agricultural Prices and Marketing

The supply of agricultural products is modeled as a consumption decision by peasants, as described in Allen (1997). Peasants can either consume their production or sell it to obtain money to buy nonfood consumer goods at a price equal to priceman. Since the total supply is determined by the decision of how much to sell on the collective farm market, total supply is made a function of that price (pricekol). Consumer preferences are modeled with a constant elasticity of substitution (ces) function where utility depends on the consumption of agricultural products (fiiksim) and purchased manufactures. Parameter values are calculated to explain the decline in marketing that occurred between

1913 and 1928. The variable split is the ratio of farm income in kind (fiiksim) to total marketings (agmarksm). Agnet is agricultural production net of seed and feed. Nonkolk is the actual level of centralized and decentralized procurements. These are treated as obligatory deliveries, and they are imposed on farmers in this model. The numbers in equation 33 link the index of prices on the collective farm market to a free market index of agricultural prices with a 1913 value of 1.00.

$$(29) \ \text{split} = 1.5043 * (\text{pricekol}/\text{priceman}) ** (-.9298)$$

$$(30) \ \text{fiiksim} = \text{agmarksm} * \text{split}$$

$$(31) \ \text{agmarksm} = (\text{agnet}/1000) - \text{fiiksim}$$

$$(32) \ \text{kolksim} = \text{agmarksm} - \text{nonkolk}/1000$$

$$(33) \ \text{pricekol} = 2.47 * (\text{kolkexp}/\text{kolksim})/.430723084$$

Equation 34 identifies centralized and decentralized procurements as the raw material supply to the consumer goods industry (agmfsim):

$$(34) \ \text{agmfsim} = 1000 * (\text{agmarksm} - \text{kolksim})$$

Equation 32, of course, implies that agmfsim equals the actual historical level of procurements.

9. Value Added in Consumer Goods

To determine farm income from government procurements, value added in producing consumer goods and the turnover tax receipts must be subtracted from retail sales in shops. Value added consists of the labor and capital costs of producing the consumer goods. Labor costs in the production of consumer goods are given by:

$$(35) \ \text{wagescon} = \text{lc} * \text{wact}$$

Following the Soviet practice of disregarding the interest cost of capital, capital costs in producing consumer goods are defined to be depreciation charges as in equation 38. These charges are the product of three terms—kc (the quantity of capital in 1937 prices in the consumer goods industry), ract (an index of the value of the capital stock in current prices relative to its value in 1937 prices), and dep (the depreciation rate). From the values of the 1928 nonagricultural capital stock in 1928 and 1937 prices (Moorsteen and Powell 1966, pp. 326–27) and the nonagricultural wage rate in 1928 and 1937, equation 36 was estimated to show how the price of capital varied with the wage. Equation 37 is intended to retrieve depreciation charges in 1937 prices from the capital stock series in 1937 prices. The depreciation rate increased with the nonagricultural capital stock since the share of equipment, which depreciated faster, was rising while the share of structures was falling.

$$(36) \; ract = (1000 * wact/3330) ** .46$$

$$(37) \; dep = .000356448 * (kp + kc) - .0035839$$

$$(38) \; capcon = kc * ract * dep$$

Equations 35 and 38 sum to value added in the production of consumer goods. However, that includes government and other services as well as consumer goods sold in shops. In 1937, multiplying wagescon plus capcon by .31 gives value added in the production of consumer goods:

$$(39) \; vacon = .31 * (wagescon + capcon)$$

10. Agricultural Incomes and Prices

Agricultural income equals collective farm market sales plus the retail sales of consumer goods minus the labor and capital costs required to produce them less turnover tax receipts and agricultural tax collections:

$$(40) \; aginc = kolkexp + (shpfdexp + shpmnexp - vacon) - turntax - agtax$$

The average price received by farmers for agricultural goods equals aginc divided by agmarksm, the level of farm marketings:

$$(41) \; priceag = 1.57 * ((aginc/(1000 * agmarksm))/.00017264)$$

The various numbers in equation 41 set the 1928 value of the index to equal 1.57 so it links with an index of wholesale agricultural prices with a 1913 base value of 1.00.

11. Standard of Living

Equation 43 defines private consumption to be the sum of household purchases of consumer goods in shops (congoods), household purchases of food on the collective farm market (kolkreal), farm income in kind (fiiksim), housing and other privately purchased services (yhs), and military subsistence (milsub). Privsol is measured in 1937 retail prices. Equation 42 converts the kolksim series (the volume of collective farm market sales measured average prices received by farmers across all marketings in 1937) to the collective farm market prices paid by consumers in 1937.

$$(42) \; kolkreal = 16 * kolksim/5.158936$$

$$(43) \; privsol = congoods + kolkreal + .8 * kolkadj * fiiksim + (26.3/11.143) * (yhs + milsub)$$

The coefficient of fiiksim is .8 * kolkadj. kolkadj is the ratio of the value of farm income in kind measured in 1937 collective farm market prices to the value in 1937 average realized prices. This ratio varies slightly from year to year due to changes in the composition of farm income in kind. Multiplication by .8 follows Bergson (1961, p. 167) and eliminates marketing and home processing costs.

Multiplying yhs + milsub by 26.3/11.143 is also a Bergsonesque adjustment intended to revalue the services whose prices were controlled at "free market" prices.

To break down overall private consumption into farm and nonfarm components, it is necessary to define the transaction terms of trade (tofttran) since that defines the rate at which farmers could exchange farm products for nonfood manufactured goods:

$$(44) \quad \text{tofttran} = \text{priceman/priceag}$$

Consequently, if farmers spent all of the proceeds from their sales on nonfood manufactures, their consumption (inclusive of income in kind) equaled:

$$(45) \quad \text{farmsol} = .8 * \text{kolkadj} * \text{fiiksim} + \text{agmarksm}(-1)/\text{tofttran}$$

Nonfarm consumption was, therefore, total private consumption less farm consumption:

$$(46) \quad \text{urbansol} = \text{privsol-farmsol}$$

Dividing farm and nonfarm consumption by the respective populations gives the following per capita values:

$$(47) \quad \text{solfmpc} = \text{farmsol/farmpop}$$

$$(48) \quad \text{solnfpc} = \text{urbansol/nonfarmpop}$$

12. Migration

Rural-urban migration is modeled as a response to differences in average consumption on and off the farm. Equation 50 is the key relationship, for it shows how the rate of rural outmigration depends on relative per capita consumption.

$$(49) \quad \text{relsol} = \text{solnfpc/solfmpc}$$

$$(50) \quad \text{migrate} = + .01875 * \text{relsol} - .018375$$

$$(51) \quad \text{mig} = \text{migrate} * \text{rurpop}$$

Equation 50 is a very rough fit to the migration data for the 1930s (e.g., Lorimer 1946, p. 150). As relsol varies from 1.6 to 2.3, visual inspection of the data indicated that the migration rate varied from .012

to .025. Equation 50 captures that movement. There are certainly errors; however, the annual values generated are sometimes in error since nonmonetary factors (dekulakization, international passports, etc.) are not modeled.

13. Other Equations

A variety of other variables — gross domestic product, for instance — can be computed in a straightforward way from the variables defined above.

II. THE MODEL OF THE NEW ECONOMIC POLICY

The model of the collectivized economy is fundamental to the study of Soviet development since that model is supposed to replicate what actually happened. By altering parameters like e, it is possible to investigate how the concentration of investment on heavy industry influenced the growth of output and consumption during the Soviet industrial revolution. However, to explore many issues — for instance, the impact of collectivization on growth — a model of the NEP is essential. The difference between the NEP and collectivization is not captured by varying one or two parameters in the collectivization model. The differences are more profound.

There are four areas of difference between my models of the collectivized and NEP economies.

First, agricultural output is higher under the NEP. I increase grain production from 1930 to 1934 to make up for the shortfall during collectivization, and I assume that livestock herds (other than horses) increased at 2 percent per year from 1928. Livestock products increased commensurately, as did the consumption of farm produce as feed. In 1933, the trough of farm output under collectivization, the value for net agricultural output under the NEP is 51 percent greater than under collectivization. In 1939, after the restoration in grain output and the rebuilding of herds, my value for agricultural production under NEP-style institutions is still 16 percent above the actual value under collectivization. Furthermore, since there is no fall in farm output under the NEP, I assume that there was no famine in the 1930s.

Second, both models include a migration function that indicates the fraction of the rural population that moved to the cities each year as a function of the ratio of nonfarm to farm consumption per capita. I posit a higher function under collectivization to reflect the impact of dekulakization, the anger at the imposition of collectivization, and the sense among the peasants that the future lay in the city (Fitzpatrick 1993, 1994).

Third, I assume that private trade would continue under the NEP, so that farmers would have received as income the value of retail sales minus any sales taxes and the labor and capital costs necessary to transport and convert farm products into consumer goods. Under collectivization, the turnover tax absorbed much of the gap between the value of retail sales in state and cooperative shops and the labor and capital costs necessary to produce them. The burden of this tax fell mainly on the rural population since the supply of requisitioned produce was price inelastic. In the NEP model, I assume that the turnover tax (and the much smaller agricultural tax) were replaced with a uniform tax on all cash incomes, including wages as well as farm sales. The cash income tax is set at a rate to bring in the same revenue as the turnover tax and agricultural tax combined. Under this scenario, some of the tax burden is shifted from peasants to workers.

Fourth, in my model of collectivization, about 80 percent of farm supply is requisitioned, but the remaining 20 percent is supplied voluntarily on the collective farm market. Hence, I model collective farm marketing as a function of the price on the collective farm market. In contrast, farm supply in the NEP model is fully voluntary, and I make it a function of the average price on all sales.

It should also be noted that there are important similarities between my modeling of the NEP and collectivization. In neither case is the focus on the organization of farming. Instead, the models concentrate on the relationship between agriculture and the rest of the economy. Moreover, I have modeled the NEP in the most "pro-growth" way possible. In particular, I presume that farm mechanization and the promotion of technical crops (e.g., cotton) would have been pursued as vigorously under the continued NEP as was the case historically.

With these considerations in mind, I have altered the model of the collectivized economy in three ways to model the NEP. Sections 5 and 7 are replaced with a section called 7A. It follows section 6. Sections 8 and 10 are replaced with a section called 8A, and equation 50 in section 12 is replaced with a new equation 50A. The details are as follows:

7A. Demand for Consumer Goods and Government Budget Balance

Changes in this section are required since the agricultural tax and turnover tax are replaced with a uniform tax on cash incomes. This tax is set to bring in the same income as the turnover tax would have collected. Since the tax is imposed on agricultural incomes and since they depend on consumer spending, the cash income tax rate (cashrate) must be determined simultaneously with consumer demand. Hence, the following four equations are solved simultaneously:

(5A-1) cashrate = (turntax + agtax)/(wagebill + trans + kolkexp + shpfdexp + shpmnexp − vacon)

(5A-2) kolkexp = .13 * (1 − cashrate) * (wagebill + trans)

(5A-3) shpfdexp = .42 * (1 − cashrate) * (wagebill + trans)

(5A-4) shpmnexp = .27 *
((1 − cashrate) * (wagebill + trans) + aginc(−1))

The solutions to these equations are values of the four left-hand-side variables.

8A. Agricultural Prices and Marketing and Agricultural Income

The changes in this section are implied by the change in tax regimes and also by the elimination of obligatory deliveries. The definition of agricultural income is changed to reflect the cash income tax:

(8A-1) aginc =
(1 − cashrate) * (kolkexp + shpfdexp + shpmnexp − vacon)

Agricultural prices, farm income in kind, split (the ratio of farm income in kind to marketings), and agricultural marketings and prices are determined by solving the following four equations simultaneously:

(8A-2) priceag = 1.57 * ((aginc/(1000 * agmarksm))/.00017264)

(8A-3) split = 1.5043 * (priceag/priceman) ** (−.9298)

(8A-4) fiiksim = agmarksm * split

(8A-5) agmarksm = (agnet/1000) − fiiksim

A regression equation was estimated to separate agricultural marketings into sales on the collective farm market and shipments to industry for processing:

(8A-6) kolksim = (−.08892 + .00000573 * agnet) * agmarksm

(8A-7) agmfsim = 1000 * (agmarksm − kolksim)

12. Migration

The only change in this section is replacing equation 50 with a new migration rate equation:

(50A) migrate = +.005 * relsol − .001

This equation generates lower levels of migration than equation 50. Equation 50 overpredicts migration rates in the late 1920s, and equation 50A corrects that error. With a value of relsol equal to 1.6, the predicted migration rate is .007. These values are like those of the late 1920s. There is of course no data for migration under the NEP with higher values of relsol. In the 1930s, relsol actually rose from 1.6 to as high as 2.3. Equation 50A implies a 50 percent increase in the migration rate under such a circumstance, while equation 50 implies an increase of 110 percent. The smaller response represents the judgment that farm life would have been more satisfying under the NEP.

III. Harris–Todaro Model

The Harris–Todaro model is a variant of the collectivization model. Equation 13 is eliminated and mpp is set equal to 3 in equations 11 and 12. They can then be solved independently for lc and lp.

Data Sources

This appendix documents additional economic and demographic data used in the simulation model and national income estimation.

I. Agricultural Data, 1913–40

Time series on agricultural output and marketings were required for the simulations and for the measurement of aggregate consumption. Except as noted, all series are constant price series in which the various quantities were aggregated with Karcz's (1979, p. 105) estimates of the average price across all marketings in 1937. (The grain price was calculated inclusive of payments to Machine Tractor Stations.) Quantities of thirteen crops — grain, vegetables (excluding melons), potatoes, flax fiber, sunflower seeds, sugar beets, cotton, milk, meat, wool, big hides, little hides, eggs — were aggregated. These comprised most of the output of Soviet agriculture. The various series were derived as follows.

1. Gross Agricultural Production

Priority was given to the values in Davies, Harrison, and Wheatcroft (1994, pp. 286–88). Other values were taken from Wheatcroft (1983). I used the "low" estimate for grain, the Davies, Harrison, and Wheatcroft estimate for potatoes, and the revised Soviet estimates for other crops. For hides, I estimated output in the late 1930s from regressions of hide output on meat production in other years.

2. Feed, Seed, and Losses on the Farm

I estimated losses and the use of agricultural products as seed and feed following Bergson (1961, pp. 325–30) and Johnson and Kahan (1959) with the following emendations: for grain, seed equals the number of hectares (from Hunter and Szyrmer 1992, p. 107; Jasny 1949, p. 790; Johnson and Kahan 1959, p. 229) times a seed rate (117 kg/hectare) from Wheatcroft (1983, p. 269). Feed equals rates per animal from Jasny (1949, p. 753) and Nimitz (1954, p. 78) times livestock numbers from Davies, Harrison, and Wheatcroft (1994, p. 289) with some detail from Nimitz (1954, Table 4). The feed rates for grain were: horses 4 years and older (400 kg per year), horses less than 4 years (133 kg per year), cows (75 kg), other cattle (25 kg), pigs (14 kg), sheep and goats (3 kg). The feed rates for potatoes were: horses 4 years and older (28 kg per year), horses less than 4 years (9 kg per year), cows (80 kg), other cattle (0 kg), pigs (403 kg), sheep and goats (3 kg).

For potatoes, seed equaled hectares from Jasny (1949, p. 790) and Johnson and Kahan (1959, p. 229) multiplied by a seed rate from Johnson and Kahan (1959, p. 236).

3. Net Agricultural Production

Gross production minus feed, seed, and losses on the farm.

4. Agricultural Marketings

Two marketing concepts were used in Soviet statistics; sales by farmers and sales by farmers net of repurchases by other farmers. Since I am concerned with the relationship between the agricultural and nonagricultural spheres, the second concept is the pertinent one. In Soviet parlance it was called the *sal'do sela*, the balance of the village. These two concepts diverge particularly for grain, meat, milk, and eggs.

Data are from Zaleski (1971, pp. 313, 338–39; 1984, pp. 728–29, 782–85), Jasny (1949, pp. 78–79), Barsov (1969, table facing p. 112), and Karcz (1957, pp. 102–3).

For grain, Barsov (1969, p. 103) gives the *sal'do sela* for 1928–32. For subsequent years, I estimated the *sal'do sela* as total collections (Davies, Harrison, and Wheatcroft 1994, p. 290) less 3 million tons. This corresponds reasonably well with Barsov's figure for 1928–32.

For meat, milk, and eggs, marketings are from Karcz (1979, pp. 102–3). To compute the *sal'do sela*, the meat figure was divided by 1.3, the milk figure by 1.15, and the egg figure by 1.1 to allow for intrarural sales. See Karcz (1979, p. 98).

For some commodities, some missing values were interpolated, some with regressions.

5. Farm Income in Kind

Net agricultural production less agricultural marketings.

6. Farmers' Market and Collective Farm Market Sales
   (Constant Prices)

The estimation proceeded in steps. First, Karcz's data (in Karcz 1957 but mainly 1979, pp. 105–8) were used to calculate the value of total

sales and of collective farm market sales in 1937 using 1937 prices averaged across all marketings.

Second, this value for collective market sales was extrapolated to
other years from 1932 to 1940 using an index of the quantity of goods
transacted on collective farm markets. For 1932–40, the index is the
official value of transactions deflated by an index of their price. Zaleski
(1971, 1984) reproduces the official returns as series 235. However, for
1940, the value shown by Zaleski is extremely large, and I use the
smaller value shown in *Sovietskaya Torgovlia*, 1956, p. 19. In his first
estimate of Soviet national income in 1940, Bergson apparently also
used the "large" value for 1940 but revised it downward to the "small"
value in his final work. Cf. Bergson and Heymann (1954, p. 21) and
Bergson (1961, p. 46). The price index used as a deflator is based on the
prices of commodities sold on the collective farm market and is pieced
together from the returns given by Malafeev (1964, p. 402) and Vyltsan
(1966, p. 61) for 1932–39. The 1940 value is from Karcz (1979, p.
334).

Third, for 1928–32, I relied on Barsov's work. He published a constant price index of the volume of agricultural marketings through all
channels and indices of procurement and farmers' market prices for
1929–32 and an overall price index that was weighted by the volumes
of the two sorts of sales (Barsov 1969, p. 107 n. 11, 108, table facing p.
112). One can work backward from his price indices and calculate relative volumes of procurements and farmers' market sales. When the total
volume of sales is multiplied by the later fraction for each year, the
result is an index of the volume of sales on farmers' markets. I assumed
the fraction was the same in 1928, for which Barsov gave no information, as in 1929. I used this index to extend the index of collective farm
market sales back to 1928.

7. Farmers' Market and Collective Farm Market Sales (Current Prices)

For 1932–40, the official series on the value of transactions on the collective farm market was used, as just explained. For 1928–31, I calculated the value of transactions by reducing the 1932 figure by the product of the quantity index of sales described previously (but rebased to
1932) and Malafeev's (1964, p. 401) index of the free market price of
food — again with a 1932 base.

8. Government Procurements

Agricultural marketings minus farmers' market and collective farm market sales (constant prices).

II. Food Balances and Calorie Consumption per Capita, 1885–1940

Calorie consumption was calculated in the manner of the UN Food and Agricultural Organization (FAO), *Production Yearbook* and *Food Balance Sheets*. Calorie consumption is calculated from agricultural and industrial production statistics rather than from household budget surveys. The balance sheet for 1984–86, pp. 351–53, gave average data for the USSR in those years and provided a template for the calculations. My calculations are based on the apparent human consumption of grain, potatoes, sugar, vegetables, beer, vodka, meat, milk, eggs, fish, vegetable oil, and butter. In 1984–86, these foods accounted for 89 percent of the calories in the Soviet diet. The most important omitted items were fruits (apples most important) and wine.

Calculation requires estimating per capita daily consumption (in kilograms) of each item by their calorie content, allowing for losses in food processing and preparation. I have used the FAO's calorie content figures that make those allowances. They are: grain (2711), potatoes (669), sugar (3565), vegetables (220), beer (483), vodka (2944), meat (1859), milk (504), eggs (1425), fish (861), vegetable oil (8385), butter (7191).

Quantities available for human consumption are estimated from the agricultural and industrial production statistics, making allowance for seed, fodder, losses, exports, and so forth. For the Soviet period, the figures were built up from the agricultural production statistics just described. For the imperial period, I relied on Gregory (1982). Details follow:

Grain

For the imperial period, net production for human consumption of wheat, rye, and barley (Gregory 1892, pp. 232–33) less grain exports less losses at 10 percent of production (suggested by Jasny 1949, pp. 751, 756; Davies 1980, pp. 427, 432) less grain used for the production of beer and vodka. The latter was estimated by multiplying beer and vodka production by grain input-output coefficients suggested by the allocation of grain to the alcohol and beer industries (Davies 1980, p. 434) and the production of those commodities.

For the Soviet period, gross production of grain less use for seed, fodder, beer, vodka, exports, army and urban horses (assumed to fall to zero in 1938). Use of grain for making beer and vodka estimated as in the imperial period. Use of grain for fodder estimated. Allowances for changes in peasant and state stocks were made. These smooth the series without changing the mean.

Potatoes

For the imperial period, net production for human consumption equals Gregory's (1982, p. 233) gross production less use for seed (taken to equal the difference between Gregory's net and gross production) less losses (at 10 percent of production) less fodder use. This was calculated by numbers of animals multiplied by the feed rates given earlier. For 1892–1902, the value implied by this formula was multiplied by one-tenth of the difference between the year and 1892. Fodder use was set at zero for 1885–92.

A similar formula was used for the Soviet period, except that seed use was calculated as the cultivated acreage multiplied by the seed rate.

Sugar

Nutter (1962, pp. 415, 451)—series 1510.

Vegetables

For 1913ff., production (revised Soviet estimate) from Davies, Harrison, and Wheatcroft (1994, p. 286) less 20 percent for expenses (Bergson 1961, p. 330). Per capita consumption for 1913 assumed to apply to earlier years.

Beer

Nutter (1962, pp. 415, 453)—series 1514. Production extrapolated by population for 1885–95.

Vodka

Nutter (1962, pp. 454)—series 1518. Production extrapolated by population for 1885–1913. Missing values interpolated.

Meat

For 1913 and subsequent years, meat consumption assumed equal to production as explained in discussion of agricultural statistics. Pre-1913 production extrapolated backward using an index of livestock. The index was the number of horned cattle plus half the number of pigs plus one-tenth the number of sheep and goats.

Milk

For 1913 and later, milk consumption assumed equal to production less expenses. These were equal to milk fed to calves. Following Johnson and Kahan (1959, p. 236), calves were assumed to eat 150 kg of milk per year and to equal 90 percent of the cows before 1930 and 85 percent thereafter.

Eggs

For 1913 and subsequent years, production for human consumption estimated as production less expenses (equal to 8 percent of production). An egg was assumed to weigh 50 grams. Pre-1913 extrapolated by population.

Fish

Nutter (1962, p. 451)—series 1507. Production extrapolated by population for 1885–1913.

Vegetable Oil

Nutter (1962, p. 450)—series 1504. Production extrapolated by population for 1885–1913. Missing values interpolated.

Butter

Estimated from the number of cows at 72 kg per cow.

III. Demographic Model Used in the Simulation Model

The simulation model of Chapter 8 contains a demographic model based on Lorimer's (1946, pp. 112–44) reconstruction of Soviet population history. This was an early effort. I have based my work on it (rather than later work) since Lorimer's estimate (5.5 million) of the number of "excess deaths" has been substantially vindicated by Wheatcroft (1990b). Moreover, Lorimer's calculations are well documented, so they can be readily extended.

At the time Lorimer composed his estimates, the firmest data for estimating the Soviet population were the censuses of 1926 and 1939, which indicate the population and allow estimates of the vital rates. Lorimer used a variety of other data to project the birth rate between

1926 and 1939. The crude birth rate followed a *U* shaped trajectory. The crude death rate was linearly interpolated between the dates. With these estimates of "normal" ferility and mortality, Lorimer projected the 1926 population forward and the 1939 population backward. When his projections met in 1934, the forecast from 1928 exceeded the backcast from 1939 by 5.5 million. This is Lorimer's estimate of "excess" mortality. Obviously, the estimate of "excess" mortality is only as good as the estimates of "normal" fertility and mortality. Lorimer believed that most of the excess deaths occurred in the period of collectivization, and allocated them to those years. He then formed annual estimates of the Soviet population between 1926 and 1939.

The question of births, deaths, and excesses deaths has been debated since Lorimer's work. (See Davies, Harrison, and Wheatcroft 1994, pp. 64–77, for a survey.) Many scholars have proposed higher numbers of excess deaths (e.g., Andreev, Darski, and Khar'kova [1990]). The increased number of excess deaths occurred among infants and offset a posited rise in the fertility rate in 1933 (Davies, Harrison, and Wheatcroft 1994, pp. 74–76). There is no point trying to incorporate this mortality into my models since it does not result in any change in the labor force.

My estimates of the rural and urban population begin with Lorimer's figures for the whole Soviet Union. Basic information includes the rural and urban populations in 1926, and annual estimates of the total population, births, deaths, and net rural-urban migration from 1927 to 1939 (Lorimer 1946, pp. 134, 150, 154, 158; Davies, Harrison, and Wheatcroft 1994, pp. 274–75). In addition, urban and rural crude birth and death rates in 1927 are employed (Lorimer 1946, p. 81).

Calculation of the rural and urban populations proceeds in steps. First, national crude birth and death rates are computed annually from 1927 through 1939. A "no excess deaths" crude death rate is then constructed on the assumptions (1) that there were no excess deaths in 1927, and 1938, and 1939, and (2) that the crude death rate in 1928–36 would have equaled the interpolated value of the actual crude death rate in 1927 and 1938 if there were no excess deaths. An annual series of excess deaths is then computed. The total equals 5.8 million. Second, all excess deaths are presumed to come out of the rural population, and a new "no excess deaths" crude death rate for the rural population is calculated accordingly. (This is surely wrong in detail since no allowance is made for deaths during and after the purges of the late 1930s, and those deaths were mainly urban. The number of purge deaths, however, was small compared to the number accompanying collectivization.) The crude birth and death rates for the urban and rural populations are then estimated by extrapolating the 1927 values to 1939 in accord with the national crude birth rate and "no excess mortality" crude death rate series. Fourth, the rural and urban populations were then calculated year by year from the rural and urban populations in 1926 by cumulating births, deaths (normal and excess), and net migration. The sum of the urban and rural populations agrees closely with Lorimer's annual estimates of the total population, and the projections of the rural and urban populations in 1939 agree with the census results of that year. Moreover, the projected 1937 population is in accord with the results of the suppressed 1937 census.

In addition to the rural and urban populations, the farm and nonfarm populations are needed for simulations. The urban population was very largely nonfarm (Lorimer 1946, p. 228), but the rural population included a fair number of nonagricultural workers in farm-related activities (e.g., flour milling, protoindustry, construction) and other activities (government administration, education, health care). Many rural residents shifted between farming and other activities. I estimated the farm population c. 1928 and c. 1939 from Lorimer (1946, pp. 222–30) and Jasny (1949, pp. 710–14). The figures are meant to be the sum of people in households engaged in farming full- and part-time. To simulate the farm population from 1928 forward, I updated the 1928 value by the change in the rural population. The nonfarm population equaled the total population minus the farm population.

IV. Other Series Required for the Simulation Model of Chapter 8

Investment, 1925–27 — 1928: investment was extrapolated backward using an index of construction materials (rolled steel, fire-clay bricks, and cement — weighted equally) from Nutter (1962, pp. 420, 427).

Production function parameters — Attempts were made to fit production functions to interwar Soviet data with little success. Consequently, the parameters were derived from the results of other statistical studies. Weitzman (1970) fit a two-factor (capital and labor) CES production function to Soviet industrial data and estimated the elasticity of substitution at about .4 and the coefficient of capital at .6. I used these values for the producer goods production function. A three-factor (capital, labor, and processed agricultural commodities) was necessary for the consumer goods function. I used a CES function again with the elasticity of substitution of .4. I made the coefficients of the three inputs approximately equal.

V. Division of the Economy into Producer
Goods and Consumer Goods Sectors

The simulation model of Chapter 8 required 1928 values for outputs and inputs in the consumer goods and producer goods industries in order to begin the simulations. All valuation was in 1937 prices. In this analysis, the economy is conceptually divided into three sectors: consumer goods, producer goods, and agriculture. GDP equals the sum of value added in the three sectors, and output in each sector equals value added in the sector plus purchases from other sectors.

Begin with producer goods. The output of producer goods is defined to be the sum of gross investment inclusive of repair expenditures,[1] consumer durables,[2] military equipment,[3] and hospital equipment.[4] I took the production of these items to have equaled the total output of the machinery and construction industries. The producer goods sector was presumed to have purchased no intermediate inputs from other sectors, so the output of producer goods equaled value added in the producer goods sector.

Agriculture was also presumed to have purchased no current inputs from other sectors, so the value of agricultural output net of seed and feed equals value added in agriculture. The calculation of net agricultural output is explained in the discussion of the agricultural database.

Since GDP equals the sum of value added in the three sectors, value added in consumer goods equaled GDP less net agricultural output and producer goods output. Value added in the consumer goods sector plus its purchases of agricultural produce equals the output of consumer goods. As noted earlier, the consumer goods industry includes the production of private consumer goods (except durables), housing, privately consumed services, health, educational, administrative, police, and military services.

To determine input use in the various sectors, input-output analysis was used. First, an input-output table was adapted from the provisional table of Kaplan et al. (1952) based on the Fourth Five-Year Plan. Some elements in this table are well founded on late 1930s Soviet data, but other elements are not. I modified the table for industries like textiles where the input-output coefficients diverged markedly from those in Leontief's U.S. tables for 1919 and 1929 (Leontief 1941). I aggregated the defense and machinery industries whose coefficients, in any event, were similar. The coefficients from this table apply to c. 1940, but I used them for 1928 calculations.

Second, to obtain 1928 starting values for the inputs, the components of final demand (household purchases, current government spending, investment) in 1928 were subdivided into purchases from the various industries distinguished in the input-output table. A vector, each of whose elements was purchases from an industry, was thus established

TABLE C.1
Division of Soviet Industries into Producer Goods and Consumer Goods, 1928
(Fraction of the industry's gross output and inputs assigned to)

Industry	Producer goods industry	Consumer goods industry
Agriculture	0.00	1.00
Food processing	0.00	1.00
Textiles	0.00	1.00
Light industry	0.00	1.00
Iron and steel	0.76	0.24
Nonferrous metals	0.22	0.78
Machinery and metalwork	1.00	0.00
Construction materials	0.59	0.41
Chemicals	0.25	0.75
Wood	0.51	0.49
Paper	0.17	0.83
Electric power	0.11	0.89
Coal	0.19	0.81
Peat	0.07	0.93
Petroleum products	0.04	0.96
Transportation	0.14	0.86
Communications	0.04	0.96
Trade	0.01	0.99
Construction	1.00	0.00
Other	0.00	1.00
Other government	0.00	1.00

for each component of aggregate demand. These vectors were then used to specify vectors corresponding to the consumer goods (in this case, agriculture plus consumer goods) and producer goods industries, as defined in this study. The producer goods vector had elements equaling the total final purchases from the machinery and construction industries; otherwise, its elements were zero. Conversely, the elements of the consumer goods industry vector were the total final purchases from all industries except machinery and construction, which were zero.

Third, the table of input-output coefficients was postmultiplied by the producer goods and consumer goods vectors. The gross output of each industry was thus split into investment goods and consumer goods. Table C.1 shows the proportions of each industry allocated to each use. The division is much as one would expect. All, or virtually all, of the output of food processing, textiles, and light industry are consumer goods. The heavy industries — iron and steel, machinery, and so on — are mainly producer goods.

Fourth, total employment by industry in 1928 was pieced together from Nutter (1962, pp. 499–504), Kaplan (1969, pp. 208–12), Weitzman and Elias (1961), Moorsteen and Powell (1966, pp. 642–50), and Bergson (1961, pp. 442–47). Multiplying each industry total by the fraction of that industry's gross output classified as investment or consumption goods yielded employment by industry in investment and consumption goods. The sum for each sector gave total employment in 1928 in that sector.

Fifth, capital was dealt with similarly, although it was necessary to break down the capital stock in the industrial sector. Moorsteen and Powell's (1966, pp. 408–18) reworking of Gosplan's estimates of the capital stock on 1 January 1928 gave values by sector but not by the various industries making up the industrial sector. I estimated capital in those industries by using the employment figures and estimates of the capital-labor ratio derived from American data (taken principally from Creamer et al. 1960, pp. 248–51, 273, 318, 323, but also from U.S. Census of Mines for 1929, p. 44, and the U.S. Census of Manufactures for 1920, vol. 8, p. 20, 146, and vol. 10, p. 920, and Jorgenson et al. 1987, pp. 380ff.). Soviet employment figures were multiplied by American capital-labor ratios and the industrial capital stock was divided among the industries in proportion to the products. This procedure assumes that the relative capital labor-ratios in the Soviet Union were the same as the relative ratios in the United States at about the same time, but the absolute levels are allowed to differ. Capital stocks in the producer goods and consumer goods industries were the sums of the industry components.

Table C.2 shows the results of this disaggregation of the Soviet economy in 1928. The economy was dedicated overwhelmingly to producing consumer goods. The producer goods sector comprised only 7 percent of the capital, 19 percent of the employment, and 13 percent of the output of the nonagricultural economy.

TABLE C.2
Division of the Soviet Economy into Producer Goods and Consumer Goods Sectors, 1928

	Capital stock	Employment	Output
Producer goods	9729	2368	12.03
Consumer goods except agriculture	126540	9977	83.25
Agriculture	21162	35000	42.60
Total	157431	47345	137.88

Note: Employment is in thousands of people. Capital stock is in millions of 1937 rubles, and output is in billions of 1937 rubles. A factor cost concept of output is used.

The Demographic Databases and Simulation Model Used in Chapter 6

I. Census Database Used for Estimation of Models of the Total Fertility Rate

1. Sample Definition and Total Fertility Rate

The sample is an extension — and in the case of 1939, a replacement — of the Coale, Anderson, and Harm (1979, pp. 20–21, 28–33, 88) data that were tabulated in their book. They reported their index of fertility (If) for the "provinces" they studied. (The term *provinces* refers to gubernii in 1897 and oblasts, krai, autonomous republics, and, in some cases, full republics in 1939 and 1959.) Geographically, the Coale–Anderson–Harm sample was primarily concerned with the fifty provinces of European Russia in the 1897 census. Only a little attention was given to other regions. The sample analyzed here was broadened to include the Caucuses, Central Asia, and Siberia.

The units of observation were the provinces of European Russia, the Caucuses, Central Asia, and Siberia in 1897, and the oblasts, krai, and autonomous republics of the Russian SSR and Ukrainian SSR in 1939 plus the other republics. The 1959 data set was similar to the 1939 data set except that the oblasts of Belorussia were also distinguished. The full data set includes 283 observations. The data were taken from Russia, Tsentralnyi statisticheskii komitet (1905), Russian Academy of Sciences (1992), and USSR, Tsentralnoe Statisticheskoe Upravlenie (1962–63).

The first step in putting together the data set was determining the total fertility rate. Age-specific fertility rates are not available for the provinces in all of the years studied, so the total fertility rate was computed from If. If is the actual number of births divided by the number that would have occurred had the female population experienced the Hutterite-age specific fertility rates given by Coale, Anderson, and Harm (1979, p. 262 n. 4). If was converted to the total fertility rate by multiplying by 12.195, the Hutterite total fertility rate.

One virtue of If as a measure of fertility is that it can be computed without age-specific data of fertility. Coale, Anderson, and Harm report their index of fertility (If) for the provinces in their study and those values have been used in this investigation. In practice, this meant redoing their figures for 1939 (which they refer to as 1940) to accord with 1939 boundaries rather than the 1959 boundaries which they used. It was necessary to estimate If for the oblasts and so on added to the list analyzed by Coale et al. The procedure was as follows.

Following Coale et al., the actual number of births in 1939 and 1959 in each oblast were estimated using the 1940 and 1960 crude birth rates reported in *Vestnik Statistiki*, 1965, no. 1, pp. 86–91. A more circuitous procedure was followed for 1897. Coale et al.'s values of If were used to retrieve the number of births in the provinces in European Russia that they studied. These births were correlated with the number of children of age less than 1 and of ages 1–9 as reported in the census in order to predict the number of births from the reported information on the age distribution of the population for the Caususes, Central Asian, and Siberian provinces. The regression with the population aged 1–9 gave much better results, since infants less than 1 year old were manifestly underenumerated in much of Central Asia.

The hypothetical number of births was calculated by applying the Hutterite schedule to the number of women in each age group shown in the census. (The age distribution of women was assumed to be uniform in each category. The 1939 census only reported the age distribution for men and women combined for each oblast. The ratio of women to men in each age group for the USSR as a whole was used to estimate the number of women in each age group in each oblast.)

2. Explanatory Variables

The explanatory variables were the fraction of the province that was urban, the fraction that was Muslim, and the years of education completed by women and men.

The urban population was recorded for each province, oblast, and so on in every census. The religious breakdown of each province was recorded in 1897, and the population was broken down by nationality in the Soviet censuses. The nationalities were classified by their traditional religion, and the Muslim percentage was computed as the percentage of the population in Muslim nationalities.

Years of education of men and women were computed from information on the educational attainment of the adult population. Three categories were distinguished in 1897 and 1939: the literate, those with some secondary education, and those with some higher education. The 1897 and 1939 censuses recorded the number of literate men and women in each province or oblast, and so on. The number of men and women with secondary and with higher education was recorded in 1897 for

broad regions—European Russia, the Caususes, and the like. Breakdowns were given for the rural and urban populations and the totals for
the broad regions were distributed among their provinces in proportion
to the urban populations. Not much error can arise since the totals were
so tiny. The 1939 census indicated how many men and women in each
oblast, and so on, had any secondary or higher education. Those with
some higher education were coded as having fourteen years of education, those with some secondary as having nine years, and those who
were literate but without secondary or higher education were assigned
two years in 1897 and 3 years in 1939 when instruction was more
widespread. Strumilin found that the earnings of factory workers with
an informal education were the same as those with two years of education, and that result guided the years of education to assign to the literate (Crisp 1978, p. 388).

The 1959 census employed a more detailed classification. Following
Karasik (1992, p. 371), it was coded as follows: completed higher (16
years), incomplete higher (14), special secondary (11), general secondary (10), incomplete secondary (9), complete or incomplete primary (3).

II. Simulations of the Total Fertility Rate and Analysis of Its Fall

These simulations required time series of the independent variables in
the Schultz equation. Education, urbanization, and religion were computed from the censuses and census cross sections just described for
1897, 1939, and 1959. Other sources include:

Education—Johnson (1969, pp. 173, 285), Timasheff (1942, pp. 82, 86, 87)

GDP/adult—GDP per head from Maddison (1995). Adult share of the population (those 20 years and older) from Andreev, Darskii, and Khar'kova (1992, p. 133ff.), Zhiromskaia, Kilselev, and Poliakov (1996, pp. 67–69), United Nations (1991, 360) for 1950–85.

Calories—See Chapter 7, Appendix C, and United Nations, Food and Agricultural Organization (1991, p. 238).

Religion—Barrett (1982, p. 689).

Urbanization—Bairoch (1988, pp. 221, 290), Lorimer (1946, pp. 154, 158), Zhiromskaia, Kilselev, and Poliakov (1996, pp. 67–69), United Nations (1987, p. 53).

Agricultural share—Shanin (1986, p. 64) Gregory (1972, p. 433), Davies (1990, p. 251), United Nations, Food and Agricultural Or-ganization, *Production Yearbook*, various years.

III. Simulation Model of Population Growth

The model begins with the age structure of the population in 1926 as given by Andreev, Darksii, and Khar'kova (1992, p. 134). It is projected forward by adding births and subtracting deaths.

Computing the births requires age-specific fertility rates for women for each year from 1926 to 1989. Andreev, Darksii, and Khar'kova (1992, p. 150) report estimates for 1926–59. Later rates were taken *Naselenia SSSR* (1973, p. 137) and *Narodnoe Khoziastvo*, various years. Reported rates are for ages at five-year intervals and were applied to all ages in the interval.

Computing deaths requires age-specific death rates for men and women for all ages. For 1926–58, the rates were abstracted from Andreev, Darskii, and Khar'kova's (1992, pp. 133ff.) reconstruction of the age distribution of men and women each year from 1920 to 1959. They report numbers of men and women in five-year age cohorts. Comparison of the numbers in one year with the numbers in the age group five years older shown five years later allowed mortality to be computed. Death rates were reconstructed for such comparisons for 1926, 1931–39, 1941, 1946, 1951, 1956, and 1958. The use of the infant mortality rate also allowed estimates of average death rates for ages 1–4 to be computed. For years after 1959, age-specific death rates were taken from *Narodnoe Khoziastvo*, various years.

Notes

CHAPTER ONE. SOVIET DEVELOPMENT IN WORLD-HISTORICAL PERSPECTIVE

1. Small countries are excluded as are countries that grew for reasons (like rich oil reserves) that are not transferable to other countries.

2. The reliability of Maddison's data is assessed in Appendix A along with other measures of Soviet economic development. I argue there in favor of his figures for Russia and the USSR since 1913. However, for pre-1913 Russia, I have used Gregory's (1972, p. 433, 1982, pp. 56–57, variant 2) estimates of Russian net national product (NNP).

3. Turkey is classified here as a non-OECD country in view of its manifest backwardness in 1928.

4. GDP per head in 1989 in each republic was computed by multiplying Soviet GDP per head in that year ($7078) by the ratio of GDP per head in the republic in 1991 to GDP per head of the former Soviet Union in 1991 as given in Maddison (1995, p. 142).

5. Kuznets (1971, pp. 250–53), Food and Agricultural Organization, *Production Yearbook*, 1952, Mitchell (1992, 1993, 1995), Minami (1986, p. 273).

6. Pipes (1974, pp. 50–51) contrasted medieval Russia with Western feudalism. The latter was reciprocal and contractual, while the former was not. Eventually, the whole society submitted to the tsar. Kivelson (1993, 1996), however, has argued for some mutuality between the tsar and the Boyers.

7. The process was gradual (Crummey 1987, p. 96).

8. See the views of Robert Brenner (1976), and the discussion they provoked (Aston and Philpin 1985).

9. This is to take the "decree" side in the debate with the "nondecree" historians. Hellie (1971) summarized the debate and defended the "decree" position, which maintains that serfdom was ineffective before the 1649 edict. The nondecree position, advanced by Kliuchevsky (1907, pp. 174–99), for instance, maintains that peasant indebtedness prevented earlier mobility. See also Worobec (1981).

CHAPTER TWO. ECONOMIC GROWTH BEFORE 1917

1. The agricultural index is Bobrov's (1925, p. 91). Bobrov also presented an industrial price index that grew at the same rate as the agricultural one. His industrial index was a weighted average of four subindices: processed foods (20%), oil and minerals (20%), chemicals (20%), and textiles (40%). Most of the rise in the industrial index was due to the textile component, which inflated at an exceptional rate due to Russian tariff policy. Oils and minerals moved erratically.

Many important industries are missing from Bobrov's industrial index. Figure

2.1 plots a new industrial index using Bobrov's subindices plus four others calculated from Gregory (1982, pp. 277–78, 296). The additional indices are nonmetallic minerals (cement, plaster, and bricks), machinery (an unweighted average of the price indices of locomotives, sickle and scythes, steam tractors, and steam engines), metals (an unweighted average of the price indices of iron and steel rails), and lumber (an unweighted average of the price indices of railroad ties and pine boards). The industrial index shown in Figure 2.1 is a weighted average as follows: processed foods (15.3%), oil and minerals (10%), chemicals (4.9%), textiles (30.6%), nonmetallic minerals (6.8%), machinery (10.2%), metals (15.9%), and lumber (6.3%). The weights are 1897 employment shares from matched industries (Crisp 1978, p. 354).

2. Labor, capital (livestock and buildings), and output from Gregory (1982, pp. 133, 268, 293). The growth of the cultivated area is measured by the growth in the area harvested of wheat, rye, barley, and oats. The areas were calculated by dividing gross production in the Empire of wheat, rye, barley, and oats by the yields per desiyatine in the fifty provinces of European Russia given in Groman (1927, Part II, pp. 2–5). Gross production of wheat, rye, and barley taken from Gregory (1982, pp. 232–33). Gross production of oats worked out from Timoshenko (1932, p. 522). In early years, no production of oats was reported for some parts of the empire outside the fifty provinces of European Russia. At the time, production in these districts was very small and was estimated here by interpolation.

3. However, see Bideleux (1990) for comparisons of Russian grain yields with those in many countries and a defense of the progressiveness of the commune.

4. Mitchell and Deane (1971, p. 90).

5. While agriculture's terms of trade improved when measured with wholesale prices, as in Figure 2.1, there is no improvement when a retail food price index is compared to a retail price index of manufactured consumer goods (Strumilin 1967, pp. 431–32). The latter is dominated by textiles, whose wholesale prices inflated exceptionally, as noted.

6. Quotations from Gregory (1994, pp. 136–37).

7. See Figure 4.1, which compares the history of wheat yields in Russia/USSR and North Dakota. Olmstead and Rhode (2002) argue that even stable average yields in North America required considerable research to find wheat varieties that were resistant to pests and capable of growing in the harsh conditions of the Great Plains and prairies. Some of the hearty varieties were imported from Russia, so it was setting the technological ceiling for North America rather than the other way around!

8. In 1913, there were 71.7 thousand kilometers of track in the area of the USSR, post–World War II frontiers. In 1989, the total was 147.7 thousand kilometers. *Narodnoe khozaistvo*, 1960, p. 535; 1989, p. 588.

9. Mironov (2000) has advanced the contrary view that Russia was launched on the European path. See Wagner (2001) for a skeptical review.

10. Gregory (1982, p. 174; 1994, p. 35) has twice published a table showing that inequality in Russia in the early twentieth century was less than that in other countries. He also pointed out, however, that the statistics were unreliable and implausible.

11. Dividing Gregory's (1997, p. 198) "Kafengauz expanded index" of industrial output by Kafengauz's (1994, pp. 307–15) employment figures.

12. The series of average annual earnings in factories is from Strumilin (1966, pp. 92, 94), the daily wage of St. Petersburg building workers is from Strumilin (1966, p. 82), and the average annual earnings of railroad workers is from Strumilin (1958, p. 642). Gregory (1982, pp. 254–55, 277, 278, 296) reports indices of the earnings of telegraph employees, railroad mechanics and maintenance personnel, Varzar's index of wages in heavy industry, and railroad construction workers. Using any of these series paints the same picture of real wage stagnation.

The series of average annual earnings of factory workers raise one issue of interpretation. The data derive from factory inspector reports, and Strumilin reproduces two series that must be linked. One relates to the Russian Empire for 1885–1900, and the other pertains to the empire less Poland and Finland for 1897 and 1900–14. They have two years in common: 1897 and 1900. The values are similar, and graphing the series indicates no break in either level or trend. There are three ways to combine them: linking them in 1897 or 1900 or simply merging them without adjustment. Doing the former produces a series very much like the Varzar series. This shows the smallest rise in earnings. Gregory (1982, pp. 254–55) does the second, which shows the greatest increase in earnings. I have done the third, which produces an intermediate result. Using Gregory's series would not change the view of Russian industrialization presented here.

13. Gregory (1982, pp. 219–220), however, assumed that the earnings of domestic servants and medical personnel moved in the same way as those of factory workers, so there is some possibility that the conclusions founded on the available data apply more broadly.

14. Six basic price series are available for deflators. More can be constructed by averaging these or from their subindices. Four of the indices apply to St. Petersburg and involve the prices of varying numbers of retail goods, while one applies to Moscow. The sixth index, the Podtriagin index, is a pseudo retail price index involving sixty-six commodities. The weights in this index reflect consumer spending patterns, while the prices are wholesale prices. The Podtriagan index has the widest geographical coverage since it uses prices from across Russia, but it is more volatile than the retail price indices since wholesale grain prices fluctuated more than retail bread prices. Aside from its greater volatility, the Podtriagin index and all of the St. Petersburg indices move similarly. The Moscow index, which is based on the fewest number of goods (fifteen), shows somewhat less inflation, but the difference is not substantial. I will use the Podtriagin index, which covers the 1885–1913 period, to deflate agricultural incomes, and the St. Petersburg index, which covers the longest period (1853–1913), for nonagricultural incomes. A further point in favor of the latter is that it is the only retail price index that includes housing rents. The two indices agree closely about the trend in prices from 1885 to 1913. The indices are tabulated in Strumilin (1966, pp. 89–90; 1967, pp. 431–32).

15. The debate has raged for two centuries. Lindert and Williamson (1983) refocused it by computing, for the first time, an economy-wide nominal wage

index and an economy-wide consumer price index. Both have been subjected to considerable critical comment and revision. Feinstein (1998) incorporates the revisions into a real wage index that shows little growth during the industrial revolution, especially when deterioration in living conditions is taken into account.

16. Atkinson (1983, p. 33), Gerschenkron (1965, p. 6), Mironov (1985), Robinson (1932, pp. 94–116), Shanin (1986, pp. 140–49), Violin (1970, pp. 52–56). However, Hoch (1994) and Gatrell (1986, p. 232) argue for rising peasant living standards.

17. Farm revenue is the sum of revenue from crops and from livestock minus redemption payments. Crop and livestock revenues are calculated inclusive of consumption by the farm family. Redemption payments from Khromov (1950).

Crop revenue is defined as the value of net production, that is, gross production minus usage on the farm for seed and fodder. Prices and net production of wheat, rye, barley, and potatoes are from Gregory (1982, pp. 234, 238–39). The total was increased by 30 percent to allow for other crops. The difference between gross and net production is an allowance for seed and animal feed. It should be noted that this scheme implicitly assumes that all of the oat crop was used as fodder. The seed and fodder assumptions were tested against seed rates and feeding norms from the 1920s and were found to be plausible.

Livestock revenue is defined as the value of livestock products. The number and current value of large horned cattle, sheep and goats, and swine were taken from Gregory (1982, pp. 268–69). Output of livestock products was computed from the number of animals using Prokopovich's (1918) assumptions about herd composition and management (with some amendments for consistency) and his yield coefficients. Annual estimates of the production of milk, beef, veal, cattle hides, sheep meat, sheep fat, wool, sheep hides, pig meat, pig fat, and pig bristles were made accordingly. These were valued with Prokopovich's 1913 prices for 1913. For earlier years, 1913 prices were extrapolated back to 1885 using the current value of the kind of livestock that produced each product as a price index, for example, the value each year in current prices of one large horned cattle was used to extrapolate the 1913 prices of milk, beef, veal, and cattle hides back to 1885.

The rural population was taken as 87 percent of the total in 1897 and 85 percent in 1913. Other years were linearly interpolated from these figures. Total population from Gregory (1982, pp. 56–57).

18. The Podtriagin index was used. The choice of a deflator becomes critical if the prices peasants received on their sales changed significantly with respect to the prices they paid for manufactured goods. This happened in the "scissors crisis" of the 1920s. In the imperial period, wholesale agricultural prices and the retail prices of food and manufactured goods like cloth and shoes were inflating at the same rates, so serious index number problems do not arise.

19. Wheatcroft (1991) reached a similar conclusion regarding real wages. Hoch (1994) correctly pointed out that the net income of farmers was the relevant indicator for most rural inhabitants.

20. Pallott (1999) discusses this concern and the wide range of peasant resistance to the Stolypin reforms.

21. The phrase is due to Stolypin (Robinson 1932, p. 194).

22. There is debate as to how the farm size distribution was actually changing — was the commune strong enough to resist differentiation (e.g., Field 1990; Löwe 1990)? — and how to interpret the motives of those who departed. Pallot (1999), for instance, thinks that the number of separations from communes overstates peasant enthusiasm for Stolypin-style changes.

CHAPTER THREE. THE DEVELOPMENT PROBLEM IN THE 1920S

1. Whether 1928 output was slightly above or slightly below that of 1913 can be debated. The issue has taken on an iconic significance since "if the Soviet industrialisation drive began well prior to recovery to pre-war levels, some of the rapid growth of the 1930s should be attributed to the higher rates of growth associated with the recovery process" (Gregory 1990, p. 238). This inference is unwarranted. If a factory that was idle for a decade and whose workforce had vanished was put back to operation in 1929, that restart amounted to new investment. It was not like recalling the workforce and restarting a mill that was idled in a cyclical downturn.

2. Ehrlich (1960), Dobb (1948), Carr and Davies (1969), and Spulber (1964).

3. Many economists have analyzed this view, including Rosenstein-Rodan (1943), Nurske (1953), Scitovsky (1954), Fleming (1955), Rodrik (1996), Ciccione and Matsuyama (1996), Puga (1998).

4. See Domar (1957) and Kaser (1964) for discussions of the model.

5. The quotations from Preobrazhensky's writings are from Ehrlich (1960, pp. 36–38, 50).

6. Minami (1986, p. 98).

7. The quotations from Rykov and Bukharin are from Ehrlich (1960, pp. 16, 82–84).

CHAPTER FOUR. NEP AGRICULTURE AND ECONOMIC DEVELOPMENT

1. Johnson and Brooks (1983) developed several well-focused comparisons between the Soviet Union and North America. Their most simply defined comparison group consists of Alberta, Manitoba, Saskatchewan, Montana, Wyoming, North Dakota, South Dakota, and Nebraska. I have excluded the latter since it is in the Corn Belt and produces so much maize that there is no counterpart in the fifty provinces of European Russia. For the same reason, the fattening of young animals bred elsewhere was central to Nebraska livestock husbandry and had no counterpart in Russia.

2. U.S. Bureau of the Census, *Fourteenth Census of the United States Taken in the Year 1920*, Washington, D.C., U.S. Government Printing Office, 1921–23, and Canada, Dominion Bureau of Statistics, *Sixth Census of Canada, 1921*, Ottawa, F.A. Acland, 1924–28.

3. See Chayanov (1966, pp. 165–66) for farms using virgin steppe and forests for grazing.

4. The Russian figures are from Prokopovich (1918, pp. 34–41). The meat yield figures for North America are Canadian averages for 1920 (ratios of dressed meat to number of animals slaughtered) from Leacy (1983). The milk

yield figures are ratios of milk production of cows in milk or calf for Canada and the United States. Wool per fleece are averages for the American plains states.

5. Canadian feed rates for 1910 are from Ward (1990, pp. 117, 138). Russian rates are from Nimitz (1954, p. 78) and Jasny (1949, p. 753). There is some variation, depending on the survey and the authority.

6. In his calculations of the net output of tsarist agriculture, Gregory reckoned all of the oat crop as feed or seed and made no allowance for the feeding of other grain or potatoes to farm animals. Thus, Gregory (1982, pp. 232–33) reports gross and net production figures for wheat, rye, barley, and potatoes. Dividing the difference between the gross and net figure by the sown area of each crop gives a value approximately equal to the seed rate, that is, there is nothing left over for animal feed. The oat crop is not treated as final output. The gross output of oats is approximately equal to the sown area multiplied by the seed rate plus the number of working horses multiplied by a feed rate of 400 kg per year.

7. Additional feed had to be imported into Montana and Wyoming. That is ignored in the calculations of this chapter, and the productivity of North American agriculture is correspondingly overstated.

8. Gosplan typically assumed a year was 290 days, but Strumilin used a figure of 245 days, and Kahan thought that was more realistic in view of Russia's climate. Thus, 17.8 million years of work is implied by a 245-day year while a 290-day year would imply 15 million years. See Kahan (1959, p. 457 n. 22).

9. In 1927–28, the farm population consisted of 114.8 million people in 23.0 million peasant households. Their potential labor supply equaled 57 million adult male equivalent years of labor, that is, 2.48 years per household. Multiplying 16 million by 2.48 gives 39.7 million years. See *Statisticheskii spravochnik SSSR za 1928*, p. 88, and Strumilin (1930, p. 9).

10. Labor was also needed to harvest barley, oats, and minor grains, but these crops were harvested after the wheat and rye and represented a smaller requirement of labor. Plowing and carting were also performed in the summer, but not necessarily during the ten-day harvest period. It might be noted that Strumilin (1930, p. 10) came to a similar conclusion, for he estimated that the mechanization of the harvest would free 15 million workers who were only needed in that short period.

11. Chayanov (1966, p. 188). The relationship between farm size and mechanization has been extensively debated by economic historians since David's (1966) pathbreaking paper launched the modern discussion. David used a threshold model similar to Chayanov's. Olmstead and Rhode (2001) have developed the most sophisticated model and applied it to tractor adoption. They found that large farms in the United States were more likely to adopt tractors than small ones, while the spread of tractors led to the growth in farm size. The economic incentives were similar in the Soviet Union in the 1920s for most types of farm machinery.

12. As people leave the countryside and farm output is divided by the smaller number of people who remain, the income—that is, available food—of the latter rises. Russian peasants were poor, so their income elasticity of demand for

food was high. Consequently, they would eat some of the rise in the food accruing to them. In other words, the Russians would not market all of the farm goods relinquished by people moving to the cities.

13. See, for instance, Erhlich (1960), Spulber (1964), Lewin (1968), Cohen (1973), Merl (1981), Gregory and Stuart (1986), Nove (1990), and Harrison (1990).

14. See Allen (1997, p. 409). Figure 4.2 plots the reciprocal of the series tabulated there.

15. Antel and Gregory (1994) have used cross-sectional data from the mid-1920s to estimate the response of grain marketing to price changes and conclude that the elasticity was .3, a value supportive of Millar's view. This rather low value, however, may be due to their using ordinary least squares to estimate the supply curve, which has price (an endogenous variable) on the right-hand side. While they argue against the likelihood of simultaneous equation bias, there remains the possibility that their elasticity is biased toward zero for this reason.

16. Mellor and Mudahar (1992, pp. 389–91) and Ghatak and Ingersent (1984, pp. 189–99) provide surveys of this literature.

17. Ghatak and Ingersent (1984, pp. 189–99) discuss several models of peasant marketing.

18. The algebraic version of the model is explained in Allen (1997).

19. This is the "predicted" series shown in Figure 4.3. Its construction is described in detail in Allen (1997).

20. In Figure 4.3, the "actual" series equals Wheatcroft's index number of marketed production (relative to its 1913 value) multiplied by the level of marketings in 1913 shown in Table 4.6.

21. The relative levels of agricultural output in 1913 and 1928 has been a contentious issue. My figures show a 10 percent increase in output net of seed, feed, and losses on the farm. This result is is line with various official Soviet series as well as the Johnson and Kahan series. These are summarized in Wheatcroft (1983, p. 48; 1990a, pp. 274–75). However, Wheatcroft (1983, pp. 45–47; 1990a, p. 279) has produced several recalculations of the data showing little or no growth in output.

22. This accounting is done from counterfactual calculations. I begin with the actual 1913 values. Leaving the level of surplus extraction and the terms of trade unchanged, the increase in production between 1913 and 1928 would have increased marketings by 9 percent, from 3334 to 3623 million rubles in 1928 prices. This tendency was offset by the reduction in surplus extraction and by the deterioration of the terms of trade, which together cut marketings to 2565 million rubles.

The exact importance of each factor depends on the order in which the calculations are performed. If the effect of the reduction in surplus extraction is calculated first, it reduces marketings by 232 million from 3623 to 3391 million, and the deterioration of the terms of trade reduces marketings by a further 826 million to the actual 1928 value of 2565. On the other hand, if the effect of the decline of the terms of trade is calculated first, marketings are reduced by 789 million (from 3623 to 2834) and the reduction in surplus extraction explains the remaining drop of 269 million to 2565. In either case, the decline in the terms of trade was about three times as important as the reduction in surplus extraction in explaining the decline in marketing, but both played a role.

23. Compare Dohan's (1969, p. 676) procurement price to Gregory's (1982, p. 234) wholesale price and the *London Gazette* wheat price (Mitchell and Deane 1971, p. 489).

24. Compare the price received by farmers in the Canadian prairie provinces (Canada, Dominion Bureau of Statistics, *Sixth Census of Canada, 1921*, vol. V, pp. 16–19) with the Kansas City and British prices shown in U.S. Bureau of the Census (1975, series E123), and Mitchell and Deane (1971, p. 489).

CHAPTER FIVE. PLANNING, COLLECTIVIZATION, AND RAPID GROWTH

1. Zaleski (1971, 1980) has studied the degree to which planned targets were fulfilled, and his data show that it was rare, so the industries in Tables 5.1 and 5.2 are representative in this regard.

2. The magnitudes depend on whether GDP is measured at factor cost or purchasers' prices. In the former, farm income in kind is valued at the average prices received by farmers on their sales—that is, exclusive of the turnover tax—and services and housing are valued at prices actually paid; in the latter, farm income in kind is valued at collective farm market prices that approximate retail shop prices—that is, inclusive of the turnover tax—and services and housing are valued at prices intended to approximate market clearing prices. The figures reported in the text measure GDP at factor cost. Using purchasers' prices lowers the investment rates by about 3 percent.

3. The reference is to the nonagricultural capital stock, gross value in 1937 prices, computed by Moorsteen and Powell (1966, p. 326).

4. These calculations assume 2 percent annual growth in the number of livestock from their peak c. 1930. If the horse population is also assumed to grow at that rate, net farm output would grow by 29 percent (on pre-1939 borders) from 1928 to 1940. If mechanization is presumed to have proceeded rapidly so the horse population declined at its historical rate, then net farm output would have increased by 46 percent. The difference is the value of the grain the horses would have eaten.

5. See Chapter 9 for a more detailed discussion of these pricing issues.

6. Prices from Karcz (1979, p. 105). The price index used for deflation is Malafeev's (1964, p. 407) retail price index.

7. Alternative estimates of economic growth are presented in Appendix A, including my own estimates of real gross national expenditure. Table 5.4 is an approximate reconciliation of gross national expenditure and gross domestic product computed from value added by sector. The economy grows slightly more rapidly by the former account.

8. On Soviet blast furace building and its relationship to existing iron works, see Balzak, Vasyutin, and Feigen (1949, pp. 238–51), Cordero (1952, pp. 623–38), Gardner (1956, pp. 64–65, 291–301, 321–23), Hogan (1950, pp. 40–41), McCaffray (1996, pp. 62–69, 155), Pounds (1959, pp. 150–59).

9. Conquest (1968) was pivotal in framing the issues. Acrimonious exchanges have occurred between Rosefielde, Nove, Conquest, and Wheatcroft since 1981.

See Rosefielde (1996), Wheatcroft (1996, 1999) for recent salvos and references to the earlier debate.

CHAPTER SIX. THE POPULATION HISTORY OF THE USSR

1. These population figures were compiled by Maddison (1995, pp. 108–16) and represent estimates on 1990 boundaries. Heer (1968) discusses many of the themes in this chapter.

2. Blum (1991, 1994) has stressed the independence of demographic phenomena like fertility from the plans of the Soviet leadership. This chapter is an exploration of that interaction.

3. Avdeev, Blum, and Troitskaya (1993, pp. 171–72) and Blum (2000) offer vigorous defenses of the integrity of the Soviet statistical services in the 1930s.

4. The actual count was 167.3 million. All censuses miss people, so the true population exceeds the census count. Two official population estimates were published — 170.1 and 170.5. These include estimates for underenumeration. There has been debate as to whether these adjustments were intentionally inflated, and Andreev, Darskii, and Khar'kova suggest that a reasonable adjustment implies a total population of 168.9 million. This is within one percent of the official figure, and that difference defines the margin for manipulation. The Gosplan estimates that led to the suppression of the 1937 census indicated a 1937 population of 174–181 million. The implied 1939 population would have been about 7 million more — 181–188 million. Any manipulation of the 1939 population estimate was far too small to close this gap. See Davies, Harrison, and Wheatcroft (1994, pp. 71–72).

5. Coale, Anderson, and Harm (1979, p. 16) tabulate their marital fertility index (Ig) from 1881 to 1970. Most of the values are interpolations, but it does show lower fertility in the mid-1920s than in 1897. This decline supports their view that the fertility transition had begun before the First World War. A pre–World War I fertility decline is called in question, however, by recent figures. Expanding the 1897 data set, as I have done, and adjusting its definition to correspond to the boundaries of the Soviet Union in the 1920s raises If to .560, which implies a total fertility rate of 6.83 for the portion of the Russian Empire corresponding to the USSR in the mid-1920s. Andreev, Darskii, and Khar'kova (1992, p. 150) have reconstructed the age-specific fertility rates from 1920 on, and their figures imply a total fertility rate of that order in the 1920s with a peak value of 6.93 in 1924. A comparison of these figures shows no fertility decline. One can always debate whether it was the 1910s or the 1920s that was the deviation from the true trend. One might also speculate that the economic growth from 1900 to 1913 should have lowered fertility and that the drop should then have been reversed with the economic collapse and deurbanization following the 1917 revolution. In any event, it is clear from Figure 6.1 that a sustained fall in fertility only began with the onset of rapid industrialization in the late 1920s.

6. These statements, as well as those in the following paragraph, are based on my reconstruction of the population for 1914–19. Andreev, Darskii, and Khar'kova's (1992, p. 129) estimate of the population on 1 January 1920 was extrapolated back to 1 January 1914 using Volkov's estimates as summarized by

Lorimer (1946, p. 30). (There is a small discrepancy between the two series for 1920.) Births were estimated by multiplying the population by the crude birth rate. Following the suggestion of Davies, Harrison, and Wheatcroft (1994, p. 57), the birth rate for 1915–19 was assumed to equal 32.9 (75 percent of the 1910–13 average). Deaths were computed as a residual and excess deaths as deaths minus the crude death rate for 1910–13 multiplied by the population.

7. The 9.7 million excess deaths are implied by extrapolating Andreev, Darskii, and Khar'kova's population series back to 1914 using Volkov's estimates. Emigration was assumed to be 750,000 in 1918 and in 1919. Other population series indicate a more substantial drop in population, implying a higher level of excess mortality. See Davies, Harrison, and Wheatcroft (1994, p. 64).

8. Deaths in prisons and Gulag camps were low in 1939 and 1940 but rose in 1941–43 as food rations were reduced during the war (Rosefielde 1996, p. 986). Most of the camp inmates were men aged 19 to 50 (Getty, Rittersporn, and Zemskov 1993, p. 1025). It might be noted that the death rate in the camps (about 22% = 663,786 deaths from Rosefielde [1996, p. 986] divided by 3 million inmates) was much less than the 40 percent mortality rate experienced by the nonincarcerated male population aged 20–49. This is not because the camps were salubrious, but because the Eastern Front was so dire.

9. These mortality rates are obtained from Andreev, Darskii, and Khar'kova's (1992, p. 138) age breakdowns of the Soviet population in 1941 and 1946. Mortality for males aged 20–24 is obtained by comparing the number of males 25–29 in 1946 with the number of males 20–24 in 1941, and so forth.

10. Discrepancies between the actual and the simulated series can arise for several reasons. The birth and death rates are averages for age ranges (e.g., men aged 30–34) rather than for every individual year of life (33-year-olds). Also, the rates are not available for every year. Inaccuracies are also introduced since births over the course of a year must all be treated as occurring on the first or last day of the year in simulations like this that are calibrated in terms of annual changes (rather than monthly or daily changes, for instance). In the event, the discrepancies are very small.

11. Many deaths in the Gulag occurred during the Second World War and accounted for less than 3 percent of the wartime losses. Compare the 663,786 deaths tallied by Rosefielde (1996, p. 986, col. 4) for 1941–45 with the total number of excess deaths. These deaths are included in the analysis of the Second World War. In principle, one could also simulate the long-run impact of deaths in 1937–39, but the number is so small compared to normal deaths that the long-run consequences are minimal.

12. Following Maddison (1995, p. 110), this comparison is on post–World War II boundaries.

13. Schultz (1997) is convenient for our purposes because his results can be easily applied to the Soviet Union. But, it should be stressed, many other studies come to the similar conclusions. Studies using international data include Barro and Lee (1994) and Barro (1999, pp. 21–25). See Drèze and Sen (1995, pp. 167–71) for a discussion of studies using Indian data.

14. The data were modeled with two structural equations. In the first, fertility was made a function of the education, economic, and religious variables as well

as child mortality. In the second, child mortality was expressed as a function of the social variables. Substituting the second equation into the first gives reduced form equations like equation 1 in Table 6.1. Exact results depend on which family planning and similar variables are added, but they have no statistical significance or explanatory power, nor does their inclusion change the other estimated coefficients in any material way.

15. Jones and Grupp (1987, p. 342) measure emancipation as the ratio of the adult female to male populations with completed secondary education or higher. I have used the ratio of the average number of years of female to male education completed by the adult population.

CHAPTER SEVEN. THE STANDARD OF LIVING

1. See, for instance, Gregory and Stuart (1986, p. 116), Ofer (1987, pp. 1778–79, 1789–91), Davies, Harrison, and Wheatcroft (1994, pp. 52–53), Westwood (1987, p. 360), Hunter and Szyrmer (1992, pp. 26–27, 34–35), Suny (1998, pp. 217, 242), Fitzpatrick (1999, p. 4), Goldman (1993), and Hoffmann (1994, p. 152). Nove (1990, pp. 236–42, 251) presents a somewhat more nuanced view.

2. See Appendix C for details. Actually, food balances were constructed back to 1885, but calculated calorie consumption from 1885 to 1895 is too low to be plausible. The implication is that the Imperial agricultural statistics understate production before 1895. I pointed out in Chapter 2 that Russian wheat yields seemed remarkably low in the period, and the calculations of calorie availability are another reason for calling their plausibility into question. If Russian yields were, in fact, higher, then much of the dynamism of tsarist agriculture becomes an illusion.

3. Wheatcroft (1999, p. 51) reports the results of a similar exercise for selected years from 1900 to 1960. The biggest difference between his calculations and mine relates to the imperial period. He reports an average calorie consumption of 2964 in 1900–13 — an extremely high figure. Discrepancies are less in the Soviet period.

4. Butter production was estimated from the number of cows on the assumption that no cheese was made. The calorie figures, thus, implicitly include cheese.

5. The base year is, thus, the later year. This shift reverses the usual intuitions regarding the Laspayres and Paasche indices.

6. Bergson sets the 1937 values at 1.00, so the 1928 values, which are the figures he reports, are .168 for the Laspeyres index and .115 for the Paasche index. See Bergson (1961, pp. 46–49, 53, 88, 313).

7. One might argue that free market prices should be used for 1928 instead of the average of free and controlled prices that she uses in her index. Using free market prices, however, requires that wages then be adjusted to reflect the consumption subsidy of controlled prices in state and cooperative shops when real incomes are calculated. That adjustment brings one back to a procedure like Chapman's.

8. The correct percentage is 74 percent. There are several approximations like this in Chapman's calculations.

9. Chapman's reported value of .115 for the Paasche price index is slightly in error. The correct value is .118 on her assumptions and incorporating the slight error in inverting 1.35.

10. Since international trade in these commodities was negligible, production indicates consumption.

11. I emended Nutter's calculations in two ways. First, I rectified his error in pricing fish, which he notes (Nutter 1962, p. 537), and, second, I added knit-wear and hosiery to his index weighted with 1928 prices. It is not clear why Nutter left out these industries. They were included in the index using 1955 price weights, and a consistent treatment of the data requires their inclusion in 1928 as well.

12. Zaleski (1971, 1984) reproduces these returns as series 235. However, for 1940, the value shown by Zaleski is extremely large, and I use the smaller value shown in *Sovietskaya Torgovlia*, 1956, p. 19. In his first estimate of Soviet national income in 1940, Bergson apparently also used the "large" value for 1940 but revised it downward to the "small" value in his final work. Cf. Bergson and Heymann (1954, p. 21) and Bergson (1961, p. 46).

13. Barsov (1969, p. 107 n. 11, 108, table facing p. 112) published a constant price index of the volume of agricultural marketings through all channels and indices of procurement and farmers' market prices for 1929–32 and an overall price index that was weighted by the volumes of the two sorts of sales. One can work backward from his price indices and calculate relative volumes of procurements and farmers' market sales. When the total volume of sales is multiplied by the latter fraction for each year, the result is an index of the volume of sales on farmers' markets. I assumed the fraction was the same in 1928, for which Barsov gave no information, as in 1929. I used this index to extend the index of collective farm market sales back to 1928.

14. As a check on this result, I have computed the increase in household purchases in retail markets by aggregating the production of fresh food and manufactures with weights equal to shares in consumer spending. The calculation encompasses shops and the collective farm market together.

The first step in this purchaser's view of consumption is to establish the shares of spending directed to each commodity. Chapman presented shares for 1928 and 1937, which I have emended in two ways. First, I reworked her 1937 weights to include estimates (derived from Vyltsan [1966] and Karcz [1979]) of the volume of sales on the collective farm market as well as sales in state and cooperative shops. Second, I have expanded the list of commodities to include consumer durables (bicycles, clocks, watches, etc.). While little money, in toto, was spent on durables, they were, in fact, a rapidly growing category. The production of bicycles, for instance, rose from 11,000 in 1927–28 to over half a million in 1937 (Nutter 1962, p. 458).

Aggregating the growth of consumption with 1928 shares gives a different answer than using 1937 shares, just as 1928 and 1955 weights gave different answers in the previous calculation. Once again, the solution is to use an index employing both sets of weights, and I have calculated a Fisher Ideal Index, which is the geometric average of indices using 1928 and 1937 spending shares as weights. This index increased by 81 percent between 1928 and 1937. Dividing the value of household purchases in retail markets in 1937 (126.0 billion rubles) by 1.81 implies a 1928 value of 69.6 billion rubles in 1937 prices. This result is close to the value of 64.9 billion rubles shown in Table 7.3.

See Allen (1998c) for full details.

15. Compare Bergson (1961, p. 327) and Barsov (1969, p. 103) and Bergson (1961, pp. 327, 329) with Karcz (1979, pp. 102–3) for the significance of Bergson's figure for that year. See also the discussion in Karcz (1979, pp. 96–98).

16. Bergson devoted a chapter to this question and urged that farm income in kind and services be valued at "adjusted market prices." For farm products, those prices were collective farm market prices reduced 20 percent to account for transport and processing costs incurred by the peasants, and I have done the same. Bergson attempted to apply the same principle to housing and other services even though markets did not exist for them or they were heavily subsidized. The exercise is intrinsically speculative, but Bergson's approach seems the best, and I have adopted his figures also.

17. Cotton and sugar beets were the other principal farm products, but their valuation is not an issue in computing farm income in kind since the entirety of their output was sold to the industrial sector.

18. This is shown by applying input-ouput coefficients from the 1920 U.S. census of manufactures to the Russian production data summarized in Nutter (1962, pp. 455–57).

19. Following Bergson (1961, p. 167), I reduce the prices by 15 percent to exclude the marketing markup.

20. The figure for shoes is particularly artificial and shows the approximate nature of these calculations. While the small hides (from sheep and goats) consumed by the rural population probably were fabricated into shoe uppers (a rather poor use of that material) by factory industry, Jasny (1949, p. 229), at least, maintains they were used for coats by the peasants. In the absence of any information on the price of sheepskin coats, I reckon the small hides as though they were converted to shoes and value them accordingly. The implicit assumption is that the value of the leather in shoes was the same as its value in clothing.

21. I checked these calculations by reworking Nutter's index of the output of manufactured consumer goods. This index, as originally calculated, included only factory production. Both large-scale and small-scale industry were included but not fabrication by the peasant community. The flour and bread made by the peasants from their farm income in kind, for example, was not included in the index of manufactured goods. These exclusions were appropriate when the object was to develop, as previously, an index of the volume of goods sold in shops. To check the estimate of rural manufacturing, I recomputed the index after adding the estimated rural production to the factory production. The result was to increase the index by 12.2 percent in 1928 and by 0.4 percent in 1937. Multiplying these increases by the 110 billion rubles of retail sales in 1937 translates into an extra 7.5 billion rubles in 1928 and .5 billion rubles in 1937—all in 1937 retail shop prices. These figures agree reasonably well with the direct calculations.

22. Bergson (1961, p. 344) valued the flax, wool, and hides by increasing the prices received for them in proportion to the overall ratio of the collective farm

market prices of foods to the average price on all marketings for the same commodities. Applying his procedure (with the most recent figures) implies that the rural manufactures of wool, flax, and hides were worth 2.2 billion rubles in 1928 and .8 billion in 1937 (all in 1937 prices).

23. The constituent series are available annually to compute all components of consumption except services. These components were, therefore, calculated by the same procedures previously described. Values for services are available for 1928, 1937, and 1940. Intermediate values were interpolated. I use the population estimates of Andreev, Darskii, and Khar'kova.

24. I assume that there were 100 million full- and part-time farmers and family members in 1926 and 92 million in the late 1930s following Lorimer (1946, pp. 222–30) and Jasny (1949, pp. 710–14). Lorimer thought there was little change in the farm population between 1926 and 1928. I assume that the drop in the number of farmers occurred during collectivization and, mainly, during the famine of 1933.

25. Unlike the previous tables, where farm cash income was computed by valuing farm production at average realized prices, the figures in Table 7.4 are constructed from other information. For 1928, I use Hoeffding's (1954, p. 14) estimate of the cash income of the farm population. For 1932–40, I compute farm cash income as the sum of cash payments to collective farm members, sales by collective farm members to state agencies and to the urban population on the collective farm market, and wages paid by state farms, machine tractor stations, and other state agricultural organizations (Zaleski 1984, pp. 280–81, 732–33, 736–37, 786–89). Agricultural taxes are taken from Holzman (1955, p. 199).

26. Malafeev's index is not annual, so it was necessary to interpolate values for 1933–36, and 1938–39.

27. Some historians find greater falls in real earnings by positing higher rates of inflation (e.g., Goldman 1993). Higher rates of inflation are obtained by using 1937 weights in the price index (e.g., Chapman 1963, p. 144; Zaleski 1984, pp. 280–81). This choice biases the measurement of inflation upward, as I have argued earlier.

28. It is something of a surprise that state agricultural employees experienced the biggest rise in real earnings in Table 7.5, but not too much should be made of this since they started from an exceptionally low base and remained among the worst paid in 1937.

29. McKeown (1976) has argued that rising incomes were the main cause of falling mortality in nineteenth-century England. Szreter (1988) has questioned that view and argued instead that improvements in public sanitation deserve the credit. It would be difficult to argue Szreter's interpretation for the USSR in the 1930s, where the urban population grew much faster than the sewage and water supply systems. Steckel's (1983, 1992, 1995) reviews of the research on nutrition and stature are also relevant and support the view that better nutrition improves health indicators.

30. Wheatcroft (1999) reviewed heights, food availability, and mortality and advanced conclusions similar to those reached here. Hoch (1999) was sharply critical.

31. As Hoch (1999, p. 69) noted, Warren Eason (1960, pp. 79–80) remarked on the rise in life expectancy in the USSR between 1926–27 and 1938–40, but the increase has generally been ignored in discussions of the standard of living.

CHAPTER EIGHT. THE CAUSES OF RAPID INDUSTRIALIZATION

1. The model contains two features that may be too reminiscent of a market economy: the use of a marginal product rule to allocate labor between the producer goods and consumer goods industries, and the calculation of market clearing prices in shops every year. Shop prices were equilibrium prices only in 1928 and 1937 during the period studied.

2. Increases in total factor productivity (TFP) make output grow faster than inputs. The present model presumes TFP growth of about 1.5 percent per year in the consumer goods sector. This is achieved by making TFP a function of the capital stock in consumer goods rather than simply a function of time. This rate of TFP growth is on a par with statistical studies of the 1930s (Davies, Harrison, and Wheatcroft 1994, pp. 192–97, 310–11).

3. There is also some nonwage income such as transfer payments.

4. The implicit assumption is that households have Cobb-Douglas preferences.

5. The computer solves a small system of simultaneous equations since farm marketings depend on the prices of farm and nonfarm goods.

6. In particular, $e = .23$ in these simulations.

7. In brief, these proportions are derived from an input-output model of the Soviet economy in the 1930s. Final demand in 1928 was divided into producer goods and consumer goods and the gross outputs of the various sectors needed to produce that final output were computed. The proportions of gross output in each sector attributable to producer goods and consumer goods were then multiplied by the 1928 capital stock in each sector (from Moorsteen and Powell 1966, pp. 408–18) and investment in each sector (from *Socialist Construction in the U.S.S.R.*, 1936, pp. 346–51). Summing the sectoral results gives the overall figures of 7 percent and 23 percent. See Appendices B and D for a more complete discussion.

8. This figure equals 3000 rubles per year divided by .93. The latter figure is my estimate of the decline in real wages in Allen (1998c).

9. In 1928, the marginal products of labor were not equal in the p-goods and c-goods industries. The figure of 2.735 thousand rubles is a weighted average of the marginal products in the two sectors.

10. Bergson (1961, p. 422) reports that the average industrial wage was 3005 rubles per year in 1937 according to the official statistics. This is a low figure since, first, real wages fell from 1928 to 1937, and, second, it excludes some wage income as discussed by Bergson (1947).

CHAPTER NINE. PREOBRAZHENSKY IN ACTION

1. Allen (1998a). The definition of investment used in this argument is a broad one and includes repairs, inventory changes, work in progress, and min-

eral exploration as well as fixed capital formation. This definition follows Bergson (1961, pp. 378–420) rather than Moorsteen and Powell's (1966, pp. 176–81) narrower one since the aim is to see if agricultural taxation was sufficient to finance industrialization. Agricultural taxation includes receipts from the turnover tax and its predecessors, as well as the agricultural tax per se (Holzman 1955, pp. 199, 216, 252).

2. For ease of exposition, the figure is oversimplified by not separately diagramming the collective farm market and the compulsory sales. The two markets are treated as one. The markets are separated, however, in the subsequent inflation calculations and in the computer simulations.

3. The alternative would be to treat the tax as though it were assessed on farmers. In that case, the demand curve would be unchanged, but the supply curve would be increased by T. The raised supply curve would intersect D_{37} at M_{37} and P_w, and the analysis would then proceed in the previous manner. This illustrates the point that the designation of the payer of the tax has no significance for the question of who bore the tax.

4. The simulations show that high rates of investment and industrialization were possible with either marketing system, but they also show that both could self-destruct. With collectivization, the problem was that rising investment required increased taxation, which could push farm incomes to zero, resulting in extraordinary — and unrealistic — migration to the cities and correspondingly unrealistic increases in output as the new arrivals were employed. With the NEP, scissors crises were possible if the production of nonfood consumer goods did not keep pace with demand. In that case, their price would rise, farmers would reduce their marketings, inputs to the consumer goods industries would decline, and the production of consumer goods would drop farther. The result would have been a spiral of rising consumer goods prices and falling production. The simulations also point to solutions. In the case of collectivization, the state had to broaden its tax base, which it ultimately did. In the case of a continuation of the NEP, the state would have had to monitor prices and to have channeled resources into consumer goods if a scissors crisis appeared imminent. Flexible administration was necessary to make both marketing systems work well. Both also had the potential of rapid industrialization.

CHAPTER TEN. THE SOVIET CLIMACTERIC

1. Harrison (1996, pp. 92, 160). The population drop is computed from mid-1941 to the end of 1945. The GDP decline compares 1940 to 1945 GNP.

2. The 1950 ratio is from Moorsteen and Powell (1966, p. 364), and the 1980 figure is from the Penn World Tables.

3. U.S. Congress, Joint Economic Committee (1982, pp. 65–67, 72–74, 76–78). Consumption includes state expenditures on education and health. It should be noted that there is disagreement among investigators as to the exact proportions. Furthermore, "investment" as reported in these and other accounts probably includes some military expenditures.

4. The well-known Harrod–Domar growth model applied.

5. Maddison's estimate of GDP in 1991 U.S. dollars is the measure of output.

The labor force is measured by the population since that indexes the potential labor supply, which is the relevant measure in assessing the impact of surplus labor and its elimination. The capital stock is calculated with equations 2 and 3 from Maddison's GDP series, the historical series of investment rates, and a value of 2 for the capital-output ratio in 1928. This value is slightly higher than the value of 1.68 calculated by Moorsteen and Powell (1966, p. 367). For 1960–89, the investment rate was taken from the Penn World Tables. Investment rates for earlier years were extrapolated from the 1960 value using Moorsteen and Powell's (1966, p. 364) series. The depreciation rate in equation 3 was taken to be 3 percent, which is consistent with Moorsteen and Powell's work. Applying these assumptions to equations 2 and 3 implies the Soviet capital stock in 1991 U.S. dollars.

6. The capital stock was cumulated from Maddison's output series and Japanese investment rates using the same procedures and depreciation rate as were used for the Soviet series.

7. An alternative approach to the data is to question their reliability. Wolf (1992, p. 135), for instance, claims that "much of the growth reported in capital investment in the 1970s and early 1980s did not occur." The reason is that inflation in investment goods was underestimated by the Soviets, so that their reported series of real investment overstates real growth. However, Rumer (1990, p. 274) estimated this omitted inflation. Deflating Soviet investment by Rumer's rate of price increase does not change the results in a historically meaningful way.

8. Reconstruction investment from *Narodnoe Khoziaistvo* (1965, p. 535; 1970, p. 485; 1975, p. 509; 1980, p. 339).

9. U.S. *Statistical Abstract*, 1962, p. 925; 1988, p. 814.

10. That is, excluding special steels and the small amount of steel made by machine building plants. See Rumer (1989, p. 54).

11. *A Study of the Soviet Economy*, vol. 33, IMF, World Bank, OECD, and European Bank for Reconstruction and Development, p. 198.

12. In addition to the three difficulties discussed in the text, there is the possibility raised by Weitzman's work that the productivity slowdown was in illusion. The discussion in the text accepts the reality of the productivity drop at least as a working hypothesis.

13. The only fault that Abouchar found with the Soviet cement industry was the large number of standards used for grading Portland cement. While only two grades account for 94 percent of U.S. production, the Soviets had half a dozen, which exacerbated inventory control problems. Cement standards were a reversal of the usual pattern, in which Americans produced a greater variety of products than the Soviets.

Appendix A. Soviet National Income

1. Moorsteen and Powell (1966, p. 622) give, for each sector, indices of the volume of output and income originating in the sector in 1937. The latter are derived from earlier calculations of Bergson and sum to GDP at factor cost. To recompute the index, I used Bergson's (1953, p. 124) estimates of net national

product by economic sector (with some minor additions from Moorsteen and Powell's figures) but otherwise followed Moorsteen and Powell's procedure.

APPENDIX B. THE SIMULATION MODEL OF THE SOVIET ECONOMY

1. A useful introduction with emphasis on applications is Dixon, Parmenter, and Powell (1992).

2. Temin's (1971a) survey of the use of general equilibrium models in economic history provides an initial reading at a time when very little work had been done. James (1984) reviews work to the early 1980s.

3. Hunter and Szyrmer (1992) have developed a programming model of the USSR with some affinities to a CGE model. Roberts and Rodriguez (1997) is a theoretical general equilibrium model of the Soviet Union.

APPENDIX C. DATA SOURCES

1. Moorsteen and Powell (1966, p. 386).

2. Nutter's (1962, p. 524) estimates of the value of output in 1928, 1932, 1937, and 1940 in 1928 prices were converted to 1937 prices using Moorsteen's (1962, p. 72) index of machinery prices. Values of intervening years were interpolated.

3. Bergson's (1961, p. 364) value of "munitions and other procurements" in 1937 was extrapolated to other years with Moorsteen and Powell's (1966, p. 629) index of "munitions procurements in 1937 prices."

4. Bergson (1961, p. 349) takes "small-valued equipment not included in fixed capital" to have been 10 percent of nonlabor outlays in the health care system. Consequently, I estimated the real value of these acquisitions to have been 10 percent of the value of nonlabor outlays in 1937 prices (Bergson 1961, p. 347) in the health care system in 1928, 1937, and 1940. Intervening years were interpolated.

Bibliography

GOVERNMENT PUBLICATIONS

Canada, Dominion Bureau of Statistics (1924–28). *Sixth Census of Canada, 1921*. Ottawa: F. A. Acland.

Russia, Tsentralnyi statisticheskii komitet (1905). *Pervaia vseobshchaia perepis' naseleniia Rossiiskoi Imperii 1897 g*. St. Petersburg: Obshchestvenaia Polza.

Russian Academy of Sciences (1992). *Vsesoiuznaia perepis' naseleniia 1939 goda: osnovnye itogi*. Moscow: Nauka.

USSR, Gosplan. *Kontrol'nye tsifry narodnogo khoziaistva SSSR na 1927/1928 god*. Moscow, 1928.

USSR, Gosplan. *Kontrol'nye tsifry narodnogo khoziaistva SSSR na 1928/1929 god*. Moscow, 1929.

USSR, Gosudarstvennyi Komitet SSSR po Statistike. *Trud v SSSR*. Moscow, 1988.

USSR, Gosudarstvennyi Komitet SSSR po Statistike. *Promyshlennost' SSSR*. Moscow, 1988.

USSR, Tsentralnoe Statisticheskoe Upravlenie. *Statisticheskii spravochnik SSSR za 1927–28*. Moscow, 1928.

USSR, Tsentralnoe Statisticheskoe Upravlenie. *Narodnoe khoziaistvo SSSR*. Moscow, 1956ff.

USSR, Tsentralnoe Statisticheskoe Upravlenie. *Sovietskaia torgovlia*. Moscow, 1956.

USSR, Tsentralnoe Statisticheskoe Upravlenie (1962–63). *Vsesoiuznaia perepis' naseleniia 1959 goda*. Moscow: Gosstatizda.

USSR, Tsentralnoe Upravlenie Narodno-khoziaistvennogo Ucheta. *Socialist Construction in the USSR*. Moscow, 1936.

UNESCO (1953). *Progress of Literacy in Various Countries*. Paris: UNESCO.

UNESCO (1957). *World Illiteracy at Mid-Century*. Paris: UNESCO.

United Nations (1948ff.). *Demographic Yearbook*. New York: United Nations.

United Nations (1987). *The Prospects of World Urbanization: Revised as of 1984–85*. Population Studies, no. 101. New York: United Nations.

United Nations (1991). *The Sex and Age Distribution of Population, 1990 Revisions*. Population Studies, no. 122. New York: United Nations.

United Nations, Food and Agricultural Organization (1984–86). *Food Balance Sheets*. Rome: Food and Agricultural Organization.

United Nations, Food and Agricultural Organization (1991). *Production Yearbook*. Rome: Food and Agricultural Organization.

U.S. Bureau of the Census (1922). *Fourteenth Census of the United States Taken in the Year 1920*, vol. VI, *Agriculture*. Washington: U.S. Government Printing Office.

U.S. Bureau of the Census (1975). *Historical Statistics of the United States,*

Colonial Times to 1970, Bicentennial Edition. Washington: U.S. Government Printing Office.

U.S. Bureau of the Census. *Statistical Abstract of the United States*, Washington: U.S. Government Printing Office.

U.S. Central Intelligence Agency (1981, 1986, 1987). *Handbook of Economic Statistics.* Washington: U.S. Central Intelligence Agency.

U.S. Commissioner of Labor (1899). *Thirteenth Annual Report of the Commission of Labor, 1898: Hand and Machine Labor.* Washington: U.S. Government Printing Office.

U.S. Congress, Joint Economic Committee (1982). *USSR: Measures of Economic Growth and Development, 1950–80.* Washington: U.S. Government Printing Office.

U.S. Department of Agriculture. *Agricultural Statistics.* Washington: U.S. Government Printing Office.

U.S. Department of Agriculture, Agricultural Research Service (1955). *Wheat: Acreage, Yield, Production by State, 1866–1943.* Washington: U.S. Government Printing Office.

BOOKS AND ARTICLES

Abouchar, Alan (1976). "Postwar Developments in the Cement Industry." *Soviet Economy in a New Perspective.* Joint Economic Committee, Washington: U.S. Government Printing Office, pp. 558–74.

Adams, F. G. (1992). *The Macroeconomic Dimensions of Arms Reduction.* Oxford: Westview Press.

Allen, Robert C. (1979). "International Competition in Iron and Steel, 1850–1913." *Journal of Economic History*, vol. 39, pp. 911–37.

———. (1988). "The Growth of Labor Productivity in Early Modern English Agriculture." *Explorations in Economic History*, vol. 25, pp. 117–46.

———. (1992). *Enclosure and the Yeoman.* Oxford: Clarendon Press.

———. (1997). "Agricultural Marketing and the Possibilities for Industrialisation in the Soviet Union in the 1930s." *Explorations in Economic History*, vol. 34, pp. 387–410.

———. (1998a). "Imposition et mobilisation du surplus agricole a l'époque stalinienne." *Annales: histoire et science sociale*, vol. 53, pp. 569–95.

———. (1998b). "Capital Accumulation, the Soft Budget Constraint, and Soviet Industrialization." *European Review of Economic History*, vol. 2, pp. 1–24.

———. (1998c). "The Standard of Living in the Soviet Union, 1928–40." *Journal of Economic History*, vol. 58, pp. 1063–89.

———. (2001a). "The Great Divergence in European Wages and Prices from the Middle Ages to the First World War." *Explorations in Economic History*, vol. 38, pp. 411–47.

———. (2001b). "Innis Lecture: The Rise and Decline of the Soviet Economy." *Canadian Journal of Economics*, vol. 34, pp. 859–81.

Allen, Robert C., and Diewert, W. E. (1981). "Direct Versus Implicit Superlative Index Number Formulae." *Review of Economics and Statistics*, vol. 53, pp. 430–35.

Amann, Ronald (1986). "Technical Progress and Soviet Economic Development: Setting the Scene." In Ronald Amann and Julian Cooper, eds. *Technical Progress and Soviet Economic Development*. Oxford: Basil Blackwell, pp. 5–30.

Amann, Ronald, and Cooper, Julian (1986). "Introduction." In Ronald Amann and Julian Cooper, eds. *Technical Progress and Soviet Economic Development*. Oxford: Basil Blackwell, pp. 1–4.

Anan'ich, Boris V. (1983). "The Economic Policy of the Tsarist Government and Enterprise in Russia from the End of the Nineteenth through the Beginning of the Twentieth Century." In Gregory Guroff and Fred V. Carstensen, eds. *Entrepreneurship in Imperial Russia and the Soviet Union*. Princeton: Princeton University Press, pp. 125–39.

Andreev, E., Darskii, L., and Khar'kova, T. (1990). "Opyt otsenki chislennosti naseleniya SSSR 1926–1941 gg." *Vestnik statistiki*, 7.

———. (1992). "L'Histoire de la population de l'URSS. 1920–1959." *Annales de démogaphie historique*, pp. 61–150.

Anfimov, Andrei Matveevich (1959). "K voprosu o kharaktere agrarnogo stroya evropeiskoi rossii v nachale XX v." *Istoricheskie zapiski*, vol. 65, pp. 119–62.

Antel, John, and Gregory, Paul (1994). "Agricultural Surplus Models and Peasant Behavior: Soviet Agriculture in the 1920's." *Economic Development and Cultural Change*, vol. 42, pp. 375–86.

Antsiferov, Alexis N. (1930). *Russian Agriculture During the War: Rural Economy*. New Haven: Yale University Press.

Aslund, Anders (1990). "How Small is Soviet National Income?" In H. Rowen and C. Wolf, Jr., eds. *The Impoverished Superpower: Perestroika and the Burden of Soviet Military Spending*. San Francisco: Institute for Contemporary Studies, pp. 13–61.

Aston, T. H., and Philpin, C.H.E., eds. (1985). *The Brenner Debate*. Cambridge: Cambridge University Press.

Atkinson, Dorothy (1983). *The End of the Russian Land Commune, 1905–1930*. Stanford: Stanford University Press.

Avdeev, A., Blum, A., and Troitskaya, I. (1993). "Démographie historique de la Russie." *Histoire & mesure*, vol. 8, pp. 163–80.

Bairoch, Paul (1988). *Cities and Economic Development: From the Dawn of History to the Present*. Trans. by Christopher Braider. Chicago: University of Chicago Press.

Bairoch, Paul, Batou, Jean, and Chèvre, Pierre (1988). *La population des villes européens: banque de données et analyse sommaire des résultats, 800–1850*. Geneva: Librairie Droz.

Balzak, S. S., Vasyutin, V. F., and Feigen, Ya. G. (1949). *Economic Geography of the USSR*. New York: Macmillan.

Baran, Paul (1962). *The Political Economy of Growth*. New York: Monthly Review.

Bardhan, Pranab K., and Roemer, John E., eds. (1993). *Market Socialism: The Current Debate*. New York: Oxford University Press.

Barrett, David B. (1982). *World Christian Encyclopedia*. Oxford: Oxford University Press.

Barro, R. J. (1991). "Economic Growth in a Cross Section of Countries." *Journal of Political Economy*, vol. 106, pp. 407–43.

———. (1999). *Determinants of Economic Growth*, Cambridge, Mass.: The MIT Press.

Barro, R. J., and Lee, Jong-Wha (1994). "International Comparisons of Educational Attainment." *Journal of Monetary Economics*, vol. 32, pp. 363–94.

Barsov, A. A. (1968). "Sel'skoe khoziaistvo i istochniki sotsialisticheskogo nakopleniia v gody pervoi piatiletki (1928–1933)." *Istoriia SSSR*, pp. 64–82.

———. (1969). *Balans stoimostnykh obmenov mezdhu gorodom i derevnei.* Moscow: Nauka.

Bassin, Mark (1991). "Russia Between Europe and Asia: The Ideological Construction of Geographical Space." *Slavic Review*, vol. 50, pp. 763–94.

———. (1993). "Turner, Solov'ev, and the 'Frontier Hyopthesis': The Nationalist Signification of Open Spaces." *Journal of Modern History*, vol. 65, pp. 473–511.

Bennett, M. K. (1933). "World Wheat Crops, 1885–1932: New Series with Areas and Yields, by Countries." *Wheat Studies*, vol. 9.

Bergson, Abram (1944). *The Structure of Soviet Wages: A Study in Socialist Economics.* Cambridge, Mass.: Harvard University Press.

———. (1947). "A Problem in Soviet Statistics." *Review of Economic Statistics*, vol. 29, pp. 234–42.

———. (1953). *Soviet National Income and Product in 1937.* New York: Columbia University Press.

———. (1961). *The Real National Income of Soviet Russia since 1928.* Cambridge, Mass.: Harvard University Press.

———. (1978). *Productivity and the Social System: The USSR and the West.* Cambridge, Mass.: Harvard University Press.

Bergson, Abram, and Heymann, Hans, Jr. (1954). *Soviet National Income and Product, 1940–48.* New York: Columbia University Press.

Bergson, Abram, Bernaut, R., and Turgeon, L. (1955). *Basic Industrial Prices in the USSR, 1928–1950: Twenty-Five Branch Series and Their Aggregation,* Santa Monica: The Rand Corporation, Research Memorandum RM-1522.

Berliner, Joseph S. (1976a). *The Innovation Decision in Soviet Industry.* Cambridge, Mass.: The MIT Press.

———. (1976b). "Prospects for Technological Progress." *Soviet Economy in a New Perspective.* Joint Economic Committee, Washington: U.S. Government Printing Office, pp. 431–46.

———. (1983). "Education, Labor-Force Participation and Fertility in the USSR." *Journal of Comparative Economics*, vol. 7, pp. 131–57.

———. (1989). "Soviet Female Labor Participation: A Regional Cross-Section Analysis." *Journal of Comparative Economics*, vol. 13, pp. 446–72.

Bideleux, Robert (1990). "Agricultural Advance Under the Russian Village Commune System." In Roger Bartlett, ed. *Land Commune and Peasant Community in Russia: Communal Forms in Imperial and Early Soviet Society.* New York: St. Martin's Press, pp. 196–218.

Binswanger, Hans P., and Deininger, Klaus (1997). "Explaining Agricultural and Agrarian Policies in Developing Countries." *Journal of Economic Literature*, vol. 35, no. 4, pp. 1958–2005.

Binswanger, Hans P., Feder, Gershon, and Deininger, Klaus (1988). "Power, Distribution, Revolt, and Reform." In Jere Behrman and T. N. Srinivasan, eds., *Handbook of Development Economics*. Amsterdam: North-Holland, vol. IIIB, chapter 42.

Binswanger, Hans P., and Rosenzweig, Mark (1986). "Behavioral and Material Determinants of Production Relations in Agriculture." *Journal of Development Studies*, vol. 22, no. 3, pp. 503–39.

Black, Cyril E., et al. (1975). *The Modernization of Japan and Russia: A Comparative Study*. New York: The Free Press.

Bloch, Marc (1931). *Les caractères originaux de l'histoire rurale francaise*. Oaris: Armand Colin, 2nd ed., 1988.

Blomqvist, A. G. (1986). "The Economics of Price Scissors: Comment." *American Economic Review*, vol. 76, pp. 1188–91.

Blum, Alain (1991). "Rupture et continuité: exemples démographiques soviétiques." *Annales: ESC*, vol. 46, pp. 169–87.

———. (1994). *Naître, vivre, mourir en URSS*. Paris: Librairie Plon.

———. (2000). "La purge de 1924 de la Direction centrale de la statistique." *Annales: histoire, sciences sociales*, vol. 55, pp. 249–82.

Blum, Alain, Ely, M., and Zakharov, S. (1992). "Démographie soviétique, 1920–1950, und redévcouverte." *Annales de démographie historique*, pp. 7–22.

Bobrov, S. P. (1925). *Indeksy Gosplana*. Moscow: Gosplan.

Brenner, Robert (1976). "Agrarian Class Structure and Economic Development in Pre-Industrial Europe." In T. H. Aston and C.H.E. Philpin, eds. *The Brenner Debate*. Cambridge: Cambridge University Press, 1985, pp. 10–63.

———. (1989). "Economic Backwardness in Eastern Europe in Light of Developments in the West." In Daniel Chirot, ed. *The Origins of Backwardness in Eastern Europe*. Berkeley: University of California Press, pp. 15–52.

Brooks, Jeffrey (1982). "The Zemstvo and the Education of the People." In Terrence Emmons and Wayne S. Vucinich, eds. *The Zemstvo in Russia*. Cambridge: Cambridge University Press, pp. 243–78.

Campbell, Robert W. (1976). *Trends in the Soviet Oil and Gas Industry*. Baltimore: Johns Hopkins University Press.

———. (1990). "Resource Stringency and Civil-Military Resource Allocation." In Timothy J. Colton and Thane Gustafson, eds. *Soldiers and the Soviet State: Civil-Military Relations from Brezhnev to Gorbachev*. Princeton: Princeton University Press, pp. 126–63.

Carr, Edward Hallett, and Davies, R. W. (1969). *Foundations of a Planned Economy, 1926–1929*. London: Macmillan.

Carstensen, Fred V., and Guroff, Gregory (1983). "Economic Innovation in Imperial Russia and the Soviet Union: Observations." In Gregory Guroff and Fred V. Carstensen, eds. *Entrepreneurship in Imperial Russia and the Soviet Union*. Princeton: Princeton University Press, pp. 347–60.

Carter, M. R. (1986). "The Economics of Price Scissors: Comment." *American Economic Review*, vol. 76, pp. 1192–94.

Chambers, E. J., and Gordon, D. F. (1966). "Primary Products and Economic Growth: An Empirical Measurement." *Journal of Political Economy*, vol. 74, pp. 315–32.

Chapman, Janet G. (1954). "Real Wages in the Soviet Union, 1928–52." *Review of Economics and Statistics*, vol. 36, pp. 134–56.

———. (1963). *Real Wages in Soviet Russia since 1928*. Cambridge, Mass.: Harvard University Press.

Charbonneau, H., and Larose, A. (1979). *The Great Mortalities: Methodological Studies of Demographic Crises in the Past*. Liege: Ordina Editions.

Chayanov, A. V. (1966). *The Theory of Peasant Economy*. Ed. by Daniel Thorner, Basile Kerblay, and R.E.F. Smith. Homewood, Ill.: Richard D. Irwin.

Chojnacka, Helena (1976). "Nuptiality Patterns in an Agrarian Society." *Population Studies*, vol. 30, no. 2, pp. 203–26.

Ciccone, A., and Matsuyama, K. (1996). "Start-Up Costs and Pecuniary Externalities as Barriers to Economic Development." *Journal of Development Economics*, vol. 49, pp. 33–59.

Clark, M. Gardner (1956). *The Economics of Soviet Steel*. Cambridge, Mass.: Harvard University Press.

Coale, Ansley, Anderson, Barbara, and Harm, Erna (1979). *Human Fertility in Russia since the Nineteenth Century*. Princeton: Princeton University Press.

———. (1977). "Bolshevism and Stalinism." In Robert Tucker, ed. *Stalinism: Essays in Interpretation*. New York: W. W. Norton & Company, pp. 3–29.

Cohen, Stephen F. (1980). *Bukharin and the Bolshevik Revolution*. Oxford: Oxford University Press.

———. (1985). *Rethinking the Soviet Experience*. New York: Oxford University Press.

Conquest, Robert (1968). *The Great Terror: Stalin's Purges of the 1930s*. London: Macmillan.

———. (1986). *The Harvest of Sorrow: Soviet Collectivization and the Terror-Famine*. New York: Oxford University Press.

Cordero, H. G. (1952). *Iron and Steel Works of the World*. London: Quin Press Ltd.

Creamer, Daniel, Dobrovolsky, Sergei P., and Borsenstein, Israel (1960). *Capital in Manufacturing and Mining: Its Formation and Financing*. Princeton: Princeton University Press.

Crisp, Olga (1978). "Labour and Industrialization in Russia." In Peter Mathias and M. M. Postan, eds. *The Cambridge Economic History of Europe*, vol. VII, part 2. Cambridge: Cambridge University Press, pp. 308–415.

Crummey, Robert O. (1987). *The Formation of Muscovy, 1304–1614*. London: Longman.

Dallin, David J., and Nikolaevsky, B. I. (1947). *Forced Labor in Soviet Russia*. London: Hollis & Carter.

Darity, William A. (1982). "A General Equilibrium Model of the Eighteenth-Century Atlantic Slave Trade: A Least-Likely Test for the Caribbean School." *Research in Economic History*, vol. 7, pp. 287–26.

David, Paul A. (1966). "The Mechanization of Reaping in the Ante-Bellum Midwest." In Henry Rosovsky, ed. *Industrialization in Two Systems: Essays in Honor of Alexander Gerschenkron*. New York: Wiley, pp. 3–39.

Davies, R. W. (1958). *The Development of the Soviet Budgetary System*. Cambridge: Cambridge University Press.

———. (1980). *The Socialist Offensive: The Collectivisation of Soviet Agriculture, 1929–1930.* Cambridge, Mass.: Harvard University Press.

———. (1989). *The Soviet Economy in Turmoil, 1929–1930.* Houndmills, Basingstoke, Hampshire: Macmillan Academic and Professional Ltd.

———. (1990). *From Tsarism to the New Economic Policy.* Houndmills, Basingstoke, Hampshire: Macmillan Academic and Professional Ltd.

———. (1996). *Crisis and Progress in the Soviet Economy, 1931–1933.* Houndmills, Basingstoke, Hampshire: Macmillan Press Ltd.

Davies, R. W., Harrison, Mark, and Wheatcroft, S. G. (1994). *The Economic Transformation of the Soviet Union, 1913–1945.* Cambridge: Cambridge University Press.

Davis, C. (1992). "The Defense Sector in the Soviet Economy during *Perestroika*: From Expansion to Disarmamaent, to Disintegration." In F. G. Adams, ed. *The Macroeconomic Dimensions of Arms Reduction.* Oxford: Westview Press, pp. 189–215.

De Vries, Jan (1976). *Economy of Europe in an Age of Crisis, 1600–1750.* Cambridge: Cambridge University Press.

Diewert, W. E. (1976) "Exact and Superlative Index Numbers." *Journal of Econometrics*, vol. 4, pp. 115–46.

Dixon, Peter B., Parmenter, Brian R., and Powell, Alan A. (1992). *Notes and Problems in Applied General Equilibrium Economics.* Amsterdam: North-Holland.

Dobb, Maurice H. (1948). *Soviet Economic Development since 1917.* New York: International Publishers.

Dogan, Charity A., ed. (1995). *Gale Country & World Rankings Reporter.* New York: Gale Research.

Dohan, M. R. (1969). *Soviet Foreign Trade in the NEP Economy and Soviet Industrialization Strategy.* Ph.D. dissertation, Massachusetts Institute of Technology.

Domar, Evsey D. (1957). "A Soviet Model of Growth." In Evsey D. Domar, *Essays in the Theory of Economic Growth.* New York: Oxford University Press, pp. 223–61.

———. (1970). "The Causes of Slavery or Serfdom: A Hypothesis." *Journal of Economic History*, vol. 30, pp. 18–32.

———. (1989). "Were Russian Serfs Overcharged for their Land by the 1861 Emancipation? The History of One Historical Tale." *Research in Economic History*, Supplement 5, *Agrarian Organization in the Century of Industrialization: Europe, Russia, and North America*, part B, pp. 429–39.

Domar, Evsey D., and Machina M. J. (1984). "On the Profitability of Russian Serfdom." *Journal of Economic History*, vol. 44, pp. 919–55.

Drèze, Jean, and Sen, Amartya (1995). *India: Economic Development and Social Opportunity.* Delhi: Oxford University Press.

Duffy, John, and Papageorgiou, Chris (2000). "A Cross-Country Empirical Investigation of the Aggregate Production Function Specification." *Journal of Economic Growth*, vol. 5, pp. 87–120.

Eason, Warren W. (1960). "Population Changes." In Cyril E. Black, ed. *The Transformation of Russian Society: Aspects of Social Change since 1861.* Cambridge, Mass.: Harvard University Press, pp. 72–90.

————. (1963). "Labor Force." in Abram Bergson and Simon Kuznets, eds. *Economic Trends in the Soviet Union*. Cambridge, Mass.: Harvard University Press, pp. 38–95.

Easterly, William, and Fischer, Stanley (1995). "The Soviet Economic Decline." *World Bank Economic Review*, vol. 9, pp. 341–71.

Ellman, Michael (1975). "Did the Agricultural Surplus Provide the Resources for the Increase in Investment in the USSR During the First Five Year Plan?" *Economic Journal*, vol. 85, pp. 844–63.

————. (1978). "On a Mistake of Preobrazhensky and Stalin." *Journal of Development Studies*, vol. 14, pp. 353–56.

Engels, Frederick (1845). *The Condition of the Working-Class in England in 1844*. Trans. by Florence Kelley Wischnewetzky. London: George Allen and Unwin Ltd., 1952.

Epstein, S. R. (2000). *Freedom and Growth: The Rise of States and Markets in Europe, 1300–1750*. London: Routledge.

Erhlich, Alexander (1960). *The Soviet Industrialization Debate, 1924–1928*. Cambridge, Mass.: Harvard University Press.

Falkus, M. E. (1968). "Russia's National Income, 1913: A Revaluation." *Economica*, vol. 35, no. 137, pp. 52–73.

Feinstein, Charles H. (1998). "Pessimism Perpetuated: Real Wages and the Standard of Living in Britain during and after the Industrial Revolution." *Journal of Economic History*, vol. 58, pp. 625–58.

Fernandez, Neil C. (1997). *Capitalism and Class Struggle in the USSR: A Marxist Theory*. Aldershot: Ashgate Publishing Ltd.

Field, Daniel (1990). "Stratification and the Russian Peasant Commune: A Statistical Inquiry." in Roger Bartlett, ed. *Land Commune and Peasant Community in Russia: Communal Forms in Imperial and Early Soviet Society*. New York: St. Martin's Press, pp. 143–64.

Figes, Orlando (1989). *Peasant Russia, Civil War: The Volga Countryside in Revolution (1917–1921)*. Oxford: Clarendon Press.

————. (1990). "The Russian Peasant Community in the Agrarian Revolution, 1917–18." In Roger Bartlett, ed. *Land Commune and Peasant Community in Russia: Communal Forms in Imperial and Early Soviet Society*. New York: St. Martin's Press, pp. 237–53.

————. (1996). *A People's Tragedy: The Russian Revolution, 1891–1924*. London: Jonathan Cape.

Findlay, Ronald (1993). "The 'Triangular Trade' and the Atlantic Economy of the Eighteenth Century: A Simple General-Equilibrium Model." In Ronald Findlay, *Trade, Development, and Political Economy*. Aldershot, Hants: Edward Elgar Publishing Ltd., pp. 321–51.

Firth, Noel E., and Noren, James H. (1998). *Soviet Defense Spending: A History of CIA Estimates, 1950–1990*. College Station: Texas A&M University Press.

Fisher, Irving (1922). *The Making of Index Numbers*. Boston: Houghton Mifflin.

Fitzpatrick, Sheila (1979). *Education and Social Mobility in the Soviet Union, 1921–1934*. Cambridge: Cambridge University Press.

———. (1993). "The Great Departure: Rural-Urban Migration in the Soviet Union, 1929–33." In William G. Rosenberg and Lewis H. Siegelbaum, eds. *Social Dimensions of Soviet Industrialization*. Bloomington: Indiana University Press, pp. 15–40.

———. (1994). *Stalin's Peasants: Resistance & Survival in the Russian Village After Collectivization*. New York: Oxford University Press.

———. (1994). *The Russian Revolution*. Oxford: Oxford University Press.

———. (1999). *Everyday Stalinism: Ordinary Life in Extraordinary Times: Soviet Russia in the 1930s*. New York: Oxford University Press.

Fleming, J. Marcus (1955). "External Economies and the Doctrine of Balanced Growth." *Economic Journal*, vol. 65, pp. 241–56.

Floud, Roderick (1994). "The Heights of Europeans Since 1750: A New Source for European Economic History." In John Komlos, ed. *Stature, Living Standards and Economic Development*. Chicago: University of Chicago Press, pp. 9–24.

Fogel, Robert W. (1964). *Railroads and American Economic Growth*. Baltimore: Johns Hopkins University Press.

———. (1967). "The Specification Problem in Economic History." *Journal of Economic History*, vol. 27, pp. 283–308.

———. (1991). "The Conquest of High Mortality and Hunger in Europe and America: Timing and Mechanisms." In Patrice Higonnet, David S. Landes, and Henry Rosovsky, eds. *Favorites of Fortune*. Cambridge, Mass.: Harvard University Press, pp. 33–71.

Fukuyama, Francis (1992). *The End of History and the Last Man*. New York: The Free Press.

Gatrell, Peter (1986). *The Tsarist Economy: 1850–1917*. New York: St. Martin's Press.

Gerschenkron, Alexander (1947). "The Soviet Indices of Industrial Production." *Review of Economics and Statistics*, vol. 29, pp. 217–26.

———. (1962). *Economic Backwardness in Historical Perspective*. Cambridge, Mass.: Harvard University Press.

———. (1965). "Agrarian Policies and Industrialization: Russia, 1861–1917." *Cambridge Economic History of Europe*, vol. 6, part 2. Cambridge: Cambridge University Press.

Getty, J. A., Rittersporn, G. T., and Zemskov, V. N. (1993). "Victims of the Soviet Penal System in the Pre-War Years: A First Approach on the Basis of Archival Evidence." *American History Review*, vol. 98, pp. 1017–49.

Ghatak, Subrata, and Ingersent, Ken (1984). *Agriculture and Economic Development*. Baltimore: Johns Hopkins University Press.

Goldman, Marshall I. (1980). *The Enigma of Soviet Petroleum*. London: George Allen & Unwin.

———. (1983). *U.S.S.R. in Crisis: The Failure of an Economic System*. New York: W. W. Norton & Company.

Goldman, Wendy (1993). *Women, the State, and Revolution: Soviet Family Policy and Social Life, 1917–1936*. Cambridge: Cambridge University Press.

Gorbachev, Mikhail (1987). *Perestroika: New Thinking for our Country and the World*. London: Collins.

Grant, James (1979). "Soviet Machine Tools: Lagging Technology and Rising Imports." *Soviet Economy in a Time of Change.* Joint Economic Committee, Washington: U.S. Government Printing Office, pp. 554–80.

Graziosi, Andrea (1988). "Foreign Workers in Soviet Russia, 1920–40: Their Experience and Their Legacy." *International Labor and Working-Class History,* no. 33, pp. 38–59.

Gregory, Paul R. (1972). "Economic Growth and Structural Change in Tsarist Russia: A Case of Modern Economic Growth?" *Soviet Studies,* vol. 23, pp. 418–34.

———. (1980). "Grain Marketings and Peasant Consumption, Russia, 1885–1913." *Explorations in Economic History,* vol. 17, no. 2, pp. 135–64.

———. (1980). "Russian Living Standards during the Industrialization Era, 1885–1913." *Review of Income & Wealth,* vol. 26, pp. 87–103.

———. (1981). "Economic Growth and Structural Change in Czarist Russia and the Soviet Union: A Long-Term Comparison." In Steven Rosefielde, ed. *Economic Welfare and the Economics of Soviet Socialism.* Cambridge: Cambridge University Press, pp. 25–52.

———. (1982). *Russian National Income, 1885–1913.* Cambridge: Cambridge University Press.

———. (1994). *Before Command: An Economic History of Russia from Emancipation to the First Five-Year Plan.* Princeton: Princeton University Press.

———. (1997). "Searching for Consistency in Historical Data: Alternative Estimates of Russian Industrial Production." *Journal of Economic History,* vol. 57, pp. 196–202.

Gregory, Paul R., and Stuart, Robert C. (1986). *Soviet Economic Structure and Performance.* New York: Harper & Row.

Groman, V. G. (1927). *Vliyanie neurozhaev na narodnoe khozyaistvo Rossii.* Moscow.

Gustafson, Thane (1989). *Crisis amid Plenty: The Politics of Soviet Energy under Brezhnev and Gorbachev.* Princeton: Princeton University Press.

Hajnal, J. (1965). "European Marriage Patterns in Perspective." In D. V. Glass and D.E.C. Eversley, eds. *Population in History.* Chicago: Aldine Publishing Company, pp. 101–43.

Harley, C. Knick (1992). "The Antebellum American Tariff: Food Exports and Manufacturing." *Explorations in Economic History,* vol. 29, pp. 375–500.

———. (1993). "Reassessing the Industrial Revolution: A Macro View." In Joel Mokyr, ed. *The British Industrial Revolution: An Economic Perspective.* Boulder: Westview Press, pp. 171–226.

Harris, J. R., and Todaro, M. (1970). "Migration, Unemployment and Development: A Two-sector Analysis." *American Economic Review,* vol. 60, pp. 126–42.

Harrison, Mark (1990). "The Peasantry and Industrialization." In R. W. Davies, ed. *From Tsarism to the New Economic Policy.* Houndmills, Basingstoke, Hampshire: Macmillan Academic and Professional Ltd., pp. 104–24.

———. (1993). "Soviet Economic Growth since 1928: The Alternative Statistics of G.I. Khanin." *Europe-Asia Studies,* vol. 45, pp. 141–67.

———. (1996). *Accounting for War: Soviet Production, Employment, and the Defence Burden, 1940–1945.* Cambridge: Cambridge University Press.

Hasegawa, Harukiyo (1996). *The Steel Industry in Japan: A Comparison with Britain*. London: Routledge.

Hatton, Timothy J., and Williamson, Jeffrey G. (1991). "Wage Gaps Between Farm and City: Michigan in the 1890s." *Explorations in Economic History*, vol. 28, pp. 381–408.

Headrick, Daniel R. (1988). *The Tentacles of Progress: Technology Transfer in the Age of Imperialism, 1850–1940*. New York: Oxford University Press.

Heer, David M. (1968). "The Demographic Transition in the Russian Empire and the Soviet Union." *Journal of Social History*, vol. 1, pp. 193–240.

Hellie, Richard (1971). *Enserfment and Military Change in Moscovy*. Chicago: University of Chicago Press.

———. (1982). *Slavery in Russia, 1450–1725*. Chicago: University of Chicago Press.

Hendlund, Stefan (2001). "Property Without Rights: Dimensions of Russian Privatisation." *Europe-Asia Studies*, vol. 53, pp. 213–37.

Hoch, Steven L. (1989). "Bridewealth, Dowry and Socioeconomic Differentiation in Rural Russia." *Research in Economic History* , Supplement 5, *Agrarian Organization in the Century of Industrialization: Europe, Russia, and North America*, part B, pp. 389–410.

———. (1999). "Tall Tales: Anthropometric Measures of Well-Being in Imperial Russia and the Soviet Union, 1821–1960." *Slavic Review*, vol. 58, pp. 61–70.

———. (1994). "On Good Numbers and Bad: Malthus, Population Trends and Peasant Standard of Living in Late Imperial Russia." *Slavic Review*, vol. 53, pp. 41–75.

———. (1998). "Famine, Disease, and Mortality Patterns in the Parish of Borshevka, Russia, 1830–1912." *Population Studies*, vol. 52, pp. 357–68.

Hoeffding, Oleg (1954). *Soviet National Income and Product in 1928*. New York: Columbia University Press.

Hoffmann, David L. (1994). *Peasant Metropolis: Social Identities in Moscow, 1929–1941*. Ithaca: Cornell University Press.

Hogan, William T. (1950). *Productivity in the Blast-Furance and Open-Heath Segments of the Steel Industry: 1920–1946*. New York: Fordham University Press.

Holzman, Franklyn D. (1955). *Soviet Taxation*. Cambridge, Mass.: Harvard University Press.

Hueckel, Glenn (1973). "War and the British Economy, 1793–1815: A General Equilibrium Approach." *Explorations in Economic History*, vol. 10, pp. 365–96.

Hughes, James (1996). *Stalinism in a Russian Province: A Study of Collectivization and Dekulakization in Siberia*. Houndmills, Basingstoke: Macmillan.

Hunter, Holland, (1964). "Priorities and Shortfalls in Prewar Soviet Planning." In Jane Degras, ed. *Soviet Planning: Essays in Honor of Naum Jasny*. New York: Praeger Publishers, pp. 1–31.

———. (1988). "Soviet Agriculture with and without Collectivization." *Slavic Review*, vol 47, pp. 203–26.

Hunter, Holland, and Szyrmer, Janusz M. (1992). *Faulty Foundations: Soviet Economic Policies, 1928–1940*. Princeton: Princeton University Press.

Jacobsen, Carl G. (1987). *The Soviet Defense Enigma: Estimating Costs and Burdens*. Oxford: Oxford University Press.

James, J. (1978), "The Welfare Effects of the Antebellum Tariff: A General Equilibrium Analysis." *Explorations in Economic History*, vol. 15, pp. 231–56.

———. (1981). "The Optimal Tariff in Antebellum United States." *American Economic Review*, vol. 71, pp. 726–34.

———. (1984). "The Use of General Equilibrium Analysis in Economic History." *Explorations in Economic History*, vol. 21, pp. 231–53.

Jasny, Naum (1949). *The Socialized Agriculture of the USSR: Plans and Performance*. Stanford: Stanford University Press.

———. (1951). "Labor and Output in Soviet Concentration Camps." *Journal of Political Economy*, vol. 59, pp. 405–19.

Johnson, D. Gale, and Brooks, Karen (1983). *Prospects for Soviet Agriculture in the 1980s*. Bloomington: Indiana University Press.

Johnson, D. Gale, and Kahan, Arcadius (1959). "Soviet Agriculture: Structure and Growth." U.S. Congress, Joint Economic Committeee, Subcommittee on Economic Statistics, Papers, *Comparisons of the United States and Soviet Economies*, 86th Cong. 1st Sess., pt. 1, pp. 201–37.

Johnson, H. E. (1969). *Russia's Educational Heritage*. New York: Octagon Books.

Johnson, Simon, and Temin, Peter (1993). "The Macroeconomics of NEP." *Economic History Review*, vol. 46, pp. 750–67.

Johnston, Bruce F. and Mellor, John W. (1961). "The Role of Agriculture in Economic Development." *American Economic Review*, vol. 51, pp. 566–93.

Jones, Ellen, and Grupp, Fred W. (1979). *Modernization, Value Change, and Fertility in the Soviet Union*. Cambridge: Cambridge University Press.

Jorgenson, D. W., Gollop, F. M., and Fraumeni, B. M. (1987). *Productivity and U.S. Economic Growth*, Cambridge, Mass.: Harvard University Press.

Jurowsky, Leo (1910). *Der Russische Getreideexport: Seine Entwickelung und Organisation*. Stuttgart and Berlin: J. G. Cotta'sche Buchhandlung Nachfolger.

Kafengauz, Lev Borisovich (1994). *Evolutzia promishlennovo proezvodstva Rossia*. Moscow: Russian Academy of Sciences.

Kahan, Arcadius (1965). "Russian Scholars and Statesmen on Education as an Investment." In Arnold Anderson and Mary Jean Bowman, eds. *Education and Economic Development*. Chicago: Aldine Publishing Company, pp. 3–10.

———. (1959). "Changes in Labor Inputs in Soviet Agriculture." *Journal of Political Economy*, vol. 47, pp. 451–62.

———. (1978). "Capital Formation during the Period of Early Industrialization in Russia, 1890–1913." In Peter Mathias and M. M. Postan, eds. *The Cambridge Economic History of Europe*, vol. VII, part 2. Cambridge: Cambridge University Press, pp. 265–307.

———. (1985). *The Plough, the Hammer, and the Knout: An Economic History of Eighteenth Century Russia*. Chicago: University of Chicago Press.

Kaplan, Norman M. (1969). *The Record of Soviet Economic Growth, 1928–1965*. Santa Monica: The Rand Corporation, Memorandum RM-6169.

Kaplan, Norman M., et al. (1952). *A Tentative Input-Output Table for the U.S.S.R., 1941 Plan*. Rand Corporation, Research Memorandum RM-924.

Kaplan, Norman M., and Moorsteen, Richard H. (1960). *Index of Soviet Industrial Output*. Rand Corporation, Research Memorandum RM-2495.

Karasik, Theodore W. (1992). *USSR: Facts & Figures Annual*. Gulf Breeze, Fla.: Academic International Press, vol. 17.

Karcz, Jerzy F. (1957). *Soviet Agricultural Marketings and Prices, 1928–1954*. Santa Monica: Rand Corporation, Research Memorandum RM-1930.

———. (1967). "Thoughts on the Grain Problem." *Soviet Studies*, vol. 18, pp. 399–434.

———. (1979). *The Economics of Communist Agriculture: Selected Papers*. Ed. by Arthur W. Wright. Bloomington: International Development Institute.

Kaser, M. C. (1964). "Welfare Criteria in Soviet Planning." In Jane Degras, ed. *Soviet Planning: Essays in Honor of Naum Jasny*. New York: Praeger Publishers, pp. 144–72.

Kaufman, Adam (1962). *Small-Scale Industry in the Soviet Union*. National Bureau of Economic Research, Occasional Paper 80.

Kelley, A. C., and Williamson, J. G. (1974). *Lessons from Japanese Development: An Analytical Economic History*. Chicago: University of Chicago Press.

Kenez, Peter (1971). *Civil War in South Russia, 1918: The First Year of the Volunteer Army*. Berkeley: University of California Press.

———. (1977). *The Defeat of the Whites: Civil War in South Russia, 1919–1920*. Berkeley: University of California Press.

Kerans, David (2000). *Mind and Labor on the Farm in Black Earth Russia, 1861–1914*. Budapest: Central European University Press.

Khanin, G. I. (1988). "Ekonomicheskii rost: al'ternativnaya otsenka." *Kommunist*, 17.

———. (1991). *Dinamika ekonomicheskogo razvitiia SSSR*. Novosobirsk: Nauka.

Khromov, Pavel Alekseevich (1950). *Ekonomicheskoe Razvitie Rossii v XIX–XX Vekakh, 1800–1917*. Moscow: Akademiia Nauk Soiuza SSR.

Kingston-Mann, Esther (1983). *Lenin and the Problem of Marxist Peasant Revolution*. New York: Oxford University Press.

———. (1990). *In Search of the True West: Culture, Economics and Problems of Russian Development*. Princeton: Princeton University Press.

Kingston-Mann, Esther, and Mixter, Timothy, eds. (1991). *Peasant Economy, Culture, and Politics of European Russia, 1800–1921*. Princeton: Princeton University Press.

Kivelson, Valerie (1993). "The Devil Stole His Mind: The Tsar and the 1648 Moscow Uprising." *American Historical Review*, vol. 98, pp. 733–56.

———. (1996). *Autocracy in the Provinces*. Stanford: Stanford University Press.

Kliuchevsky V. O. (1907). *A Course in Russian History: The Seventeenth Century*. Trans. by Natalie Duddington. Armonk, N.Y.: M. E. Sharpe, 1994.

Kontorovich, Vladimir (1986). "Research and Development Productivity in the USSR: Causes of Decline since 1960s." *American Economic Review: Papers and Proceedings*, vol. 76, no. 2, pp. 181–85.

———. (1990). "The Long-Run Decline in Soviet R&D Productivity." In H. Rowen and C. Wolf, Jr., eds. *The Impoverished Superpower: Perestroika and the Burden of Soviet Military Spending*. San Francisco: Institute for Contemporary Studies, pp. 255–70.

Kornai, Janos (1992). *The Socialist System: The Political Economy of Communism*. Princeton: Princeton University Press.

Kotkin, Stephen (1995). *Magnetic Mountain: Stalinism as a Civilization*. Berkeley: University of California Press.

Kotsonis, Yanni (1999). "The Ideology of Martin Malia." *Russian Review*, vol. 58, pp. 124–30.

Kumar, Dharma, and Desai, Meghnad (1983). *Cambridge Economic History of India*, vol. 2, *c. 1757–c.1970*. Cambridge: Cambridge University Press.

Kuniansky, Anna (1983). "Soviet Fertility, Labor Force Participation, and Marital Instability." *Journal of Comparative Economics*, vol. 7, pp. 114–30.

Kuznets, Simon (1971). *Economic Growth of Nations: Total Output and Production Structure*. Cambridge, Mass.: Harvard University Press.

Leacy, F. H. (1983). *Historical Statistics of Canada*. Ottawa, Statistics Canada, 2nd ed.

Lenin, V. I. (1984 [1972]). *The Development of Capitalism in Russia*, vol. 3, *Collected Works*. Moscow: Progress Publishers.

Leontief, Wassily W. (1941). *The Structure of the American Economy, 1919–1929*. Cambridge, Mass.: Harvard University Press.

Lewin, Moshe (1968). *Russian Peasants and Soviet Power*. London: Allen & Unwin.

———. (1977). "The Social Background of Stalinism." In Robert C. Tucker, ed. *Stalinism: Essays in Interpretation*. New York: W. W. Norton & Company, pp. 111–36.

———. (1985). *The Making of the Soviet System*. New York: The New Press.

Lewis, Frank (1975). "The Canadian Wheat Boom and Per Capita Income: New Estimates." *Journal of Political Economy*, vol. 83, pp. 1249–57.

———. (1979). "Explaining the Shift of Labor from Agriculture to Industry in the U.S." *Journal of Economic History*, vol. 39, pp. 681–98.

Lewis, W. A. (1954). "Economic Development with Unlimited Supplies of Labour." *Manchester School of Economic and Social Studies*, vol. 22, pp. 139–91.

Liashchenko, P. I. (1927). *Russkoe zernovoe khoziaistvo v systeme mirovogo khoziastva*. Moscow: Izdatelstvo kommunisticheskoi akademii.

Lindert, Peter H., and Williamson, Jeffrey G. (1983). "English Workers' Living Standards During the Industrial Revolution: A New Look." *Economic History Review*, 2nd series, vol. 36, pp. 1–25.

Lockwood, William W. (1968). *The Economic Development of Japan*. Princeton: Princeton University Press, expanded edition.

Lorimer, Frank (1946). *The Population of the Soviet Union: History and Prospects*. Geneva: League of Nations.

Löwe, Heinz-Dietrich (1990). "Differentiation in Russian Peasant Society: Causes and Trends, 1880–1905." In Roger Bartlett, ed. *Land Commune and Peasant Community in Russia: Communal Forms in Imperial and Early Soviet Society*. New York: St. Martin's Press, pp. 165–95.

Maddison, Angus (1995). *Monitoring the World Economy*. Paris: OECD.

Malafeev, A. N. (1964). *Istoriia Tsenoobrazovaniia v SSSR*. Moscow: Mysl'.

Male, D. J. (1971). *Russian Peasant Organization before Collectivization*. Cambridge: Cambridge University Press.

Malia, Martin (1994). *The Soviet Tragedy: A History of Socialism in Russia, 1917–1991*. New York: The Free Press.

Marer, Paul (1985). *Dollar GNPs of the U.S.S.R. and Eastern Europe*. Baltimore: Johns Hopkins University Press.

Martens, John A., and Young, John P. (1979). "Soviet Implementation of Domestic Inventions: First Results." *Soviet Economy in a Time of Change*. Joint Economic Committee, Washington: U.S. Government Printing Office, pp. 472–509.

Marx, Karl (1867 [1959]). *Capital*, vol I: *A Critical analysis of Capitalist Production*. London: Lawrence & Wishart.

McCaffray, Susan (1996). *The Politics of Industrialization in Tsarist Russia: The Association of Southern Coal and Steel Producers, 1874–1914*. DeKalb: North Illinois University Press.

McDaniel, Rim (1988). *Autocracy, Capitalism, and Revolution in Russia*. Berkeley: University of California Press.

McEvedy, Colin, and Jones, Richard (1978). *Atlas of World Population History*. London: Penguin Books.

McKeown, T. (1976). *The Modern Rise in Population*. London: Edward Arnold.

McKeown, T., and Record, R. G. (1962). "Reasons for the Decline of Mortality in England and Wales during the Nineteenth Century." *Population Studies*, vol. 16, pp. 94–122.

Mellor, John W., and Mudahar, Mohinder S. (1992). "Agriculture in Economic Development: Theories, Findings, and Challenges in an Asian Context." In *Agriculture in Economic Development, 1940s to 1990s*, ed. by Lee R. Martin, *A Survey of Agricultural Economics Literature*, vol. 4. Minneapolis: University of Minnesota Press, pp. 331–544.

Merl, S. (1980). *Der Agrarmarkt und die Neue Ökonomische Politik. Die Anfange staatlicher Lenkung der Landwirtschaft in der Sowjetunion, 1925–1928*. Munich: Oldenbourg Verlag.

———. (1990). "Socio-Economic Differentiation of the Peasantry." In R. W. Davies, ed. *From Tsarism to the New Economic Policy*. Houndmills, Basingstoke, Hampshire: Macmillan Academic and Professional Ltd, pp. 47–63.

Metzer, Jacob (1974). "Railroad Development and Market Integration: The Case of Tsarist Russia." *Journal of Economic History*, vol. 34, no. 3, pp. 529–50.

———. (1976). "Railroads in Tsarist Russia: Direct Gains and Implications." *Explorations in Economic History*, vol. 13, pp. 85–111.

Millar, James (1970a). "A Reformulation of A.V. Chayanov's Theory of the Peasant Economy." *Economic Development and Cultural Change*, vol. 18.

———. (1970b). "Soviet Rapid Development and the Agricultural Surplus Hypothesis." *Soviet Studies*, vol. 22, pp. 77–93.

———. (1974). "Mass Collectivization and the Contribution of Soviet Agriculture to the First Five-Year Plan: A Review Article." *Slavic Review*, vol. 33, pp. 750–60.

———. (1976). "What's Wrong with the 'Standard Story'?" *Problems of Communism*, vol 25, pp. 50–55.

Miller, Robert F. (1970). *One Hundred Thousand Tractors: The MTS and the Development of Controls in Soviet Agriculture.* Cambridge, Mass.: Harvard University Press.

Minami, Ryoshin (1986). *The Economic Development of Japan: A Quantitative Study.* New York: St. Martin's Press.

Mironov, Boris N. (1985). *Khlebnie tseni v Rossii za dva Stoletiia (xviii–xix bb.).* Leningrad: Nauka.

———. (1985). "The Peasant Commune after the Reforms of the 1860s." *Slavic Review*, vol. 44, pp. 438–67.

———. (1999). "New Approaches to Old Problems: The Well-Being of the Population of Russia from 1821 to 1910 as Measured by Physical Stature." *Slavic Review*, vol. 58, pp. 1–26.

———. (2000). *The Social History of Imperial Russia.* Boulder: Westview Press.

Mitchell, B. R. (1992). *International Historical Statistics: Europe, 1750–1988.* 3rd ed. Basingstoke: Macmillan.

———. (1993). *International Historical Statistics: The Americas, 1750–1988.* 2nd ed. Basingstoke: Macmillan.

———. (1995). *International Historical Statistics: Africa, Asia, and Oceana, 1750–1988.* 2nd ed., Basingstoke: Macmillan.

Mitchell, B. R., and Deane, Phyllis (1971). *Abstract of British Historical Statistics.* Cambridge: Cambridge University Press.

Moorsteen, Richard (1962). *Prices and Production of Machinery in the Soviet Union.* Cambridge, Mass.: Harvard University Press.

Moorsteen, Richard, and Powell, Raymond P. (1966). *The Soviet Capital Stock, 1928–1962.* Homewood, Ill.: Richard D. Irwin.

Moriceau, Jean-Marc (1994). *Les fermiers de l'isle de France.* Paris: Fayard.

Moriceau, Jean-Marc, and Postel-Vinay, Gilles (1992). *Ferme, enterprise, famille: grand exploitation et changements agricoles, xviie–xixe siècles.* Paris: Écoles des Hautes Etude en Sciences Sociales.

Morris, Morris C. (1983). "The Growth of Large Scale Industry to 1947." In Dharma Kumar and Meghnan Desai, eds. *The Cambridge Economic History of India*, vol. 2: *c. 1757–c. 1970.* Cambridge, Cambridge University Press, pp. 553–676.

Murphy, Kevin M., Shleifer, Andrei, and Vishny, Robert W. (1989). "Industrialization and the Big Push." *Journal of Political Economy*, vol. 97, pp. 1003–26.

Nicholls, William H. (1964). "The Place of Agriculture in Economic Development." In Carl K. Eicher and Lawrence W. Witt, eds. *Agriculture in Economic Development.* New York: McGraw-Hill, pp. 11–44.

Nimitz, Nancy (1954). *Statistics of Soviet Agriculture.* Santa Monica: Rand Corporation, Research Memorandum RM-1250.

Nolting, Louvan E., and Feschbach, Murray (1979). "R. & D. Employment in the U.S.S.R.—Definitions, Statistics, and Comparisons." *Soviet Economy in a Time of Change*, Joint Economic Committee, Washington: U.S. Government Printing Office, pp. 710–58.

Noren, J. (1995). "The Controversy over Western Measures of Soviet Defense Expenditures." *Post-Soviet Affairs*, vol. 11, pp. 238–76.

North, Douglass C. (1990). *Institutions, Institutional Change, and Economic Performance*. Cambridge: Cambridge University Press.

North, Douglass C., and Thomas, Robert Paul (1973). *The Rise of the Western World: A New Economic History*. Cambridge: Cambridge University Press.

Nove, Alec (1962). "Was Stalin Really Necessary?" In his *Was Stalin Really Necessary?* London: George Allen & Unwin Ltd. 1964, pp. 17–39.

———. (1990). *An Economic History of the U.S.S.R.* London: Penguin Books.

Nove, Alec, and Morrison, David (1982). "The Contribution of Agriculture to Accumulation in the 1930s." In Charles Bettelheim, ed. *L'industrialisation de l'URSS dans les années trente*. Paris: Éditions de l'École des hautes Études en Sciences Sociales, pp. 47–63.

Nurske, Ragnar (1953). *Problems of Capital Formation in Underdeveloped Countries*. New York: Oxford University Press, 1961.

Nutter, G. Warren (1962). *Growth of Industrial Production in the Soviet Union*. Princeton: Princeton University Press.

Odell, Ralph M. (1912). *Cotton Goods in Russia*. U.S. Department of Commerce and Labor, Bureau of Manufactures, Special Agents Series, no. 51. Washington: U.S. Government Printing Office.

Ofer, Gur (1987). "Soviet Economic Growth: 1928–1985." *Journal of Economic Literature*, vol. 25, pp. 1767–1833.

Olmstead, Alan L., and Rhode, Paul W. (2001). "Reshaping the Landscape: The Impact and Diffusion of the Tractor in American Agriculture, 1920–1960." *Journal of Economic History*, vol. 61, pp. 663–98.

Olmstead, Alan L., and Rhode, Paul W. (2002). "The Red Queen and the Hard Reds: Productivity Growth in American Wheat, 1800–1940." National Bureau of Economic Research, Working Paper no. w8863.

O'Rourke, Kevin H. (1991). "Rural Depopulation in a Small Open Economy: Ireland, 1856–1876." *Explorations in Economic History*, vol. 28, pp. 409–32.

———. (1997). "The European Grain Invasion, 1870–1913." *Journal of Economic History*, vol. 57, pp. 775–801.

O'Rourke, Kevin H., and Williamson, Jeffrey G. (1999). *Globalization and History: The Evolution of a Nineteenth-Century Atlantic Economy*. Cambridge, Mass.: The MIT Press.

Owen, Thomas C. (1995). *Russian Corporate Capitalism from Peter the Great to Perestroika*. Oxford: Oxford University Press.

———. (1998). "Autocracy and the Rule of Law." In Jeffrey D. Sachs and Katharina Pistor, eds. *The Rule of Law and Economic Reform in Russia*. Boulder: Westview Press.

Pallott, Judith (1999). *Land Reform in Russia, 1907–1917*. Oxford: Clarendon Press.

Pavlovsky, George (1930). *Agricultural Russia on the Eve of the Revolution*. New York: Howard Fertig.

Percy, M. B., Norrie, K. H., and Johnston, R. G. (1982). "Reciprocity and the Canadian General Election of 1911." *Explorations in Economic History*, vol. 19, pp. 409–43.

Pipes, Richard (1974). *Russia under the Old Regime*. New York: Charles Scribner's Sons.

Poliakov, Iu.A., Zhiromskaia, V. B., and Kiselev, I. N. (1992)., "A Half Century of Silence, The 1937 Census." *Russian Studies in History*, ed. by Robert E. Johnson, vol. 31.

Pounds, Norman J. G. (1959). *The Geography of Iron and Steel*. London: Hutchinson & Co. (Publishers) Ltd.

Prados de la Escosura, Leandro (2000). "International Comparisons of Real Product, 1820–1990: An Alternative Data Set." *Explorations in Economic History*, vol. 37, pp. 1–41.

Preobrazhensky, E. (1926). *The New Economics*. Trans. by Brian Pearce. Oxford: Clarendon Press, 1965.

Pritchett, L. (1997). "Divergence, Big Time." *Journal of Economic Perspectives*, vol. 11, pp. 3–17.

Procyk, Anna (1995). *Russian Nationalism and Ukraine: The Nationality Policy of the Volunteer Army during the Civil War*. Edmonton: Canadian Institute of Ukrainian Studies Press.

Prokopovich, S. N. (1918). *Opyt ischisleniia narodnogo dokhoda 50 gubernii evropeiskoi Rossii v 1900–1913 gg*. Moscow: Soviet vserossiiskikh ko-operativnikh siezdov.

Puga, D. (1998). "Urbanization Patterns: European versus Less Developed Countries." *Journal of Regional Science*, vol. 38, pp. 231–52.

Putnam, Robert B. (1993). *Making Democracy Work: Civic Traditions in Modern Italy*. Princeton: Princeton University Press.

Ramsey, Frank (1928). "A Mathematical Theory of Saving." *Economic Journal*, vol. 38, pp. 543–59.

Rashin, A. G. (1956). *Naselenie Rossii za sto let (1811–1913 gg): statisticheskie ocherki*. Gosstatizdat.

Rele, J. and Alam, Iqbal (1993). "Fertility Transition in Asia: The Statistical Evidence." In Richard Leete and Iqbal Alam, eds. *The Revolution in Asian Fertility*. Oxford: Clarendon Press, pp. 15–37.

Roberts, Bryan W., and Rodriguez, Alvardo (1997). "Economic Growth under a Self-Interested Central Planner and Transition to a Market Economy." *Journal of Comparative Economics*, vol. 24, pp. 121–39.

Robinson, Geroid Tanquary (1932). *Rusal Russia under the Old Regime*. Berkeley: University of California Press.

Rodrik, D. (1996). "Co-Ordination Failures and Government Policy: A Model with Applications to East Asia and Eastern Europe." *Journal of International Economics*, vol. 40, pp. 1–22.

Roemer, John E. (1994). *A Future for Socialism*. Cambridge, Mass.: Harvard University Press.

Rosefielde, Steven (1981). "An Assessment of the Sources and Uses of Gulag Forced Labour, 1929–56." *Soviet Studies*, vol. 33, pp. 51–87.

———. (1982). *False Science: Underestimating the Soviet Arms Buildup: An Appraisal of the CIA's Direct Costing Effort*. New Brunswick, N.J.: Transaction Books.

———. (1996). "Stalinism in Post-Communist Perspective: New Evidence on Killings, Forced Labour and Economic Growth in the 1930s." *Europe-Asia Studies*, vol. 48, pp. 959–87.

Rosenstein-Rodan, Paul N. (1943). "Problems of Industrialisation of Eastern and Southeastern Europe." *Economic Journal*, vol. 53, pp. 202–11.

Rowen, H., and Wolf, C., Jr. (1990). *The Impoverished Superpower: Perestroika and the Burden of Soviet Military Spending*. San Francisco: Institute for Contemporary Studies.

Rumer, Boris Z. (1984). *Investment and Reindustrialization in the Soviet Economy*. Boulder: Westview Press.

———. (1989). *Soviet Steel: The Challenge of Industrial Modernization in the USSR*. Ithaca: Cornell University Press.

———. (1990). "What Happened to Soviet Investment?" In H. Rowen and C. Wolf, Jr., eds., *The Impoverished Superpower: Perestroika and the Burden of Soviet Military Spending*. San Francisco: Institute for Contemporary Studies, pp. 271–86.

Rutland, Peter (1984). "The Shchekino Method and the Struggle to Raise Labour Productivity in Soviet Industry." *Soviet Studies*, vol. 36, pp. 345–65.

Sah, R. K., and Stiglitz, J. E. (1984). "The Economics of Price Scissors." *American Economic Review*, vol. 74, pp. 125–38.

———. (1986). "The Economics of Price Scissors: Reply." *American Economic Review*, vol. 76, pp. 1195–99.

Sanders, John Thomas (1984). "Once More into the Breach, Dear Friends." *Slavic Review*, vol. 43, pp. 657–66.

Schultz, T. Paul (1997). "Demand for Children in Low Income Countries." In M. R. Rosenzweig and O. Stark, eds. *Handbook of Population and Family Economics*.Amsterdam: Elsevier Science B.V.

Schultz, T. W. (1964). *Transforming Traditional Agriculture*. New Haven: Yale University Press.

Scitovsky, Tibor (1954). "Two Concepts of External Economies." *Journal of Political Economy*, vol. 62, pp. 143–51.

Scott, John (1942). *Behind the Urals: An American Worker in Russia's City of Steel*. Ed. by Stephen Kotkin. Bloomington: Indiana University Press, enlarged edition, 1989.

Seligman, Adam (1992). *The Idea of Civil Society*. New York: The Free Press.

Sen, Amartya (1981). *Poverty and Famines*. New Delhi: Oxford University Press.

Shabad, Theodore (1976). "Raw Material Problems of the Soviet Aluminum Industry." *Soviet Economy in a New Perspective*. Joint Economic Committee, Washington: U.S. Government Printing Office, pp. 661–76.

Shanin, Teodor (1983). *Late Marx and the Russian Road*. London: Routledge & Kegan Paul.

———. (1986). *Russia as a 'Developing Society.'* London: Macmillan Ltd.

Siegelbaum, Lewis (1988). *Stakhanovism and the Politics of Productivity in the USSR 1935–41*. Cambridge: Cambridge University Press.

Simms, James Y. (1977). "The Crisis in Russian Agriculture at the End of the Nineteenth Century: A Different View." *Slavic Review*, vol. 36, pp. 377–98.

Solow, Robert M. (1956). "A Contribution to the Theory of Economic Growth." *Quarterly Journal of Economics*, vol. 70, pp. 65–94.

Spulber, N. (1964). *Soviet Strategy for Economic Growth*. Bloomington: Indiana University Press.

Suny, Ronald Grigor (1998). *The Soviet Experiment.* New York: Oxford University Press.

Steckel, Richard H. (1983). "Height and Per Capita Income." *Historical Methods,* vol. 16, pp. 1–7.

———. (1992). "Stature and Living Standards in the United States." In *The Standard of Living in Early Nineteenth Century America.* Chicago: University of Chicago Press, pp. 265–308.

———. (1995). "Stature and Standard of Living." *Journal of Economic Literature,* vol. 33, pp. 1903–40.

Strumilin, S. G. (1930). "Sotsialno-ekonomicheskie problemi." In *Piatiletnii plan narodno-khoziastvennovo stroitel'stva SSSR* vol. 2, part 2. Moscow: Izdatelstvo. "Planovoe khoziastvo," pp. 7–91; reprinted in *Na Planovom Fronte,* pp. 448–502.

———. (1957). *Problemy ekonomiki truda.* Moscow: gosudarstvennoe izdatelstvo politicheskoi literaturi.

———. (1958). *Statistiko-ekonomicheskie ocherki.* Moscow: Gosstatizdat.

———. (1958). *Na planovom fronte, 1920–1930 gg.* Moscow: gosudarstvennoe izdatelstvo politicheskoi literaturi.

———. (1966). *Ocherki ekonomicheskoi istorii Rossii i SSSR.* Moscow: Nauka.

———. (1967). *Istoriia chernoi metallurgii v SSSR.* Moscow: Nauka.

Swan, Terence (1956). "Economic Growth and Capital Accumulation." *Economic Record,* vol. 32, pp. 334–61.

Szreter, Simon (1988). "The Importance of Social Intervention in Britain's Mortality Decline c. 1850–1914: A Re-Interpretation of the Role of Public Health." *Social History of Medicine,* vol. 1, pp. 1–37.

Taira, Koji (1978). "Factory Labour and the Industrial Revolution in Japan." In Peter Mathias and M. M. Postan, eds. *The Cambridge Economic History of Europe,* vol. VII, part 2. Cambridge: Cambridge University Press, pp. 166–214.

Tasky, Kenneth (1979). "Soviet Technology Gap and Dependence on the West: The Case of Computers." *Soviet Economy in a Time of Change.* Joint Economic Committee, Washington: U.S. Government Printing Office, pp. 510–23.

Tauger, M. (1991). "The 1932 Harvest and the Famine of 1933." *Slavic Review,* vol. 50.

Temin, Peter (1966). "Labor Scarcity and the Problem of American Industrial Efficiency in the 1850s." *Journal of Economic History,* vol. 26, pp. 361–79.

———. (1971a). "General Equilibrium Models in Economic History." *Journal of Economic History,* vol. 31, pp. 58–75.

———. (1971b). "Labor Scarcity in America." *Journal of Interdisciplinary History,* vol. 1, pp. 251–64.

Thoen, Erik (1993). *Technique agricole, cultures nouvelles, et économie rurale en Flandre au bas moyen age.* Ghent: Centre Belge d'histoire rurale, no. 107.

Thurston, Robert W. (1996). *Life and Terror in Stalin's Russia, 1934–1941.* New Haven: Yale University Press.

Timasheff, N. S. (1942). "Overcoming Illiteracy: Public Education in Russia, 1880–1940." *Russian Review* vol. 2, pp. 80–88.

Timoshenko, Vladimir (1932). *Agricultural Russia and the Wheat Problem.* Stanford: Food Research Institute.

Todaro, M. (1968). "An Analysis of Industrialization: Employment and Unemployment in LDCs." *Yale Economic Essays,* vol. 8, pp. 329–492.

———. (1969). "A Model of Labor Migration and Urban Unemployment in Less Developed Countries." *American Economic Review,* vol. 59, pp. 138–48.

Treml, Vladimir G., et al. (1976). "The Soviet 1966 and 1972 Input-Output Tables." *Soviet Economy in a New Perspective.* Joint Economic Committee, Washington: U.S. Government Printing Office, pp. 332–76.

Tucker, Robert C. (1977). "Stalinism as Revolution from Above." In Robert C. Tucker, ed. *Stalinism: Essays in Interpretation.*New York: W. W. Norton & Company, pp. 77–108.

Vainshtein, A. L. (1924). *Oblozhenia i platezhi krest'yanstva.* Moscow: Ekonomist.

Viola, Lynne (1996). *Peasant Rebels under Stalin: Collectivization and the Culture of Peasant Resistance.* New York: Oxford University Press.

Violin, Lazar (1970). *A Century of Russian Agriculture from Alexander II to Khruschev.* Cambridge, Mass.: Harvard University Press.

Volkov, A. (1992). "Le recensement de la population de 1937, mensonges et verité." *Annales de démographie historique,* pp. 23–59.

Vyltsan, M. A. (1966), "Obshestvenno-ekonomicheskii stoi kolkhoznoi derevny v 1933–1940 gg." *Istoriia SSSR,* no. 2, pp. 44–65.

Wagner, William G. (2001). "Law and State in Boris Mironov's *Sotsial'naia istoriia Rossi.*" *Slavic Review,* vol. 60, pp. 558–65.

Walras, Léon (1984). *Élements d'économie politique pure.* Lausanne: Imprimerie L. Corbaz & Cie, Éditeurs.

Ward, Anthony John (1990). *Extensive Development of the Canadian Prairies: A Micro Analysis of the Influence of Technical Change.* Vancouver, B.C.: Department of Economics, University of British Columbia, doctoral dissertation.

Weitzman, Martin (1970). "Soviet Postwar Growth and Capital-Labor Substitutability." *American Economic Review,* vol. 60, pp. 676–92.

Weitzman, Murray S., and Elias, Andrew (1961). *The Magnitude and Distribution of Civilian Employment in the U.S.S.R.: 1928–1959.* U.S. Bureau of the Census, International Population Reports, series P-95, no. 58.

Westwood, J. N. (1987). *Endurance and Endeavour: Russian History, 1812–1986.* 3rd ed. Oxford: Oxford University Press.

Wheatcroft, Stephen G. (1983). "A Reevaluation of Soviet Agricultural Production in the 1920s and 1930s." In Robert C. Stuart, ed. *The Soviet Rural Economy.* Totowa, N.J.: Rowman & Allanhead, pp. 32–62.

———. (1990a). "Agriculture." In R. W. Davies, ed. *From Tsarism to the New Economic Policy.* Houndsmills, Basingstoke, Hampshire: Macmillan Academic and Professional Ltd., pp. 79–103.

———. (1990b). "More Light on the Scale of Repression in the Soviet Union in the 1930s." *Soviet Studies,* vol. 42, pp. 355–67.

———. (1991). "Crises and Condition of the Peasantry in Late Imperial Russia." in Esther Kingston-Mann and Timothy Mixter, eds. *Peasant Econ-*

omy, Culture, and Politics of European Russia, 1801–1921. Princeton: Princeton University Press.

——. (1996). "The Scale and Nature of German and Soviet Repression and Mass Killings 193–45." *Europe-Asia Studies,* vol. 48, pp. 1319–53.

——. (1999). "Victims of Stalinism and the Soviet Secret Police: The Comparability and Reliability of the Archival Data—Not the Last Word." *Europe-Asia Studies,* vol. 51, pp. 315–45.

——. (1999). "The Great Leap Upwards: Anthropometric Data and Indicators of Crises and Secular Change in Soviet Welfare Levels, 1880–1960." *Slavic Review,* vol. 58, pp. 27–60.

Wheatcroft, S.G., and Davies, R. W., ed. (1985). *Materials for a Balance of the Soviet National Economy, 1928–1930.* Cambridge: Cambridge University Press.

Williamson, Jeffrey G. (1974). *Late Nineteenth Century American Development: A General Equilibrium History.* Cambridge: Cambridge University Press.

——. (1985). *Did British Capitalism Breed Inequality?* Boston: Allen & Unwin.

——. (1988). "Migration and Urbanization." In H. Chenery and T. N. Srinivasan, eds. *Handbook of Development Economics.* Amersterdam: North-Holland, pp. 425–65.

——. (1990). *Coping with City Growth during the British Industrial Revolution.* Cambridge: Cambridge University Press.

——. (1995). "The Evolution of Global Labor Markets since 1830: Background Evidence and Hypotheses." *Explorations in Economic History,* vol. 32, pp. 141–96.

Williamson, Jeffrey G., and Lindert, Peter H. (1980). *American Inequality: A Macroeconomic History.* New York: Academic Press.

Wolf, Charles, Jr. (1992). "Defense and the Macroeconomy in the Soviet Union." In F. G. Adams, ed. *The Macroeconomic Dimensions of Arms Reduction.* Oxford: Westview Press, pp. 133–56.

Worobec, Christine (1981). "Contemporary Historians on the Muscovite Peasantry." *Canadian Slavonic Papers,* vol. 23, pp. 315–27.

Wright, Gavin (1990). "The Origins of American Industrial Success, 1879–1940." *American Economic Review,* vol. 80, pp. 651–68.

Yakovlev, Alexander M. (1995). "The Rule-of-Law Ideal and Russian Reality." In Stanislaw Frankowski and Paul B. Stephan III, eds. *Legal Reform in Post-Communist Europe: The View from Within.* Dordrecht: Martinus Nijhoff.

Yasuba, Y. (1996). "Did Japan Ever Suffer from a Shortage of Natural Resources Before World War II?" *Journal of Economic History,* vol. 56, pp. 543–60.

Young, Alwyn (1995). "The Tyranny of Numbers: Confronting the Statistical Realities of the East Asian Growth Experience." *Quarterly Journal of Economics,* vol. 110, pp. 641–80.

Zaleski, Eugène (1955). "Les fluctuations des prix de détail en Union Soviétique." *Études et Conjunctures,* pp. 329–84.

————. (1971). *Planning for Economic Growth in the Soviet Union, 1918–1932.* Chapel Hill: University of North Carolina Press.

————. (1980). *Stalinist Planning for Economic Growth, 1933–1952.* Trans. and ed. By Marie-Christine MacAndrew and John H. Moore. Chapel Hill: University of North Carolina Press.

————. (1984). *La planification stalinienne: croissance et fluctuations économiques en U.R.S.S., 1933–52.* Paris: Economica.

Zhiromskaia, V. B., Kilselev, I. N., and Poliakov, IU.A. (1996). *Polveka pod grifom "Sekretno": Vsesoiuznaia perepis' naseleniia 1937 goda.* Moscow: Nauka.

Index

Abouchar, Alan, 208
Afghanistan, 10
Agnet, 231
"agricultural involution," 41–42
agriculture, 65–67, 86–87, 236, 258nn. 6, 7, 259n. 21, 266nn. 25, 28; and agricultural surplus, 176–78; collectivization of, 2, 4, 97–102, 109–10, 173–74, 183–85; compared to North American agriculture, 66–67, 69–73, 254n. 7, 257n. 2; decline in farm marketing, 79, 81–82, 84; and farm labor, 72–74, 76–78, 258n. 10; and farm marketing, 66, 78–79, 82–86, 180–81, 236, 259–60n. 22, 264n. 13; and farm output, 41–42, 65; farm population, 76, 258n. 9, 266n. 24; and farm revenue, 256n. 17; and horse population, 70, 87, 260n. 4; mechanization of, 100; oat production, 254n. 2, 258n.6. *See also* wheat production
Alexander II, 17
Allen, Robert C., 215–20, 230
Amann, Ronald, 190
Anderson, Barbara, 113, 123–24, 249–50, 261n. 5
Andreev, E., 150–51, 252, 261–62nn. 4–7
Antel, John, 259n. 15
Argentina, 6, 13, 34, 35, 37, 39, 133; real estate prices in, 43
aristocracy. *See* Nicholas II; Peter the Great; Russia, economics in Tsarist Russia
Army Corps of Engineers, 175
Australia, 5, 34, 35; real estate prices in, 43

Bangladesh, fertility rates in, 111, 121–22
Barsov, A. A., 144, 172–73, 264n. 13
Belorussia, 249
Bergson, Abram, 3, 52, 112, 133, 144, 214, 215–20, 240, 248, 265–66n. 16, 22, 267n. 11, 269–70nn. 1, 3; 270n. 4; and definition of investment, 267–68n. 1; reassessment of, 137–41

Berliner, Joseph S., 124, 129, 207–9
Bideleux, Robert, 254n. 3
Big Push, the, 53, 58–59
birth and death rates, 116–23, 243–44, 261–62n. 6
blast furnaces, 104
Blum, Alain, 261n. 2
Bobrov industrial index, 253–54n. 1
Bolsheviks, 3, 47–48, 81, 83; and control (nationalization) of the industrial economy, 47–48
Brazil, 133; fertility rate in, 111; literacy rate in, 36
Brest-Litovsk treaty, 48
Brezhnev, Leonid, 204, 207
Brooks, Karen, 66, 257n. 1
Bukharin, Nikolay, 58–59, 60, 91, 132

calories. *See* food balances and calorie consumption
Campbell, Robert W., 210
Canada, 5, 34, 35, 39, 51, 67; literacy rate in, 36; real estate prices in, 43; wheat boom in, 224–25
capital, 33, 56–57, 59, 152, 193, 248; diminishing returns on, 197–98; human, 96–97. *See also* capital accumulation
capital accumulation, 58, 60, 94–96, 191–93. *See also* Fel'dman model
capital stock, 55–56, 96, 154, 158, 161–62, 189, 198–99, 227, 228, 231–32, 248
capitalism, 14, 35, 50, 52, 58, 206; and the "civil society," 14; in Russia, 2, 21–23, 32. *See also* capitalist economies
capitalist economies, 51, 53
Carstensen, Fred V., 21, 23
Caucuses, the, 128
cement, 208–9, 269n. 13
censuses, 112–13, 124, 249
Central Asia, 9–10, 13, 35, 124, 128; fertility rates in, 122, 124
Central Figures (Gosplan), 91
Central Intelligence Agency (CIA), 213–14